Eastern Europe in the World Economy

SOVIET AND EAST EUROPEAN STUDIES

SOVIET AND EAST EUROPEAN STUDIES

Series list continues on p. 404

Eastern Europe in the World Economy

by

LÁSZLÓ CSABA

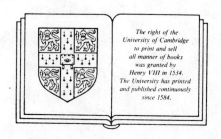

The right of the
University of Cambridge
to print and sell
all manner of books
was granted by
Henry VIII in 1534.
The University has printed
and published continuously
since 1584.

CAMBRIDGE UNIVERSITY PRESS

CAMBRIDGE

NEW YORK PORT CHESTER MELBOURNE SYDNEY

This edition is
published by the Press Syndicate of the University of Cambridge
The Pitt Building, Trumpington Street, Cambridge CB2 1RP
40 West 20th Street, New York, NY 10011, USA
10 Stanford Road, Oakleigh, Melbourne 3166, Australia
and Akadémiai Kiadó, Budapest, Hungary

This is a revised and enlarged edition of the author's original work: *Kelet-Európa a világgazdaságban — Alkalmazkodás és gazdasági mechanizmus*, published by Közgazdasági és Jogi Könyvkiadó, Budapest, 1984

British Library Cataloguing in Publication Data
Csaba, László, 1954
Eastern Europe in the world economy. — (Soviet and East
European studies; v. 68).
1. Europe. Eastern Europe. Soviet Union. Eastern Europe &
Soviet Union. Economic conditions
I. Title II. Series
330.947
ISBN 0 521 33426 8

Printed in Hungary by Akadémiai Kiadó és Nyomda Vállalat, Budapest

TO MY WIFE,
CSIA

Contents

Foreword
to the Hungarian edition and acknowledgements

The line of thinking in this book is one of critical analysis. In writing it my purpose was to develop a new approach. What I have tried to do is to understand the CMEA not *per se*, but as an integral part of the world economy. Rather than camouflaging institutional and other peculiarities by wide-ranging generalization, I have attempted analyses based on the study of the most distinctive features of my subject. It was not my objective to present a complete list of the accomplishments of the past decades, though I do not question their existence. Nor do I wish to reinterpret certain arrangements from a historical perspective. My sole concern was to find an answer to whether or not the existing system of cooperation is able, in its present, in some modified or in a thoroughly reformed form, to promote the more successful adjustment of the Council's member states to the changes in the world economy. It seems to me that elaborating proper and feasible answers to these problems has by the early eighties become a real exigency for the CMEA countries, as they face increasingly fierce competition on world markets. The present volume might contribute to accomplishing this comprehensive task.

This book is a synthesis of my research conducted in the Department for Regional Economic Integrations in the Institute for World Economy of the Hungarian Academy of Sciences. Many of my colleagues from this and other institutions have helped me with their advice and criticism. A number of them read the first version of the manuscript for the discussion on it held at the Institute. I wish to thank them all for their comments, communicated to me both there and afterwards. Of the greatest help were the comments and criticism of László Szamuely, pertaining to both conceptual and editing matters. I am also indebted to the referee of this book, Rezső Nyers, who helped a great deal with the points he made in his report, as well as suggesting phraseologies that have helped correct some of the shortcomings of the original manuscript.

My other constructive critics, the late Bálint Balkay, Tamás Bauer, Béla Kádár, András Köves, István Salgó and Iván Szegvári have helped me the most in finalizing the book. My immediate superior, András Inotai, has provided me with ideal conditions for elaborating, presenting and discussing my ideas at scientific fora.

Budapest, October 1983
The author

for Technological Progress and the possibilities for expanding direct interfirm relations in the CMEA.

To one who studies the Contents and the Bibliography, the question might well occur why Eastern Europe and not the CMEA figures in the title. The answer is this: numerous studies have appeared in both the socialist and Western literature which have analyzed CMEA matters from the point of view of the Soviet Union. This work—without pretending to be an exclusive or official approach—analyzes the questions of adjustment to the world economy primarily from the point of view of the small nations. It examines the East European countries' external trade policy alternatives and their capability and opportunities for action. Since, from the standpoint of foreign trade, the East European countries' determinant environment is the CMEA, and since, in my opinion, a number of questions have remained unanswered or have not even been raised in the relevant literature, it is perhaps warranted that the two primary subjects—the East European countries' external trade policies and the CMEA—are intertwined. The peculiarity of the present analysis is what most of the Soviet and American literature fails to emphasize that the small East European countries are, if not more open, certainly more vulnerable, to international economic disturbances. Therefore I find it important that their indigenous problems, which are transmitted to their regional cooperation, be analyzed in the context of the epochal transformations and ongoing structural changes in global trade.

Some of the analyses contained in this book have already been published in various languages in the form of articles. Chapter Three which deals with investment contributions, appeared in April 1985 in *Soviet Studies* (XXXVII/2); Chapter Six in February 1984 in *Economies et Sociétés*, Série des économies planifiées, No. 40 (joint edition of Presses Universitaires de Grenoble—Cahiers de l'I.S.M.EA, Paris), as well as in German, by permission, in a collection of studies edited by A. Drexler, *Modernisierung der Planwirtschaft* (SOVEC, Göttingen, 1985). Chapter Seven appeared first in India in December 1985, in the quarterly of the Gokhale Institute of Economics and Politics, Poona *(Artha Vijnana*, XXVII/4), and later revised in French, in the 2/1987 issue of *Revue d'Etudes Comparatives Est-Ouest*, as well as in Italian in the 3/1986 issue of the quarterly *Economia e Banca* (Trento); its substantially shortened German version appeared in *Europäische Rundschau*, No. 2/1986. The latter text was translated into English by permission of Europa Verlag—but without the author's prior knowledge—in the 1/1988 issue of *Soviet and East*

European Foreign Trade (U.S.A.). A preliminary to Chapter Four and the original version of Chapter Five appeared in 1983 and in 1986 respectively in the Deutsche Gesellschaft für Osteuropakunde's quarterly, *Osteuropa-Wirtschaft* (Nos 2 and 3). Chapter Ten was first published in French by *Le Courrier des Pays de l'Est*, in December, 1986 while what has been revised to form the concluding chapter appeared originally in the quarterly of the Trieste-based ISDEE institute, *Est-Ovest*, in the 4/1987 issue. I should like to take this opportunity to express my gratitude to the above publishers and copyright holders for their consent to the publication of these studies, of their revised and updated version, in this book.

Although I originally set out to write several of the chapters upon requests from various Hungarian and foreign publishers, I mean this book to be not merely a collection of studies, but an intellectual product which reflects the author's way of thinking and gives a structured analysis of some of the as yet less explored areas of the East European countries' external trade policies. It is both a description and a diagnosis, reflecting as it does the search for self-awareness and solutions, as well as its stumbling-blocks, along with the intellectual struggles involved. Its aim is to find more fruitful ways of alternative action. As to how far it has succeeded—only time and the reader can tell.

Budapest, September 1, 1988

L. Cs.

Introduction

"In scientific work, just recognizing the limitations of our knowledge is already an important progress; a significant step forward from the time when while we 'knew' all the answers, yet we did not know all the questions."
(Goldmann and Kouba, 1969)

"In the CMEA integration, economic science developed much slower than economic policy; nor did the general application and practice or the critical analysis of these economic policies develop sufficiently. . . There was no critical analysis of the CMEA integration's progress, nor any in-depth study of the prospects of further development. The backwardness of the theory was significant in the methods and forms of the CMEA countries' economic cooperation developing inadequately." (Kiss, 1973, p. 116). Interestingly, the most prolific Hungarian economist on the subject wrote these lines at the very time of the series of debates which preceded the adoption of the Comprehensive Programme of 1971, when the gap between theory and practice was the smallest since the establishment of the Council in 1949. In this period of economic reform, a flourishing Hungarian economics joined forces with the economists of the other CMEA countries which had not yet lost all their reform momentum to eliminate the shortcomings of the previous period. Practice had come to recognize the need for analysis, and researchers turned from abstract theories to the realities, and engaged in practical studies instead of apologetics. The market model and the corresponding theory of integration were formulated, and Ausch (1972) explored with enduring validity and classic conciseness the laws, categories, and forms of action of the CMEA's traditional cooperation mechanism.

Then, after 1971—in Hungary after 1973-74—the overall recentralization gave rise to a certain reticence, to regulations which affected both the cognitive and communicative methodology of scientific research, and characterized most of the seventies.

Yet it was in this very period that there emerged—first in the world economy, as global trends, and later in the East European region as well—those fundamental and irreversible changes which constituted a process of epochal transformation. New phenomena surfaced, old relationships were replaced by new ones, trends changed and scales of value were modified. Within the CMEA cooperation, however, with a few notable exceptions, economic analysis kept within the limits of the politically determined compromise solutions embodied in the wording of the Comprehensive Programme of 1971, even after the real processes and scientific developments had gradually rendered them obsolete. Beyond this, the relevant literature was confined mostly to reporting and popularizing various points made in the joint communiqués of the CMEA Council Sessions, and to attempting to provide theoretical "justifications" for positions reflecting nothing but everyday commercial interests.

No doubt, certain of the prerequisites of advancing beyond this, as János Szita (1971, p. 41) pointed out in his study on the Comprehensive Programme, were lacking: an internationally open, free atmosphere of discussion, the availability of the most important data on CMEA cooperation, narrowing the class of secret and confidential documents, and clearing up the "frequently recurring misunderstanding" that each and every published study fully reflects the official stand of the author's country (and only that). Unconditionally identifying a theory with the official stand is inexpedient even in the case of statements published by government representatives. "To facilitate this distinction, a public agreement or at least an understanding should be arrived at to treat each and every publication—especially those of a theoretical nature—as being a reflection solely of the author's personal views, and not of government positions. Governments have various avenues open to them to voice their views at any time and in any form they deem appropriate", while "a freer expression of views might, in the end, prove helpful also for governmental activities", noted Szita.

This suggestion was, regrettably, disregarded during the seventies. Nor can it be claimed that a sober, objective scientific analysis of the subject, free from the undertones and considerations of officialism, was the general norm by the eighties. Still, after the Twenty-Sixth Party Congress of the CPSU, and also during the preparations for the Economic Summit of 1984, there was more open discussion of those theoretical and practical issues that had not been covered by the Comprehensive Programme of 1971. Economic analysts are wont to focus on the fifteen year interval between the two economic summits, as this has permitted a long-range overview which was not tied to the timing and other considerations of some Party Congress, or to the adoption of some new Five Year Plan.

In reviewing the major trends of the post-1970 period, I shall be trying to answer the following questions. 1) What has, in fact, changed in a system of cooperation where nothing has changed on the surface (i.e. what measures might solve those difficulties)? 2) How did policy choices (including inaction) influence the theoretical constructs reflecting the thinking of the 1960s, or conversely, contribute to their ideological rejection? 3) What were the past and future trends of the CMEA countries' involvement in the world economy? 4) What is new in the planning and monetary arsenal of integration among the planned economies? 5) What were the prospects of the CMEA, and what partial or comprehensive measures were possible and/or necessary to improve the region's performance during the 80s? 6) How did the CMEA member states use their increased room for manoeuvering in the mid-eighties, and what does the Gorbachevian programme for renewal hold for them and for the cooperation?

Discussing these issues is made both easy and difficult by the abundance of literature available on the subject. I have tried as much as I could to examine the available source material, since in dealing with a subject like this, there is a great danger of re-inventing. Because of this, I chose a method uncommon in Hungarian economics but widely practised in other social sciences and humanities and also abroad: that of comparative analysis. I have not only compared theories one to another, but have also matched them against reality. This way we may be better able to separate the relevant from the irrelevant, and the cyclical from the secular in the empirical material. With the widest possible use of the source material, I have tried to document previously available evidence, as well as conflicting schools of thought and statistical trends, in order to make my personal views more pronounced. An overview of the literature, primarily of that of the CMEA countries, has served as a starting point, since a realistic view can hardly be elaborated without taking into account the plurality of approaches in this polycentric organization composed of countries so different both in terms of their systemic models and their policy priorities. Following this, I have presented my own (normative) concept of how the CMEA could become an organic part of the world economy, and have elaborated the conditions and prospects of such an alternative scenario. I wish to call attention to my independent use of the source material. This means that my interpretations often differ from those of the quoted authors who have published the data I rely on, or who represent a view characteristic of a period, a view which I do not share, but have had to document, since many of its former supporters would not re-state it today. This seems to be the only way one can show the context in which theories and proposals have evolved, without producing apologetics. It is this method which has suggested my use of quotations, a practice quite common in Britain and the US, but much less in Hungary.

Given the very wide topic I cover, this book primarily centers on issues of economic policy and the closely related theoretical problems. This is certainly only one of the possible options, and one that involves abstracting from a series of important subjects for reasons of space. To list some of the subjects I shall not be discussing: the problem of equalizing the level of development among the CMEA member states; the functioning of the law of value in the CMEA market; the general convergence among member countries; the general and specific laws of functioning within the world socialist economy, and the interrelationship of these regularities with the national economy and with a number of other theoretical matters. Some of these areas have already been sufficiently covered by previous writings. In others, we lack adequate information and further research must precede any relevant discussion.

The parameters of my subject are also determined by the range of issues that have been solved, or conversely, left unanswered, by the Hungarian economic literature. The book by the late Sándor Ausch (1972) has thoroughly discussed the traditional issues of the integrational mechanism; thus, I have confined myself to analyzing new developments. András Köves (1985) has described the process of world economic opening primarily from the point of view of the Soviet economy, whereas my angle of analysis is that of the small East European states. I also deal with the issue of how the mechanism of regional integration functions when I search for the conditions of a more efficient integration into the world economy. Finally, the exhaustive information provided by Meisel (1979) on the organs, setup and functioning of joint institutions applies for the whole period under scrutiny, making superfluous those descriptive parts and appraisals that are otherwise necessary in monographs.

In elaborating my ideas, I have proceeded as follows. After surveying the problems that appear on the surface of CMEA cooperation, I approach the reasons gradually. Having determined the causes, I recommend the therapy. I have tried to separate normative from descriptive parts, even though the possibilities for such an approach are quite limited: the very description of certain processes suggests alternatives to the existing methods. A more consistent separation of the two aspects would substantially increase the size of this volume.

I consider the financial problems of CMEA cooperation as evident: both economic policy and business practice are confronted with those most tangibly. In the literature on the CMEA, it used to be common to find semi-critical views which attribute the problems in a given area to the underdeveloped state of finances. This was ritually followed by an optimistic prognosis that was substantiated by a vague hint at the need for "improving" or "further developing" this element of the integration's mechanism. What was less frequently discussed were the following issues: a) How exactly if the monetary sphere to be "perfected", i.e. what are the preconditions of introducing currency convertibility, something that would do away with the growth of bilateralism and the attendant predetermination of supplies in physical terms; b) What are the reasons for precisely this area's lagging behind, why are the results so meagre, if any, despite the fact that both Hungarian economic policy and the provisions of the monetary-financial chapter of the Comprehensive Programme of 1971 are quite specific in this area? Without addressing these questions, statements urging the "improvement" of financial arrangements in the CMEA or the "development" of the money function of the accounting unit, the transferable ruble (TR), were bound to remain empty declarations, with no consequences for either economic policy or business activities.

In analyzing intra-CMEA finances, I had had two objectives: 1) to point out concrete ways and means of enhancing the efficiency of this area both for companies and for the population at large; 2) to prove the *naiveté* of the widespread belief of those days that modifications in financial techniques could really induce a radical—or what is even worse, gradual—market-oriented overhaul of the entire mechanism of cooperation.

It is quite legitimate to question the general theoretical implications of the peculiarities of the CMEA's financial sphere. How can the advantages of regional international trade assert themselves? Are these advantages mutual, or, does one party or the other incur losses on occasion due to the distorted prices? This somewhat theoretical chapter tries to prove, by analyzing representative views from both East and West, that the disadvantages are, indeed, mutual. Though it is hardly possible to quantify the magnitude and distribution of advantages, the general tendency to mutuality does exist in intra-regional trade.

Despite the once recurring statements to the contrary, the inefficiency of the Comecon financial system has been amply proven. Producers of certain commodities feel that contractual prices do not cover their costs; therefore, they make the sale of their products conditional on investment contributions. Analyzing this peculiar form of integration, I attempt to prove in Chapter Three that it has nothing to do with capital exports. Nominal intra-CMEA prices have long not been taken at face value even at the macroeconomic level of intra-CMEA bargaining. Thus, any theory based on the comparison of nominal intra- and extraregional prices is, by definition, misleading and out of touch with East European realities. This is substantiated by the fact that the economies with mandatory planning have been forced to invent and apply for decades a wide variety of methods substituting for the market clearing function of contractual prices. Investment contributions, thus, have nothing to do with the particulars of the raw material and energy sector, but reflect the underdeveloped state of the system of payments and settlements within the CMEA. It was manifest in the primary products sphere only because of the peculiarities of physical planning. The shortage of primary products was recognized, first and foremost, at the level of macroeconomic decision-making. In fact, the essence of investment contributions was not the consumers' bearing part of the actual production costs of a priority, but the suppression of the demand for it. This is *par excellence* a function of prices in a market economy.

Like other market categories, this function of prices has been restricted in the CMEA region by the prevailing system of mandatory physical planning. How did the integration of planning hierarchies function in reality? What did integration in planning mean in a period when neither planning nor the market function in practice as they had convertionally been postulated to? What was the actual and possible role of firms which, in theory, are in a completely subordinate position? What are the implications of divergent trends in intra- and extra-CMEA developments for the organizational forms of economic activity? In the world economy, small and decentralized larger organizations have taken the lead both in terms of competitiveness and in technological change and innovation in the vast majority of sectors, and flexibility has been revalued. In the meantime, both in the CMEA and in the constituent national economies, an attempt has been made to ward off the spillover of these and other externally originated signals by a spatial and temporal extension of the role of physical planning, and by an emphasis on creating ever larger economic units (in decreasing numbers, of course, which reflect the administrative needs of detailed mandatory planning). Stability was supposed to be the major priority—although it could only be secured in very relative terms (for immanent reasons). How does all this affect the relationship between firms and the hierarchy, especially in foreign economic relations? These questions are addressed in Chapter Four, focusing on the repercussions of the oft-heralded priority of physical planning during a period of accelerated changes in the entire world economy.

The modernization of intra-CMEA cooperation became necessary not only on logical grounds, but also because of real economic developments. Eastern Europe and the Soviet Union became integral parts of the world economy in the 1970s. However, the countries of the region have experienced the disadvantages rather than the benefits of this development. This was due to the unilateral nature of their integration into the world economy: their export performance was so poor that it was unable to finance even an import that has grown at a considerably slower pace than the international average. What has changed between 1970 and 1985? Primarily the intra-CMEA conditions of trade, more precisely, the role and possibilities of the Soviet economy. This factor has always exerted a decisive influence on the East European economies, and has moulded their structures. An additional, though far from irrelevant, factor has been the impact of the epochal transformations in the world economy that have also had to be absorbed by the basically unchanged policies and structures of the region. The statistical series illustrating these developments place the fifteen years of relative intra-CMEA stability in an international context.

In the 1980s, when a peculiar sort of "adjustment policy" has overwhelmed the previously unchallenged growth policies in the CMEA countries, the marginalization of the region within the world economy has become even more pronounced than before. In the development of the Soviet economy, losing ground to the advanced Western nations in the international division of labour emerged as a lasting trend even prior to the "reversed oil price shock". Due to underlying trends in Soviet economic development as well as to the slow pace of adjustment in the East European states, an essentially new situation emerged within the CMEA even prior to the inception of the Soviet modernization endeavours. A description of some of the commercial policy implications of this fact concludes Chapter Five.

Demands for a conceptual overhaul of the entire intra-CMEA cooperation have been voiced all through the first half of the 1980s.

This was due to the changed position and interests of the member states as well as to the deterioration of the East–West political climate between 1979–84. Chapters Six and Seven analyze national approaches to and proposals for intra-CMEA change, and try to trace the interrelationship between the national positions and interests and their reflection in official standpoints. These analyses are followed by a summary and evaluation of the proposals for alternative forms and methods of harmonizing conflicting interests. Then some conclusions are drawn about the types of solutions that could realistically be suggested under the then existing arrangements, and why nothing short of radical reforms can bring about a more competitive performance than that of the previous fifteen years.

The concept of radical reform was first introduced at the Twenty-Seventh Congress of the CPSU. It is therefore expedient to review the series of practical measures that immediately followed, and to attempt to prognosticate the dynamics of this change.

First, in Chapter Eight an attempt is made at a comparative analysis of the 1986–1990 Five-Year Plans that were elaborated under the impact of *perestroika*, and of a temporary relaxation of the debt burden. It is proven that the enhanced room for manoeuvring has been used by the East European leaderships to further postpone painful decisions on adjustment and reform. On the other hand, *perestroika* itself has been a mixed blessing: more ideological leeway coupled with a stiffer Soviet commercial policy stance.

In Chapter Nine, an attempt is made to understand the Soviet reform as a historical process, something going beyond the specific economic and legal measures. Although its social and historical dynamism has been remarkable, it will take a long time for the fundamental changes to reach the Soviet foreign trade sector.

This conclusion is substantiated by the detailed analyses of Chapters Ten and Eleven. The former describes the drive to establish new East–East joint ventures and to develop direct contacts among firms within the framework of the long-term technological Programme of the CMEA. Adopted in the spirit of the Gorbachevian obsession with accelerating technological change, it was part and parcel of the new economic strategy. Our analysis of the CMEA's long-term Programme shows the inherent conflict between the novel aims and the traditional methods of cooperation: adequate financing was not secured, and technological objectives were set prior to decisions on financing. We find that the regulation of direct contacts does not, as a rule, increase the firms' elbowroom, since on the macroeconomic level there are no indirect methods of securing bilateral trade equilibria in ways analogous to plan coordination. Thus, we are back to where we started: the problems of market, and the related arsenal of economic categories that do not evolve by *fiat*. This problem has been recognized at the Forty-Third (Extraordinary) Council Session, where a new concept of integration, the unified socialist market, has been drafted (the final version was approved by the 1988 Prague Session of the Council). The concluding chapter analyzes the evolution of the concept, and after a comparative survey of the national standpoints, it outlines the medium-run economic and trade policy implications of the new concept for Eastern Europe.

This book is applied theory. Based on empirical evidence, it draws new theoretical conclusions, but it also relies on theory in its attempt to understand new phenomena. The conclusions it draws are far from being tantamount to options which, obviously, would be more directly related to day-to-day considerations of national interest. However, I believe that only a theory which is not an apology for, but a criticism of, practice, one which is not remote from realities, can become an efficient tool for an economic policy trying to solve the problems of overdue adjustment. Reversing the acceleration of unfavourable trends in the CMEA member states is of interest to the Western countries as well, especially to those on the European continent, since it is economic prosperity, rather than decline, that can, in the long run, serve as a solid basis for cooperation.

Budapest, September 1988

The author

CHAPTER ONE

The CMEA's monetary system and the epochal transformation of the world economy

In this context, epochal transformation in the CMEA pointed not only to the noticeable aggravation of earlier difficulties but to the evolution of a fundamentally new set of problems as well. However, for the time being, the mechanism of international cooperation has been able to react to the new conditions of East European and Soviet economic growth only within the traditional framework. Clearly, adequate adaptation to new situations requires new ways and means, new methods and procedures. The ever more frequent incidence in the CMEA of increasing delays in shipments, of non-delivery of goods and of weak production performance, the superficiality of technological and scientific cooperation, the inadequacy of product development, the chronic spare part and component shortages, the lack in stimulating export of agricultural products for rubles, i.e. the shortcomings that had been the subject of political-level criticism of the CMEA's sessions throughout the last decade, are inherently related to the backwardness of the CMEA's monetary system.

THE SUBJECT AND ITS FRAMEWORK

The CMEA's monetary system has been the sum total of its unique regional monetary institutions, accounting methods, credit- and currency categories and relations. The system had two determinants: a) monetary and market categories are part and parcel of a unique cooperation mechanism determined primarily by methods of mandatory planning. These stood apart from both the national and international markets. b) This multi-currency international system was managed directly by the socialist states through their national banks and other agencies of economic control; therefore, it could—*strictu senso*—not be considered either supranational or autonomous. The above definition, following Konstantinov (1982a, pp. 18–19), emphasizes two facts. First, it was typical of the CMEA's monetary system that, unlike in the international capitalist one, no actions were initiated by the monetary sphere that could result in somewhat automatic real economic (adjustment) processes within the member states' economies.[1] Second, it follows, that every one of the CMEA's monetary categories were unique in themselves. In other words, even in the case of intra-CMEA trade in convertible currency, though they might be nominally identical to the corresponding categories of the capitalist international monetary system, they did differ both in their function and in their economic essence due to their different motivations and mechanism. Since, as we know, this peculiar monetary system was influenced primarily by the degree to which the respective CMEA national economies were monetized, we had to examine the possibilities also from the standpoint of the current and prospective levels of the national monetary functions.

Along with, and beyond, the problems elaborated in the introduction, the day-to-day practice of CMEA cooperation seems to continuously collide head on with the backwardness of the integration's monetary and financial order. In the absence of a convertible currency it was hardly worth arriving at a surplus in intra-CMEA ruble export, as the transferable ruble (TR) could not substitute for convertible currency even in the most rudimentary purchases on the world market. Nor is it accepted as a means of clearing different types of indebtedness, be this in the form of direct transfers, or indirectly in import substitution for goods otherwise obtainable for convertible currency. This, from the late 70s, has prompted the member states to closely monitor the convertible-currency shares of their overall exports to the CMEA, and to intensify their attempts to modify the pattern of their exports for TR according to these points of view. Clearly, this also reflected the demonetization[2] of cooperation, a phenomenon consonant with the decade-long development trends of the CMEA-mechanism. In the 80s, *in lieu* of direct monetary evaluation in terms of the TR, the vindication of convertible import content as an independent determinative factor—a trend followed by all CMEA countries—manifested itself as a complementary plan indicator. This fitted in the growing arsenal of unique physical "solutions" substituting for market evaluation, the matching of "hardness" (mostly by narrow commodity items), tying shipments to countershipments (by the month or by even a shorter time span). In essence, they took over the role of the monetary and other features of the market economy, such as image, interest, or penalty. We also have to qualify the term "solutions". On the one hand we are talking about the only possible and logical steps that could by and large assure at the macroeconomic level equal reciprocal values in the exchange of commodities within the given system of cooperation. On the other, these often lead to highly irrational "solutions" on both the enterprise-level, and from the point of view of the national economy.[3]

In the final analysis it is the inadequacy of economic valuation and motivation in terms of, and through, the TR which is manifest in the negative phenomena criticized by the political fora of the CMEA. These include the strengthening of bilateralism, and also the empirically documented fact that the long-term CMEA agreements on specialization and cooperation concluded within the framework of the given monetary system have actually resulted in the conservation of the existing levels of technology (Drechsler and Szatmári, 1982, p. 3). In typical instances the partners disallowed the additional costs of technological development and product improvement, and this led to product inferiority and obsolescence. This explains, to some extent, the often and severely criticized very slow pace of introducing existing technological achievements into the intra-CMEA trade. Also this is why it is difficult to share the point of view that "Without the CMEA (our) successes would certainly be smaller while (our) past or existing problems would be there just the same" (Nyers, 1983a). In fact, the problems which are present in the above phenomena and have become palpable also in business practice stem immediately (among other things) from those methods of cooperation mechanism that most clearly manifest themselves in the monetary system.[4] Having clarified the terminology, I shall try to find answers to why the CMEA's monetary system has remained what it is and, given this situation, what the alternatives are: what practical steps could be taken both by Hungarian economic policy and in regional cooperation to improve it.

I assume (and shall prove later) that a more intensive joining into the global division of labour is not only a desirable but a compelling alternative for the CMEA. Is it really justified to state: "Signals of crisis in the world economy and the disturbing signs of maintaining the factor intensive type of growth have put the accomplishment of short-term—on an economic scale, daily—tasks to the fore. The national economic policy efforts to find short-term solutions to (these) conflicts did not promote the timely attainment of long-term objectives aimed at the improvement of the cooperation mechanism

as outlined in the Comprehensive Programme" (Kővári, 1982)?
In other words: was this short-range "perspective" really the cause,
or was it the effect of a conceptual ruling—subsequently proven
erroneous, yet very definite at the time—which gave monetary
categories a much smaller and less active role than designated by
the inconsistent guidelines of the Comprehensive Programme, itself a
step backward even from the mentality of the sixties? Isn't it the fact
that within the particular framework created by this conceptual
ruling the adjustment to the new real economic situation by
necessity took the form of physical—i.e. non-monetary—and short-
range measures as there were no other alternatives?

What I shall try to substantiate in the following is that it is simply
impossible to effect pinpointed partial "perfection" *(sovershenstvovanie)*. Suggestions to this end can either be fitted into the situation
at the time, in which case they are automatically inconsistent with
the "concept of future reform", or they can highlight the parameters
of a real and meaningful future reform—inevitably pointing beyond
the earlier system of cooperation—in which case they cannot be
moulded "to fit into the system". Adjustment to the world economy
demands that we accept the "outside world" the way it is, and readjust
the regional arrangements of the CMEA so as to stop its losing ground
in the world economy. For this, the point of departure from the aspect
of the monetary system is convertibility (Rédei, 1973; and Wiesel and
Wilcsek 1978, p. 162).

CONVERTIBILITY, TRANSFERABILITY AND EXCHANGEABILITY

The term "convertibility" is used in a variety of diverse senses. Mark
Allen (1980, p. 142) mentions twenty-four different interpretations.
In this work, the term is used in accordance with the International
Monetary Fund's basic ruling, whereby convertibility exists when, at
their request, non-residents can get their claims deriving from items of
the current account exchanged by the central banks to convertible
currencies. This does not preclude all kinds of restrictions on financial
transactions. These, as we know, are being practised by many of the
IMF's—especially poorer—member countries. What it does preclude
is that currencies which "unlike those of the capitalist countries cannot
independently regulate real economic processes" be called "convertible"[5] in any sense of the word as Ehlert (1978, pp. 144, 161) suggested.

In keeping with the aims of the Comprehensive Programme, the GDR author proposed establishing limited exchangeability within the region from a strictly monetary aspect. This, in turn, would, of course, ensured the "transferability" of the common currency. This would have meant that, within the multilateral clearing system, credits arising from any one transaction could be applied to another, i.e. be used for the purchase of any merchandise in any bilateral relation which is in a deficit. While on a narrow interpretation of multilateral clearing this option would exist for the central banks only, through wider application this avenue would also be open to companies, as it would monitor the real value of the bilateral clearing units through their premium or discount rates of exchange on the respective domestic money markets.[6] Exchangeability—as opposed to transferability— pertains to national currencies, and it is present to a limited extent in the tourist trade and in some non-commercial payments where the actual exchange of national currencies takes place. *De facto* and full-scale exchangeability—if realized— within the CMEA could make this a possible practice for companies and individuals alike for all items of the current account without applying quantitative restrictions. This suggestion in fact essentially reiterated, although under different circumstances and many years later, some provisions of the Comprehensive Programme's financial and monetary chapter. Therefore, I shall come back to the feasibility of this concept when I examine the financial parts of the Comprehensive Programme, including the possibilities for developing the money functions of the common currency.

THE TRANSFERABLE RUBLE SYSTEM

At the end of the sixties, the CMEA integration was considered non-monetary in character, i.e. a cooperation system without a *de facto* monetary system (Ausch, 1971; and Csikós-Nagy, 1973a). Though the provisions of the Comprehensive Programme did not guarantee that the CMEA would, in the seventies or by the early eighties, achieve monetary integration, neither did they definitely and conclusively rule out this possibility. However, expectations as to the integration's monetization have turned out to be vain. *In lieu* of an explanation, I should like to submit two summarizing statements.

1. At the end of the 1960s, no one questioned the presumption of the stability of the international economic environment and of growth as it pertained to both the world economy as a whole and the

CMEA region. Nor were the epochal changes of the seventies fore-seeable —at least not in their full weight and dimension. Nowadays, however it is these very changes that are determining the success or failure of the growth and management models adopted by one or the other CMEA country.

2. When the Comprehensive Programme was being elaborated, the view—maintained primarily by Hungarian economists—that the trends to centralization already dominant at the time the Programme was adopted could mean but a temporary digression in the development of the CMEA member states' economic mechanism seemed justified or at least defensible. So was the assumption that the dissimilarities evolving among the CMEA countries' economic mechanisms were only of a temporary nature and therefore would, sooner or later, be "replaced by a *rapprochement* on different bases" (Csikós-Nagy, 1973a; and Nyers, 1970). This, in fact, is not what happened. In Hungary a tendency toward centralization gained the upper hand instead, as became obvious following the November 1972 decision of the Hungarian Socialist Workers' Party's Central Committee.[7]

As it logically follows from the above, not even the moderate changes outlined in the monetary and financial chapter of the Comprehensive Programme have been implemented (the Programme itself institutionalized the political disavowal of monetary integration and the *de facto* predominance of integration through physical planning). To say that the entire financial chapter of the Comprehensive Programme failed would, however, be an exaggeration. Some of the outlined objectives were achieved. A comprehensively harmonized system of coefficients (quasi-rates) of the national currencies' exchange into one another and to the transferable ruble has been established. A common methodology has been developed for evaluating the efficiency of joint investments. Pricing methods have become more flexible, and the IBEC's procedures for extending credit have been simplified. The conditions under which third countries (outside the circle) could join the TR system, as well as the methodology of clearing non-commercial payments have been worked out. Both CMEA banks have become more active in their TR and convertible currency banking and credit transactions (the latter has entailed primarily the financing of joint investments) (MIEP, 1981).

A partial and mainly attitudinal change has taken place in the evaluation of the possibilities of international financial and global monetary cooperation—this reflecting the changes in the CMEA countries' real economic situation.

Today, we find anachronistic what was still the dominant approach of the early 70s, namely, that the very idea of even the common currency's convertibility should be dropped, as "it does not stem from the peculiar internal needs of CMEA cooperation and would only introduce the capitalist world's financial uncertainties into the integration's monetary system" (Allakhverdyan, 1976, pp. 225–236). This view held that the closed, non-convertible, clearing nature of the CMEA countries' currencies was an asset rather than a shortcoming. In the early 80s even professionals such as the late Soviet Minister of Finance urged the solution of the numerous irritating problems—such as interest, credit, balance of payments—within the CMEA's monetary system, and they spoke up for the expansion of East–West credit relations (Garbuzov 1983). If these ambitions were, indeed realized, they argued, we can no longer consider the issue of a common currency a regional matter, but must see it in a global context. Soviet economists usually close to the official line have done what seems to be a *volte-face*, and in the late 70s were urging that the CMEA's mechanism of cooperation serve to enhance (the CMEA countries') mutually beneficial relationships not only with each other but also with the developed capitalist and the developing countries (Shiryaev 1981, p. 131).

In spite of all the improvements, it is hard to dispute the validity of an assessment by the CMEA's International Economic Research Institute which, based on an analysis of the 70s, concluded that the changes in the monetary sphere were only of a technical and organizational nature. At the October 1980 meeting of the CMEA's Executive Committee, it was concluded that while the accounting and credit functions of the transferable ruble system were basically consistent with the then prevailing (directively) planned exchange of goods among the CMEA members, the efficiency of the monetary system as a whole and in its constituents was far from the desirable level, and a wide range of problems remained unresolved. Among them, the most pressing ones, in the view of the team of the CMEA International Economic Research Institute, were the following: the lack of actual multilaterality in payments; that no third party had joined the TR system of payments; that automatism remained typical of the placing of IBEC's credits; that rates of interest remained low and the practical possibility of spending the nominally charged rate of interest remained nil. Furthermore, the practical role of the multilaterally-coordinated coefficients remained insignificant. "The modification of the rules of setting contractual foreign trade prices was not comprehensive. It lacked the thorough evaluation of their impact on financial flows, and was not followed by appropriate modifications in other, closely related spheres of the financial system. That these changes were only partial ones contributed to bringing about the imbalances in intraregional trade, and compounded the difficulties the respective member states had in quantifying how, in the end, the jointly adopted measures (especially the longer-term ones) would affect the individual national economies" (MIEP MSS, 1981, p. 14).

Clearly, even if the transferable ruble had not remained a strictly bilateral accounting unit, direct government-level intervention could not have lessened, as has been suggested by both the Comprehensive Programme and its propagandists in the relevant professional literature. *Dirigisme*, in fact, has escalated unavoidably and independently of the differing basic principles of the respective national economic mechanism, despite the numerous and well-known shortcomings, nay, irrationality of such high-level interference. This also means that in the 80s, the TR mediated a trade that was not only 90 percent predetermined, but—by the coordination of plans—was nearly 100 percent so in terms of quantity, of choice, and of the bilateral trade relations in effect at the time. Since this predetermination was due primarily to the ever increasing number of day-to-day decisions by the central management organs,[8] the TR was not in the position to exert an independent feedback-effect on the actual evolution of trade turnover. Thus, the common currency "strictly follows the physical movement of goods, and this eliminates even the remotest chance of its becoming an independent, anonymous representer of value".[9] Enev, (1980a) and Ausch (1972) have rightly characterized this situation, which was growing ever more acute, as the TR's being totally void of all functions of money (in the Marxian sense). What we are saying here is "that a relationship in a physically determined commodity exchange, in a barter deal, is inevitably always bilateral. Monetary or value relationships, on the other hand, are, by definition, multilateral, even if they develop between two partners. In the latter case a commodity is, in fact, not measured against one another, but the commodity as value is measured against money, against a general equivalent and a general representative of value" (Špaček 1982).

It is common knowledge (Kiss, 1973) that in the course of coordination of plans bargains between bilateral monopolies and monopsonies take place. From this very fact it follows that the bargaining parties are usually insensitive to costs of, and profits on, the individual products—or even to their relations, since the bargain focuses on aggregate costs and profits. Hence, the individual (contractual) commodity prices exert no influence on either production patterns or on the choice of products. Prices thus degenerate into mere accounting instruments. No room is left for microeconomic automatisms and adjustments, so mistakes in planning took the place of the spontaneity of the marketplace (Chvojka, 1982, p. 108).

This situation has made somewhat anachronistic the repeated reiterations in the late 70s and early 80s of that thesis of the Comprehensive Programme which envisaged the establishment of organic links between national producer prices and CMEA contractual prices.

On the contrary: if a CMEA member state were to develop a more market-oriented price system, one which is more responsive to the signals of external trade, as indeed Hungary has done, it would necessarily have to filter out and neutralize the effects of actual CMEA prices.[10] The Comprehensive Programme had assumed a parallel evolution of marketizing reforms in the respective national economic mechanisms. Things, however, turned out differently. A rise in CMEA prices does not restrict demand; the abundance of supply does not bring down the prices of soft goods. Therefore contractual price movements can't and must not spill over into the national price structures. To look at it in another way: the structures of the various national producer and consumer price systems, their interrelation to taxation, to income policies and to consumer, agricultural and export prices, as well as their ways of functioning are so different from one country to another that the economic essence of even the nominally identical elements of price, cost and revenue differ substantially. Consequently, they can under no circumstances and to no extent serve as a cost basis for separate regional CMEA contractual prices,[11] as it has been proposed again and again in the last two decades or so.

THE REGIONAL DIVISION OF LABOUR
AND THE COMMON CURRENCY

In the 1980s, the European socialist countries found themselves with a different set of economic policy priorities, and in world economic conditions radically changed from what they were at the time of founding the CMEA. As the sometimes even too complex national industrial structures developed, as the embargo policies of the cold war faded into the background and as the tendency to peaceful coexistence came to dominate international political relations, it has proved possible for these countries to set their economic policy priorities taking into consideration the advantages of a division of labour on a global scale.

Thus, in the 70s, a process analogous to world-economic developments (Kádár, 1984) took place in the CMEA primarily as a function of the member-states' adjustment to the changed and changing system of exogenous conditions. Regionalism has, to some extent, been pushed into the background. This trend of real economic development has been somewhat contrary both to the expectations voiced in the economic literature of the 50s and 60s, and to the consensus of professional opinion.

It has been proven in the relevant professional literature that worldwide and multilateral regional division of labour alike—be it in commerce, in technology, in capital flows or in interfirm cooperation—can best be served by the use of a convertible currency. It is therefore worth examining just *which* currency's convertibility[12] would promote regional integration.

WESTERN EUROPEAN EXPERIENCES

The Western European countries attained the free convertibility of their currencies within the framework of international monetary cooperation (EPU+Marshall Plan). This was achieved through simultaneous and parallel steps to structurally change their individual national economies. They eliminated the domestic economies' subordination to defence priorities and the ensuing system of rationing, and did away with its derivative, the bilateral clearing form of international economic intercourse. This, roughly speaking, was tantamount to a return from the methods of physical allocation of resources to a commodity-monetary, i.e. market, economy. It meant the gradual termination of direct administrative (save for regulative) interference with both internal and external economic activities, with an internationally coordinated set of measures. International cooperation helped to bridge temporary imbalances and promoted the process of structural adjustment. This was made possible by the financing provided primarily by the considerable dollar surpluses of the US at the time.

All these preconditions are totally lacking in the CMEA countries. It is a well-known fact that in the 60s, the changes in economic management in most of the East European countries were still in the direction of the gradual expansion of the scope of commodity and monetary (market) relations. In the 70s, however, the changes enhanced centralization, and the plurality of national ways increased rather than decreased. Working out their own systems of economic management has always been part of the member states' sovereignty, as is reflected in the Comprehensive Programme of 1971 and the Documents of the Economic Summit of 1984. Due to the individual countries, widely differing endowments, plurality will remain a lasting feature. Furthermore, there is no country or international organization of ample liquidity that could—in pursuing its own economic and political interests—finance the changeover and the structural adjustment.

The Western European countries introduced the convertibility of their national currencies, despite their intimate monetary cooperation and the parallel modifications of their economic systems. They did this precisely because their monetary, fiscal and cyclical policies continued to be strongly national in character, and dependent on the individual national power structures, and the particular balance of social forces in each member country. The thesis that decentralization and the free flow of commodities—both essential factors for convertibility—are not incompatible with the planned management of the economy established in practice by the NEP era in the Soviet Union, and in theory in the 60s. In a nutshell: a modern planned economy can in no way be identified with its earlier command centralized form, with the physical rationing of resources, which indeed *ab ovo* rules out all free flow of commodities and currencies. It has been suggested that the East European countries ought to strive, as an initial step, for a "lower level" of convertibility, that of their national currencies.

The more difficult "higher level" of convertibility, i.e. a convertible common currency, has not been attained, and is not likely to be attained, as a dominant form of settling accounts even by the highly monetized member countries of the Common Market. The world economic changes of the 70s have prompted either global or national reactions, as opposed to regional ones. This process was enhanced in the mid-70s by the temporary desynchronization of the national business cycle. Desynchronization took place in the financial sphere as well. While the EMS (European Monetary System) is, after all, an instrument of integration within the EC, its rules are often more closely adhered to by the monetary and exchange rate policies of Switzerland and Austria than by the EC member states of Great Britain and Italy. The 1981–83 international liquidity crisis tended to give impetus to multilateral and global approaches. It became clear that international interest rate fluctuations, i.e. the matters of the business cycle and exchange rate risks, could not be stabilized without political understanding and cooperation with the United States. What is more, the establishment, even the possibility for the establishment, of the EMS was conditional upon an American decision: ending the dollar dumping (floating dollar which had been the policy of the early Carter administration. "Dependence" upon the US dollar was also demonstrated by the fact that within the EMS's basic currency, the ECU, the proportionate value of the individual currencies could only be determined in terms of their ratio to the US dollar. Hence the floating dollar kept upsetting the ECU's equilibrium. The West European system of relatively stable currencies and exchange rates was, thus, found to be inherently unstable, for its basis was open to unilateral manipulation by the monetary authorities of the US (Becsky, 1982, pp. 1216–1219). Furthermore, as it happened, the liquidity crises of the world's most indebted countries (Brazil, Mexico, Argentina and Yugoslavia), as well as of the overextended Venezuela, Nigeria and Indonesia who had overestimated their oil wealth, coincided with the culmination of the CMEA countries' debt problems. All this led to a significant revaluation of the standing and influence of the multilateral international banking organs, primarily of the IMF, of the World Bank and of the BIS (Bank for International Settlements).

Rather than regional monetary solutions it is the internally revamped IMF along with other forms of international monetary cooperation, more often than not involving the major US banks and sometimes even the US Government, that have gained the decisive role in managing international financial difficulties. As the developments of 1981–83 indicate—most palpably the much-discussed interrelationships among national interest rates—the mere possibility of the functioning of a regional monetary arrangement is conditioned by general world economic processes and expectations, most prominently by those in the USA. This holds true even if the EMS has set much more modest targets of monetary cooperation than its forerunner, the Werner Plan, did. Namely, instead of establishing an independent West European key currency, it is attempting to create a system of cross rates floating between quite narrow limits — a far cry from the goals of the earlier postulated monetary union, and from its summary reflection in a common currency. In other words, in contrast to the thoughts and targets of the 1971 Werner Plan, in the mid-80s, the

economic autarky set the framework for development. A whole series of new interests acquired a stake in the preservation and cementing of this peculiar system in the past few decades. The mechanism of international cooperation has remained overcentralized, and operates without there being a convertible currency in terms of which the partners' gains and losses could be unambiguously quantified, and without their being a real, full-fledged exchange rate mechanism. Thus, both on the micro- and macro-levels, we often find quite uncompromising organs representing the various national interests clashing with one another, and not only formally. By the mid-70s, the epochal changes in the world economy had aggravated the so-called "raw material problem", further deepening the conflicts of interest between the various countries. Over and above all this, advanced technology and the state of the balance of payments *vis-à-vis* the West reached a bottleneck in all the CMEA countries.

Suggestions for the liberalization of trade and the simultaneous hardening of the terms of payments had been made soon after the common currency and the formally multilateral clearing system were introduced in 1963. It is evident that these steps would have been necessary to make truly transferable the "transferable ruble" that took the place of the bilateral clearing currencies. Such measures would have made the TR more than an accounting unit. They would have provided and institutionally guaranteed the reserves necessary to make a claim established *vis-à-vis* one partner acceptable coverage for a claim earned by another partner. The suggestions were, in fact, never put into practice, on grounds of their putative incompatibility with the interests of the national producers. In fact, it was much more a matter of the inflexible interpretation of what these interests actually were. They were not put into practice despite the fact that the economic management of a number of the CMEA countries—and the economic theorists of practically all of them—were calling for the relaxation of the rigid, centralized system of physical planning and distribution. From the mechanism point of view, the period between 1965 and 1970 would have been appropriate for the institutionalization of partial multilaterality and convertibility within the framework of a transition to a monetized CMEA integration—one on its way to becoming an East European common market (Nyers, 1970; and Kiss, 1973, pp. 112–163). In other words—as all the contemporary literature pointed out—the chance of convertibility was there if the above changes were accompanied by appropriate measures to liberalize planning, pricing, and trade. The changes proposed were never put into practice, not for objective "real economic" reasons, but for strictly protectionist, budgetary and ideological considerations formulated in terms of "national" interest, considerations so dominant that there was no place for payments in convertible currency even for a part of the year-end bilateral balances.

The 1971 Comprehensive Programme's chapter on currency and finances nevertheless declared that the CMEA countries would look for ways to make their common currency not only exchangeable, but also (partially) convertible outside the CMEA region as well.[15] It is evident from what has been said above that the position of the CMEA countries in the 1980s was radically different from that of the countries of the EPU in the mid-50s. There was no international monetary cooperation, no parallel domestic economic steps have been taken to increase monetization and delegate decision-making authority to the company level, nor is there abundant liquidity provided by an interested outside source. Since we can hardly consider the productive forces of the East European countries today to be less developed than those of Western Europe in the 1950s, we can be fairly certain that it is not the different level of development, but economic policy priorities and institutions that have prevented, and continue to prevent the preconditions of currency convertibility from evolving in the CMEA region as a whole.

It is worth noting that even the West European economic community of interest among substantially more monetized capitalist national market economies has not been strong enough to bring into existence an economic and monetary union based on a common currency. For the world economic changes have, in general, served to strengthen the centrifugal forces in the world economy, and have tended to push regional solutions into a background.

Thus, from the financial point of view, even the long-term prospects of the convertibility of any integration's common currency seem rather bleak. In the case of the Common Market, it is the national antagonism aggravated by the community's enlargement, by the lasting discrepancies between economic and social policy priorities, and by the permanent differences in the competitiveness of the various member states that have worked againts the finding of a regional monetary solution. In the case of the CMEA, it is also the changes in the world market and the growing intra-block discrepancies in development due to enlargement, as well as the ever stronger trend to centralization within the national economies, that were serving to conserve the former system of physical planning within the integration. For this reason, the majority of the member countries felt that the advantages they derive from multilateralism, i.e. the higher level of foreign trade, do not compensate them for the disadvantages deriving from the modifications that are its precondition (Bartha 1975). While these priorities, regulations and real processes endure the concept of a financial integration that would permit the convertibility of the transferable ruble stands no chance of realization. Like practically all Hungarian economists dealing with the subject, I, too, believe that the probability of change in this respect in the foreseeable future is nil.

In the final analysis, it is justified to call the transferable ruble the manifestation of the "international relations of production", as Konstantinov (1982b) does, noting, I believe quite rightly: "The currency will be like its economic environment. It cannot be different from it. All this means that in theory, the transferable ruble is a principally new phenomenon among the currencies of the world. There never has been, nor is there at present, a currency like it." Thus, as long as the environment—i.e. the international relations of production—does not change to meet the demands of the epochal change in the world economy, the essence of the common currency shall necessarily remain unchanged. *Whatever* other currency might be introduced, it, too, would, of necessity, have to adapt to this environment, and not *vice versa*, as some theorists would have it.

In theory, the common currency would become convertible if all the CMEA countries—or at least a number of them, with the Soviet Union definitely among them—would introduce a system of measures that would permit the convertibility of the national currencies as well. Then and only then would it make sense to aim at developing the transferable ruble's money functions, and to this end to introduce internationally coordinated economic regulations and financial measures. (Essentially ones in keeping with the proposals in the 1971 Comprehensive Programme's financial chapter.) At best, measures of this kind can be introduced in the middle of the 1990s. Until then, however, it makes sense *only* to think in terms of how best to expand the money functions of the national currencies, and to take the appropriate steps to make it happen. For this and only this can provide a basis for the effective development of a regional international monetary system, something that might well prove to be more conducive to the region's competitiveness on the world market than the practices of the post-1975 period.

THE IMPACT OF THE SWITCH TO SLIDING PRICING
ON THE TRANSFERABLE RUBLE SYSTEM

The traditional situation outlined above was further complicated by the 1975 modification of the methodology of pricing within the CMEA. In 1975, this seemed to be no more than a short-term compromise between net raw-material exporter and the net raw-material importer countries. By 1976, a change seemed to be in order. For in keeping with the recommendation of the CMEA Executive Committee, no overall, comprehensive price revision had been worked out for the 1971–75 period, only small, bilateral changes had been made, so that in 1975 prices were still as they had been set in 1965 (Meisel, 1979, p. 149). Some economists saw the switch to sliding pricing as the first step to the reform of the entire system of cooperation (Zwass 1978, p. 179), if for no other reason than that it seemed to be the diametrical opposite of the CMEA's traditional overriding concern for stability. Others felt that the new pricing policy was an incentive to flexibility, and transmitted world-market valuation in serving to approximate the intra-CMEA to the extra-CMEA prices, which was, in the final analysis, a good thing (Lakos, 1975, p. 33).

This optimism, too, proved to be unfounded. For a number of reasons—primarily owing to the system of financial bridges which each and every CMEA country was obliged to resort to, and also due to the unchanged methods and role of joint planning—the new pricing formula did not, essentially, influence enterprise activities but "only" led to the redistribution of national incomes within the CMEA because of the changes in the terms of trade (Kiss–Pavelcsák 1981, p. 95). The practice of annually changing prices remained extraneous to the mechanism of cooperation as a whole (Ptaszek 1981, p. 33), inconsistent as it was with the methods of national economic planning practised by most of the member states, methods, that were highly stability-oriented, particularly as regards prices. It was, thus, hardly surprising that soon suggestions appeared for the stabilization, or at least long-term pegging of contractual prices within the CMEA. Only four months after the February 1975 session of the CMEA Executive Committee where the switch to sliding pricing was proposed, the first Bulgarian objections were raised, and suggestions made for changing to a stable price base (Mateev 1975). Subsequently, a number of Bulgarian, Romanian, and GDR publications urged a return to stable prices, and from the references, we find that there were Czechoslovak and Hungarian economists, too, who objected to sliding pricing. It would be a mistake to trivialize these objections as attempts to give theoretical underpinning to the immediate commercial interests of the net raw material importer countries. As is well known, the former system of national economic planning does require stable prices, requires, in fact, that prices stay stable for the entire plan period. In practice, annually changing prices prevent the member countries from evaluating the effect any measure taken as part of the long-term cooperation programme has on the national economy, and the same holds true of the joint investments. The annual recalculation of a plethora of individual product prices and the related bargaining about changes in subsidies and in levies often involves an incredible amount of extra work for the bodies directly responsible for finances and trade, without, however, all this work having any direct, positive microeconomic effect. For this reason, already in the 1976–80 period, contractual prices in the bilateral trade of a number of small CMEA countries did not "slide", but were fixed for two or three years by intra-governmental agreements, and when they did change, changed only slightly (in spite of the general formula).[16] This was undoubtedly the most sensible solution, for the trade between the small East European countries was structurally balanced, and this balance—arrived at through much painstaking effort within the framework of the coordination of medium-term plans—seems to have been mutually accepted to both parties at least for the duration of the plan period. It would, thus, have been superfluous to calculate anew every year what were, in fact, satisfactory, or at least, mutually acceptable terms of trade, for the commodity patterns of trade were fixed by the plans, and the changes in its terms —due precisely to structural bilateralism—were, for the most part, insignificant. Constant bargaining is, essentially, an intolerable chore for an inflexible state apparatus whose main tasks are quite different, especially when it involves the inescapable bureaucratic horsetrading frequently dominating the course of multilateral CMEA negotiations and the activities of CMEA organs. It is, thus, hardly surprising that four years before the beginning of the new plan period, i.e. at the most initial stage of the coordination of plans for 1986–1990, the question was raised again whether the use of sliding pricing was, indeed, expedient (Holeček 1982, p. 65).

THE "PURCHASING POWER" OF THE TRANSFERABLE RUBLE

From the financial point of view, the above practice also means that the "purchasing power" of the transferable ruble—which had always been different for different bilateral trade relations and commodity groups—was even further differentiated. The nominal "value" of the TR became "inflated" in the various bilateral relations to varying measures and at varying rates. For this reason, we can only agree with the Bulgarian economist, Stoyan Enev, that "within the CMEA, the value of the transferable ruble for the various national economies is a function of a number of processes and factors. Thus, it cannot be described in terms of a single indicator, as for instance, purchasing power, but only by using a whole series of economic indicators" (Enev 1980b).[17] In other words, "joint planning objectively limits the effectiveness of trade and monetary relations in general, and in particular in relation to the common currency, when it confines its operation to square with the parameters set by the plan. For this reason, there is absolutely no grounds for likening the transferable ruble to gold or to the US dollar" (Konstantinov 1981c, p. 109). It seems justified to conclude, therefore, that it was, for the most part, the adverse effects of the yearly changes in price levels that were felt (Špaček 1982), though not primarily, as the Czech author maintains, because of pricing problems, or because of the "decline in the real value" of the TR.

In spite of the explicit provisions of the jointly accepted pricing principles, thus, in practice it is never the case that a given product has the same price in the various bilateral trade relations. In other words, the common currency has no uniform purchasing power (Dubrowsky and Zschokelt 1980; and Zhivkova and Kazandzhieva 1980), which in itself impedes the efforts at transference (especially given the lack of a money market, and that there is no appropriate substitute for premium and discount). Under the circumstances, there is no telling ahead of time what goods of what quality can be obtained in what quantity and on what terms of delivery for a unit of transferable ruble credit. Understandably, this in itself strengthened the earlier trends to physical planning and bilateralism within CMEA trade in the 1980s. The leader of the GDR delegation at the Thirty-Sixth session of the CMEA held in Budapest explicitly formulated as a normative requirement the demand that export and import deliveries be more closely tied to one another (Stoph 1982).

The fact that the transferable ruble functions, in effect, as a bilateral clearing currency is the immediate reason why "every common, multilateral programme breaks into a set of bilateral programmes in the course of its implementation" (Shiryaev 1981, p. 166). Thus it is difficult even simply to comprehend, let alone to accept, the periodically recurring exaggerated claims that "the transferable ruble successfully serves the cooperation of the socialist countries, fulfilling every monetary function there is" (Geidarov 1981, p. 35; and Zverev 1981, pp. 39–41). Much more logical is the view of the German economist, Christa Luft (1982), who gave the following rationalization[18] of the existing practice: "The introduction of multilateral forms of trade and accounting—among others, the convertibility of the transferable ruble—cannot be regarded as the main way to develop socialist integration". After roundly condemning those economists who present bilateralism as obsolete, Luft concludes that "multilateral coordination and balancing can be used along with bilateral coordination, as a supplementary possibility", which, given the earlier mechanisms, seems an accurate description of how things used to be. (Luft's formulation, however, seems to carry a degree of normativeness which is definetely quite out of place.)[19]

EXCHANGE RATE ISSUES

The switch to sliding pricing has resulted in a number of new exchange rate problems. The matter of exchange rates, as we have seen, received special attention in the financial chapter of the Comprehensive Programme of 1971. Under the above-detailed circumstances, however, the proposed measures seem to have lost their relevance. By its very nature, the transferable ruble was not homogeneous. Thus, it had no content that can be defined in economic terms such as, for instance, the ratio of the nominal value of the transferable ruble to the dollar. Consequently, it makes no sense to speak of a transferable ruble exchange rate policy in the classical economic sense of the term. True, changes in the TR: $ ratio were significant in the setting of nominal contractual prices within the CMEA, and in maintaining the value of credit nominated in transferable ruble terms, especially when the $ input contents of the products delivered on credit was high. In spite of this, in strict economic terms we cannot call "exchange rate" a ratio that exerts no immediate influence on the income of an enterprise, nor on its investment decisions.[20]

In order to establish a "realistic exchange rate" for the TR at the regional (CMEA) level it has been suggested (Bánfi, 1981, p. 226; and Botos, 1980) that the average be taken of the, for the most part unpublished, national coefficients that were actually used by the respective states to evaluate convertible currencies. The suggestion seems logical, for every national economy has an interest in being able to realistically evaluate for its own purposes the costs of acquiring a unit of convertible currency. An evaluation of this sort, imprecise though it be, is still of more real economic value than the official TR: $ "exchange rate" based on the nominal gold content ratios of these currencies, which reflects no real economic content whatsoever.

Bánfi's and Botos's suggestion, however, was based on the misunderstanding of the foreign-exchange multipliers used in the CMEA countries. For it is only appropriate to call attention to the fact that "in the majority of the CMEA countries, the role of exchange rate has been assumed in part by coefficients differentiated according to export and import as well as according to trade relations and commodity groups, and in part by the budgetary regulation of exports and imports, making import opportunities conditional on export performance, all of which immediately affects the CMEA market and the exchange rates that obtain there" (MIEP MSS, 1981, p. 24). Bulgarian economists have called attention to the incommensurability of the exchange rates and multipliers used by the various CMEA countries as a result of which they fail to form a unified valuation system. The various multipliers each influence different partial areas of cooperation. There was no unified CMEA methodology of setting them; each country had its own ways of calculating. This pluralism of the rates of exchange has persisted, although the 1971 Comprehensive Programme had envisaged the contrary (Enev, 1980a, pp. 23–24).

Put another way, we encounter the same problems in the course of averaging exchange rates (in fact, even before we come to averaging them) as we do in the course of averaging the various national producer's prices. Even identical financial categories are calculated in different ways, i.e. even identical entries reflect divergent cost structures, so that they cannot even be compared, let alone averaged. All of this applies equally to the suggestion that the transferable ruble be made into a composite currency through basketing the national currencies (Botos 1982). Clearly, from the point of view of financial technique, the problem could be solved by introducing a unified method of calculating hard currency coefficients, as indeed the Comprehensive Programme had proposed. Multipliers derived from such a unified methodology have, in fact, been elaborated. For the reasons outlined above, however, these never acquired the economic substance that would warrant our considering them a realistic exchange rate. There continued to be no organic relationship between CMEA prices and domestic prices, and the multiplier continued to have no direct influence on either enterprise decisions or incomes. Thus, it comes as no surprise to find that "there was no practical demand" (Faluvégi, 1977, p. 351) for the use of the multilaterally coordinated coefficients. Nor should we forget that in different systems of economic management even similar goals can be achieved only by a variety of different means. Any suggestion to adopt uniform instruments therefore seems to be unfounded. At this point, we might well ask what economic sense could be made of an average which, on the one hand, consists of a Hungarian commercial exchange rate which, in theory, is a marginal equilibrium exchange rate; and on the other hand, is comprised of a Soviet currency multiplier based on the theory that "in a planned economy, the exchange rate cannot be the linear function of the ratio of foreign and domestic prices, and of the balance of payments . . . Under socialist conditions, the currency's rate of exchange loses its independent role as a separate economic regulator" (Konstantinov, 1981a, pp. 37–38).

NON-COMMERCIAL PAYMENTS

The need for the CMEA countries to exchange their national currencies among one another arises in the course of non-commercial settlements. Here, actual conversion takes place, which has prompted certain economists to speak of "planned convertibility" (Konstantinov, 1982 a) operating in this sphere. Others feel that this more or less inevitable degree of exchangeability shows how far the CMEA countries have gone along the road to convertibility and realistic price formation (Brainard 1980, p. 134). In fact, however, this is far from being the case. As the ever-growing number of administrative, customs, currency, exchange, and commodity export restrictions regulating intra-CMEA tourism since 1979 show, the *de facto* exchanging of one national CMEA currency for another has been coming up against ever greater difficulties. Though non-commercial items account for but 3 to 4 percent of foreign trade, it has extraordinary (political) weight from the point of view of the whole process of socialist integration, directly touching, as it does, millions of people, and having an impact on their thinking and behaviour.

The system of multilateral accounting has been in practice since 1963. The essence of the 1963 Prague agreement was that the purchasing-power parity of the various currencies was calculated on the basis of the "consumer basket" of a four-member diplomat family. The value of the goods purchased was expressed in terms of their consumer price in each of the CMEA countries, and each of these values was compared to the value of the identical goods at Soviet consumer prices. The resulting figure yields the coefficient of each national currency as against the Soviet ruble. It is this coefficient that is used to convert to Soviet rubles the non-commercial year-end balance in each national currency. Then, though the nominal value of the Soviet ruble was identical to that of the transferable ruble (something that has never had any justification, the value arrived at in Soviet consumer prices was converted to the common currency of intra-CMEA trade (whose value, in theory, is supposed to derive from world market prices). To facilitate this conversion, a special coefficient (divider) was introduced already in 1963, whereby 3.4 Soviet rubles = 1 transferable ruble.

The goal of the Prague agreement was to introduce a multilaterally coordinated and technically not overly complicated system of accounting. The simplicity of the system lay in the fact that, due to multilateral coordination, the rates of exchange between the various national currencies derive immediately, as cross exchange rates, from the coefficients of the various national currencies to the Soviet ruble. (Thus, no CMEA country could be "expensive" or "inexpensive" from the others' point of view simply for exchange rate reasons.) Equally simple was the conversion to transferable rubles of the various claims arising between the various countries. (This, had a truly transferable currency come into being, would have greatly facilitated the clearing of balances.)

Over the years, however, the shortcomings of the system have become evident. A number of the difficulties have been due to there being no truly transferable currency. Others, to the transferable ruble's above-outlined lack of homogeneity and to the problems caused by the changeover to sliding pricing. Yet others have been caused by the growth of tourism, which has laid bare the immanent weakness of the system (i.e. comparing the food bills of diplomat families) by which the exchange rates were set in 1963. No less important, however, has been the inflexibility with which the economically unfounded coefficient between the Soviet ruble and the transferable ruble has been applied.

It is evident that the consumption pattern of people residing within a country (thus of diplomats) will be radically different from that of tourists, who will spend a few days or weeks within the given country. Moreover, in a number of CMEA countries, diplomats are given special treatment in respect of provisions: they have access to goods not, or not always, available in the stores. The variety of the goods available, stability of supply, the range of scarce goods, the degree to which consumer demands are satisfied differs significantly from one CMEA country to the next at the current official consumer prices. In other words, there are very great differences in the degree to which these consumer prices are able to guarantee the stability of the domestic market. This is tantamount to unrealistically weighting the various items in evaluating the "consumer basket" (Vincze, 1984). The *de facto* consumption pattern can also be significantly different from what was taken into account at the time the "consumer basket" was "filled". Empirical investigation has shown that this is, in fact, the case. The "basket" approach puts too much emphasis on subsidized staples (e.g. flour, lard, sugar) that tourists do not require, and underestimates the significance of items that are decisive in the tourist trade (e.g. the price of hotel accomodations, which is frequently available only with 100–200 percent surcharges for foreigners). Furthermore, consumption patterns and standards differ considerably from one CMEA country to the other, something, which makes hard to justify an exchange rate uniformly (multilaterally) calculated on the basis of uniform baskets. This assumption that all consumption patterns are identical and all markets equally saturated within the CMEA countries put countries with more equilibrated domestic supply conditions at a disadvantage (Faluvégi, 1980, p. 219). The problematic nature of the artificial "basket" approach became especially evident when tourism got to be a large scale phenomenon, just at a time when—in consequence of the very divergent priorities maintained by the various CMEA economies in the 1970s—very great differences had developed in the degree to which the domestic market equilibrated, how the official consumer price indexes shaped up, and how realistically they were presented in the different member countries.

Tourism—being an important convertible currency earner for each of the East European countries—has raced ahead of the CMEA countries' capacity to accommodate it. The possibilities for influencing the macroeconomic efficiency and quantity of socialist tourism through exchange rates failed precisely because these coefficients had been produced by an insensitive, uniform methodology. Actual bilateral rates of exchange were mere derivates from a multilaterally coordinated inflexible methodology, based on several unrealistic assumptions. The cross-rates were the results of periodic political-level bargaining, where the better-supplied countries could raise their prices only to a point, and not as far as the excessive demand would warrant. (A fine case in point used to be the great and permanent discrepancy between the official zloty/forint exchange rate, and the black market rate.) In this area, too, then, the direct valuational function of money had been "supplemented" by a variety of not always very civilized measures: currency export prohibitions, restricting the amount and even the types of foreign currency available for tourist exchange, lengthy lists of commodities whose export is strictly prohibited (including garlic, potatoes) etc.

The switch to sliding pricing caused difficulties in non-commercial accounts as well. In theory, it is clear that if the coefficient (divider) for converting Soviet rubles to transferable rubles remains unchanged even when contractual prices have risen this adversely affects the countries with non-commercial assets (Brainard 1980, p. 130; Špaček 1979; and Pachta 1980). This indeed is what happened in practice: since the Moscow agreement of 1974 elaborating on the Prague agreement, the coefficient has been modified only in 1978, 1981 and 1987. Presently, it is at 1.7. In this connection we must note that already in 1978, when it was lowered from 2.3 to 1.9, the official joint calculations were calling for 1.6 as the warranted figure (Špaček 1979). This, for the most part, explains why the countries with surpluses have been seeking since 1976 for adequate ways to offset their non-commercial assets *ex ante*, i.e. already at the time of the coordination of plans. This was justified enough, for the countries with liabilities had made no efforts that would have enabled them to do without the non-monetary restrictions on tourism. On the contrary, most of them have even introduced unilateral restrictions, instead of making attempts to revive the economic interest of the receiving countries. All in all, at the planning level they have managed, for the most part, to offset their liabilities in adequately hard commodities, and to avoid—or at least to minimize—the inflationary losses due to the static TR:Soviet ruble coefficient. But this was possible, again, only at the cost of increased bilaterality and physical planning. This, naturally, has led to certain tensions, at the planning level as much as at the level of the man in the street. Bilateral agreements in physical terms, thus, have come to complement and supplement the monetary valuation at official rates to an ever growing degree. The former, however, precisely because they are non-monetary in character, have always been open to dispute as to the size and distribution of the advantages they involve. The countries with liabilities have felt that their partners, in demanding that they offset their debits in commodity shipments of above-average hardness, were compelling them to make financial sacrifices of an unwarranted magnitude. So far as I can see, a country might well find that it is worth making even some financial sacrifices for the political end of an increased and free flow of people among the CMEA member states. In practice, however, the countries with liabilities, many of whom have long been paying lip service to the ideals of internationalism at the level of general propaganda, have chosen to act on quite another set of priorities, and a number of them have not exploited the possibilities of tourism even to the degree that is economically feasible. It is for this reason, too, that the equilibrium in non-commercial payments has been arrived at a below optimal level, and this in an atmosphere of mutual self-sacrifice instead of mutual advantage, all of which have led to a growing shortage of CMEA currencies in a number of the member countries, and have served to strengthen the black market.

On purely theoretical grounds, one might make a further objection. In a system of multilateral cooperation, it is hardly warranted to evaluate every bilateral non-commercial relation in terms of the price structure of one and the same country. Furthermore, the 1974 Moscow agreement allowed for fluctuations of plus or minus 20 percent in the various relations. At any rate, the strictly bilateral clearing of balances, which focused on securing the equivalence of exchange more and more in physical terms, and concentrated increasingly on the detailed preliminary setting of the commodity mix of counter-deliveries, had rendered the role of Soviet consumer prices virtually nominal by the early eighties.

All the problems outlined above essentially stemmed from the fact that a typical market category, the rate of exchange, has been substituted artificially for a bureaucratically devised multiplier. This causes problems because the consumer demand functions as a real market in a command economy, too. To the extent that the population is not restricted in its movement, its purchases and its exporting activities, it will evolve into an international market as well. The laws of motion and the motivational forces of this peculiar kind of restricted, but real, market have inevitably come up against the specific, different kind of logic of directive planning and bilateral balancing. In other words, the "spontaneity" or real economic factors has come into conflict with the non-commercial accounting practices that mirror the changing needs of the "planned trade turnover" which used to make up 96–97 percent of the CMEA countries' intra-block trade. In any given case, it is, of course, the particular regulation in question that proved to be inadequate. In essence, however, it is just another form of the fundamental question of the domestic as much as of the international market of the CMEA countries, namely, how far unplanned decisions, or spontaneous decisions out of keeping with the plan, could lead to re-allocative decisions, both in terms of production and of scale. What lent the issue special political weight is that the processes outlined above reflect the immediate consequences of a number of partner countries' sovereign decisions on prices, wages and production, which spill over to another country in the form of effective demand for supplies that had originally been planned to meet national consumer needs.

Two types of solutions are possible. One is to go in for more detailed specific regulation in keeping with the logic of mandatory planning, and thereby further restrict the market character of this spontaneous international exchange. This has been the practice to date.[21] The other is to recognize the market substance of non-commercial payments, and to introduce a regulation which corresponds to its inherent features, one that essentially differs from the above outlined arrangements both in its logic and its methods. Choosing the second alternative is facilitated by the fact that most CMEA economists agree that the non-commercial coefficients bear every feature of an exchange rate. They have direct influence on the income position of tourists, they can make a country attractive or too expensive, and thus motivate the choice of country for purposes of tourism, the duration of time spent there, and the structure of the outlays. Under ideal circumstances, thus, the best solution, in theory, would be to introduce floating rates which immediately reflect supply and demand (Botos, 1978, pp. 182–185). It is clear, however, that under those conditions this proposal could not be implemented directly. Given the former currency and foreign-trade monopolies, some countries could, for instance, inflate floating prices to unrealistic levels through creating an artificial shortage of currency. In passing, we should note that when the surpluses deriving from tourism were converted into goods (formally into transferable rubles), non-commercial payments were also being channelled into the entire "planned trade turnover". Having become a part of the latter, it, too, must bear all of its characteristics. In spite of this, official intra-CMEA exchange rates that follow the cross exchange rates established *via* Western convertible currencies would certainly be a step forward.

Another important area of non-commercial payments was working out the methodology of calculating the coefficients applied to settling the special payments related to joint investments, and its modification in 1981.[22] The advantage of the multipliers arrived at lies in the fact that they allow for the conversion of the national outlays even in the absence of a realistic exchange rate and of a convertible currency. Their drawback lies in the extraordinary slowness and awkwardness of the calculations (separate calculations must be made for each and every cost-element), and in the fact that the resulting concrete coefficient can be used only for the given investment project. It is not only a matter of a calculation for every international project—each instance being an opportunity for renewed bargaining about earlier settled issues in the guise of methodological debate. For some projects, for instance the Orenburg pipe line, dozens of uniquely applicable calculations had to be made (Špaček, 1982).

Detailed analysis has shown that in the sphere of the convertibility of national currencies, too, the CMEA cooperation is on the road to growing demonetization. It is difficult to avoid the conclusion that as in planning, commerce, and commercial settlements where bilateralism dominates, here, too, bilateralism would be a step ahead: it is primarily in setting exchange rates that multilateral decisions should be confined to the basic principles of methodology, leaving it to the respective countries to negotiate with each other the exact magnitudes to be effectuated (Asztalos, 1981, pp. 132–133).

SOME ASPECTS OF INTRA-CMEA TRADE IN CONVERTIBLE CURRENCIES

Oddly enough, this subject is generally not included in the professional and official literature which analyzes the monetary system of the CMEA. This, without exception, holds true of the writings of the highest ranking administrative people of the Soviet Ministry of Finance. The first official Soviet *de facto* acknowledgement of even the existence of intra-CMEA convertible currency trade was the 1981 article by Konstantinov (1981c, p. 113). The author maintained that trade in convertible currency constitutes but "sporadic, transitory agreements which have no substantial effect on the export or import patterns of the CMEA countries". He further stated that this foreign currency trade constituted a mere 0.3 percent of the total intra-CMEA turnover.[23] Bogomolov's (1983a) elaboration was the first Soviet attempt to look at the intraregional trade in convertible currencies in a way that, seen from Hungary, appears to be consonant with its magnitude and relevance, i.e. in a way that relates it to the regular problems of trading in the official TR system. Of the volume and composition of this trade, none of the CMEA countries, other than Hungary, supplies any public information.[24] Hence, no lump-sum evaluation can be made as to its region-wide significance (although on occasion, such figures do get produced in some Western studies).

While the "dollar trade" represents 8–15 percent of Hungary's Comecon commerce, a great number of important writings stated *expressis verbis* that the transferable ruble actually transmits the whole of intra-CMEA turnover. For one, "the transferable ruble is an ideal means of accounting for *all* transactions on the international socialist market" maintained Bochkov (1982). Following this train of thought, it is somewhat difficult to understand why indeed it was the group of the "hardest" commodities that ceased to be part of the TR trade. As a reflection of the growing strains in the CMEA countries' current accounts, also expressing the doubts as to the actual worth of the transferable ruble and the concern about the size and distribution of the mutual benefits derived from the transferable ruble trade, there was a significant growth in the intra-CMEA trade which was handled through Western intermediaries. During the EC's 1974 ban on beef imports, Hungary lost a considerable amount of export revenues in convertible foreign exchange, but since the internal Soviet market conditions allowed for this, it was made up for within the CMEA. Later, similar arrangements developed with some other CMEA partners, and became permanent due to their being mutually advantageous. In Hungarian—Soviet trade, for instance, they made it possible for the Soviet Union to realize world market conditions—as far as her oil deliveries were concerned—even beyond the levels set by the plan targets and the established practice. The intra-CMEA hard currency trade took a number of forms.[25] Of these, most important were the options for delivery contracts over and above the planned deliveries as well as the *ad hoc* business deals. From a microeconomic standpoint, the latter may be viewed as a pragmatic alleviation of a number of sources of tension: the excessive length of the plan periods, the inflexibility as concerns new products and new requirements, and the fact that an almost necessary product obsolescence is part and parcel of the over-detailed specification of mutual deliveries.

For most of the 1970s, interstate optional agreements formed the backbone of the intra-CMEA "dollar trade". This practice was useful on a number of counts. a) It secured the import of hard commodities over and above the plan targets.

b) sought goods were acquired from suppliers who were members of the same political and defence alliance. In other words—unlike many sonorous but uneconomical or unviable solutions—it guaranteed the security of the above-plan supplies, primarily in goods of strategic significance (raw materials and agricultural produce in particular). c) The purchaser, in accordance with the basic stipulations, of the option, was not required to buy any of the surplus. This way the buyer was not burdened by having to store superfluous supplies, while he was assured of a flexible and secure source. d) The country running a surplus got to acquire convertible currency. Consequently, the balance of payment problems of the countries with a surplus were eased, while the countries with a deficit saved on transportation and intermediary costs and also enjoyed manifold indirect benefits from the easing of the bottleneck. Though the original agreement presupposed strictly equilibrated deals, the above holds all the same.

Convertible currency trade is transacted at "non-cleaned" current world market prices. This in itself acted on an incentive on both the national and company levels, given that the advantages of the TR trade with all its complications have been quite difficult to define, and the distribution of its benefits has not been quantifiable.

Therefore, in my opinion exchanging free currency into a convertible ruble, transferable ruble II or something else issued by either the CMEA banks or the Gosbank, as has been suggested in some of the pertinent Hungarian literature,[26] would be not only senseless but, in fact, damaging. Obviously such artificial money—which, by virtue of its name and its issuer would resemble the common currency—would not have the universality of acceptance characteristic of a free currency. The multitude of technicalities involved in the emission and functioning of such a new monetary unit aside, it is quite likely that the convertible ruble would be discounted against its nominal value after issuance at least for some time. Unless this *disagio* were continuously quoted on the money market (thus reflecting the TR's actual value), it could not even in theory displace the presently used convertible currencies. Its acceptance would therefore gradually decrease, then cease, and it would regress into the transferable ruble.

The various suggestions made in connection with the convertible ruble do, however, bring into focus the theoretical difficulties which the somewhat apologetic CMEA financial literature has been facing in trying to explain away the prolonged presence of an external trade practice in which increments of trade on the hardest commodities have been exchanged for hard currency. No traditional approach can offer a theoretical explanation for this. It is hardly surprising, therefore, that the financial literature—if and when it deals with intraregional trade in convertible currencies at all—has treated it with disdain and reluctance. According to one of the oft-repeated arguments, this trade is directly influenced by imbalances of trade and the currency fluctuations on the capitalist world market (Enev, 1980a). Other theories maintain that since it limits the scope of functioning of the common currency, it is, by nature, incompatible with the objectives of integration (Botos, Patai and Szalkai, 1980, pp. 93—94; and Kazandzhieva, 1980, pp. 4–5). Some authors caution that the extensive use of convertible currency may upset the equilibrium of the socialist monetary system which rests on the collective (common) currency (Enev, 1980a, p. 14; and Lyubskiy et al. 1978, p. 149). Still others consider it useful if it creates additional trade, but dangerous if it does not do so in absolute terms, but merely rearranges trade i.e. if it withdraws merchandise from the TR clearing trade (Nyers, 1983a).

In evaluating the trade in convertible currency, I, too, am of the opinion that "increasing the role of the transferable ruble should never become an end in itself; it has to be subordinated to the needs of the socialist economic integration" (Konstantinov 1981c, p. 114). As was borne out by the 1973–75 upsurge in intermediated commerce, the intra-CMEA convertible currency "market" did not, for the most part, draw merchandise away from the conventional clearing trade. Rather, it reduced somewhat a well-known aspect of bilateralism, i.e. that it hinders the evolution of the optimal volume and welfare effects of international commerce. In other words, it created trade which, under the traditional arrangement of payments, would not have come about. Further, it created an incentive for a CMEA country to increase its export potentials beyond the limits of the counterdeliveries that a partner of lesser export capability could offer, an incentive—not provided by the transferable ruble trade—to attain a balance of trade surplus. And finally, it lent CMEA trade a modicum of multilateralism which extends beyond regional boundaries, to the extent that the year-end balance of payments was cleared by payments in actual convertible currency, and as far as the *ad hoc* deals were concerned. Should convertible currency trading be built into the planning mechanism between now and 1990—a suggestion which already surfaced in the 1976–1980 period and received political consideration at the 1982 Session held in Budapest (Dăscălescu, 1982)—all these benefits would cease, and Hungary, for instance, would probably lose her interest in, depending on circumstances, 8–15 percent of her previous intra-CMEA trade.

Nowadays, convertible currency trade is an organic part of the former mechanism of CMEA cooperation rather than an alternative to it. The traditionally prevalent "specially constructed deals" have given way to an exchange of a very limited number of products that were mutually strictly predetermined in physical terms by the respective national planning agencies (primary raw materials and agricultural produce). Here, the role played by convertible currency was symbolic, as only the measuring rod of the world market has been adopted, without its mechanism (Csikós-Nagy 1983).

One should not lose sight of the fact that convertible currency trade is aimed primarily at the optimization, between the two trading entities, of the very limited commodity bases which are saleable on both major markets. Noting this, Richter (1980) is quite right to pinpoint that its appearance indicated the growing strains in CMEA trade, and this can only be interpreted as a criticism of the traditional cooperation system. This, however, in my opinion does not warrant their overall negative appraisal. What a theoretical critique should focus on is the viability of the whole of the system of traditional physical and bilateral cooperation in an era of epochal transformations taking place on both world markets, rather than the tenability of a partial, and in itself warranted, financial solution.

The relevance of this wider context, i.e. the determining role played by the non-market type of intra-CMEA arrangements, as well as by the unfavourable changes in the international liquidity position of the CMEA countries, is reflected in a novel turn of events in the mid-80s. With the substantially diminished power standing of OPEC, oil, too, has joined other fuels in losing its relative price against finished products. The relative prices of other primary products, i.e. their terms of trade, either failed to improve in the 70s, or if they temporarily did improve, their 1973–75 profits were already depleted by 1979. Since fuels account for two-thirds of the Soviet hard currency earnings and given that even in 1983, at a time of declining prices, the Soviet Union maintained her traditional practice of selling its oil 2 dollars per barrel below the OPEC price, the effects of diminishing prices could only be offset by increasing export quantities. Even the reorientation of certain sales formerly sold to CMEA countries for TR offered but a slight possibility for this, as oil production has hardly increased at all, coal production is going down, and natural gas can substitute for oil only to a very limited extent (even that only after the completion of the controversial pipeline between Siberia and Western Europe). The export of more electric power would have been a possibility, given that grids had been built in the 60s and 70s. This, however, was precluded by the increasing strains on the Soviet domestic energy balance —as indicated by the growing frequency of blackouts since the 70s (Poteryam, 1983).

This situation was further aggravated by the fall in gold prices. Soviet manufactured exports were unable to counterweigh the combined effects of all these factors (See Appendix, Table 11). This explains why, beyond the previously mentioned ideological reasons and those of monetary policy, from the Soviet Union's point of view, convertible currency trade, which by nature perpetuates (structural) trade deficits, has become less and less attractive. The attempt to cope with their liquidity difficulties has become a central problem to all CMEA countries, especially since 1981.

This is a further reason why—after the hopeful signs of the late 70s and early 80s—the outlook for intraregional convertible currency trade has become rather bleak. Some countries have even attempted to require payments in convertible currency for certain items whose delivery was fixed in the protocols of medium-term coordination of plans, and it was only through the traditional surplus countries' refraining from further sales for convertible currency that these attempts could be curbed. Hence contrary to the expectations of certain quarters, we were seeing convertible currency trade shrink, rather than expand, in the 80s. If it does not altogether disappear, its role as the producer of surpluses for the current account in convertible currencies will nevertheless diminish substantially. In other words, only zero sum dollar transactions are likely to continue, which—as a further manifestation of the well-known peculiarities of bilateralism—has a limiting effect on this particular type of intraregional trade. It increases the likelihood that transactions will be predetermined in physical and bilateral terms, and thereby contributes to their conforming to the overall CMEA mechanism of cooperation.

ON CONVERTIBILITY

The matter of "external convertibility" arises on both regional and national levels. Realistically speaking, however—because of the above outlined situation—it has been an unlikely alternative. It is hardly surprising therefore, that Konstantinov (1981b, p. 51), five years after IBEC's 1976 initiative, discussed the use of the transferable ruble in East-West trade as a technically workable, but in practice as yet untried, future possibility. Under the current regulations, a Western creditor whose claims were denominated in TR would not only be faced when trying to liquidate it with the same obstacles as the enterprises of any CMEA country would be (van Brabant, 1977). He was positively disinterested in joining the earlier system of multilateral settlements. For an extraregional creditor it is definitely more advantageous from the liquidity point of view to sign a series of bilateral agreements with each of the debtors than to join a system of multilateral settlements where, in the final analysis, no one is responsible *"in concreto"* for the liquidation of his claim (Pörzse, 1979, p. 105; and Nikolova, 1982).

Still, this does not mean that it was in no outsider's interest to join the transferable ruble system. As the German economists Dubrowsky and Zschockelt (1980, p. 6) have rightly pointed out, "The transferable ruble has been created for settling the planned trade among the socialist countries, taking into account the peculiar pricing rules and the regulations providing its plan-based coverage. Consequently, it is other socialist countries or developing countries with a socialist-orientation which might be interested in joining the system. For this, too, however, further steps must be taken in the direction of real multilaterality of settlements."

Wiles (1973) was the first to introduce the idea of the transferable ruble's purely financial convertibility. He suggested that, capitalizing on the transferable ruble's pre-1975 nominal stability, it would have been developed into a sort of reserve currency. At the time, the CMEA countries' interest could have been secured as they could have obtained additional foreign exchange deposits, although the problems connected with interest rates and with valorization which would have had to follow the contractual price revisions of every five-year plan, would have required special arrangements. Since the post-1975 changes within the CMEA shook the very foundations on which the proposal had been built, it is rather strange to find it reappearing years later in the pertinent socialist economic literature (Shmelyov, 1979b, p. 283; and Botos, Patai and Szalkai, 1980, p. 133).

On a national economic level, convertibility is a logical step following the elimination of a command economy. As early as 1968, the economic reform plans included the introduction of the Hungarian forint convertibility. Although this target could not immediately be met, however, it remained a not too distant prospective goal of the new economic management (Csikós-Nagy, 1973a). Recentralization emerged as the dominant trend of the 1970s in the CMEA, Hungary being no exception to the general rule. Therefore the idea of the convertibility of the forint remained an issue to be advocated by researchers only. Renewed calls for convertibility came to the fore again in Hungary after the return to the 1968 guidelines for economic management, and following the political-level recognition of the need for export orientation.

It does not seem expedient to go into the details of analyzing whether and to what extent current Hungarian financial regulation corresponds to the systemic preconditions of currency convertibility. The balance of payments position of the country renders this suggestion out of place for some time to come. But for the purpose of clarifying conceptual alternatives, it should be discussed irrespective of the immediate practical significance of the issue. In the context of the intra-CMEA financial system it seems sufficient to note that convertibility of a national currency is a step which stems from the sum of those radical economic reform measures whose necessity is (has been) derived from the immanent analysis of a multitude of spheres of the economy. Most of the counterarguments voiced in the financial literature on the CMEA are of an ideological, rather than a professional nature. These either postulate some non-existent quality of the traditional system—such as the uniformity of the system of payments within the CMEA—or defend precisely those obsolete forms of economic control that are to be modernized by the comprehensive overhaul of the management system. (For example, the state monopoly on foreign exchange, and a "sovereign", i.e. clearing, form of settling accounts, both integral parts of the traditional planning system which permit the implementation of voluntaristic priorities.)

Of the authorities who are, in principle, sympathetic to the concept of national currency convertibility in the CMEA states, Rusmich (1983) has warned against the possible spillover of the spontaneous, unplannable processes of the world market into the CPE's; while Rédei (1973) has argued that convertibility would render the national economy "open and vulnerable".[27] Others, in voicing their reservations, have questioned not so much the particular monetary instrument as the general policy of export orientation, which is, however, an organic part of the concept of thorough reforms. These objections reflect the vested interests of those adversely affected by a consistently implemented adjustment policy. They complain of convertibility's "increasing the effects on the uncertainties prevailing on international markets"; its being a "giving up of the protective function of the state monopoly on foreign exchange"; or, for that matter, of its "exposing" the allegedly "underdeveloped" productive forces of the socialist community to the merciless laws of the competitive world markets. (Cf. Kazandzhieva, 1980; Lyubskiy et al. 1978, pp. 137–150; and Konstantinov 1981a, pp. 37–39.)

Though the need neither for radical reforms nor for export orientation can be substantiated by an argument confined to the subject of intra-CMEA finances, be it sufficient to recall that in the discussions on convertibility, it is often issues of principle rather than of financial economics that are being debated. More often than not, they are no more than a rehash of age-old disputes over the inherent nature of the socialist economy, or over the unity or the division of the world market.

Rather than reviving such interminable controversies, I should like to point out that a limited, central-bank-level convertibility of the forint had once been officially contemplated. Even if it had been realized, however it would not have affected intra-CMEA relations (Fekete, 1980). In its more substantial form, convertibility would institutionalize an organic link between the domestic and competitive markets. Convertibility would compel Hungarian producers to adjust to world market demand, and would heighten their sensitivity to market signals. The resulting growth in the share of universally marketable produce in the total output of the country would mean that many more Hungarian hard commodities would be available for exchange in intra-CMEA trade. Should any other CMEA country succeed in making her currency convertible, a bilateral trade relation would emerge, where a uniform and undisputed measure prevailed irrespective of the actual unit of account.[28] In this particular bilateral solution, integration at the interfirm level could substantially expand.[29] It would make running a surplus worth the effort, and even the quota system could be abolished. For the integration, this development would imply a trend towards a regional currency system as proposed by the Czech economist, Petr Špaček.[30] In this concept the TR would become exchangeable for national currencies, and their convertibility, in turn, would function as a bridge to the Western monetary system. It is clear that if all CMEA currencies became convertible, the TR would also become convertible (or would cease to exist). This, however, does not seem to be within easy reach, if for no other reason than the specific problems involved in the convertibility of the Soviet ruble, and of the currencies of the non-European developing CMEA member states.

Would not Špaček's proposed line of action (to which I also subscribe) imply tangible dangers, especially for the smaller members of the CMEA? Would this not be tantamount to the institutionalized renunciation of a major advantage of the integrational currency system, based on the TR, namely its international nature, which is described by the earlier-quoted publications of Professor Konstantinov as the most immediate proof of the superiority and democracy of the CMEA financial arrangements? Would this not mean vulnerability for the small countries, their defencelessness in the face of manipulations initiated by the countries emitting the key currencies?

In answering these questions the following factors deserve consideration. The power status of small countries—and therefore also the possibilities open to them for asserting their interests—is inherently different from that of big countries. Irrespective of the international legal regulations and postulates, small countries have to live with this without their necessarily being powerless objects in the process. The leading world economic and financial role of the United States is reflected, in the final analysis, in the "dominant role" of the US dollar in the international monetary system. Under the present international economic order there is absolutely no viable substitute for the US currency (Enyedy, 1979) whatever reform the international monetary system undergoes. The only realistic choice is between joining in or staying out of the international financial flows (and staying out is not a viable alternative, given its intolerably high costs). Equally, the dominant role of the USSR within the CMEA was also the result of a number of factors: the postwar international order, the implementation of the radial type of integration concept, the decisive role played by the Soviets in socialist industrialization both in terms of market, of structures, of sales patterns and methods, as well as of technical levels and of being the sole supplier of primary products to name just a few. This is a given fact also from the economic point of view, whose disregard—with reference to abstract internationalism or to "equal rights"—would be rather naive and unrealistic.

True, this determinant influence has been formally filtered out by the traditional "monetary" system serving the autarkic policy priorities as long as it did not let the impacts of either CMEA or of world markets to spill immediately over the domestic economies. Analyses of the 60s have, however, already proved: it is precisely the inward-looking, the separation of domestic and external markets both in economic and monetary policies, that is a chief ingredient in the growing technological lag between East and West as well as in the insufficient international competitiveness of the results of industrialization endeavours. International experiences of the seventies are also indicative of seclusion and protection of the domestic producers from external shocks being a disadvantage, rather than an achievement. And intra-CMEA experiences of the same period have shown that even a modest opening up of these economies to the world market will be a failure if monetary seclusion, the bilateral clearing arrangements, remain in force, especially if integration into the world economy is also on the agenda.

Last but not least, it should be noted that it is precisely the former intra-CMEA financial arrangements which act as a disincentive to running surpluses in integrational trade. Its much-heralded international character never really existed, and is less and less likely to come into being, given the growing structural bilateralism. Real multilaterality, that truly international system neutral to pairs of bilateral relations postulated by the CMEA's principles, has never materialized, and consequently the "democratism" argument is not a very strong one. Neither the advantages, nor the disadvantages customarily enumerated by the traditionalist opponents of the system based on convertible national currencies exists. As has been demonstrated, what was perceived as the major threat of the 60s, and fear of which prompted much of the resistance to progressive changes, i.e. income redistribution among the CMEA member countries, has actually materialized. Since this income redistribution happened through the changeover to sliding pricing, i.e. through a partial modification, the growth in redistributive elements was not attended by the sort of pressures for better microeconomic adjustment that convertibility could have activated.

The Documents of the 1984 Summit[31] as well as the resolutions of the 1987 Council Session are a reiteration of the economic programme of the Comprehensive Programme of 1971. Official statements made at the Council Sessions of the 80s are indicative of continued diversity of national concepts, approaches and interests. Recent attempts at more radical renewal seem to show that there has been no energy for debates more substantial than the ones of 1969–71. Short-term readjustment problems seem to dominate in the minds of the member states and also at the Council Sessions. Among these, the problems of energy supplies, agricultural self-reliance, the use of existing industrial capacities and the issue of aid might be mentioned, along with the issue of conflicting trade interests. Problems of the economic mechanism of cooperation are hardly mentioned at all, and when they are, the national positions diverge. The thesis of the CMEA's having to be an instrument of international economic competitiveness has frequently been voiced in joint documents in the 80s, but this has had no tangible connection to concrete decisions as to integrational means. To make this connection could be a task of the Long-term Concept for Socialist International Division of Labour for the 1991–2005 period. The rehabilitation of the concept of national currency convertibility may be a step in the right direction.

NOTES

1 The exchange rate fluctuations that followed the soaring American interest rates in 1982 did, in direct contradiction to conventional economic theory, have a determinative effect on international commerce: the tail, so to speak, wagged the dog. This type of change-about was unimaginable in the monetary system of the CMEA.

2 The use of this particular term by no means implies that, the arguments of Ausch (1965) and Csikós-Nagy (1973a) notwithstanding, we should look at the CMEA of the 60s as being monetary in character. On the contrary: the cooperation's monetization grew ever weaker from the 60s to the 80s. In short, since the early 50s, a generally negative trend has predominated.

3 A rather randomly selected extreme example being that energy-poor Hungary had to offset its coking coal imports by exporting brown coal briquet to Czechoslovakia. In citing this particular example, I do not mean to be making a value judgement on this arrangement. I merely wish to point out that Hungary's exporting brown coal can in no way be regarded as even indirectly compatible with the theory of comparative advantages.

4 This statement does not lose any of its strength by the fact that it is not only the issue of cooperation, but also issues like the internal, national mechanisms, the national economic policies, historic and world economic factors that come into play when one examines certain problems in detail. When I talk about the "mirroring" character of the monetary system, I am thinking of the interrelations elaborated by Vincze (1984).

5 Nyers (1975, p. 20) similarly to Rédei (1973) took a similar stand, with the exception that as against the earlier expressed views, he looked at the viability of the common currency's convertibility much more positively, and considered it an even more plausible possibility than making the national currency convertible. Yet already at the 1980 CMEA conference in

Sopron, in agreement with the views here presented, he argued for the national currency's convertibility to be realized in the shortest possible time. (For a report on the conference, see *Acta Oeconomica* 1981, Vol. 27, No. 3–4.)

6 This topic is explained and analyzed in detail by Kozma G. (1976).

7 A detailed account of the complexity of the insights and contemporary developments making way for the November 1972 political turning point is presented in the illuminating analysis by Soós (1987).

8 It is a different story that Szegvári (1987, p. 94) notes with some justified irony that the system of long-term agreements based on the *ex ante* setting of physical flows may actually function, in the end, thanks to constant deviations from it in various stages of its implementation. What is relevant from our point of view is that it is not the financial feedback, but other considerations that prompt central control organs—not companies—to adjust plans to changes.

9 Thus it cannot measure value, as Kiss (1973) departing somewhat from his own logic, polemically states. The clearing (synthesizing, accounting) function is an entirely different matter: it exists in every type of economic mechanism, independently of whether the synthetic indicator is suitable for determining the measure of necessity of social expenditures.

10 A contradictory requirement was advanced by Kozma F. (1978b, p. 356). He maintains that the regulatory system should be sensitive, in fact, highly sensitive (op. cit., p. 367) to impulses originating from within the CMEA. This requirement was fulfilled in the extreme when in 1979 Bulgaria introduced its "world market pricing" which reflected its prime market the CMEA-s prices, to the extent of 75 percent in the country's transactions. Because of this the agricultural sector—most of all animal husbandry—showed heavy losses. Quite understandably, it was not animal husbandry, but their peculiar "world market pricing" that they abandoned from 1982, when they returned to cost-based producer prices (Bautina, 1983), which were to some extent influenced by the capitalist export-import prices. Since the CMEA prices did not reflect shortages, or the interrelations of supply and demand, they were *ab ovo* unsuited for providing a basis for microeconomic market-related decisions. Of course, filtering out the effects of pricing does not, in itself, solve the problems of the CMEA market's adjustment to the world market, nor of reconciling the differences that the structural policies of the two international markets entail.

11 This became obvious in practice during the fruitless debates in the 60s about the "cost basis" of separate CMEA prices, which really put mental endurance to the test. Csikós-Nagy (1975) gave an enduring analysis of the nature of the differences between price systems, and of the problems they presented. For a critique of more recent similar approaches, see Vincze (1983).

12 When it comes to the question of adjustments in the CMEA's monetary system, the literature more or less confines itself to dealing with only partial measures, which would provide only slight possibilities for convertibility. I have elaborated on this literature in my three studies on the CMEA. *Trends in World Economy*, No. 52. 1985, Hungarian Scientific Council for the World Economy, Budapest.

13 For example, the devaluing country has to adopt a tight financial policy, while the revaluing country needs to intensify its efforts to counterbalance

its growing export problems. The former is faced with growing inflation or unemployment, the latter has to introduce redistributory measures favouring capital, albeit all three of the above developments are politically risky.

14 True, in his later published excellent and rightly famous article, Shmelyov (1987) himself calls the TR an aborted baby, the proper purpose of whose conception and birth no one can account for today, as its "father", V. Garbuzov, is no longer alive.

15 The Forty-Third (extraordinary) Council Session, convened already under the impact of the unfolding Gorbachevian reforms in order to restructure the intra-CMEA multilateral arrangements has, in fact, gone no further than to reiterate this particular position in October 1987 (cf. Communiqué 1987).

16 Similar information is given by Meisel (1979, p. 149).

17 According to Konstantinov—(1981d), the IBEC's credit mechanism *ab ovo* ruled out inflation, but in the same work he acknowledges that "purchasing power is diminishing". However, since the basic situation described by Ausch (1972) has not changed, but has in fact, been worsened by the problems enumerated in the main text, in the absence of "purchasing power" we cannot talk about its "diminishing", either. In a later work, Konstantinov (1982b) does not mention diminishing purchasing power any more, but relying on the earlier arguments, categorically re-states: "The TR is not subject to inflation."

18 In the psychological sense of the expression, whereby our effort to *ex post facto* rationalize our deeds is an immanent human characteristic.

19 It is interesting to note that in his "marketizing", liberally-toned article, Rédei (1973) although reasoning in the opposite value system, found it necessary to state his conviction that "a certain degree of bilateralism and the quota system derive from the essence of planned relations, and they do not constitute a primitive barter agreement. In a system of bilateral trade, multilateral clearing is technically workable". Neither the latter statement, nor the extent of the "certain degree", nor the way this observation can be reconciled with the idea of convertibility are explained anywhere in any part of the article.

20 Reasoning in a similar economic frame of mind, Hágelmayer (1976, p. 78) argues the above ratio's exchange-rate status on a different basis, saying that if, in fact, an actual TR: $ conversion never materializes, there is no need to call the clearing coefficient anything but what it is. As a counter-argument, Botos (1982) maintains that the coefficient "nevertheless carries a certain economic content". Shelkov's (1980) point that it does, in any event, determine the level of contractual prices and is "capable of safeguarding the real value" of the ruble does not sound very convincing, since its level is not influenced by price factors, by the region's balance of payments situation, or by supply and demand (Špaček, 1982). Furthermore, the size of the multiplier does not influence the volume of exports and imports between the member states (Kiss, 1973) as these are determined by the coordination of plans based on physical parameters. An interesting contribution to this discussion is the opinion of Botos (1979, p. 592), that "if a multiplier does not affect actual and far-reaching decisions,

if it does not have a part in establishing domestic prices, it cannot be regarded as a rate of exchange, but only as a coefficient". I, of course share this view completely. Rusmich (1983) adds to this that the economic precondition of a rate of exchange's functioning is that it influence not only existing imports and exports, but production decisions oriented to external markets; and furthermore, that on its basis, the consumer be free to make decisions about his import capacity. The Czech expert rightly notes that this is not the situation in any of the CMEA countries, let alone in the community as a whole.

21 This also means a step back to the practices of the 50s, when "unplanned" private tourism ceased altogether.

22 For a detailed account of the Berlin method and its shortcomings, see Lantos and Pörzse, 1975.

23 The author specifies neither the sources, nor the method of calculation through which he arrived at this figure, which seems remarkably low.

24 In the course of the 1982–83 negotiations for rescheduling, Romania and Poland did provide the IMF and the creditor banks with such data, but these have been confidential.

25 For a typology of these forms and an empirical analysis of this trade, see Richter 1980.

26 The idea—as Pécsi (1983) pointed out at the 1982 international CMEA conference held in Sopron—dates back to a Soviet proposal of the early 1960s. Pécsi joined Bársony (1980) and Farkas (1978) in reviving the proposal. By way of comment, we can only note that at the time the proposal was originally made by the Soviets, there was, as yet, no convertible currency trade within the CMEA. The Soviet proposal was, thus, to institute something that did not yet exist; the latter three authors, however, were proposing the (nominal ?) transformation of an existing practice.

27 Today, it seems that openness and vulnerability are immanent features of the national economies of small nations, features which are independent of the particular political direction and monetary system of a given country.

28 In this case, too, the US dollar or the DM would continue to be the unit of account — as indeed it is in the trade relations of the small capitalist nations. The point, however, is not this, but the consistent application of the "if you have domestic currency, you have foreign currency" principle, and a system of subsidies (e.g. industrial protection) that conforms to the market.

29 This possibility was already raised by Kiss (1973). However, the overall halt that was put to the reforms has meant that it has never been tried in practice.

30 In his book *Platebne — Úvěrovy mechanismus RVHP* (The accounting and credit mechanism of the CMEA), Prague: Academia, 1981. See Válek 1982.

31 For details, see Csaba 1985, pp. 71–89.

CHAPTER TWO

A contribution to the theory of prices in a demonetized environment

The mechanisms of quota-based bilateral trade reflect the needs of import oriented growth. Its mechanisms rely on balances drawn up in physical terms and are actually an extension, on an international level, of the material-technical supply system of domestic directive management and of the system of delivery contracts. Thus it assigns to both the categories and laws of the market a subordinate role that fits in with the logic of the centralized planning model. In other words, it should be clear, even on a cursory examination, that commodity and monetary conditions within the CMEA are, with regard to their nature, fundamentally different from the same categories as defined on the basis of what philosophically is a free competitive market, but historically is a neoclassical interpretation of it. So "subordination" here certainly does not mean the virtual presence of conditions identical with the ones assumed by the neoclassical theory, where differences are manifest only in magnitude. One of the corollaries resulting from the dialectics of the objectivity of socialist commodity production and the non-expression, or rather, restricted, and partly distorted expression of market categories is, precisely, that in a centralized economic mechanism, it is not the free market categories, laws, processes (and motivations!) that dominate either at the national or international level, but the interest structures inherent in commodity production express themselves in a different way. How do the "subordinated" market categories then express themselves and what do they reflect? It is very important to examine this question when trying to interpret the benefits gained from a regional international division of labour. Since the nature of the advantages has already been characterized, in a general sort of way, by the relevant literature and any specific answer we might come up with could only be formulated in the context of the peculiar mechanism by which the advantages are distributed, it seems warranted, and indeed logical, to resist, for the moment, exploring any other possible avenues and concentrate instead on the mechanism itself, of the distribution of advantages.

"FAIR PRICES", "CLEANING UP" WORLD-MARKET PRICES, BUSINESS FLUCTUATIONS

An expression of the way in which export prices are determined by the economic mechanism is the fact that prices, valid in bilateral relations, are fixed according to the uniform price calculation principle adopted for trade between the CMEA member countries, a sliding scale that is a modified version of the price principle of Bucharest (the modifications were introduced in February 1975). The old and the new pricing methods share two basic features.

First, in intra-CMEA trade, prices were based on capitalist world market (chief supplier) prices. This was because world market prices ultimately express the internationally defined socially necessary and recognized input. Second, these prices have to be "cleaned up", since the capitalist world market was seen as subject to certain monopolistic trends, speculation, power considerations and also extreme fluctuations, from which, in the opinion of government leaders in all the CMEA countries, the economies of the socialist countries must be protected. It is to be stressed that the means by which to achieve this was to average the actual prime market prices over a five or three-year period. This did not rule out, in theory, the use of other methods, if the need arose to do so. "Need" here was to be taken to mean, according to the price principle and the resolutions of the 1975 and 1976 sessions of the CMEA, all cases where the above factor is demonstrably and dominantly felt.

From this point of view, what are we to make of the two price explosions on the world market? This subject would deserve a special study, but—given the extensive coverage of the topic in analyses published in the 1970s—we shall here limit ourselves to summing up the conclusions. Accordingly, the skyrocketing of oil-prices was attributed to two equally important factors: an economic one (the scarcity of a natural resource as a limit to the previous path of growth expressing itself in the restructuring of relative prices) and a political one (on the one hand, the considerations of OPEC both as producers and as a political power grouping, while on the other, the business-policy considerations of the transnational companies controlling raw material production).[1]

At the same time, it is to be recalled that there were some economists who tried to explain the dramatic escalation of prices entirely and exclusively by economic reasons. Hence they regarded the increase of raw material prices within the CMEA and also the modification of the price principle not as a timely adjustment to the changing fortunes of the world economy but rather as a step towards an economically "equitable" price structure (Bakhtov—Zoloev 1977).

But equity, in this sense of the word, is an ethical, rather than an economic, concept. Accordingly, there is not much room in economics for the category of fair or equitable price, a category rooted in Emperor Zenon's antimonopolistic constitution. As for what can be regarded as a theoretically appropriate price—well, it is that which equilibrates market and secures the mutual advantage of those participating in the exchange. It is economically unsound for prices to rise fourfold overnight, while production costs and the conditions of supply and demand remain fundamentally—structurally—unchanged. This can only have been a "political price"—and sure enough, it was just that, born as it was under persistent pressure from the transnational monopolies, as part of some global strategy, even if it did express some real and, to a certain extent, well-founded economic trends.

To the extent that the price changes were brought about by monopolistic and political factors, they had to be considered—according to the CMEA principle—the sort of fluctuations which were to be filtered out. The application of the sliding pricing as a temporary compromise solution might have provided a sound basis for harmonizing the interests of raw material producers and consumers.[2] However, with the above in mind it does seem something of a contradiction that this price principle was introduced in the context of precisely the events of 1973–74, for, in the logic of the same price principle, the 1974–75 prices should have been screened out, for the very reason of their freak nature (Biró, 1976, p. 10).

The switchover to sliding pricing did not involve a modification of any of the fundamental elements of the price principle, nor did it at all affect the reason for applying the principle. For this the resulting higher nominal price level did not render the relationship between export prices and domestic prices, nor did it enhance the potential for expanding production. If something still did, that was obviously not a consequence of the new CMEA pricing practice.

By taking the prices of only three years, those of 1972–74, as the basis—with a view to a swifter transition—they made it clear that the new pricing methodology was to serve the adjustment to world market trends, i.e. capitalist prime market prices. Therefore there was not a hint of the afore-mentioned "fair price structure", which is not surprising at all, given that we live in a world burdened with national and regional conflicts of interest, rather than in an era of a unified communist world economy. Because of the differing interests, it is impossible to determine, especially *ex ante*, what sort of prices would subserve (and for what reasons) a harmonious development of the world economy as a whole, as well as that of the constituents of that overall structure. The crux of the matter is this: had it not served a better adjustment to world market trends, the transition to sliding pricing would have been politically impracticable.

Let us mention here a few practical consequences, too. Clearly, so long as raw material prices were rising on the world market, the CMEA's internal raw material prices—due to that grouping's pricing practices—were nominally lower than the capitalist world market prices. (This, of course, does not automatically imply that importing from CMEA countries was unconditionally more efficient; to judge that, import costs would have to be balanced against export earnings.) Still, recent developments show that raw material and energy source prices do not necessarily stay at a high level; indeed, there have been notable precedents in the past where even the nominal prices declined significantly. In such cases, intra-CMEA raw material prices exceeded world market prices. This—in view of the interrelationship between the structure and the volume of all imports with those of total exports under the bilateral arrangements—need not pose a problem. What is worrying, though, is that, under the theory of "fair prices", at the peak of a nominal intra-CMEA raw material *hausse*, trends could assert themselves which, by declaring this price structure as fair, seek to perpetuate it, under the slogan of stability. This, in turn, would prevent the otherwise unavoidable spillover of higher prices for manufactures.

It goes without saying that international trade prices are ultimately always the result of a bargain. In theory prices in international trade are to bridge and harmonize the conflicting interests of buyer and seller. This is precisely the reason why the price principle of intra-CMEA trade did apply the capitalist market prices as these are indicative of the point where the conflicting interests of buyer and seller are balanced. To the extent that this makes for a rejection of autarkic solutions and continuous reliance on world market prices reflect the CMEA's being a subregion of a homogeneous world market, the changeover to sliding pricing did imply some favourable shift in economic thinking. In practice, however, it was a one-off isolated move, felt through its disadvantages rather than its theoretical benefits.

PRICES AND ADVANTAGES

Owing to the peculiarities of the monetary system of the integration, favourable or unfavourable CMEA price relatives alone are by no means equal to the actual benefits or disadvantages from foreign trade for a particular member country. Intra-CMEA trade is characterized by the member countries' aiming at bilaterally balanced trade in physical terms.

"In this respect, the rigid tying to each other of hard goods (measured in world market prices) does, indeed, make the exchanges among CMEA countries more 'equivalent' by the year, though, from the viewpoint of the joint advantages to be gained from the international division of labour and from that of the special benefits to the particular countries, it makes that exchange less than rational. This is because it forces the individual countries to disregard existing natural endowments and priorities associated with national productivity levels and relative capital-intensity. Hard goods must, in part at least, be repaid in kind, or, if that should prove unfeasible, should be produced domestically, at any cost. Of the large number of available examples, let us remember here that it was this factor that has promoted the development of Hungary's coal-mining industry and Bulgaria's non-ferrous metallurgy sector." (Ausch, 1972, pp. 112–113). On the basis of the foregoing, we might perhaps venture to say that, in this particular medium, hardness is a more important factor of advantage than price. This is true even if, as a result of the peculiarities of CMEA trade, hardness reflects the member countries' mutual demand for each other's commodities in a rather indirect and subjective manner. Still—as opposed to world market prices—it does ultimately reflect *regional* supply and demand. This seems to reinforce the view that the existence of investment contributions is linked to the subordinate role of prices and of market categories in general. Investment contributions, whose role spectacularly increased after 1973, and which, under a proper economic regime, could be a mutually advantageous form of CMEA cooperation, are intrinsically tantamount to a price increase. Its rate can be quantified: in a market economy it corresponds to the discounted value of a credit as calculated for the corresponding moment (t) of the time of expiry (Tardos 1969, p. 164). It follows that investment contributions and a price increase can only be considered as alternative ways of eliminating a given imbalance.

WESTERN EXPERTS ON MUTUAL ADVANTAGES

In western literature in the field, Horst Mendershausen and later Franklyn Holzman and László Zsoldos were the pioneers of the debate on price discrimination.[3] The gist of Mendershausen's (1959) argument is that the Soviet Union charged Eastern European countries higher prices for her exports and paid lower prices for her imports than to Western Europe. Holzman (1962) contested this view. In his opinion, the CMEA countries form a peculiar customs union aimed at a high level of autarky. This, however, they seek to attain not by using discriminatory customs tariffs but through direct control of foreign trade. This policy has two important consequences. First, internal prices differ from world market prices, and, second, the members do not sell at higher prices outside the CMEA, while buying at lower prices outside the organization. However, they often sell at prices lower than those on the world market and also frequently buy at higher prices. To this, Zsoldos (1962) added some comments specifically concerning Hungary. He carried out hypothetical calculations in order to determine the possible export revenue of Hungary, had the goods sold within the CMEA been exported to the West. He claimed that this, in the 1950s, would have left Hungary with losses of billions of foreign exchange-forints. He likewise contended that his conclusions did not contradict those of Mendershausen, for, in the relevant product range, Hungary was buying from her CMEA partners at higher than world market prices, while selling to them at lower than world market prices.[4]

But this argumentation does not hold water. It is a well-known fact, accentuated, incidentally, by Holzman, too, that every CMEA country achieved poorer results in selling their really marketable commodities to western nations than in their ruble-accounting sales. This reflects primarily the mutual economic preferences that member states accord each other, e.g. by accepting each other's products even if they are of a lesser quality or if delivery conditions or servicing are less favourable than is usual with western products. This is true across the board and it affects each and every country. Therefore, a peculiarly interpreted specific terms of trade index, illustrating the mutual advantages, can be calculated for the range of products actually sold on both markets. This is done as follows: for example, we compare the socialist and the capitalist market prices of the Hungarian export commodities directed towards both markets. Then, for the same range of products, we compare the export prices that the Soviet Union charges on the socialist and the capitalist markets respectively (using the official exchange rates). If the value of the index is bigger than one — and this seems to be borne out by the calculations (Tardos and Nagy, 1976)—then we are faced with a clear case of either mutual discrimination or mutual preferential treatment, which proves the *reciprocity* of the results and effects of the trade between the countries concerned.

The above analysis, the first in western literature on the subject, was followed by several further studies which—like the first attempt— ignored, for the most part, the peculiarities of commodity, monetary and market categories as they prevail under socialism. Their conclusions rested mainly on comparisons between the nominal levels of intra-CMEA and "world market" prices. Understandably enough, it was mostly after 1973 that such analyses proliferated. Most authors rely on the econometric methodology of international economics. They often disregard, however, the fact that even if it were statistically possible to come up with identical economic indices for the CMEA integration and for other regions of the world, the risk is there that the impact of institutional factors is so strong that it may undermine the end result of the whole statistical exercise (Marer and Montias 1980a, p. 5).

And this is far from negligible, indeed, it is the determining factor in the studies that rely on comparisons between intra-CMEA and world market prices, in proportion to the passing of time. As a matter of fact when Mendershausen was carrying out his separate investigations peculiar to intra-CMEA prices, he had a history of a mere six or seven years. That period had not yet been enough for the earlier motivational system of the market indeed, axiomatically presupposed in the econometric methodology,—to disappear in the CMEA. At any rate, it was then not quite so absurd for theorists to try and make sense of conditions within the CMEA in terms of the traditional motivational system. It did make some sense to assume, for instance, a profit-maximizing attitude on the part of these countries. The political developments of 1956 did no doubt play a part in the adoption of the Bucharest price principle, and by the same token, in the changes which took place in these countries' practices as well. However, the price principle was invoked fairly infrequently. Actually, over a period of nearly two decades, it was applied only on two occasions. Hence, the earlier motivations and the theory strongly related to them has gradually become irrelevant. Since the economy—nowadays a living organism, being, in a constant state of flux—is, by its very nature, irreconcilable with a set of prices that are fixed for long. If, however, prices are frozen for long periods, the inherently changeable economic interests are bound to assert themselves in a different form. In consequence: the motivations of economic decision-makers have growingly been oriented towards those peculiar *price-supplementing* elements in this medium that have effectively *replaced* the function of price.

This is also reflected in the shaping of the traditional planned economy's sociologically discernible relative power relations. Management organs controlling factors of production in physical terms continuously gain weight and influence over monetary authorities. It is the central planning board that sets up macroeconomic balances in physical terms, that breaks down and finalizes mandatory plan-objectives. The central board and the regional party organizations dispose over inputs vital for meeting plan targets. All these authorities are being revalued *vis-à-vis* the financial organs and the banks. The latter, though quite influential on paper, are in fact relegated to playing no more than an ancillary supervisory role. Theoretically, the banks have, in many instances, the right of veto even in certain stages of the investment process. In practice, however, even the watchdog role they have in keeping an eye on adherence to the plan is limited, inasmuch as the plan—which is the yardstick—may itself change, something over which they do not have much control.

This state of affairs, characteristic of the mandatorily planned economies of Eastern Europe, is common knowledge among the economists of CMEA countries. It appears, in a number of instances, to be quite incomprehensible for some western analysts, steeped as they are in a world of "money-fetishism", where banks often have a decisive say. Taking the latter for granted and extrapolating these conditions into actual intra-CMEA arrangements (that are not really transparent for most outside observers) we arrive at the fashionable theories, explaining integrational developments in Eastern Europe on the basis of nominal price-differentials between intra- and extra-regional trade flows. Needless to say, such a method applies a logic artificially imposed from outside and quite alien to the environment under examination. It should be fairly clear, then, that the longer the time span is since the introduction of the peculiar institutional system of the planned economy in Eastern Europe and the longer its specific interests and power structures have been around, the better its participants know those real power relations, that are not always manifest on the surface. Therefore, with the passing of time, the non-price benefits, along with the possibilities and techniques of gaining advantages in other than price considerations, become more widely known. This type of information has gradually been "internalized" and has thus become, as it were, part of the natural reflexes of decision-makers. Therefore, the degree to which any theoretical analysis based on the former motivations of market economies becomes irrelevant for explaining intra-CMEA developments is a linear function of time, since 1949.

In market-economy terms, the trader in the CMEA is one only in a rather restricted sense; as owing to the extreme centralization in decision-making, he is, for the most part, reduced to executing formalities and particulars in an essentially prearranged deal. The "higher nerve functions", including the negotiation of global deals, are performed by the higher echelons ranging from prime minister to general managers in the Ministry of Foreign Trade. What is involved here is not just that the specific transaction price is not even known to them (moreover, it is objectively impossible for them to know it in due time, as it is established, for a significant part of the product range, in civil-law contracts only in a later stage, i.e. after other terms of deliveries have already been set). In other words, the price is a constituent of a multi-dimensional bargaining system characterized by an overall duopoly situation, and therefore the individual transaction price thus distorted is not a decisive factor at all. In most cases, a price gain or loss is not even quantifiable, since it figures as an element to be balanced against factors associated with other transactions (e.g. the hardness of an item linked to another commodity group on the other side of the global deal). Obviously, a price for a given product cannot be compared—in spite of the provisions of the price principle—with the corresponding product price of any other bilateral relation within the region, for it is part of a different system of bargains, linkages and advantages. It would make still less economic sense to compare a barter price characteristically (and increasingly) bound to bilateral relations only, with real world market prices. With the latter, the price, and the price alone, expresses the totality of the advantages (including, of course, credits, mode of payment, conditions of delivery, and the relation of the price to performance and to the competitor's price). Moreover, in the absence of a money market, there is no sound basis for a barter price to be measured against real market prices.

Hence, even if for considerations of negotiation tactics, it is understandable why Konstantinov (1982a, p. 21) strongly emphasizes the statistic, presumably arrived at by comparing nominal ruble prices and world-market raw material prices, that, in the CMEA, the Soviet Union lost an annual 3 billion rubles between 1974–1979. What is less understandable, and must be considered a superficial grasp of the issues involved, is that western authors, too, regularly come up with similar data: for example, Böhm (1981, p. 191) puts the loss at 8.5 billion transferable rubles, with Dietz (1979) and others extending the list.

To this group belongs one of the most controversial western writings on the subject, a book co-authored by Michael Marrese and Jan Vanous,[6] quoted earlier on. Their main conclusion is that, between 1960–80, the Soviet Union subsidized her East European allies to the tune of 87.2 billion US dollars (Marrese and Vanous, 1983, pp. 3 and 49).

The chief merit of this writing, which used an extremely impressive econometric apparatus, is the straightforward, axiomatic[7] exposition of the authors' hypotheses. They clearly dared to "stick their necks out", and, unlike some other authors, presented their axioms not as scientific conclusions. The most important point they made is that—in clear contrast to the analysis presented by Bogomolov (1967) representing the standard Soviet view of a longer period, according to which it is primarily in comparison to her own manufacturing industry that, for the Soviet Union, it is less than profitable to invest in extractive industry—they computed alleged Soviet losses along the lines of comparative advantages. In other words: world markets, rather than other domestic sectors, serve as a yardstick; therefore the maximum profit attainable through a better marketing of available fuels is their objective function. To be precise: they assume *expressis verbis*, that Soviet economic decision-makers have, in fact, always been out for maximum profit. Moreover, being aware of the distortions of intra-CMEA prices, the Soviet Union, in its internal calculations, was, in the end, reacting to world-market prices (Marrese and Vanous, 1983, pp. 65–66). Put in highly simplified terms, what they attempted in their work was to reconsider the actual processes of intra-block trade at world market prices. Having "world-marketized" raw material prices, a formally fairly easy procedure, they sought to discount the value of East European manufactured goods, regarded as poorer than their West European equivalents but on a par with the Soviet industrial average. The figure mentioned was the end result of these procedures. Two additional results of their detailed investigations—results that appear to be pivotal—deserve to be mentioned from the viewpoint of our present analysis. On the one hand—as with the East European authors of the late 1960s—they, too, "discover" the nominal disparity (corrected in the manner described above), between raw material and finished product prices, between CMEA and world-market levels (op. cit., p. 93). On the other hand, in contrast with certain other interpretations, they do not consider the "implicit subsidy" given through price level differentials a gift: "The 36.4 billion dollars of direct subsidy granted to Eastern Europe between 1960 and 1978 is matched, in the Soviet Union's western imports, by a negative cumulative machinery balance of 38.4 billion dollars and a cumulative trade deficit of 19.4 billion dollars. But this cannot be taken to mean that, without the burden of Eastern Europe, the Soviet Union might have doubled its machine imports from Western countries, or that, in its trade with the West, it could have achieved a surplus of 17 billion dollars, instead of a deficit. Without the subsidies, the Soviet Union would have been forced, both directly and indirectly, to proportionately increase its military spending, because these subsidies increased Eastern Europe's willingness to cooperate, which is part of the Soviet security concept" (op. cit., pp. 39–42 and pp. 67 and 149). So the American authors interpret the price disparity within the CMEA as, from the Soviet viewpoint, "the price of power". According to their calculations, "both in terms of current 1980 dollars and of the unchanged prices of 1970, the subsidies show an order of GDR—Czechoslovakia—Bulgaria—Poland—Hungary—Romania", which, in the authors' view, "is to be regarded as a countervalue dependent on, and proportionate with, the non-price benefits rendered by these countries in return for the implicit subsidies" (op. cit., pp. 69 and 146).

Quite apart from the numerous political and ideological arguments that could be marshalled to contradict the above analysis, just how shaky this explanation is could be gauged from the contradictions inherent in the results of the partial calculations showing the distribution between particular periods and particular CMEA countries of the total amount of the subsidies (op. cit., p. 48). For example, Czechoslovakia, which ranks second, in this respect, after top-of-the-league GDR, received the biggest part of Soviet subsidies, i.e. 27 percent, at a period when she was considered to be the weakest point in

the military alliance of the WTO. By contrast, she received the least—
17.2 percent—in the period of 1970–1973, usually regarded in the
socialist press as a period of successful normalization. Even between
1974–1978, this value rose to no more than 20 percent, although
Czechoslovakia is known to be a major importer of raw materials.
And, according to the American authors, Bulgaria was comparatively
in the most disadvantageous position precisely at the periods when
she was most eager to promote the closest possible integration with
the Soviet Union. Between 1960 and 1969, even negative subsidies
are shown (a staggering 45.7 percent), and in the subsequent period of
1970–73, a mere 2.2 percent of the subsidies fell to their share.
When evaluating these data, it should be borne in mind that the
former is considerably less than the value calculated by the American
authors to have fallen to Romania in the same period, which seems
politically absurd. As for the 1970–73 values, the two countries are
on a par, whereas, both in general terms and even more in their attitudes towards multilateral integration, the two countries could be
considered as representing the two extremes of the time within
CMEA. The American authors do not even attempt to provide a
plausible explanation for these blatant disproportions. The arguments
put forward on pages 146–147 about the Bulgarians being Russophile
anyway, for which reason there is no need to subsidize them, is in
harsh contrast even with their own explanation (it, too, in a similar
vein) regarding the 1975–78 period. Relying on the calculations—
which show a very steep rise, indeed, in both the amount and the
proportion of the subsidies of the formerly so "unimportant" ally—
they conclude that a large-scale living-standards policy to be conducted in this period (!) by the Bulgarian leadership would have been
the precondition of preventing a Poland-type crisis.[9] This "explanation", which, on the evidence of the developments of the subsequent
period, even if one possesses but a sketchy knowledge of Bulgarian
reality, seems so unsound as to be unfit to be discussed, amply illustrates how econometrics, when used indiscriminately as a sort of in-
fallible method, may serve at times but to disguise, under a cloak of
scientific presentation, highly superficial and ill-founded impressions,
and how, as sometimes happens, it serves only to fill the gap between
academic researchers' ambitions and the evidence that is available
to them.

But even if one stays with the American authors' own economic
thought-process, open to much criticism though it is, one can't help
raising objections to the way they have left unanswered two funda-

mental conceptional criticisms which—*à propos* of an earlier, similarly inspired econometric work by Rosefielde (1973), Bergson (1980, pp. 300 and 304) had already been published when the famous work was written. These are as follows:

—Relative prices in the CMEA countries are so distorted compared to world market prices, taken by the two authors as the sole yardstick, as to preclude any sort of trade optimization according to competitive norms, even if—as is definitely not the case—central planners wished to determine the quantity, the geographical and price structure of foreign trade on that basis. According to this system of norms, the Soviet Union and Eastern Europe have a, by any standard, excessive share in each other's foreign trade, thus the additional charges also mean the price of the priorities followed by this very trade policy.

—From the East European point of view (to continue within the same sphere), the static nominal terms of trade-gain should also be set against the dynamic and competitive losses arising from a non-optimal geographical and price structure of production and of foreign trade, that evolved as a result of policies and priorities followed over a 30-year period (1950–80). It is methodologically unacceptable to disregard this loss—namely, the fact that, in addition to foreign trade, the structure and quantity of domestic production, too, have evolved according to contemporary Soviet priorities, that did not follow these competitive norms that Rosefielde and Marrese and Vanous also regarded as the yardstick. All the more so, if its size is probably greater than the sum total of cumulative "implicit subsidies" which is a static gain anyway. And provided the marginal rate of transformation and the marginal rate of substitution is not the same, then both the Soviet and the East European side were running further efficiency losses arising from the trade practice based on non-competitive norms.[10] Marrese and Vanous, in the final version of their investigation, admitted that their results could not be regarded as a comprehensive balance of trade between the Soviet Union and Eastern Europe (which, they insist, is definitely not what their results were intended to be). On page 145 of their book, they stress that, with the latter considerations in mind, it is impossible to decide if, due to the effects of "implicit subsidies", the small countries of Eastern Europe were the real beneficiaries, faring better "than otherwise".

Given the size and publicity of the unprecedented controversy around this theory it would not have been a queer venture if Marrese and Vanous published a second volume devoted to the same topic and addressing the conceptual counterarguments. It is also somewhat surprising to the present author that the international discussion in conferences and other gatherings, as well as in a considerable part of the English-speaking literature continues mostly along the methodological lines, i.e. concentrating on the ways of determining the exact size of the implicit subsidies. This seems rather curious, since from early 1985 the whole set of problems got into the reverse, but this phenomenon, shaking the very foundations of the entire intellectual construction has not been addressed either by Marrese and Vanous, or by most other participants of this quite emotional exchange of views. However, the mere fact that at least in 1986–90 due to sliding pricing the problem of inverse subsidization (of the Soviet Union by its allies) has taken place, should raise serious *ex post* doubts about the validity and scientific merits of the entire exercise. It is also noteworthy, that the first versions of this theorem have been subject to public debate since 1980, still its authors haven't even tried to address the conceptual objections or answered such sweeping criticisms as those of Köves (1983) or van Brabant (1984). Nor did they reflect on the underlying question restated quite rightly by Holzman (1986): if the CMEA is basically a customs union implemented through non-tariff methods—as interpreted by Holzman (1962) and proved by Ausch (1972) and not disproved by anyone in the relevant literature—then why should intra and extra regional trade prices be the same? Under the neoclassical model used by the implicit subsidy (East European burden) theories this is positively excluded, and if they happened to coincide for a longer period of time, that would, indeed, require a theoretical explanation.

THE DEBATE OVER MUTUALITY OF ADVANTAGE IN THE CMEA COUNTRIES

Mutual advantages in CMEA trade have also been called into question from a different standpoint. In a widely accepted view net finished product exporters secure unilateral advantages given that, until 1975, contractual raw material prices were low in a dual sense (both in relation to finished product prices and world market prices), and also because of the high capital intensity of the raw material exports. The Soviet Union advances 3 to 3.5 times as much of her fixed assets because of foreign trade as she would if she were substituting her imports from the CMEA, that is, produced these commodities domestically (Bogomolov, 1967, p. 15).

Let us ignore for the moment the fact that this sort of reasoning implies a politically as well as economically outdated theory of the 1930s, suggesting that foreign trade, for the Soviet Union, is just a necessary evil; that it is useful only for obtaining the products that it is quite impossible to produce domestically. In this concept, foreign trade is not a means of the optimal utilization of scarce factors of production, but, in effect a sacrifice made for peaceful coexistence and for the socialist community. Soviet economics and economic policy have already shed this view; hence, to criticize it here would be unnecessary. Let us concentrate instead on analyzing the two main arguments, i.e. the questions of raw material prices and capital savings.

As far as the first argument is concerned, we must remember that, according to the calculations of the Soviet economist Savitskii (1976), in 1975, the per ton prime cost of petroleum (franco-western border) was 10–12 rubles. This means that, even under the CMEA price of 17 rubles per ton, valid in 1971–74, and even taking into account the depressed price level of capital equipment, the exporting of petroleum was not a loss-making activity. However, since this is a question of theory and not just of statistical computation, it requires a more detailed investigation.

Given that, on a fixed-price market prices and advantages are not identical, to equate, in such an environment (mechanism), unequivocally and directly, low prices with losses—and the other way round—would be a rather superficial procedure. As is known, even before the price explosion, raw materials were considered hard goods, to be repaid in hard goods (as a manifestation of the law of value, which, though in a peculiar fashion, did express itself in the peculiar bilateral barter trade).

This could only be refuted by the Soviet Union's position as a net exporter of raw materials if there were not five, but only two main commodity groups and if it were possible to mutually and unequivocally match raw material with hard commodity, and machinery or finished product with soft commodity. But this would be an exaggerated and ill-founded generalization, because it is patently untrue: beef, for example, is neither raw material nor finished product, but still it is a hard commodity. Or, as an example to disprove the second qualification, pharmaceutical products are definitely finished goods and yet they are hard commodities.

But wasn't the contradistinction between hard goods and soft goods given too much weight in that reasoning? In this connection, we could quote a few well-known relationships, including the one that "the products that, in the price bargain, the seller is willing to grant reductions on are usually those he knows are not going to figure in next year's trade, because, in the annual specification of long-term contracts, these products, for some reason, will not be delivered in the relation concerned. Therefore, it is frequently the prices of more valuable products or commodities in short supply that are reduced, while the price of a less valuable product may be left to remain high. Thus, in spite of companies being involved in these negotiations, given that, in this type of economic mechanism prices have no objectively delimitative economic basis, little attention is paid to ensuring that the resulting relative prices reflect the values in exchange or the substitutability among products or the technological processes for that matter. As a result, relative prices differ not only from those on capitalist world markets, but they also come into a diametric contradiction with the relations of CMEA-wide input, demand and supply" (Ausch 1972, pp. 97–98).[11] This, incidentally, is an immanent contradiction of applying capitalist world market prices, and follows from the price principle as such (Hágelmayer 1974, p. 394), therefore it persisted after 1975 as well. Coordination of plans continues to go on predominantly in physical terms, unilaterally determining prices (in the sense that they reflect rather than influence the selection of objectives). In trade based on quotas, failure to agree on the price even today cannot be a reason for withholding or cancelling deliveries. This situation was not changed even by the transition to sliding pricing; indeed, the transition itself was retroactive. That is, the commodity flows still significantly precede monetary flows; the latter do not shape but reflect the former.

Since the mechanism of functioning is an immanent element of the price, and a medium in which the advantages manifest themselves, in our case price and hardness should be considered jointly. From this, it follows that the low pre-1975 raw material price level in itself does not prove the disinterest or unilateral disadvantages of net exporters of raw materials. This is true if only because, in this system of cooperation, price has neither a restrictive nor an expansive impact on trade, nor does it reflect the conditions of supply and demand. Even if it did, over-demand would not help but bring about a situation where price increases would enhance the producer's interest in and real possibilities for (incremental capital investments to enterprises) of the extractive industry for increasing supply (Ausch 1972; and Csikós-Nagy, 1975). This is true not only in theory, but also in practice. As is well known, in spite of rising prices on both markets until 1982, when potential gains would have been the greatest, the Soviet Union's raw material deliveries decreased or stagnated in both Western and CMEA relations.

Further it may be justified to ask: is it possible to construct a hardness-profitability joint indicator, that is, one simultaneously reflecting both the price and hardness of commodities? Ostensibly, nothing is simpler in the form of product-by-product and relation-by-relation exchange premium and discount, as it translates into the language of prices in bilateral trade between market economies, assuming regulation by the bilateral exchange rates (Kozma G. 1976, pp. 70–92 and pp. 117–133). This, however, is infeasible both theoretically and in practice. It is theoretically infeasible because, in order for the index to be devised, the existence of an intimate, market-type correlation between hardness and the price would have to be a prerequisite. But that is not the case, for then the gap between supply and demand would express itself not in the manner characteristic of the fixed-price market but, in the familiar ways of real markets, automatically in the price. At least, it would have to be true that any price increase automatically increases both the producer's interest and the supply. However—apart from the consumer goods market and the labour market—this is not the case in a traditional centrally planned economy the essence of the system being precisely, that enterprises are not entitled to decide on matters of investment (this right being reserved by the centre for itself). Companies do the calculations not before but after the fact. Thus the projected financial result becomes a passive mirror of the system of compulsory prices and indices. Therefore the calculations expressed in monetary terms do not provide the central authority with an accurate picture of the profits and the losses (signifying the real effectiveness of company management). In other words, price and profit are not necessarily the proper indices of efficiency. They do not indicate the effectiveness of enterprise management (Brus 1972, pp. 76–80 and pp. 129–131). In reality, such a role of prices clearly foreshadows doubts about any (theoretical) attempt at basing investment efficiency calculations on domestic prices.

CAPITAL SAVING AND PRICES IN THE INTERNATIONAL
SOCIALIST DIVISION OF LABOUR

Another type of argument querying the mutuality of CMEA trade advantages refers to the inequality of capital saving possibilities. These calculations are undoubtedly correct mathematically, the economic and theoretical conclusions drawn from it are already less so. What's involved is this:

a) Methodological and theoretical problems

As is known, in the Soviet Union, the efficiency of investments is calculated according to the formula:

$$\frac{\text{investment costs}}{\text{gross production}} \text{ (both valued at domestic prices).}$$

Well known, moreover, is the fact that Soviet price theory and price policy until recently flatly rejected the concept of market-clearing prices. In accordance with the general practice of the centralized mechanism, the central organs decide directly, in physical terms, upon the structure of economic accumulation. In other words, it is not on the basis of market considerations that they distribute their investments (Yakovets, 1974, pp. 172–182 and pp. 228–234; Glushkov 1982, pp. 3–4; and Osnovnye . . . 1987). Still, if they wished to do so, then, taking their cue from Oskar Lange and the Soviet mathematical school, they would simulate the capital market, evaluating the assets and the alternative efficiency of their investment at prices calculated from the model (rather than at actual current prices).

Consequently, authors who base their computations on current prices in the Soviet economy, and posit the "Leontieff paradox as valid for the Soviet Union" (Abonyi and Sylvain, 1977, p. 143; and Rosefielde, 1973, pp. 127–130), commit two methodological errors.[12]

For one, they use for purposes of efficiency calculations accounting prices, thus (mis)interpreting them for equilibrium prices. Also, it is on the basis of the formula:

$$\frac{\text{cumulated investment cost of the given phase}}{\text{net production (= value added)}} \text{ (both taken at world market prices)}$$

that investment-efficiency calculations suitable for international comparison can be correctly carried out, in which case agriculture and engineering nowadays are as capital intensive as is extraction of raw materials.

The "raw material production = below-average efficiency" thesis is open to question theoretically as well. Nobody doubts the technological-economic fact that various activities are of differing organic composition (of capital), thus also of varying capital intensity. From this, however, no one draws the conclusion that, in a capitalist economy, the shipbuilder, for instance, makes a sacrifice in the interest of the textile industrialist only because he advances more fixed assets for production than the latter. According to the labour theory of value rather the opposite is the case: the capitalist in the branch with the higher organic composition appropriates the surplus value produced in the branch with the lower organic composition in the form of average profit. If the differing capital intensity meant differing levels of efficiency, the long-term growth in the organic composition of capital would not be understandable. Nor would it be clear why capital does not flow into the sectors with a lower organic composition of capital. The absurdity of these suggestions is fairly obvious, since technological progress is generally "embodied" in the increase of the organic composition. An answer has been given already by Marx, when, summarizing the lessons of the Ricardo-Malthus debate, he demonstrated how and why value was transformed into production price. It follows that branches with differing organic compositions would show different efficiencies only if value were what immediately determined actual market price movements, that is, in the case of simple commodity production. It is, therefore, surprising that when the question arises in the context of socialist international trade, numerous economists regard it self-evident that particular branches differ in efficiency purely for technical reasons.

What are we to make, then, of the statistical fact that, at Hungary's or the Soviet Union's actual prices, a per unit investment produces different returns in different activities?

b) First approach: price and economic efficiency

The peculiarities and disequilibria of the fixed-price market, different from those of a real market with flexible prices, are well-known. It is generally accepted that not only the CMEA, but —by virtue of its system of management—the Soviet Union's internal economy, too, maintains a fixed-price market. The fixed prices of a centralized mechanism are by no means success indicators either in principle or in practice. Hence, any calculation that takes the differing capital-intensity of the particular branches as implying differences in their efficiency, is, by definition, highly inaccurate.

Still, a number of authors maintain that intra-CMEA division of labour would only be mutually advantageous if the products of each branch and each country were equally capital intensive, for—so they argue—only in that case would the development of production for exports "impose equal burdens" on all the countries involved.

To take a numerical example, country I, in order to produce 20 dollars worth of product A, has to invest 100 dollars; while country II, for the same value of product B, will have to invest 100 dinars. Assuming that one dollar equals two dinars, this means that country II obtains a unit of exchanged products at half the investment cost. Or, country I takes twice as much time to recover its investment costs. Or, country II's investment per unit is twice as efficient as country I's, so country II gains unilateral advantages, because it is not they who produce the more capital-intensive product A. In other words, the return per unit on their capital is twice as much as it would be if they had to produce A. Thus, as a result of the international division of labour, they save 100 dinars worth of capital. Is that so? And under what conditions?

It is obvious that the principle of "equal profits on equal capital" is peculiar to the production-price-type price system. That is, it operates if the net social income produced is allocated in proportion to the capital advanced by producers. In socialism, prices are mostly centrally fixed. In this way, net social income (m) can also be distributed following other price formulae: according to Strumilin and Kronrod, for instance, profits should be calculated proportionately with v (wages). Also known from the practice of the socialist countries is the prime-cost-type price system, where m is reflected (allocated) in prices in proportion to ($c' + v$), with c' equalling depreciation.

Even without a detailed analysis of the particular price types it should be fairly obvious that if the net social income is *ab ovo* allocated not on the basis of c', but profits are calculated according to a different rule, as e.g. in proportion to v, ($c' + v$), or a combination of these, then by definition the return on capital per unit is bound to differ. That is, the varying yield on investment per unit is, in all non-production-price-type price systems, only right. Taking a numerical example, let social production be: $100\,c + 10\,v + 10\,m = 120$, which is produced by three branches. Let the capital intensity of the individual branches be 70, 20, and 10 units, and their labour intensity 3, 3, and 4 units. Let us distribute the total of net social m of 10 among the particular branches following the formulae of three different price types, i.e. proportionately to c, v, and $(c' + v)$. In the latter case, for reasons of simplicity we assume the capital engaged and the capital utilized as identical, which is not a realistic assumption, but is not confusing in the present instance:

on the ratio of c:	7	2	1
on the ratio of v:	3	3	4;
on the ratio of $c + v$:	6.63	2.09	1.27

Are the individual sectors in the various cases of allocation of different efficiency? Nothing can be said on that score, for the result of a single period has been distributed in three different ways. The requirement of "equal returns on equal capital" is enforced only in the first instance, because only there has the 10 m-s been distributed following that consideration. But, if the 10 m-s are divided between the three branches according to inherently different criteria, it would be naive to demand that the investment per unit everywhere ensure the same returns, because, by the very nature of arithmetic, it cannot ensure that. In concrete terms, in the case of the value-type price, the unit of returns on a unit of capital is respectively 3.7, 1.5 and 4. In the case of the prime-cost-type price, the returns on capital per unit are 0.947 (= 6.63 : 7), 1.045 and 1.27, which is a natural consequence of the choice of price type.

Relying on these findings, there is one thing we can safely state about the efficiency criteria of investments in prime-cost-type price systems, namely, that a rational utilization of scarce resources does not mean that any alternative use ensures equal profitability. It follows from this that, at the actual prices of the Soviet Union in an essentially prime-cost-type price system, neither the principle of "equal profit for equal capital" nor the demand of the equal return on the last invested unit's alternative use can be a yardstick in trying to decide over efficiency, and neither in theory nor in practice can these two demands be accepted to any degree.

c) Second approach: differences in capital intensity under market-type pricing

If the result that the production of product A is twice as capital-intensive as of product B, and to invest in producing the former is half as efficient as producing the latter were arrived at in an actually functioning price system that fully allowed a rational distribution of resources—which, in short, is the correct means of orientation for economic planning—then the following conclusions seem warranted.

First of all, it needs to be stated that value and production-price are categories of the long-term centre of price movements, i.e. of "natural price". The market price is a category of a completely different quality, characterized among other things precisely by the circumstance that it may only coincide with the natural price accidentally. What we have to consider is a price system, functioning in reality, i.e. market prices reflecting scarcities. What do different returns on capital imply in this context?

It means that the investment of one unit yields different profits in different activities, that is, the scarce resources were not optimally allocated, because the optimum state of resources, as most generally defined, is characterized by the fact that an additional (incremental) unit of resources invested in any of the various activities yields the same.

The levelling of advantages is a general principle of business management in use-value and is completely independent of value-production, which is a result of abstract work (Petrakov, 1966, pp. 52–55, pp. 100–125; Erdős, 1982, pp. 104–106, and Csikós-Nagy, 1975, pp. 65–67). Such an allocation of resources thus reflects economic disproportions consciously created by the decision-making central agency.

In the second step, the question arises how this disproportion is reflected in prices. Or taking specifically the above-discussed calculations of the efficiency of investment in the Soviet Union's actual prices, is it the scarce resources that the price, which is used for evaluating the efficiency of the investment, revalues? In the given price system, it is definitely not the case. Quite the contrary, it is the diversion of resources from the production of the scarcest resources, that of the hardest commodity, that seems advantageous, and not what both economic rationality and daily practice call for, i.e. supplementary investment in raw material production.[13]

In view of the relationships mentioned, in the environment of a centralized system, it is not surprising that prices signal as a rather peculiar sort of "thermometer". It is surprising, however, that, on the basis of its readings, it has long been a widely accepted thesis, advocated by certain economists, that the Soviet Union was interested not in investing its capital but in diverting it and investing it somewhere else, or in forcing net importers of raw materials to raise the exporter's interestedness (Dobozi 1973, pp. 22–23; and Kozma F. 1978b, p. 363).

Failing that, trade can come about only at the price of sacrifices made for political reasons. It is obvious—and this is not denied by the western calculations criticized, either—that, because of its factor endowments, it is in the extractive industry where the Soviet Union has significant comparative advantages (Bergson 1980, p. 298).

SOME CONCLUSIONS

1. It is true that the Soviet Union is the world's greatest producer of raw materials. However, it is also true that specific use of raw materials is much higher in the Soviet Union than in the developed capitalist countries, indeed, it exceeds the comparable figures of some CMEA countries (GDR, Hungary) as well. Therefore, and because of certain inherent features of mandatory planning, the raw material problem has, for the Soviet economy, too, become a source of tension, that is, a bottleneck. This is true in the market sense, because of the decreasing returns on capital and the growth in the already high material intensity of growth at the macroeconomic level. It is similarly true in regional terms, since already in the 1976–80 five-year plan the bulk of raw material production was located in Western Siberia, whereas manufacturing industry is concentrated in the European parts of the USSR.

2. Because of the foregoing, it is difficult to argue with the analysis that it would be a mistake to perceive Siberia's industrialization as but an awkward encumbrance on the Soviet economy.[14] Rather, it should be regarded as the development of the Soviet Union's most successful export branch in world-market terms. Ninety percent of the Soviet Union's export to the West is made up of raw materials (petroleum alone making up a full 45 percent), which are, and for the medium-run, will remain the main source of paying off her predominantly non-competitive (grain and technology) imports and the main guarantee (in conjunction with gold production) of her credit standing (Köves 1980, pp. 236–237).

3. It follows from all this that, contrary to the conventional wisdom discussed so far, the Soviet Union—both independently of, and in equal proportion with, the effect of CMEA markets, which play an ancillary role—is impelled by her own real economic interests, too, to develop the extractive industries, although if actual, accounting prices are misused for determining the efficiency of investments, it certainly appears the most irrational investment possible.

Therefore we have a two-directional argument to demonstrate that, in intra-CMEA trade, despite the exchange of products with varying capital intensity, mutual disadvantages did accrue in the earlier periods as well.

Assuming hypothetical, ideal prices, and regarding these as equal with the marginal costs, it can be demonstrated by examining linear combinations, in what price band (under restrictive conditions) the exchange of products of differing capital intensity ensures mutual advantages (Tardos 1969, p. 164).

To use the actual prices, hardness would have to be quantified, which cannot be done with precision. The position of net exporter of raw materials does not by itself involve a loss, as, under conditions of structural bilateralism, the profit accruing from the relatively higher level of soft machine export prices cannot at all be spent on obtaining necessary (hard) commodity. The examination of the terms of trade, by countries, corroborates the economic argument that export to higher price level markets is concomitant with higher import prices, and conversely, that even differences in nominal export earning do not really prove a difference in market efficiency.

Finally, we must not lose sight of the fact that the actual possibilities for substituting imports are frequently restricted (grain), and, furthermore, that the interpretation of import substitution used so far in the context of capital savings is correct only assuming an infinite availability of capital. Otherwise the final total costs of import substitution would have to be compared (at world market prices) with the opportunity costs of producing exclusively for export, assuming that the investments are, indeed, to be allocated on the basis of this calculation. Without this motivation, the above alternative calculations are meaningless, except as a sort of intellectual exercise.

THE INTERNATIONAL FLOW OF INVESTMENT RESOURCES AND THE DEVELOPMENT OF THE CMEA'S MONETARY SYSTEM

One of the conclusions that can be drawn from our discussion so far is that—contrary to certain views widely held in the mid-1970s—investment credits, so far from being some kind of "compensation for losses", could—given the right conditions—be a method of the socialist countries' mutually advantageous international division of labour. It should be noted that time was when quite a considerable body of opinion held that this was the only way of ensuring of raw material and energy supply.[15] This concept is debatable from several viewpoints.

1. All joint investments into raw material production require a considerable amount of capital and technology imports and credits. In Hungary's case, for example, the immediate dollar content of investment credits to Orenburg was, in the 1970s, 54.4 percent (Keve-vári 1977).[16] In other words, in this field, too, the danger—generally observable in the world economy as a whole—of the inward looking development strategies does manifest itself. Products of investments aimed at "self-reliant" development, "independent" of the demands of the world market, do not in fact meet such requirements, while a large part of their inputs does have to be imported from the West, thus, increasing, rather than decreasing, import dependency. The net balance effect of these projects, taking into consideration the prohibi-tion on re-export, valid for the products of joint investments, is ob-vious. It appears that it is precisely this phenomenon that bears out the maxim: "maize production, too, can be a form of energy policy" (Köves 1978), that is, a coordinated handling of integration policy with East-West relations is indispensable.

2. By now, the literature on economics seems fairly unanimous in recognizing that the significance of the above-mentioned security of supply, as defined in the everyday sense, was rather overestimated at the time of the oil shock. Security and risk are quantifiable economic factors (in the case of commodities trade on the organized markets, for instance, the differential between the daily price and that of the futures, interest etc.), while a so-called "strategic" handling would be tantamount to an open disregard of the "value-side", that is, the costs of the solution. Nor is strategic handling justified because the oil weapon is all too prone to boomerang. It is held, after all, prima-rily by countries vitally interested in maintaining and increasing their monocultural exports (Nyilas J. 1978, p. 149). Without this, their ambitious development plans based largely on foreign credits would collapse. Also noteworthy is the fact that the countries capable of adjusting to the new price relations by structural reorganization did not put security of supply at the centre of their economic policy. On the contrary, they treat raw material and energy production as a subordinate part of their export-oriented overall economic policy, subordinating it to their world-market competitiveness.

3. In the international division of labour, exchange takes place among different proprietors. Accordingly, there is an obvious impor-tance attached to the cooperation mechanism ensuring a *modus vivendi*

for the mutual interest of the commodity producers. The CMEA countries are not interested in granting long term credits, indeed, it would be contrary to their interests, since under the present terms, it involves an enforced lending out of national income. The level and coverage of the interest credited give small compensation for the opportunity costs of average domestic returns, which, in Hungary's case, is put at 10 to 12 percent, but the normative return requirement is put at 15 percent. In the case of the Soviet Union in the period under discussion, the normative rate of return—the opportunity cost of the integrational credits extended with 2 percent interest—would have been 15 percent (Glushkov 1982, p. 15). Since, however, the two percent interest figures among those items of the synthetic transferable ruble account which cannot be broken down according to bilateral relations, even raising the interest to the world market level would not solve the problems of incentives and distribution of income.

Therefore, a peculiar possibility of improving the accounting system presents itself in repaying investment contributions, as there the coverage of the interest is granted. Hence it does make sense to raise here the question of economically justified interest rates. This would not be an interest charged according to the current banking rules, but, like the initial capital repayment of joint investments, a physical share in the product of the capacity built of joint resources.[17] Because of the homogeneity and/or clear identifiability of the products, this is quite practicable. And if a decision is made to distribute its products proportionately to the capital advanced, this would solve, for this special range of questions, the as yet unresolved problem of the valorization of credits given at the sliding price scale.

4. Peculiar as it may sound, the wide application of investment contributions did not just impose certain limits on, but also led to a strengthening of physical bilateral trade, for investment credits involve, in practice, not so much the delivery of products actually used in the specified investments as an extremely high share of hard commodities exported in a prefixed structure (Vincze 1977, p. 825).[18] Essentially, this method strengthens structural bilateralism in physical terms. In other words, we have been witnessing an excessive demonetization of intra-CMEA trade, reduced to direct exchanges of commodity for commodity, which has nothing to do with capital exports or other international financial flows.

Precisely because of its bilateral nature and the stringent determination of deliveries in kind it is surprising that the point has been made that the recipient of credit cannot spend the investment credit on the commodities he needs (while, for the creditor, this form is more expensive than a purchase in a normal foreign trade transaction), because the contents of the credit are prefixed in physical terms (Shiryaev 1973, p. 98). Owing to the lack of the money functions of the TR, i.e. that it cannot be spent freely, this complaint would have been justified if credit had not been tied to a purpose and its coverage fixed in a physical structure. In fact, precisely because of this feature, only hard goods have been included in it, which is probably not in conflict with the interests of the recipient of credit.

5. In conclusion, the relationship between investment contributions and the system of economic management should be mentioned. This form of CMEA cooperation is given and may only be implemented as a characteristically central task. It requires that the product, the supplier, etc., be centrally determined, and thus, in the last analysis become part of a kind of central development programme (both in its level of decision-making and its physical approach). In its degree (between 1976 and 1980 it amounted to 8 percent of all central investments), this, too, contributed to the recentralization process of the Hungarian economy. Insofar as this continues to be strengthened—beyond its short-term effects—in the future, too, it will also make more difficult the evolvement of the sort of domestic economic management mechanism that could create conditions for a "massive international flow of capital".

NOTES

1 Remarkably, Soviet experts later not only admitted the political determination of energy prices, but considered it a characteristic feature of the period until the year 200 (Mangushev 1983, p. 149).

2 It might have, had it not been an isolated ruling, but had it been coupled with the thorough revision of at least those aspects of the monetary policy which conform with the thinking of the given integration mechanism (the yearly revision of the R: TR coefficients, interest, credit valorization, the oil-ruble recycling mechanism, etc.), and more so, had it been a prelude to some "world-marketization", i.e. modernization of the entire arsenal of the means of cooperation (which was out of the question).

3 The description of this debate is the basis of all Western writings on the subject. For example, see Marer 1974, and Marrese and Vanous 1983. It is much less known in Hungary. Only Tardos and Nagy 1976 touch upon it in their chapter on methodology.

4 Marrese and Vanous 1983, and Tardos and Nagy 1976 rightly point out that in both countries the number of commodities involved in both rela-

tions is very small, and that substituting Austrian or other prices would somewhat overrate the Hungarian economy's competitiveness. Any analysis based on "two-market" commodities would produce less than representative results which, reflected on the entire trade turnover, could only be accepted with reservations. Marrese and Vanous underrate East European commodities in rough aggregates and without differentiation, which not only creates a conceptual problem, but—using their own terminology—makes their analysis an "intelligent guesstimate". The statement is valid only as it pertains to a minor segment of trade; it is of marginal value, and disregards the very complicated Hungarian-Soviet interrelations of the time.

5 I have tried to bring attention to some remarkable results in my review of Marer and Montias, 1980b in *The Journal of Comparative Economics,* 1982/4.

6 For a comprehensive critique of this approach from the point of view of trade policy, see Köves 1983b, pp. 32—40, and Köves 1983a.

7 They state *expressis verbis* in the subtitle of their book that they are examining the advantages and costs of CMEA trade from a Soviet and not an East European—and even less from an abstract economic—standpoint.

8 This does not contain the earlier considered "opportunity costs" stemming from the alleged overvaluation of East European machinery, or the "subsidies" which followed the second oil price explosion, which amounted to $ 10,393, billion and $ 17,772, billion dollars in 1979 and 1980 respectively (Marrese and Vanous 1983, p. 52).

9 Köves (1983b, p. 37) and Lavigne (1983, p. 138) rightly state that the size of the implicit subsidies was a function of OPEC's, and not of the Soviet Union's, decision, and the switch to sliding pricing was to moderate just this; although, according to Marrese and Vanous, it was precisely after 1975 that the amount of the subsidies rose most sharply.

10 Similarly, Graziani (1982) also expressed theoretical doubts—beyond his methodological observations—about the costs of the division of labour, and about these costs being borne disproportionately by the Soviet Union.

11 Taking market economies and the parallel use of bilateral and multilateral clearing as constituents, it can be proven that the prices of many commodities of the clearing partners necessarily differ from one relation to the other, as well as from the multilateral prices of the world market. See Kozma G. 1976, Ch. 4.

12 These are mistakes over and above the ones Bergson (1980, p. 249) points out in criticizing Rosefielde's calculations, namely, that in its motivations and conditions, Soviet—East European trade is radically different from the complex of motivations and conditions postulated in the Heckscher—Ohlin theory, which presupposes the free flow of factors, complete specialization, prices equalling marginal costs, and the allocation of investments on the basis of relative profitability. Thus, there is no theoretical justification for the statistical approach Rosefielde and subsequently Marrese and Vanous used.

13 This factor has been subject to severe criticism during 1986—87 in the debates on the Soviet price reform, especially by representatives of the

Central Economico-Mathematical Institute. As a result, it will be the main task of the overall price reform to overcome this most fundamental deficiency of Soviet pricing (Osnovnye 1987).

14 It is a different story whether and to what degree this statement holds if low raw material prices prove to be a secular trend in the 1990s; the statement was certainly valid of the period under discussion (1965–85).

15 This approach was rightly criticized by Kiss (1971a), yet it is worth dealing with, as it became the majority view, not in the literature, but among decision-makers.

16 Similar problems emerged with the Yamburg-Tengiz joint investment projects in the 1980s. For details see the following chapter.

17 It is difficult to understand how Hannigan and McMillan (1981, pp. 261, 267, 272)—who generally depend on vast source material—can discuss this proposal as if it were a *fait accompli*, especially in relation to the entire invested capital. This would mean that the joint project would be jointly operated, which would be warranted by the joint efforts, but this is not the case. Similarly, there is no foundation for their using the unchanged January 1980 gas prices (op. cit., p. 385) in their repayment calculations for the Orenburg project: as is well known, (Bagudin 1983) current (contractual) prices are being used without any valorization clause. These two unfounded assumptions form the basis of their "proving" that joint investments secure a 19.5–31 percent profit margin for the small CMEA countries.

18 Both the quoted source and Tesner's 1982 study make it clear that this export means the export of commodities and services that had no relation whatsoever to the raw-material sector (e.g. Tokay wine and the building of kindergartens), and this refutes the claim of Hannigan and McMillan (1981, p. 260), unfamiliar with the fact that the most important novelty of the cooperation is direct participation in the establishment of primary producing projects. In fact, it is the lack of this participation that is noted with disapproval by Inozemtsev (1981) and Bagudin (1983).

CHAPTER THREE

Joint investments and mutual advantages in the CMEA—retrospection and prognosis

The topic of mutual advantages is an evergreen one in the CMEA context. Starting with the old Holzman—Mendershausen price discrimination debate that followed the dispute over whether or not Eastern Europe had become a liability to the Soviet Union after the oil price increases, up to the controversy brought about by Marrese and Vanous's book on the size and trends of the "implicit subsidies" granted by the Soviet Union to its CMEA partners, a great number of Western researchers have addressed themselves to the issue of mutual advantages.

Within the CMEA, too, the debate goes back to the 1950s, and especially to the 1960s. This was the time when—in connection with the subsequently aborted attempt to establish an "own" regional price basis—Hungarian and Soviet scholars published extensively on intra-CMEA price discrepancies: both price levels and relative prices (Ausch 1972; Bogomolov 1967; and Kiss 1971). During the debates on the Comprehensive Programme there arose the question of what type of price mechanism would be adequate for achieving mutual gains in sectors of the economy with different kinds of planning (Csikós-Nagy 1973, pp. 179–190). Finally, following the changeover to moving average prices, a vast number of articles were published on whether or not mutual advantages were achieved, and if so, then by whom and to what extent. The impact of world economic changes, the need for more successful adjustment policies, and the challenges of the 1980s have all raised again some of these basic issues, and the search for adequate solutions to the above dilemmas has intensified both at the specialist and political levels. The protracted preparation for a CMEA summit was a sign of this in the latter realm. In the former, a most interesting exchange between two leading Western experts in Soviet studies (Lavigne 1983; and van Brabant 1984) was indicative of the renewed interest.

I have had the opportunity, in the preceding chapter, to present my criticism of the more traditional approaches that question mutual advantages on the grounds of the obvious discrepancy between nominal intra- and extra-regional prices. I have also outlined my views on the general issues of future CMEA development. A comprehensive critique of the Marrese—Vanous book has recently been undertaken by a fellow Hungarian researcher (Köves 1983a). So, it seems to me most expedient to join in the Lavigne—van Brabant exchange in an indirect manner. In this chapter, instead of commenting on comments, I shall attempt to survey the emergence and life cycle of joint investments, or in CMEA terminology, of "investment contributions", from a purely practical point of view. This form of cooperation is most closely related to the underdeveloped state of the monetary sphere of socialist integration.

"INVESTMENT CONTRIBUTIONS" AND THE UNDERDEVELOPED STATE OF THE MONETARY SPHERE IN THE CMEA

Joint investments in the CMEA are practised primarily[1] in the extractive industries and the energy sector, mainly in the form of investment credits.

Conventional wisdom sees this as related to the peculiarities of the energy and raw materials sector, i.e. its capital intensity and slow return, which require the advance investment of large sums. This form of long-term credit is called "investment contribution" in CMEA jargon, reflecting the majority belief that this embodies a form of compensation granted by raw material importers to the exporters to make up for the latter's losses (opportunity costs) incurred because of the nominally low level of contractual prices. It is of great importance that, in theory, investment credits are extended in order to create incremental capacity to produce definite export items, thus alleviating the capital burden of the exporter.

One of the basic functions of a regional integration's monetary system is to act as a medium in harmonizing the conflicting interests of buyers and sellers. It is primarily the financial system which transforms comparative cost advantages into absolute gains in prices. It is demonstrable in pure theory (Szegvári 1972) that, with a mistakenly chosen exchange rate or some other financial intervention to this effect, comparative advantages in labour inputs do not turn into price gains. In this case, profit-oriented enterprises do not, in fact, realize a theoretically feasible international division of labour.

International economic intercourse among CMEA countries has never been based on considerations of comparative advantage. Even the theory of comparative advantage has been emphatically refuted as aimed at conserving structural dependencies established under imperialism.[2] Furthermore, in the absence of a meaningful exchange rate mechanism within intra-regional trade, coupled with the incompatibility of national price structures, comparative advantages cannot even be established under the CMEA mechanisms of cooperation. It is hardly a surprise, therefore, that the size and distribution of gains from CMEA trade have been a subject of discussion since the introduction of "stop-prices" in 1951. By the late 1950s—partly due to the impact of the 1956 events—it had become a generally established fact that, for example, coal exporters incurred substantial opportunity costs, as they were unable to profit from the world market boom triggered by the Korean War (Poland received compensation). Other East European countries also suffered losses because of the price freeze. The relevance of this issue is demonstrated by the fact that it was precisely this that led to the adoption of the simulated world market pricing principle (still in force in a modified form) by the Ninth Session of the Council in Bucharest in 1958. This principle states that instead of a price justified by actual supply and demand conditions in the region, sellers can (should) charge a price based on that offered by the buyer's chief potential Western supplier. To this is added half of the hypothetical freight cost.

This formula, no matter how simple it may seem, was unable to put an end to the haggling that preceded its adoption, first of all in the two traditional areas of bargaining: raw materials and agricultural produce. Exporters of both commodity groups maintained that contractual prices did not cover their costs, and furthermore that these items were relatively underpriced compared with the often mediocre output of the region-wide priority area, manufacturing.

THE EMERGENCE AND THE FIRST WAVE OF INVESTMENT CONTRIBUTIONS

The problems involving the above commodity groups have been articulated with varying degrees of vigour. It has primarily been Bulgaria who has been fighting for a preferential treatment (mainly in the form of price incentives) for its agricultural products since the early 1960s. Meanwhile, the integration of the farming sector has progressed very slowly in Eastern Europe. Several observers contend that its present level hardly justifies the use of the term. The final form of the long-term target programme for agricultural cooperation, broken down to sub-programmes, also emphasized the primacy of national self-sufficiency (Meisel 1979, p. 135). The Thirty-Seventh Berlin Session of the Council in 1983 adopted supplementary measures to this programme. Although there was agreement among the speakers at this Session concerning the importance of promoting integration in this area, and the Bulgarian, Romanian and Hungarian speakers also supported the project put forward by the Committee for Cooperation in Planning calling for new incentives for intra-regional agricultural exports, the joint communiqué did not mention any specific measure to this end. It simply reads: "[The participants] have found it necessary to coordinate measures by the interested parties in the matter of economic incentives for agricultural production, in order to promote mutual deliveries of foodstuffs."[3] There is no mention of a jointly accepted incentive scheme, not even a promise in general terms by net importers to do something specific to create new, additional incentives. The formula quoted does not even serve as a point of reference to net exporters, since the allusion to the "interested parties" means that the question of additional incentives (say by convertible currency payments) remained as much a matter of bilateral bargaining as before. Again, the economic document of the 1984 Moscow Summit in principle allowed for extra incentives for incremental intraregional agricultural exports. However, no mention of this was made in the communiqué of the October 1984 Havana Session of the Council, although this meeting concentrated on the practical implementation of the Summit discussions.

Several national agricultural markets have shown a disequilibrium which has constantly been increasing. A growing portion of the deficit is being covered by imports from the West, as is illustrated by the growing share of this commodity group in Western exports to the CMEA states. Table I, which could be the source of a number of interesting observations, illustrates that while the CMEA countries, after 1977–78, tended to restrict their imports from the West, an ever larger percentage of the shrinking import is in the form of traditionally disfavoured agricultural products. In the meantime, the share of agricultural exchange in East European intra-regional trade has decreased further (from 6 to 4.5 percent according to CMEA statistics).

The difference between the raw material and energy sector on the one hand, and agriculture on the other, derives from the fact that in the 1949–80 period the former played a dynamic role in intra-CMEA cooperation. What is more, dynamism in this field was a prime factor in explaining the impressive growth rates achieved by the East European countries in the above period. Consequently, the well-known changes in this area were instrumental in the deceleration of the East European growth rate in the 1980s. Owing to its size, its raw material and energy supplies, the peculiarities of demand on its vast market, as well as its centralized foreign trade system, the USSR has played a structure-determining role in respect of other CMEA national economies in this entire historical period. This holds true for both the direction and—with the exception of Romania—the extent of the structural changes. It is appropriate to recall (Meisel 1979, pp. 8–10) that political factors have played a dominant role in the formation of the regional integration. In the late 1940s, the USSR was largely self-sufficient, whereas the level of development of the productive forces in East Central Europe had not yet attained the degree of international cooperation that "integration" in the full sense of the term requires. Since in the choice of both the integration model and its techniques (Berend 1971; see also Salgó 1982), as well as in the formation of national industrialization policies and management methods the (often too direct) adoption of Soviet solutions prevailed, quite obviously the "raw materials for finished products" type of division of labour was a by-product, or rather an immediate consequence, of Soviet priorities. This is most important to pinpoint, since various theories contesting the mutuality of advantages in CMEA trade aim to prove that this model is inherently unfavourable from the Soviet point of view. In this context, this seems to be a paradox.[4] It is all the more paradoxical since, until the middle of the 1970s, the official positions taken by both the national governments and the joint organizations approached CMEA cooperation from an overall politico-economic angle, rather than from particularistic considerations, i.e. the cyclical changes in the position of the fuel sector.[5] This reasoning placed a high value on industrialization along identical patterns in each country, and gave priority to the equalization of development levels. An official brochure from the mid-1970s is worth pointing out. It listed the achievements of the CMEA as follows: "Cooperation in the CMEA has enabled individual countries to develop the most progressive industries, including those playing a key role in technological development, irrespective of their domestic natural resource endowments, as they could rely on mutual raw material deliveries." Further on, the high share of material and energy-intensive industries (such as ferrous metallurgy and petrochemicals) in the overall economic structure, the extensive development of engineering by the less-developed CMEA member states, and the high per capita consumption of intermediate products like steel and cement were all mentioned with special pride (Pálfai 1974, pp. 35–37, and p. 50). If Hungarian—Soviet bilateral relationships are indicative of the general situation, the cumulative balance of credit flows was around zero between 1945 and 1975 (Pécsi 1979, pp. 122–123),[6] and it is quite obvious that the "raw materials for finished products" model of the intra-regional division of labour was based on contemporary political and economic deliberations rather than on altruistic considerations.

From this it does not follow that disproportions between the extractive and manufacturing industries were non-existent within either the individual CMEA countries (including the USSR) or the region. As early as the mid-1960s it was established by the first analysts of the "quasi-cycles" of socialist economic development, Goldmann and Kouba 1969, that under centralized, directive methods of planning there was a built-in tendency to overstrain growth targets, which time and again came into conflict with constraints embodied either in hard currency foreign trade, or in raw material and fuel production. Press reports on energy and raw material shortages abound in the CMEA countries. A further study of the developments of the 1970s has proven that when a practical alternative to investment cycles was elaborated in Czechoslovakia and in the Soviet Union in the framework of the centralized planning model, this meant a growth path where the "normal degree" of shortages in general and shortages in energy and raw materials in particular was considerably higher than in the traditional case (Bauer 1981). From this it follows that even apart from the extremely material-intensive macro and microeconomic structure of the East European economies, the peculiarities of the industrialization and management model "ensured" that competition for the increasingly scarce raw material and energy resources become a major feature of trade among East European centrally planned economies. Hungary, for instance, as early as the mid-1950s— a period seen in retrospect as the age of abundance of raw materials—found that those raw materials which were most needed were not always available, or not at the most appropriate time. Occasionally, the required quantities were not obtainable at all, to say nothing of the general problem of quality, which also applied to finished products. By the end of the 1950s "had become more and more difficult to satisfy raw material and intermediate product needs. By 1960 one quarter of the imported intermediate and agricultural products was of Western origin, and this share was on the increase" (Pálfai 1974, p. 58). Since emerging scarcities were not reflected in the financial system of regional cooperation, the increased macroeconomic significance of the deficit items was perceived and mirrored by central planning. This was the time when the concept of hard versus soft goods evolved, meaning the emergence of a second (price-substituting) weighting system. From then on, a hard commodity could only be exchanged for a similarly hard one, no matter what the price of a soft item was. The point here is that there is no markup and discount mechanism by which a commodity falling in one category can be converted to the other, perhaps with a discount. The lower price achieved in exporting a hard commodity, which is by definition underpriced, never leads to a loss, since the underpricing is automatically compensated by the tying together of sales, i.e. to a similar discount in the import price of the item received in exchange.

After the adoption of the Bucharest pricing principle, contractual prices remained stable from 1957 to 1964 and then again from 1966 up till 1975 (with minor modifications). This was in conformity with the requirements of physical planning techniques. However, it is hardly a surprise that "Member countries attempt to ease strains stemming from the existence of shortage items in intra-CMEA trade neither by exploiting possibilities included in the pricing principle itself (such as granting incentive prices or markups), nor by enhancing the role of prices as economic regulators, but through non-price methods such as, e.g. investment contributions" (Pécsi 1979a, p. 174). From the above it follows that under the given circumstances there was no substitute for an effective price rise apart from increasing structural bilateralism (sales for convertible currency were usually out of the question).[7]

As a consequence, from the early 1960s raw material exporters increasingly tended to make incremental supplies conditional on investment contributions (Bogomolov 1964, p. 520).[8] In the late 1950s and early 1960s, a great number of investment credit agreements were signed. Czechoslovakia—and to a smaller extent, the GDR—were particularly active in this field: besides the Soviet Union, they granted investment contributions to Poland and Bulgaria too, in exchange for a long-term stable supply of various kinds of raw materials. In addition to the well-publicized oil and gas deals, Czechoslovakia extended further long-term investment credits to the USSR in return for long-term import possibilities of iron, steel, non-ferrous metals and asbestos (Stračar 1980, p. 6). Joint efforts created such exemplary projects of CMEA cooperation as the Friendship oil pipeline and the Peace international electric power supply system. Investment credits, in fact, were often embodied in the supply of quite different goods from those required by a power station or by an establishment in the extractive industries. In other cases, the contribution was made by additional settlements of a clearing account at the end of the year (when there was not even the theoretical possibility of adhering to the often-emphasized "target character of credit"). It was quite clear in the meantime that investment credits were by no means a form of subsidy, assistance or compensation for losses (Pécsi 1964, p. 424). But in the absence of a convertible currency it was impossible to calculate the efficiency of joint investments in a reliable manner. To overcome this difficulty, in 1963 a methodology was introduced which prescribed a way in which inconvertible national currencies could be brought to a common denominator. However, this could only be done in a most complicated manner, through a plethora of calculations, since each cost item had to be separately calculated. The joint methodology was constrained by accounting principles, and offered several alternatives as far as actual regulation was concerned. So it is not surprising that, under a methodological guise, intense in-fighting went on to decide the actual size of the national income redistribution induced by a particular agreement on an investment contribution. At this stage, it became evident that this form of cooperation was, in fact, a substitute for the market clearing function of the price mechanism, though the final distribution of gains in a given deal was much more a function of random factors than in the case of a market bargain.

It is understandable that by the end of the 1960s raw material importing countries were vigorously contesting the attempts to use investment contributions as a general integration practice. They pointed out that every CMEA state was short of capital, so they could extend credits only by reducing their own investment. As far as Hungary was concerned, 60 percent of her imports from CMEA partners consisted of fuels and raw materials in the late 1960s; 80–90 percent of these items were either absolutely impossible to replace by domestic production, or the costs of substitution would have been disproportionately high. So it was out of the question to grant investment contributions for such a high share of imports, and Hungarian officials were not slow to point this out (Kiss 1971a, pp. 78–80).[9] To

counterbalance excessive endeavours to extend the scope of investment crediting in a radical manner, raw material importing countries
for the first time demanded investment contributions for the development of capital-intensive agricultural production and also for
capital-intensive engineering industries (Kiss 1972, p. 82). Although
this issue was later also reiterated at CMEA sessions and in the relevant literature alike, it has to be borne in mind that since the commodity structure of such counter-investment contributions would most
probably consist mainly of mediocre ("soft") machinery and other
finished products, it is questionable whether this practice would actually be beneficial to the recipients.

It is instructive in this context that the issue of joint investments
was raised (and also partly solved) years before its theoretical vindication appeared in the literature, most extensively in the book by
Bogomolov (1967) already cited. His reasoning was based on the use of
the official TR/\$ coefficient of IBEC, and he found that finished pro-
duct prices exceeded world market price levels by much more than raw
material and fuel prices did (although nobody doubted that a significant portion of these comparisons was conceptually unsound).[10] It
is important to note that to the way of thinking of this period — when
there was no talk of a Soviet opening to the world economy along the
lines of the 1970s, when the relative world market prices of fuels and
raw materials were not favourable at all, and a high degree of regional
self-sufficiency was a political priority in the Soviet concept of the
CMEA—the above-mentioned "opportunity cost" argument was definitely secondary compared with the "less efficient relative to manufacturing" argument. The latter was emphatically used by those days'
Soviet foreign trade policy, with a view to increasing the share of
manufactures in the Soviet exports to the CMEA. This conviction
was in line with both the nominal relative prices in the region and
with the then generally shared unilinear industrial structural policy
concept, which considered the high share of certain "leading", "progressive" sectors in the national economy as a sign of, and a precondition for, success in catching up with the advanced industrial states.
Consequently, any theory that attributes an implicit profit-maximizing behaviour based primarily on reactions to world market signals
to Soviet decision making (Marrese and Vanous 1983, p. 13; Hanson
1982, pp. 75–76, 93–94)[11] is out of keeping with the realities of the
CMEA.[12]

THE IMPACT OF THE COMPREHENSIVE PROGRAMME OF 1971
AND THE SECOND WAVE OF JOINT INVESTMENTS

As there were only minor changes in contractual prices for the period 1971–75, and no change either in structural policy priorities nor in the institutional factors conducive to shortages in fuels and raw materials, the discrepancy between extractive, processing and manufacturing industries increased rather than decreased. Because of growing shortages, the Comprehensive Programme also devoted a lot of energy to urging joint efforts to ease this bottleneck, while at the Council Sessions of 1972 and 1973 several joint investments were approved. The Comprehensive Programme itself is a sign of the high priority attached to fuel and raw material issues all over the region, as reflected in the practical decisions laid down in this document. Note that in the 1970s, it became general practice for fuel, energy and raw material exporters to make incremental deliveries conditional on investment contributions. What is more, every measure of the Comprehensive Programme aiming at increases in fuel and raw material deliveries was conditional on the extension of investment credits (Meisel 1979, p. 86). This also meant that there was no such thing as "depressed" prices for new raw material projects in the 1970s. In fact, selling prices plus the considerable investment credits (whose full size became known only in the late 1970s) together guaranteed incremental supplies for Eastern Europe. This also led to the reemergence of some unresolved problems of the early 1960s: the rate of interest, which was far below world market level, and a number of other issues related to safeguarding the interests of creditors (Pécsi 1964, p. 425). A decade later, even an official observer has had to concede that "owing to unrealistic domestic prices and exchange rates, it was nearly impossible for the member countries, and even more so for the enterprises, to evaluate the benefits or disadvantages of any given joint measure in an economically sound manner" (Pálfai 1974, p. 63).

This situation remained unchanged during the 1970s, when the second "round" of joint investments took place. However, certain new developments did take place. This was connected with the fact that the contracts for joint investments were signed without detailed technical documentation (construction plans), and were finalized only several years later, when conditions had significantly changed (Tesner 1982, p. 207).[13] The delay was all the more important since the time lag included the first oil price shock, as well as its transmission to intraregional trade by the changeover to moving average prices. Hannigan and McMillan are quite right in pointing out that joint investments in the 1970s were not a part of a strategy of regional adjustment to the international economic disturbances, but the delayed implementation of an integration priority formed in an earlier period. It was a strategy doggedly implemented under the completely changed economic circumstances of after 1975 (Hannigan and McMillan 1981, p. 265).

The use of investment credits as a general tool of integration was the really new feature of the first Multilateral Concerted Plan for Integration Measures, adopted in 1975 (Szita 1975, pp. 92–94). During the 1960s, investment credits were granted on a bilateral and mostly occasional basis. From 1975, huge multilaterally coordinated joint projects enjoying political priority were undertaken in the framework of the Concerted Plan, and they received preferential treatment in national planning methodologies as well. In 1975, the two approaches came together. On the one hand, the discrepancy between the nominal CMEA and Western market prices of raw materials, especially fuels, reached unprecedented magnitudes, which led a number of economists and decision makers to the somewhat perfunctory and hasty conclusion that exporters of the above commodities incurred significant losses and/or opportunity costs. On the other hand, the impact of the oil shock brought supply security considerations to the fore in the East European countries, which favoured long-term agreements as guarantees of a planned way of meeting these strategic needs. This overlap of interests produced the Concerted Plan, which differed from standard CMEA practice in that a final state-level compulsory obligation was undertaken in a multilateral form, and a finalized agreement was signed prior to clarifying technical and financial issues in detail.

A further novelty of the Concerted Plan, from the point of view of planning technique, was that an immediate link was created between national and integration plans, which took the form of a special chapter on integrative aspects in almost all of the national macroeconomic plans. In Hungary there was no such provision, but the overall goals of the non-compulsory plan did include the Hungarian share in the Concerted Plan, to be implemented through the generally applied set of direct and indirect measures. At first sight, the Concerted Plan may seem a mere repetition of certain provisions of the existing national economic plans, such as the sections on investment, labour, material-technological supply and foreign trade. However, such "repetition" is far more than a formal act. It is well known that in a planned economy some divergence between planned and actually achieved developments is a usual phenomenon, and that inconsistency among different plan targets, as well as among different considerations of the foreign trade plan itself, is far from rare. In CMEA trade, divergence from long-term trade agreements may occur not only in cases of *force majeure* (e.g. floods, earthquakes), and not only in respect of commodities of minor significance, but also of the highest priority goods, the so-called commercial policy items as well. By way of the revealed political preference and the *a priori* integration of major physical flows on the input side, it was possible to ensure that the respective sections of the national plans were indeed coordinated or, if they were not, the inconsistencies would not be mitigated at the expense of international obligations (i.e. unconditional preference for domestic plan targets, the track usually taken).

At the time of the elaboration of the Concerted Plan, attention was drawn to the fact that investment credits should not overstrain the investment fund of the lender countries; further expansion of this form of integration would lead to domestic difficulties (Bálek 1976). This was quite a problem, since CMEA member states are primarily interested not in the maximization of the total output resulting from international cooperation, but in the size of the gains directly contributing to efficiency in their own economies (Shiryayev 1977, p. 107; Brendel 1979). It is the financial conditions of a deal that determine the degree of "interestedness" of the individual parties. As experience shows, these requirements have not been met. The adverse consequences of this have been voiced in the relevant literature of several CMEA countries. Hungarian authors have pointed out that investment credits are not valorized: the rate of interest is well below the economically justified level; they cannot be spent, so they do not fulfil their redistributory functions; and furthermore, after repayment, options to purchase at the internationally used discount rates are not granted to the creditors (Vincze 1978).[14] Bulgarian sources have added that at the time a decision was made, neither the technical, nor the economic indicators of the joint investment, such as the final cost of the project, were known. Efficiency calculations were still too inadequate to determine whether or not it is worth participating in a project. Further, the target character of credits cannot be observed. As East European industries are frequently unable to meet technological requirements, creditors either have to re-finance their share from Western sources on less favourable terms, or they have to contribute products that could be sold to Western countries (Dimov 1983, pp. 50–62).[15] This was a burden for the creditors, since their balance of payments in convertible currencies was already strained.

How has this situation, so closely resembling the "first wave", evolved? Why could not the advantages of this method (e.g. the long-term, stable supply of raw materials and fuels for consumers; a *de facto* price increase for the producer) supplemented by the mitigation of those—mainly efficiency—problems that were already well-known from earlier experience, outweigh its difficulties? We might find, as we try to answer these questions, that a survey of the Hungarian experience may lend some extra insight.

THE EXPERIENCES AND LESSONS OF THE 1970S

As was already well known in the early 1970s (Kiss 1972, pp. 80–81), in Hungary the domestic protagonists of expanding investment contributions have always been the branch ministries and their bedfellows. These remnants of the directive planning system are, as a rule, indifferent to considerations of structural policy and of macroeconomic equilibrium. Bilateral trade balance and efficiency or profitability do not matter to them. It is inherent in their narrow departmentalist approach that major macroeconomic considerations of this kind are relegated to second place. Instead, particularist interests (such as convenience of administration, planning techniques, quantitative and sometimes also one-sided technical indicators) tend to come to the fore. These intermediary organs of state administration are bent on establishing and legalizing such economically void, artificial concepts as sectoral optimum, or even international sectoral optimum (at the CMEA level). These endeavours aim at enhancing the role of sectoral management organs to a disproportionate degree at the expense of the functional management organs (Ministry of Finance, Planning Office). This process would culminate in the more or less unrestricted delegation of proprietary rights to the branch ministries. Owing to its political significance, international intercourse in general and CMEA cooperation in particular is a perfect means to document, legalize and enhance the prestige and importance of the branch ministries relative to the other management organs.

In 1969 and 1974, the growth of unintended surpluses in CMEA trade led to campaigns to increase machinery imports from the CMEA partners in Hungary. This campaign augmented the relative strength of the Ministry of Metallurgy and Engineering. (In 1969 it

helped to prove the usefulness of a state organ whose very reason
to exist was in question at the time.) In 1973–75, the course of ignoring world economic changes was adopted, based on the assumption
that the use of budgetary means plus CMEA contacts could shelter
the Hungarian economy from external shocks. In this context, secure
supplies from the CMEA were a high political priority, and boosted
the comparative strength of the Ministry for Heavy Industry in
charge of this matter. The reinforcement of the position of this branch
ministry was due to the domestic processes of recentralization, too.
Industrial management in those years was, in general, more interested
in the details of enterprise activity than in the major issues of industrial policy, or the synthetic final product of the enterprises, i.e. profits,
as would have followed from the politically then still valid principles
of the New Economic Mechanism. The prevailing anti-reform tendencies brought about a decline in the professional standards as well as
in the economic soundness of macroeconomic planning. Following the
decision of the CMEA Executive Committee in February 1975 on the
changeover to moving average prices, the panic of confrontation
with the actual situation and the increased difficulties in securing
adequate raw material and fuel supplies created favourable conditions
for the resurgence of the use of macroeconomic physical balances
both for psychological and real economic reasons. The absolute priority of supply security considerations, coupled with endeavours to
find a planned outlet for the products of a dynamically expanding
industry in a stagnant international economy, were a more or less
automatic result of the eclipse of the New Economic Mechanism.

A theoretical by-product of these changes was a temporary mush-
rooming of approaches advocating in principle a "massive international flow of capital" among CMEA countries. This boiled down in fact
to an apology for a very specific form of capital flow under physical
planning, namely investment contributions. This type of approach
considered it normal rather than anomalous that "since the domestic
economies themselves lack an efficient mechanism of selection among
investment aims, the choice in fact is not between the 'good' and the
'not so good' alternatives of development, but simply whether or not
there is a continuous supply at all" (Tömpe 1979). During that period
it was a general fact of Hungarian economic management that the
meticulous weighing of costs and benefits was replaced by "more
important" considerations, e.g. meeting various technico-economic
parameters, or attempts by enterprises to achieve a good ranking in
the comparisons made by the supervising branch ministry. All in all,

adjustment to the expectations of higher management organs (expressed in the "comprehensive evaluation of managers", in "responsibility for supply" of non-profitable, but in the judgement of the authorities necessary, products, etc.) became far more important than adjustment to market signals. In this context, there was nothing wrong if in an area with such high political priority as securing energy and raw material supplies, penny-wise calculations played a tertiary role.

The climate of the mid-1970s is well illustrated in an article by the leading officials of the Hungarian National Planning Office, who interpreted as a sign of fraternal help the fact that the Soviet Union honoured its obligations to supply the amounts of raw materials and fuels envisaged by the coordination of plans plus the long-term CMEA delivery contracts for 1971–75 (Kővári and Mosóczy 1976, p. 84).[16] This explains why part of the economic literature abandoned the earlier critical evaluation of investment contributions as "the least good" form of cooperation, and rather described them as an advanced integration measure (Dobozi 1978).

Some Soviet authors went so far as to see in it one of the numerous "general laws" of the political economy of socialism (Shiryaev 1981, p. 105).[17] The aims of security of supply and of maintaining dynamism of growth took precedence over adjustment to the world economy. When, in order to justify this economic concept, leading politicians asserted that "the national interests of the individual CMEA countries are in the end identical with those of the other member states" (Szekér 1976, pp. 15–17),[17] then "penny-wise" weighing by individual cost items of each joint project seemed improper for some time—but only for some time. Since the financial sector in Eastern Europe is inherently national, as the price and monetary systems are autarkic, separated by inconvertible currencies, it is quite clear that proprietary interests are formulated primarily in national financial terms. Incompatibilities necessarily emerged even before the full scale of the epochal transformations of the world economic system and the absolute constraints of Soviet incremental supplies became apparent in 1979.

Following the endorsement of the Concerted Plan, critical evaluations began to proliferate in the CMEA countries (although the tone of these varied, of course, depending on the general customs of the respective countries). These included statements at the political level, too, justified by the experience gained during the elaboration of the long-term target programmes. Without plunging into the details of this separate issue, be it sufficient to note that the documents of the

1976 Berlin Session of the Council were not all that specific about what exactly the contents of the long-term target programmes were to be. The wording of the published documents as well as a significant body of the relevant literature reflecting on the issue lead one to assume a theoretical and also economic policy approach implying the expansion of joint investments.[19] This has not turned out to be the case. Authoritative sources gave 90 billion TRs, i.e. ten times the amount spent in 1976–80, as the sum earmarked for financing the long-term target programmes till 1990 (Konstantinov 1980). Other well informed sources also treated the subject of LTPs as a part of the unrealistic attempts to expand investment credits beyond any reasonable limit (Pécsi 1980–81, pp. 72–81).

The above seems sufficient evidence that such attempts were, in fact, made. They were resolutely countered by the GDR, the Hungarian and especially the Czechoslovak participants at the 1976 Session. From 1977 onwards, Bulgarian economic literature gives detailed accounts of continued unresolved problems (indicating official displeasure at the developments). In Poland during the 1970s, experts maintained a subdued critique of the whole international monetary system of the CMEA (which they had voiced more explicitly in the late 1960s). Polish economists criticized joint investments implicitly, together with CMEA joint ventures, by pointing to the obstacles posed by the monetary sector for both forms of cooperation.[20]

We have already surveyed the literature of this period on the above subject. Analytical publications—while subscribing to the theoretical usefulness of this form of cooperation—mostly reiterate the controversial financial issues known from earlier experience. Analysis of the practical lessons of the 1970s allowed some further conclusions. The majority of these problems arose from the phenomenon indicated earlier, i.e. that contracts deciding on the basic issues were signed at the political level two or three years before the final elaboration of the technical and economic details. This produced phenomena similar to those experienced within the individual economies, where construction started with so-called preliminary permission, but without detailed technical documentation, and costs—such as those of deliberately omitted, but functionally necessary infrastructural outlays—were hidden and only "discovered" later. Other well-known practices in the process of domestic plan bargaining for investments also appeared (Bauer 1981, pp. 33–56). The starting of projects without prior documentation foreshadowed the resurgence of the "usual" discrepancies between costs and outcome of joint investments. This had been the experience of the 1960s, too (Pécsi 1980–81, p. 74). Since the size of producing capacity in output terms was fixed by intergovernmental agreements, it could not be varied. This does not imply, however, that it was only the cost side that involved uncertainties. From the creditors' point of view, the output side had its problems, too. As is documented by case studies (Tesner 1982), in the case of the Ust-Ilimsk joint project, for instance, there was no possibility of preferential purchases for the creditors after repayment, unlike what is usual in international practice. In the case of the Orenburg pipeline, a more general problem emerged, since moving average pricing was introduced when construction was already well under way. As a consequence, the valorization of credits is unresolved even in nominal terms, and the final price of the gas is still unclear, since the reduction of the planned repayment period (which would also imply a solution to the first problem) was not accepted by the Soviet side (Hannigan and McMillan 1981, p. 282).[21]

The output side is also affected by what was suggested above as only a possible eventuality, but what by now is known for certain. Namely, in several cases the "receiving" capacity of the creditors is, in fact, not capable of utilizing the imported items. Utilization involves additional (unplanned) investments in those sectors whose expansion should, instead, be curtailed under the world economic conditions. This is quite a problem in a period when investment rates have dramatically fallen in every East European country, and a large share of the remainder is already being spent on domestic energy and intermediate product development, infrastructure maintenance, and preserving the (not very impressive) level of social services already achieved. So the utilization of imported items further decreases the already insufficient funds remaining for actual export-oriented projects.

The basic problem, of course, is related to the extra outlays. One element has been mentioned earlier, namely, that the convertible currency content of joint investments has increased to well above planned proportions and under unsettled conditions for TR/$ conversion. Furthermore, creditors can hardly influence the cost calculations of debtors, since the jointly built project is owned by the country where it is situated, and the Soviet investor tends to pass on the "usual" cost increases on to the East European creditors (Pécsi 1980–81, p. 75).[22]

Further factors affecting cost increases centred around two issues. First, since neither the concept nor the size of additional investments was clear, it was disputed which objects of what construction value should be considered as integral parts of a given project. This problem was obvious with items like kindergartens, schools, living quarters and so on, which are part of the general development of any region, and whose contribution to actual economic results is very indirect. Second, it has turned out that the construction industries of individual East European states are not prepared to work under the special conditions of Siberia. This was augmented by two further problems: the use of the 1929 Soviet construction norms in costing (which Soviet enterprises themselves are unable to meet), and the insufficient size of the fund for unforeseen contingencies. All in all, the question emerged whether it was worthwhile at all for these industries to engage in activities so far from their base, and if not, what other economic performance by the given country could be accepted by the Soviets as a substitute (Tesner 1982, pp. 207–211). Since the second alternative prevailed as more rational in the great majority of cases, it is quite obvious that the "target character" and "capital burden easing function" of investment credits, much heralded by part of the theoretical literature, are completely formal in real life. Authoritative Soviet sources (Inozemtsev 1981) were critical of East European industries as being mostly (!) unable to deliver the specific items required for the development of the raw materials sector. When they did deliver, it was at the expense of normal clearing supplies. This, in their view, has meant that the development of this sector has remained mostly the task of the Soviet organs, while the emergence of a structural surplus in the Soviet balance of payments *vis-à-vis* Eastern Europe has deprived investment credits of their original substance. These Soviet criticisms can be taken as further evidence that investment contributions in fact constitute a combination of an additional price rise and a "hardening" of the structure of counter-deliveries received for fuels and raw materials (which is by definition a non-price method of further increasing prices).

This, in fact, is the core of our whole reasoning: it is substantiated by practical evidence that "investment contributions" are not a theoretically new integration form, a socialist version of capital exports, but exclusively a substitute for the sharp rise in prices under the present conditions of the CMEA monetary relations. In other words, they have nothing to do with the peculiarities of the raw materials and energy sector, as they spring from the underdeveloped state of the regional monetary sphere.[23] Investment credits were granted in the fuel sector because the shortage in this commodity group was most keenly felt in the system of physical balances that play a central role in macroeconomic planning. Other shortages, for instance in agriculture and foodstuffs, can be equally acute, without evoking any reaction by planners. This is partly due to industrialization priorities, partly to the different nature of the two fields from the point of view of "planability". Production of basic items can, in theory, be coordinated by a system of physical balance, but this is a far cry from balancing supply and demand on the consumer market. In the meantime, this equilibrium can be achieved in the less assortment-sensitive raw material and intermediate product sector.

THE REEMERGENCE OF THE ISSUE IN THE 1980S

A practical manifestation of the above-described discontent was the temporary decline in the extension of investment credits during 1978–83. This meant, first of all, that the earlier, over-ambitious aims were filtered out of the finally approved version of the five long-term target programmes. From the practical point of view, the sum of 90 billion TRs referred to as earmarked for financing these programmes can only be interpreted as a total comprising investments in engineering formally or actually implemented under CMEA cooperation, plus the accompanying infrastructural (transport) development by the CMEA partners (e.g. modernization of railways and highways), as well as those sums which have been earmarked for the development of the domestic resource base (e.g. Hungarian development programmes for lignite mining). The LTP for fuels and raw materials explicitly calls for greater reliance on domestic resource use, and in most cases does not contain specific pledges for incremental Soviet fuel, energy or raw material supplies.[24] What is more, according to the communiqué issued by the 1983 Berlin Session of the Council (Communiqué, 1983), the supplementary measures approved seven years later by the member states did not even deal with issues other than energy saving and conservation. These measures—conservation and increased domestic production—were in fact a substitute for earlier imported items. All these different measures added together result in the 90 billion TR figure.

However, it was improper to conclude that the issue of joint investments has become suspended in the 1980s.[25] On the one hand, there was the Concerted Plan for 1981–85. Its scope was less ambitious than the LTP projects would have indicated, and even less ambitious than the 1976–80 actual Concerted Plan was. Its value was

2.5 billion TR (compared with the 7 billion TR for 1976–80), but it did include joint investments, such as the Khmelnitsky and Konstantinovka nuclear power stations, the high-voltage electric line to Rzeszów, another to Bulgaria (through Romania), the joint construction of the Mozir fodder factory, plus a nickel project in Cuba. The Concerted Plan included 13 cooperation agreements, some of them exerting a structure-determining impact on industrial development in some CMEA states (e.g. the one on atomic engineering and the one on the computer industry) (Bagudin 1983).[26] At the Thirty-Seventh Session in Berlin in October 1983, Czechoslovakia, Hungary, the GDR and the Soviet Union signed an agreement on a further joint investment in the construction of an iron ore enrichment combine in Krivoi Rog (from which Hungary withdrew in 1985). In October 1984, in Havana, several joint investment projects were discussed, the most significant being the Yamburg pipeline. According to the Czechoslovak Premier, the cost of the joint investments advocated by the Chairman of the Committee on Cooperation in Planning at that session would have been in the range of 45–55 billion TR by 1990 (Štrougal 1985b). This figure has proved to be beyond reach. However, the planned costs of the Yamburg pipeline, in the, construction of which Hungary has been taking part since January 1986, are put at 20 billion TR (Obodowski 1985).

A second major factor influencing the future of investment credits in the CMEA is the increasing demand of the Soviet economy for the products of the Eastern European countries. This problem had already arisen quite insistently in the 1981–85 period. Not only were the East European countries to have halted the further increase in their balance of payments deficits *vis-à-vis* the USSR which occurred in the 1976–80 period due to the introduction of moving average prices. They were supposed to attempt to repay their debts, notwithstanding the further, and more dramatic, deterioration in their terms of trade (Inozemtsev 1981; and Szikszay 1982). Neither of these has occurred, but the failure is explained by such external shocks as the Polish and Romanian reschedulings in 1981–82, Vietnam's in 1980, and Cuba's in 1982 and 1983, 1984, 1985 and 1986. Knowledgeable observers judged the financial difficulties experienced by Hungary and the GDR in 1982–83 to have been of comparable magnitude (Schröder 1983), although they did, in fact, manage to meet all their financial obligations. While these factors were becoming independent sources of tension for the world economy as a whole, Eastern Europe's deficit of trade with the Soviet Union increased rather than decreased. This indicates that if the Soviet Union had decided to apply current world market prices to avoid "implicit subsidization" of its trade with Eastern Europe, this gain in prices could hardly have been spent on purchasing Eastern European hard commodities, but would have resulted in a soaring (nominal) trade deficit for the smaller countries (Köves 1983b, p. 38). It is interesting that while criticizing the developments of the 1976–80 period, the deputy chairman of Gosplan agreed with this interpretation of intra-CMEA trends (Inozemtsev 1981). It is more than doubtful whether this surplus could have been used for financing Soviet imports from the West, as some analysts maintain (Drábek 1983). Under the given politico-economic conditions, the opposite is the case, as is shown by the actual balance of payments trends. In order to overcome this difficulty, in the first phase of plan coordination for 1986–90, the Soviet side formulated the requirement of investment contributions to maintain the level of supply of hard commodities already reached. This was first expressed after the 1982 Session in various meetings of specialists, and at the 1983 Session at the political level, too.[27]

This cannot be taken for a purely tactical exercise, since—as demonstrated in Chapter 1—the opportunity for hard currency deals could not increase in intra-regional trade. While Soviet indebtedness to the West is on the increase—notwithstanding the curbs on technology imports—and to contain this trend is a high priority for the Soviet leadership, a growing share of the mostly stagnant Soviet raw material and fuel production has to be earmarked for Western exports (especially since relative prices for primary products did not increase in the 1980s). As there is little indication that there will be management changes capable of achieving a drastic reduction in the Soviet domestic consumption of primary energy and raw materials in this decade, and since the disequilibrium on the domestic consumer market will not be eliminated before the late 1990s (even if all the provisions of the Food Programme had been realized on time), the basic state of the intra-CMEA market is given. While the Soviet supply of hard commodities was objectively restricted, there was a growing demand for CMEA products, especially in the consumer sector. In view of the well-known duality of the Soviet economy, it is quite clear that any theory treating Soviet and East European industrial products as being generally of equal quality (hardness) (Marrese and Vanous 1983, p. 14) is out of contact with the real world. Even if this assumption were generally valid, it would surely not hold for the industrial products normally traded. This means that, especially with the further growth of the Soviet surplus in 1981–85, there is growing demand for East European industrial produce.

None of the above implies that a change in the new structure of Soviet import priorities—first formulated for the 1981–85 period by an authoritative Soviet author usually close to official sources (Shiryaev 1981, p. 31)[28]—was maintained in the second half of this decade. This priority consisted in preferring food, agricultural produce and consumer items, coupled with investment contributions for maintaining exports of hard commodities. The latter appear to be the sole effective means of reducing the East European demand for Soviet fuels and raw materials. This seems to express a basic Soviet interest: a cutback in raw material and fuel exports to the CMEA, with a parallel increase in agricultural and consumer imports. This interpretation contradicts, the argument that lack of effective demand (purchasing power) on the side of Eastern Europe is the prime cause for the present developments (Bethkenhagen 1985, pp. 185–187). If it were the price mechanism that constrained demand, no additional non-price control measure would have been necessary (investment contributions, quantitative limits on hard commodity exports, etc.), and CMEA contractual prices would be of a market character. But this is not the case. Thus, I cannot subscribe to Bethkenhagen's conclusion that the East European countries in fact postponed the required real transfers to the USSR. Since these are prices whose whole functioning is void of the logic of the market, it is wrong to introduce an alien logic in a differently constructed system. Theoretical considerations apart, the crux of the problem was not the lack of East European demand (purchasing power), but the physical constraints on Soviet supplies pointed out several times by Soviet economists themselves, plus, as we have demonstrated above, the lack of an efficient financial means (a hard budget constraint) to depress demand to the level justified by the potentials of Soviet production and export interests. In intra-regional hard currency trade, where payments are cleared in effective payments, Hungary has had a surplus in 1981–83 in the range of US $ 500 m., which itself disproves the "lack of effective demand" theory.

In other words, consumption of certain products in a non-price-sensitive foreign trade system had somehow to be made price-elastic, while the system as a whole remained intact. This is precisely what resurgent investment contributions were able to deliver.

The above point is a most serious one. If Bethkenhagen were right, the East European countries could and should intensify their structural adjustment according to Soviet rather than other priorities. This would be a reasonable strategy, were the TR a convertible currency so that surpluses achieved in it could be used to offset debts accumulated in Western trade. The experience of the 1970s has made all East European decision-makers aware of this theoretical problem. Consequently, the divergence of structural adjustment requirements on the two main markets posed a most difficult dilemma for every East European economy.

NOTES

1 There are other forms of joint investment too, such as establishing socialist multinational enterprises and coordinating centres. Literature on this subject abounds, but the practical significance of these forms with market integration potentialities is, unfortunately, small and decreasing. In the very strict sense of the term, maintaining the whole joint institutional system of integration (as, for example, financing the Standing Committees, the Secretariat, etc.) also constitutes common investment activity.

2 Numerous Bulgarian, Romanian and Soviet sources could be cited; for a Czech assertion of this point, see Tauchmann 1983b, pp. 769–778. In fact, the theory of comparative advantages in its most generalized form is a universally valid technico-economical interrelationship, and the only principle capable of ensuring the rational allocation of scarce resources. For an elaboration of this point, see Szegvári 1981.

3 Author's translation from the Hungarian edition of the Communiqué 1983.

4 A further—technical—paradox is that while the world market prices of raw materials are unambiguous, those of finished products are not; bargaining apparently tends in both cases to disfavour the Soviet Union. (See Bergson 1980.)

5 This was consistent with the logic of a foreign trade system characterized by bargains among duopolies, where individual transaction prices do not matter a lot. They cannot even be separated from the prices of other products, since they together comprise the conditions of a deal (as a discount in the selling price of one commodity might well be made up by a discount on buying a technically completely unrelated but scarce product).

6 I have not come across any studies evaluating—often unreported—trade flows between the USSR and other East European countries in the same manner, so the generalization cannot be substantiated with empirical evidence. However, knowing intra-CMEA relations, it does not seem to be an unsound or arbitrary generalization.

7 In fact in 1973–75, it was the incredible growth of intermediary trade that prompted the acceptance of intra-regional hard currency trade (as a means of short-circuiting intermediaries) in daily practice. It is instructive, however, that the overwhelming majority of the theoretical literature has never conceded the usefulness of this practice, and efforts are constantly being made to put an end to it at the trade policy level.

8 The article is also available in Russian in the May issue of *Planovoe Khozyaistvo*.

9 At the time of writing, T. Kiss was general manager of the International Department of the National Planning Office.

10 It is not at all clear how to interpret a world market price for the non-standard finished products that comprise a large share of intra-regional trade, especially when there is no analogous product in the chief potential supplier countries. To cite one example, technical experts consider the special ships developed by Hungarian engineers for specific use on the vast and icy Siberian rivers to embody a technology meeting all international standards. However, just because of its specific nature it has no alternative market, and so no world market price either, since on Western European rivers it does not have a use value.

11 It is to the credit of these researchers that they formulate their assumptions so explicitly, while a great body of the literature implicitly takes it for granted that Eastern Europe is a liability to the Soviet Union.

12 Van Brabant 1984, p. 128, reiterates the basic systemic interrelationships that prove the opposite at this point, and support my conclusions in the main text.

13 These changes included, for example, the fact that the construction and engineering industries of the East European countries, contrary to original expectations, were able to produce and install machinery, pipes and projects meeting specific Siberian conditions to a minor extent only. This is a prime cause of the much higher than anticipated dependence of these projects on Western supplies. So it strikes me as odd that Hannigan and McMillan treat this as something obvious on p. 261 of their study. During an interview after the 1973 Session (which approved Kiembaiev and prepared for the Orenburg natural gas pipeline project), Fock (1973), the then Hungarian Premier, explicitly stressed Hungarian industry's readiness to produce engineering components for oil and gas pipelines. Furthermore, he emphasized: "We have stated our wish to carry out further developments with a view to the needs of fraternal countries." This interview illustrates a resolute determination to supply the components by relying on Hungarian engineering, rather than on (unfavourably refinanced) Western imports.

14 I. Vincze was then Deputy Minister of Finance). It is not quite clear to me why van Brabant 1984, p. 131, states the opposite, as all of his examples come from the 1960s, when conditions for joint investments were of course more favourable for raw material importers and when option purchases after repayment actually were granted. Four years later than Vincze, a knowledgeable expert of the Institute of Social Sciences of the Central Committee of the Bulgarian party also advocated the restoration of the conditions of the 1960s: "It would be desirable, after repayments, for the interested countries to continue to receive the same part of the jointly established project's output in the framework of the normal turnover", which is a proposal to create what van Brabant treats as an accomplished fact. Cf. Lozanov 1982.

15 This problem is also acknowledged by some authors of the capital-importing countries. Cf.: Karavaev 1979, p. 167. So it is not clear what makes van Brabant 1984, p. 131. claim that commodities supplied on investment

credit could not have been invested in the creditor countries, i.e. that they were quite "soft" items.

16 For a similar judgement by another importing country, Bulgaria, see Savov 1975, p. 3. (This source is a monthly bulletin, jointly published by the Hungarian news agency MTI and the Soviet agency APN.)

17 He states the following: "The evolution of planned proportional development at the community level means that a growing share of national [financial—L. Cs.] resources is being jointly utilized in order to achieve common objectives." Since no time-frame or other constraint is defined, and the overall character of the treatise is theory of political economy, in this context the statement quoted above can hardly be interpreted in a different way. Unfortunately, no indication of the date, place, publisher and title of the Russian original is provided in the Hungarian edition quoted here.

18 Gy. Szekér was Deputy Premier in the Hungarian Government at the time of writing.

19 Apart from the numerous Soviet sources that could be quoted, see also Meisel 1979, pp. 134–135. At the time of writing, he was Hungary's deputy permanent representative—i.e. *de facto* Ambassador—to the CMEA in Moscow.

20 An excellent example of this is the article by the head of the Economic Advisory Committee to Edward Gierek published in the 1977 joint integration issue of the leading economic monthlies of the CMEA countries (Bożyk 1977).

21 In their calculations, they use a repayment period of 4.5 years instead of the actual 12 years, and this is the basis for their conclusion concerning the higher-than-world-market rate of return for the East European countries. For a Western critique of this calculation, see Schönfeld (1984, pp. 116–117).

22 It is not clear to me why Pécsi (1980–81) contends in the same place that a solution to these difficulties could be found through political therapy, since most of the above-listed problems seem to stem precisely from politics.

23 This major conclusion has already been convincingly demonstrated by the pioneering work of van Brabant, 1971, especially p. 94, which I became familiar with only during the revision of this chapter for the present book.

24 Apart from the obvious exception of natural gas (the Orenburg pipeline having been finished only in 1979). Commenting on this issue, Furmanová (1981) correctly draws attention to the fact that this LTP called for an increase in the share of solid fuels in the energy balance, the additional energy sources being mostly nuclear energy (the ambitious nuclear energy programmes have since been considerably slowed down), and called for limitations on the use of oil and gas for purposes other than the chemical industry. It is, therefore, surprising that a prolific Hungarian energy economist, Dobozi (1984, p. 15) attached a "supply side approach" to the LTP in 1984, calling for extensive new joint investments. In fact, as I try to document in Chapter 4, the Bucharest Session of 1978 was already a turning point in the opposite direction.

25 This prognosis is based by Hannigan and McMillan (1981, p. 291) on a Western press report of the communiqué issued at the January 1979

Session of the Executive Committee. Dobozi (1984, p. 16) interprets the communiqué of the 1982 Budapest Session of the Council as containing a "change of emphasis" to coordination of investments "not leading to a significant international redistribution of investment resources", this being a substitute for investment contributions. Although in the Soviet literature there was indeed such a line of thought, it has to be emphasized that this was only one of the competing interpretations of the concept of coordination of economic policies. For more details, see Chapter 7.

26 For further details, see Jecminek, Petráš, and Takács 1982.

27 Nikolai Tikhonov N., speech at the Berlin Session of the Council, *Népszabadság*, 19 October 1983. (The version published in the Soviet dailies does not contain this allusion.)

28 The priority was reformulated for 1986–90 in Shiryaev 1983.

CHAPTER FOUR

Planning, enterprises and trade
with the West

THE INTERDEPENDENCE OF REGIONAL AND GLOBAL
INTEGRATIONAL PROCESSES

The 1970s saw several important changes in the system of international economic relations. In Hungarian economic literature—using the wording of József Bognár—these are called epochal transformations in the world economy. In this process of major restructuring, several notions of international economics underwent change. It is obvious that categories and interconnections abstracted from the realities of a given historical period cannot be applied in an unqualified way to a very different period. All the less so when what distinguishes the latter is that the trends and interrelationships of the earlier period no longer apply. This thesis has been established and substantiated in detail by Hungarian research as concerns global issues: the social transformations of the advanced countries, as well as the structural changes in the world economy. Small wonder that it has not left the theory and practice of regional economic integrations untouched.

Until the early 1970s, conventional wisdom in economic theory considered regional economic integration among nations a process analogous to the integration of the local division of labour into a national market, such as took place in the eighteenth and nineteenth centuries. On this interpretation, the phases of free trade area, customs union and common market evolve into economic union among the participants. With the adoption of common monetary, cyclical, growth and external commercial policies, the regional organization of economic activity and its respective institutions take over the roles played earlier by the nation states. In practice this vision—rooted in an emotional reaction to the hardships of World War II—has proved to be but an illusion. It was in the middle of the 1960s, i.e. 1964–65, that an interesting coincidence of integration development took place in both parts of Europe. There was the so-called "constitutional crisis" of the EC, meaning that France, under the leadership of General de

Gaulle, for more than a year absented herself from the Ministerial Council, and thus blocked the Brussels Commission's receiving the partial supranational prerogatives called for by the Treaty of Rome. Concurrently, upon the resolution adopted in May 1964 by the Central Committee of the Communist Party of Romania, the idea of joint supranational planning initiated by Khrushchev in the autumn of 1962 disappeared from the "agenda" of the CMEA. These two major events demonstrated most conspicuously that the contemporary majority conviction of economists and political scientists of the obsoleteness of the nation-state framework definitely overestimated both the speed and the extent of the international economic integration attainable on a regional scale.

A particularly remarkable discrepancy emerged between the practice and the theory of regional integration. While the participants in both European regional groupings paid meticulous attention to preserving the prerogatives of national sovereignty,[1] the scientific literature was overwhelmed by the "conditions are not sufficiently ripe *yet*" approach. In other words, it was not the infeasibility of all regional supranational endeavours that was postulated, only the timetable of implementation was modified by setting a somewhat later date for attaining the substantially unchanged goal. The presumption of the regional "densification" of international trade as the inevitable main path of world economic development remained the position taken by the vast majority of the literature appearing in East and West alike. As far as the CMEA was concerned, it is interesting to note that this approach dominated even works not written by the advocates of supranational mandatory planning. The emergence of proposals along these lines, every 5–6 years or so, must be taken as a more-or-less inevitable by-product of the prolonged existence of command planning[2] in the majority of the CMEA member states. The inherent logic of this kind of planning has been extrapolated to the regional level, irrespective of the latter's marked differences from the single, nationally owned, centrally planned state-run economy. Some proponents of market-type reforms in the CMEA have also voiced similar convictions. Kiss (1971, p. 105), for one, envisions full-fledged integration as the target model, when political boundaries become symbolic, or "spiritualized". A typical theoretical statement for the 1970s reads: "In a longer historical perspective, the process of integration leads to the merging of formerly separated national economic complexes into a unified international economic complex. Progress in integration is primarily reflected in the identical or near identical reaction of the participant countries' economies to individual economic impacts; external influences induce similar processes in them all" (Pálfai 1974, p. 26).

The real economic development of the seventies did not support the assumptions based on developments in an earlier period, specifically the one relating to the regionalization of the international division of labour. Already the papers of the World Congress of Economists on international economic integration (Budapest 1974)[3] called attention to the fact that the process of integration takes place not only regionally, but also sectorally (in the cross-section of the branches) and globally (that is, on a world scale in the widest sense). Later empirical analyses have pointed out that a regional "condensation" of the international division of labour could not be observed even in the European Community, which is usually considered to be the model for integration theory. The flow of labour was slight and unidirectional (from South to North), the flow of capital and technology was worldwide, while the most important manufacturing branches of the dynamically adjusting countries of the EC exported increasingly and even decisively to markets outside the region. Due to structural changes in international trade, the world turnover of products that could not be subject to intra-regional trade regulations expanded at an above average rate. The sectoral and market pattern of the international relocation of industries created unfavourable conditions for seclusive regional cooperation (Inotai 1978; and Kádár 1984, pp. 136–146).

Within the CMEA, in spite of the defensive (primarily import-substituting) reaction to the changes in world economy, the degree of regional self-sufficiency did not increase in the seventies. On the contrary, even in respect of needs that could be satisfied earlier from within the region, suppliers from outside the community had to be relied upon increasingly (e.g. agricultural products, fuels and partly— depending on modernization intentions—advanced technology and the related spare parts and special materials). That is, an opposite, "outward turning" import substitution took place (Köves 1979).

In consequence, the conclusion justly emerged from a comparative analysis of the integration practices of the various groups that the existence of a "world economic umbilical cord" was an essential condition for the success of regional integration, for strengthening the community's position in the world economy. That is, in case of a successful world economic adjustment, the regional and global integrations can be considered as two sides of the same coin.[4] And since the CMEA countries—due in part to their economic structure and their system of economic control—are, for the time being, organic parts of the world economy only on the import side and through raw material exports, particularly the smaller European CMEA countries are faced with the task of organically joining the world economy also from the export side. Such a completion of the ongoing process of their world economic integration is also the condition of their successful regional integration.[5]

Reforming their economic mechanisms became the order of the day for most of the European socialist countries as their adjustment difficulties continued to grow in the late 70s. Other considerations, too, impelled them in this direction: the exhaustion of the resources of factor intensive growth, the recognition of the shortcomings of their systems of planning and control, the deceleration of the rate of their economic growth, and their growing difficulties in producing adequate domestic supplies.

To join more effectively in the worldwide division of labour has become an economic policy priority in several member countries, though it might appear to some that this has not affected the macrolevel cooperation between the planning bodies of the centralized national economies of the CMEA members.

Adjustment to the epochal transformation in the world economy undoubtedly places certain behavioural requirements on the individual economies, requirements which considerably determine the scope and type of the planning, control and institutional instruments that can succeed in attaining these objectives. It is, therefore, not immaterial to examine to what extent the main instrument of CMEA cooperation, i.e. plan coordination, requires and secures the flexibility so much needed for the adjustment to the world economy. Furthermore, to what extent could those much discussed instruments of cooperation in planning—the long-term target programmes (LTPs)—contribute to an export oriented economic development policy? How closely did they involve the old goal of regional autarky?

Cooperation in planning has, of course, several other elements as well, such as consultations on economic policy matters, and the so-called "joint" or "common" planning, which some economists have considered to be the way of the future, leading to "true" integration. It does not seem to be expedient to challenge these views here. The possibilities of joint planning are, for the foreseeable future, limited. The practical attempts at joint planning that have taken place since 1972 have been restricted to individual products, or to areas even narrower than an industrial subsector (e.g. containerized shipping). Moreover, in other cases—as in plant-medicaments—joint planning is being practised within the framework of a joint CMEA enterprise, Interchim in this case. This has led Kuznetsov and Nartsissov (1983, p. 10) to conclude that the underdeveloped state of the integration's financial system, the differences in national price systems, the various technological and economic policy priorities of the respective CMEA member states from a practical point of view seriously limit the possibilities of joint planning.

PLAN COORDINATION AND FLEXIBLE ADJUSTMENT

The coordination of macroeconomic plans is the most important form of cooperation within the CMEA. This is not because it was so defined in the Comprehensive Programme, but because the volume of foreign trade—the main area of cooperation—its structure and rate of growth are determined primarily through the coordination of plans. Plan coordination relies on consultations on economic policy and economic development concepts (five-year plan concepts), and the forecasts of the individual countries. In practice, long-term trade coordination emerges from a convergence involving national plan objectives and international possibilities and commitments. It is partly determined by the interests of the countries, by their willingness to compromise. Conversely, what national plan targets can be considered realistic is delimited to a great extent by the possibilities for international coordination and its results from both the resources and the marketing aspects.[6]

It is the primacy of plan coordination and the subordination of finances that manifests itself also in the method of establishing mutual trade. It is in the course of a series of high-level plan coordination that agreements are reached on the most important delivery conditions of the so-called commercial policy items.[7] This, for all practical purposes, means the quantitative determination of deliveries. This method—characteristic of the entire armoury of instruments of physical (i.e. in terms of goods and quantities, as opposed to monetary terms, planning—works well for the planned turnover of homogeneous products, where the assortment changes very slowly, if at all, or where the turnover is composed of generally not marketing-intensive items, above all of raw and semi-finished products.

In the case of manufactures, particularly engineering products, it is doubtful whether the highest organs making the final decision can really appreciate all the alternatives of the complicated network of quality, price and delivery conditions, as well as of cooperative relations, and thus, whether, setting out from the mutual coordination of quantities, they always arrive at the best possible solution.[8] On the world market of manufactures—particularly as regards marketing-intensive products—the volume to be supplied is determined in the last step, when, having weighed all viewpoints, the partners have already found a common denominator.

On the other hand, infrastructural decisions point beyond the horizon of a five-year period in respect of both technological and economic preparation and implementation. Thus these decisions are made outside the formal framework of the five-year plan.

It seems, therefore, that plan periods of five years are partly too short, partly too long[9] both in themselves and from the aspect of plan coordination.

We can only agree with the evaluation that the present level of plan coordination among the CMEA member countries—which requires an unambiguously "exact" determination of the demand, and of the related mutual deliveries in almost every field—in reality reflects the shortage of commodities within these countries, as well as the inflexibility of the producing and planning organizations.[10] We may add: given that this physically planned bilateral system exists—and the avoidance of trade surpluses has become a basic national interest—until this set of conditions is radically changed, every participant will necessarily aim at establishing bilateral balance and at increased physical determination of trade flows.

The solution is to develop a flexible system of plan coordination, since today the integration also has to serve as an instrument of export orientation. That is, cooperation on third markets was proposed to become one of the main prospective areas of CMEA cooperation (Bognár 1979). This would require, however, that the means of integration change beyond the parameters of the present model of cooperation.

Efforts aimed at improving plan coordination—writes the leading Romanian expert, R. Moldovan (1970, p. 120)—should take the final purpose of coordination into consideration: it has to contribute to the rapid and steady growth of the economies of each and every one of the member countries. This has to be emphasized, because views emerge from time to time in the literature that it was possible and expedient to optimize the economies—or part of the economies—of several countries as if they were parts of the economic organization of one single state.[11] This kind of questionable approach is reflected by the concept of "international economic policy", its substance being that "... the peripherally coordinated national external economic policies, given that they constitute a separate entity, put demands [?] on the national external economic policies of the individual countries, and through them on the domestic economic policies of those individual countries. Thus, the international socialist economic policy is not simply the set of the main features of the national foreign economic policies of the individual countries, but appears as an autonomous category". (Pavelcsák and Kiss 1977, pp. 91–92).

This concept has several times been criticized in the economic literature for presuming "planned and proportional development" at the regional level. This inevitably implies the existence of a subject administering and managing the process, i.e. of an international/supranational planning authority. Planned development, an economic policy based on planning, thus, an international economic policy of the planned economies, are some of the relatively few well-defined concepts of socialist economic theory. The last concept follows unambiguously from the categories of planned development *(planomernost)* and plan-based economic policy, both implying in the CMEA context the mandatory character of the activity even within the confines of a single country.

Is it not possible to interpret the concept of international economic policy more broadly, and use it in the sense of "international industrial policy" and other like "policies" are used in Western literature? One of the above-quoted authors in a later writing (Kiss–Pavelcsák 1981, p. 42) attempts to do precisely this. She interprets the notion as follows: "A system of interrelated and plan-based measures, means and methods aiming at the realization of the economic, political and social objectives of integration, and the principal decisions concerning these made by the respective authorities of the (member) states". As practical embodiments, she lists the jointly adopted documents, the joint investments, the joint ventures and common institutions, noting among other things that "the Comprehensive Programme, in fact, does not yet contain a real 15 to 20 year development programme for integration" (1981, p. 45). Furthermore "an explicitly integrated structural policy at CMEA level exists only indirectly" (1981, p. 48). In other places, however, echoing the majority view of the writings on the CMEA, she reiterates positions favouring further centralization at the regional level. In clarifying the contents of the international economic policy aiming at joint action by the member states, she lists "long-term issues such as setting rates of growth, and structural changes", further "the main lines of developing the world economic activities of the CMEA countries, (e.g. involving problems of international trade, of relations with the EC, of the international monetary system)" (1981, p. 63). These are major areas that were definitely—and quite rightly—left under national decision-making competence in the Comprehensive Programme of 1971, and in all other documents that were adopted jointly at the political level afterwards, including the Documents (1984) of the Economic Summit. "The more important examples sufficiently demonstrate that decisions taken in the CMEA are at least of equal significance to the ones adopted by the EC. Moreover, given the socialist *étatist* character of the CMEA countries, both they and the CMEA proper possess greater competence in making decisions" (1981, p. 50), although she adds that none of the integrations can bring decisions binding on the sovereign states.

Based on the above, it is evident that the concept of an international economic/industrial policy remains ambiguous even if abstracted from the accepted terminological conventions of socialist economics, since the standpoint taken by the author over some fundamental issues of regional integration varies in the different passages of her book. It is only right if the applicability of this concept—along with the other concepts and methods of Western economics—is not determined by traditional reference to the ritual categories of what is "permissible" under socialism, but by its contribution to resolving earlier unclarified aspects of the previously available evidence on this subject. It might be interesting to recall that authoritative US analysts define international industrial policy as "state intervention into the structure of the economy, comparatively lasting arrangements on the distribution and use of resources" (Diebold 1980, pp. 6 and 10). They do not fail to note in the meantime that this applies only to situations where "the sources of structural changes that induce industrial policy actions are mostly fully independent from the government, since they are the products of modifications in technology, in incomes, in the level of needs and requirements in fashion and in productivity, or alternatively they are motivated by external and domestic entrepreneurial activities or the lack thereof" (ibid.). It is clear that in this context, the CMEA region nowadays is even less of an appropriate area to apply the concept of "international industrial policy" to in a sense other than "supranational". Thus it is not prejudice, but the ambiguous content and the unacceptable practical consequences of other notions that caution against renaming the CMEA countries' cooperation in planning, and the consultations on economic policy among them.

Equally contestable is the use of "joint planning", the fashionable theoretical concept of the 1970s, in any but the earlier discussed limited sense. It is not clear what would legitimate speaking of joint planning in describing the practices of the CMEA. Since there is no supranational planning authority, and coordinative activities are restricted to a part of the foreign trade section of the national macroeconomic plans, the use of the traditional terminology "cooperation in planning" seems appropriate.

"Joint planning" is, however, a correct theoretical description of the multilaterally concerted integration measures. There, a joint *ex ante* setting of targets takes place in a physical form (including the technological and economic parameters). Concrete contractual supply obligations are elaborated and broken down to the individual participatory countries, conditions of repayment are set, and problems of ownership and of running the plant are also jointly set *a priori*. In this case, capital outlays and the use of manpower and of convertible currency is realized in a coordinated way, in order to attain a common goal, i.e. covering their needs for the given products from a jointly created source.

It is not, however, justified to apply the term "joint planning" in any wider sense, since the socialization of labour among the CMEA countries has not ever led to a frontal, all-out cooperation. It does not extend to the entirety of the respective national economies, or to all their economic activities. Depending on their degree of "interestedness", i.e. on the ownership relations, the member countries join regional cooperation projects only if this involves palpable additional gains for them (Valouch 1979).

In interpreting the notion of "planned development on an international scale" *(mezhdunarodnaya planomernost)*, it is expedient to set out from the peculiarities of the international plan-mechanism of integration. Planned development—following the conventions of the literature in the CMEA countries—is a specific feature of the system of plan-based economic management under conditions of the state ownership over most of the means of production.

The economic mechanism of the CMEA integration is also to be understood as the sum of planning, commodity-monetary market and organizational-institutional factors. On the other hand, it differs substantially from the national management systems in that, unlike in the case of the national control systems, it is not the institutional element that plays a dominant role. The system of common institutions in the CMEA consists of bodies functioning on the basis of

sovereignty, where participation follows the interested party principle
and decision-making is, as a rule, indicative, i.e. in the form of re-
commendations.

In most cases only bilateral agreements are of a binding nature.
Thus, the joint institutional system is not a determinant of, but a
supplementary element to, the international planning, trade and commodity-monetary (market) forms of cooperation. This is why in this
respect the standpoint of the Czech economist D. Machová (1976)
is convincing: "In connection with the economic life of the CMEA
community as a whole, we cannot speak of a 'planned economy'
in the sense of there being relations of production of the kind specified by the definition, and such as can be brought about only by
the social ownership of the means of production. And yet, elaborate
theories profess and try to prove the opposite. Voluminous studies
discuss the problem how the CMEA as a whole can be controlled by
a single plan."

"The problem is not", continues Machová, "whether such procedure
is feasible in practice. Experience shows that the CMEA countries and
the CMEA organs—based on their theoretical knowledge and political
experience—have always recognized the substance of supranational
directive theories, in whatever packaging they have been presented.
The difference lies quite elsewhere. The above reviewed theory and
those like it give the impression in economic circles that today the
road to the acceleration of integration and to the economic development of the world socialist system leads through greater centralism
and the enhancing of the mandatory character, for the solution to the
economic problems of integration is to be sought in institutional,
organizational and similar measures. In reality, this would only draw
attention away from the need to solve the actual economic problems,
among others those arising in the existing joint organizations of the
socialist countries—the various 'Inters' and other associations. These
problems can and have to be solved on the basis of the existing relations of production, as no other basis exists. It is this basis which
determines the range in which institutional, organizational, methodological etc. measures can be effective."[12]

Plan coordination has thus been the main instrument of cooperation
among the sovereign states of the CMEA. While acknowledging the
great achievements of cooperation, "We have to recognize the fact that
plan coordination is not yet the most rational way to organize production and trade, nor is it the most efficient way to allocate labour,
to optimally satisfy needs among the socialist countries. Nor can we

be deliberate enough to bring into the scope of plan coordination all the diversified activities of economic life" (Kiss 1973, p. 118).

Plan coordination and its basic factor, specialization in production, "cannot be an exhaustive form and mode of joint economic activity, one suited for the solution of every kind of production and technical-scientific task", points out Shiryaev (1977). Indeed, no other element of the cooperation mechanism, torn out of context, can be considered "an instrument exclusively suited for solving every kind of task"; but nor is this suggested in the literature in connection with any other element of the mechanism of cooperation.

For some economists[13] coordination of plans is directly identified with the conscious social regulation of production. This directly or indirectly implies a one-sided emphasis on the traditional forms of high-level cooperation in physical planning, or can serve as the apology for this practice. And in the course of improving cooperation in planning, it is of practical importance to decide whether it is warranted to identify the central planning organs' deliberate cooperation with the conscious social regulation of production. It is, therefore, expedient to survey the relationship between plan coordination and planned development.

It is noteworthy that most practical planners have distanced themselves from this theory even in countries relying on relatively inflexible management methods. This is illustrated by a statement made by a then deputy chairman of the Bulgarian Committee for Science and Technology in the year preceding the 1979 turn to the new economic approach: "We have emphasized time and again that planning is a subjective activity, and is, thus, by definition not free from the elements of subjectivism and voluntarism" (Davidov 1978). In the present practice of international coordination of plans, the way of dovetailing the various national economic mechanisms is far from satisfactory, nor is sufficient account being taken of the dissimilar "planability" of the diverse areas of economic activity. This is the situation in spite of the fact that these problems were already evident in the economic literature over twenty years ago.

PLAN COORDINATION AND PLANNED DEVELOPMENT

Economists criticizing the phenomena of the centralized system of economic control have frequently pointed out the following paradox. In the classical directive system, formally, i.e. as laid down in the

legal regulations, every substantial decision necessary for the operation of the system is taken at the centre. In practice, however, the
very moment that central economic policy aims not only at the
achievement, at any price, of a few, well-delimitable and quantifiable
objectives, its system of goals becomes complex. Depending on the
increasing complexity of its system of goals and on the size of the
country, the planning agency is increasingly dependent on the detailed
knowledge of the local leadership already in the stage of preparing
the plans. Since the interest of the enterprise is a slack plan, the centre
tries to strain the plan targets based on the information received in
the process of plan bargaining. The possibility of the enterprise's
manoeuvring is well illustrated by the frequent modifications of plans,
of prices and of regulators. Along with the centralization of decisions,
we often find a parallel (and unintended) decentralization of incomes.
Moreover, nearly every CMEA member country is characterized by
the fragmentation and cyclical development of investments (Bauer
1981).

One of the classical arguments for decentralization is, thus, that
the centre could then concentrate on decisions truly in need of high
level intervention. It could better prepare the latter by delegating to
the lower levels operative tasks and those of minor importance, as
well as those not necessarily demanding settlement at the highest
level. Since the early seventies, signs of decentralization have appeared also in the practice of plan coordination. In Hungary plan
coordination is being done not only in the Planning Board, but also
by several subcommittees, by the sectoral ministries and by the large
enterprises as well.

Reliance on lower-level proposals and separate negotiations by
such bodies, however, cause problems, because ministries are not
profit-oriented economic organs (nor, for the most part, are the enterprises). Their interests are mostly related to obtaining extra investment funds and to increasing the volume of foreign trade. They
are not interested in the profitability of individual deals, nor in the
balance of trade.

It is well known from Hungarian practice that enterprises willingly
export to the socialist countries since, circumstances being what they
are, there they attain a unit of domestic income with much smaller
input than on the Western markets. This enterprise-level inclination
is only further strengthened by the ministry's interest in volume.
"Yes", goes the familiar argumentation, "that is why it is necessary
for plan coordination to assert the interest of the national economy

at the highest level". But the large enterprises[14] and the ministries pre-allocate a considerable part of the long-term trade already in the stage of preparing the plan. Thus the organs representing the macro-economic equilibrium, the National Planning Office and the Ministry for Trade, are faced with a *"fait accompli"*. This is partly because the claim of "security of production" counts in the present systems of management of the CMEA countries as a serious and positive argument. Supported by considerations of employment policy and planning techniques, it is an argument which even the functional organs, emphasizing the need for equilibrium and efficiency, have difficulty countering. The highest level might be faced with a *fait accompli* also because it is extremely difficult—certainly at the highest level—"not to coordinate", i.e. not to sell, certain articles when the partner needs them, especially if he knows that such products exist or can be produced in Hungary, and there would even be a producer available, if not already found. In short, contrary to the expectations of the sixties, drawing in the enterprises does not necessarily improve the success of plan coordination, because it provides an opportunity for extending plan-bargaining to the international sphere.

The ranking of investment possibilities and of production programmes becomes impossible if the planning agency is faced with such *fait accompli,* and the real independence of macro-economic planning is thus curtailed. In practice, this means that during the coordination of medium-term foreign trade plans, in many cases it is merely the lists submitted "from below" that are summarized. Thus the danger of a foreign trade surplus is real. Clearly, it is also undesirable, because it would mean an unintended and uneconomical "placing" of a part of the national income. This is an inflationary factor, and necessitates a certain amount of forced imports which—because it involves the import of products which are not of the required quality or assortment—means a relative reduction of living standards. In the case of multilateral settlements—convertible currency—the situation would be quite different, since the surplus could then be used in any country and spent on any commodity.[15]

The directively planned economy requires detailed five-year volumes of commodities to be exchanged. It is well known what difficulties this causes on the micro-level simply because in some cases (i.e. in the case of commercial policy items) the technological parameters of the machines also have to be more or less defined 3–8 years in advance, which—depending on the product—is a multiple of the product obsolescence time on the world market. The usual answer is: "It is thus

that the necessary proportions are achieved on the macro-level'',
although necessary for what and to whom is generally not specified.

In practice, various "solutions" have been found. In some cases,
entire factories are left out of the fulfilment of foreign trade contracts,
which is not surprising since the plan coordinator is faced with insoluble tasks. He has to buy machines—technologically more or less
specified ones—for development for which the investment plan has
not yet been approved (or even drawn up). His predicament follows
from the nature of the case: decisions on development cannot be
taken or scheduled without due attention to the investment and
budgetary equilibria of the given (short-term) period. But delays in
the realization of investment projects, overspending on investment,
its cyclical movements, neglect of terms of delivery and parameters
are deplorable, yet well-known features of the economies of socialist
countries. Therefore, the problem the plan coordinator has to face
is practically insoluble. Only if all the above problems could be solved
simultaneously would the theoretical possibility exist that all investment projects to be implemented in the course of a given plan period
(broken down by sectors, areas and the extent of implementation)
would be known in advance and reckoned with by the negotiating
partners. I should like to note, however, that even if this theoretical
possibility existed, it would not be expedient to act on it, since it is
objectively impossible, for instance in 1987, to make a good prognosis
about the technological parameters that will obtain in computer production in 1995.

The practical situation was, of course, not so tragic. In the annual
foreign trade protocols, the problems were partly corrected according
to the necessities of life, which is natural. This, however, cannot be
considered as a process promoting the minimization of deviations
between the long-term plan and its outcome. Thus, in the practice
of plan coordination the formal, planned character of the process is
constantly being violated. This is hardly in keeping with the expectations raised by a part of the extensive literature on the problem,
which depicts plan coordination as the embodiment of planned development in a formal sense. The former framework provides but one
possibility of keeping more closely to what was planned. Efforts could
be made to specify more and more of the agreed long-term trade in
terms of value.[16] In addition in the interest of defining the foreign
trade tasks deriving from the national five-year plan, a quota had to
be set on socialist export possibilities, which can be transgressed only
when adequate imports are secured. Of course, this challenges in

principle the possibility, necessity and expediency of one-sided long-term planning in physical terms. As regards the organizational problems of trade and its mechanism,[17] a comprehensive solution can be provided by planning in terms of value[18] on the international level as well, which will necessarily be coupled with an economic (not administrative) system of regulation and control. As in the case of the internal economic mechanism, so, too, on the international level it is questionable whether it is expedient for foreign trade market research to be conducted on the highest level. Would it not be better the other way round? If familiar with the state plan and the regulators, the enterprises decided whether they wished to buy complete equipment, and if so, from where. Generally speaking, no concrete source of purchase follows automatically from the state of the balance of payments, particularly if enterprises keep economic efficiency in mind and improve their market research.

In the earlier system of plan coordination, it is precisely direct market evaluation of this kind that is ruled out.

THEORETICAL BASES OF THE LONG-TERM TARGET PROGRAMMES (LTPs)

Section 2 of Chapter IV of the Comprehensive Programme of 1971 proposed the complex solution of the problems arising in planning co-operation through uniting the financial means of the member countries. The Thirtieth Session of the CMEA held in Berlin in 1976 decided that the countries should draw up 15-year target programmes of co-operation (up to 1990) in five areas which were of common interest.

The target programme as a means and method of planning and organization developed in the course of analyses of internal economic problems. It was an interesting experiment at solving the contradictions of sectoral control. It is described in the economic literature of the East-European countries, primarily of the GDR and the Soviet Union. Thus it would seem logical to assume that the long-term cooperation target programmes of the CMEA are international projections, or more exactly, regional applications of the target programme approach. In fact, however, the relationship is more indirect in respect of both economic history and planning techniques.

The CMEA target programmes were not motivated by some "organic" internal economic development. Rather they were motivated by the wish to give a common regional answer to the basic changes in the "external" world economic system.

It was in the framework of a common regional reaction to the oil price explosion that the CMEA countries in 1975 changed the practice of price formation that had been used in mutual trade. It was in the same year that the plan for multilateral integrative measures was accepted. Through a joint effort in the form of granting investment credits, it was intended primarily to solve the fuel problem for the years 1976–80. This was a problem which had beset the CMEA since the sixties. Investment contributions have been given comprehensive treatment in a previous chapter. Here, I shall discuss only the development of the long-term cooperation programmes.

Why should the target programme be the instrument suited for implementing the above-mentioned objective of the CMEA countries? The regional solution certainly fits well into the planning model used in the majority of the member countries. In centralized planned economies, the main effort is concentrated—if only on account of the planning techniques, that is, the method of compiling the material balances—on securing "primary" raw material needs, and material needs in general, from the smallest possible number of sources and for as long as possible. As is known, keeping prices unchanged or the efforts to do so serve the same purpose.[19] The arguments were formulated in terms of the security of supply, and there was a time when this consideration seemed to be so weighty that some economists were even inclined to abstract from the "value aspect", that is, from the (opportunity) costs of the solutions. In the majority of the CMEA countries this idea today counts as an extreme and archaic approach, since at present every theory of planning relies on the unity of planning in physical and value terms,[20] independently of the importance attributed to commodity (market) and monetary relations.

As a further consideration, the priority of sheltering the domestic economy from world inflation may be mentioned. This is related partly to incomes policy and other political considerations, and follows closely from the system and methods of control.

Hungary in the mid-70s differed from the other CMEA countries, where the economic mechanism was based on the breaking down of the plans. She was a textbook example of something Nove had called attention to in another context. Namely, that the decentralization of decision-making will not lead to efficiency unless the price system provides objective local criteria for the decisions of the manager. With no objective criteria to guarantee the rationality of lower-level decisions, we can have the incongruous situation that although the political leadership would like to see some of the authority and some decisions delegated to the local level, this does not happen (Nove 1964, pp. 119–123).

It is well known that the world market prices did not infiltrate the Hungarian price system in 1973–75 at all, and even between 1976–78 only moderate adjustments were made (which in no way affected investment decisions). Thus the orientation the price system gave producers and users was quite misleading, for it did not encourage economizing on raw materials. The timing of the "infiltration" was a matter of economic policy. The fact of "non-infiltration", that is, the disorienting prices and their impact, was an integral part and peculiarity of the given system of control, namely that there were no objective criteria to guarantee the rationality of local decisions. That is why adjustment required a central decision in the case of Hungary as well; it followed from the nature of the system of control.

The third group of reasons explaining the development of CMEA target programmes is the above-mentioned prevalence of the programme-like or target programme approach of the countries with directively planned economies.

The target programme approach is an attempt to solve the problems deriving from sectoral control in the framework of the centralized planning model. We can mention here some of the well-known problems that follow from the state control of industry through branch ministries: the petty interference in enterprise matters and administrative over-regulation which works against the evolution of enterprise initiative; the "empire-building" activity of the branch-ministries; the narrow-mindedness of the central authorities which hinders the achievement of the national economic optimum through conflicts of authority; organizational problems and prestige fights; and finally, the administrative competition of the various branches for scarce investment funds, which goes a long way towards explaining the general and chronic propensity to overspend, and the fragmentation of investments.

To eliminate these deficiencies, two variants have been elaborated in the economic literature. The first relies on the decentralized model of management, and according to the logic of the socialist market economy, proposes the separation of the ownership and the power functions of the state. In this model, the ownership functions would be fulfilled by profit-motivated companies, holdings or managing enterprises and commercial banks. The power functions, those of control included, would be exercised by the central functional organs (National Planning Office, Ministry of Finance, Industrial Ministry, and

Central Bank).[21] In this view, there are no theoretical differences in respect of control among the light, heavy, engineering and metallurgical industries. Hence there is no need for the branch ministries which had been created in response to the needs of physical planning (Szamuely 1974, p. 20).

The other variant is based on the centralized model of economic control and, accordingly, looks for the solution within this framework. Its basic idea is the recognition, known from organization theory, that it is the organizations that have to be reorganized for the solution of given tasks, and not conversely; tasks found for the existing organizations. In the latter case, the uniform operation of organizations called into being for some earlier tasks will be more or less disfunctional, irrational and costly. Control of the socialist economy was also to be organized in a way aimed at targets in a programme-like manner. In the GDR this was called "planning according to complexes of needs"; in the USSR, "programme-like approach" or "complex planning".

The Hungarian central development programmes of the 70's correspond to the above, though with certain organizational and dimensional limitations.

Complex planning means several things: interbranch (interindustry) planning, societal planning, long-term programmes, etc. From the organizational aspect, this means that in order to avoid competition among the branches, the plan is drawn up "backwards" from the target—in the debates of the 1920s this was called "teleological planning"—and the tasks are distributed in the same way. For their implementation, partly the Planning Office, partly inter-branch committees are responsible.

The programme-like approach has never become exclusive, neither in the literature nor in the practice of the countries with directive systems of economic planning. It is not difficult to recognize its basic contradiction. If every task becomes a "priority", being a priority no longer carries any weight. Furthermore, any concrete area—e.g. that of living standards—is simultaneously a part of several issues (social policy, incentives, growth policy, etc.). In the case of the traditional mechanism of breaking down the plans, plan-bargaining is an ongoing process. In the case of a mechanism where the regulators are broken down,[22] regulator-bargaining is an ongoing process. However, it is conducted not (only) with the sectoral and functional ministries, but also with the intergovernmental committees, the price board and other state organs. The approach through target programmes does not alter the underlying interest relations of a centralized economic mechanism which is made manifest in plan-bargaining. The lower level continues to have an interest in withholding performance.

SOME PRACTICAL ASPECTS OF THE LONG-TERM CMEA TARGET PROGRAMMES (LTPs)

The target programmes are not identical with the plans for multilateral integration measures. The latter covered a shorter period (1976–80 and 1981–85) while the target programmes covered the period 1976–90. The former was organically built into the national economic plan of every member country, and concentrated—in the interest of increasing fuel deliveries—on investment projects on Soviet territory. That is, they were aimed at the joint development of fuel production and of the related infrastructure. Thus, they embraced less than the "raw materials and fuels" target programme, which also extended to long-term uses, the production of raw materials, the exploitation of domestic energy resources, the joint building of nuclear power plants and the building of related equipment, the pattern of long-term energy utilization, etc., and could not be linked to the time-proportional part of the long-term plan (where such a plan exists). Further, the special purpose programme itself and its subprogrammes did not include the bilateral delivery contracts (broken down into physical units).[23]

Yet, on the basis of the methodology worked out in 1977 by the International Institute of the CMEA[24] and from the literature published after the Thirtieth Session,[25] the impression could be got that the draft target programmes aimed at some international "branch" optimum. Conversely, they have also been frequently interpreted as an attempt to introduce a long-term, directive and partially supranational planning practice. Their supranational nature was seen to have been secured above all by the branch optimum calculated on the international (CMEA) level, and by the obligatory nature of the joint plan document. The target programmes were interpreted by some as entailing a large-scale international flow of capital much exceeding the extent of the usual investment credits. More exactly, on the analogy of the plans for multilateral integration measures and their extension, the building of large common projects with the joint financial means of the member countries were seen as the principal material content of the long-term CMEA target programmes.[26] Thus the special-purpose programmes as instruments of a multilateral international joint or common planning were expected to become instruments of integration of identical or nearly identical importance with plan coordination, and leading to the formation of essentially common planning documents implying interstate commitments based on long-term physical indicators.[27]

The implementation of the international sectoral optimum in its actual form focussed attention on two methodological issues: the questions of national sovereignty, and of optimization in physical terms. Within the CMEA, which is an integration of sovereign nations, the international optimum can be arrived at only as the resultant of the national optima. On the other hand, it also seems self-evident that in a commodity-producing society, in consequence of commodity contradiction[28] no optimum can be determined *ex ante* in physical terms. In optimal planning, needs and means, as different use values, can be compared and measured only in terms of value. Finally, it has to be noted that the notion of branch-optimum has no economic substance, since the branch is not the owner of the fixed assets, and the subject of the planned economy which optimizes is not the branch, but the state.

These two theoretical problems set the task of making national and international plans compatible, and of developing international mechanisms of cooperation within the CMEA which take into account that different economic mechanisms exist in the various member countries. It is therefore not surprising that in the resolution of the 1978 CMEA Session (Communiqué 1978) which put an end to the discussions, the heads of government of the member countries formulating the individual and joint interests of the CMEA countries did not take into account those elements of the proposal which did not reckon with realities.

Thus, the jointly accepted resolution does not state that the long-term target programmes were multilateral agreements comprising physical commitments. The special purpose programme was a joint international planning document which, in respect of its content, was a framework agreement in order to "work out and conclude multilateral and bilateral agreements on cooperation in concrete questions". The agricultural target programme, since it was dominated by bilateral agreements, characteristically differed from the drafts conceived on the analogy of the plans for multilateral integration measures. Another way of putting this is that the plan adopted as the comprehensive document of multilateral cooperation among CMEA countries was, in fact, an internal document of the Council, whose purpose was to help coordinate economic cooperation. It was not, however, a planning document of the national economies of the CMEA countries (Stancu 1978).

This clearly disproves a once fashionable trend in economic literature which tried to depict the LTPs as a qualitatively new stage in the development of the CMEA integration. Already, Kiss (1972, p. 86) described as "established practice" the joint planning which translates the long-term target programmes into interstate agreements. In reality, however, joint planning is a method of proceeding that is used only in certain narrow spheres. In the late 1970s, too, it was only setting the objectives and the main lines of the draft agreements that was done multilaterally; interstate agreements and final delivery obligations were fixed in private international law contracts on a bilateral basis. It is, thus, indicative of a basic misconception that even years after the 1978 Council Session we find many authors maintaining that a decision taken in the framework of a LTP automatically [!] becomes a mandatory plan-task for the participatory countries (Ladygin 1981). No less mistaken is the following: "The LTP can be taken for an obligatory plan document jointly elaborated by several member states, one that embraces the development of a given area of production including [!] the chain of related areas . . . Target programmes denote a higher stage of international coordination of plans as they comprise priority development projects [?], and their international harmonization requires the closest [?] cooperation in planning" (Kiss–Pavelcsák 1981, p. 46). Equally mistakenly, Rácz (1982, p. 22) maintains that the substance of the LTP is "the elaboration of a long-term unified strategy in a given sector for all CMEA countries". The following statement by a prolific authority on the LTPs is downright misleading: "It is the first time that the most important delivery conditions are set for several five-year-plan periods" (Shiryaev 1981, p. 214).

Knowing the methodology of the LTPs, we must realize that it has absolutely nothing to do with "optimizing individual sectors of the various national economies as if they were constituent parts of a single economic organization", or as if LTPs were magnified investment contribution agreements, as implied by another earlier-quoted statement. The implausibility of these interpretations will be evident if we recall that long-term plan projects do not aim at specifying the details of the pattern and choice of mutual trade flows, since it is objectively impossible to predetermine such an assortment 10–15 years ahead in most product categories (Motorin 1980). Nor, despite recurring claims to this effect by certain authors, e.g. Konstantinov

(1980), have LTPs induced substantial international capital flows within the CMEA. Financing was decided upon by the national financial organs as a function of the degree of interest shown by the national planning organs[29] in finalizing the agreements in the course of the coordination of plans for 1981–85. It is noteworthy that for the 1986–90 plan coordination period, LTPs did not serve even as points of reference for determining mutual deliveries.

In sum, we can conclude that given the predominance of the traditional planning method of *zakaz-naryad*, the use of target programming as a modernized instrument of centralized planning never got off the ground. All in all, it was not implementation that was adjusted to the new tasks, as had been presumed and proposed by the target programme approach. On the contrary, the existing set of interests and institutions managed to mould the new planning technique to their established ways. In other words, it was the given form of international relations of production that reshaped the targets imposed by the economic policy decisions. This might come as a surprise to the traditional apologists of mandatory planning, but will be seen as only normal by all with an understanding of modern economic theory, and with some knowledge of sociology and of the workings of large non-market organizations.

The lack of the external resources necessary for shifting to the intensive type of development (i.e. the shortage of capital), the absence of modern technologies, the lack of competitive products and of market organization, the ignorance of modern management methods, and the dearth of managers of the enterprising kind can be observed in several CMEA countries. Thus it seems clear that, in spite of the beautiful slogans, the recurring proposals to replace East—West cooperation by CMEA cooperation (arising from time to time particularly in the extractive industries and in engineering) have not much to do with the real possibilities. Only very meagre results can be expected on this score, although such proposals were still abroad, in the late 70s (Kozma F. 1978a).

In concrete terms: the long-term target programmes of the CMEA on cooperation were framework agreements which comprised sub-programmes. These sub-programmes attained concrete formulation in the course of the interested CMEA member countries' coordinating their medium-term plans at the decisive stage of bilateral agreements. Thus, the target programmes fitted into the process of the CMEA countries' integration into the world economy. They were not aimed at large-scale collective import substitution, and have not been implemented with the methods of supranational directive planning. Therefore, the target programmes cannot be considered as constituting a qualitatively new phase in the development of CMEA cooperation. As was pointed out in 1978 in the joint publication on integration put out by the planning periodicals of the member countries by G. Georgiev of Bulgaria and Z. Šedivý of Czechoslovakia, both then deputy presidents of their respective planning offices: "It is common knowledge today that the target programmes cannot and will not become a wide complex of balanced relations, nor can they become a substitute for bilateral plan coordination between the CMEA countries in the fields in question" (Šedivý 1978, p. 1166).

As we find out from the article by the Bulgarian author, the countries interested in the individual sub-programmes concluded contracts in the course of plan coordination in which they specified the details, e.g. the extent of the investment contributions to the nuclear power plant in Khmelnitsky. The quantity of the energy to be produced was clarified in a protocol attached to the plan coordination. The annual supplies of energy were bilaterally determined each year and were also adjusted to take into account the value of the commodities actually delivered by the interested member countries.

This shows palpably that the implementation of the long-term target programme of cooperation was not an alternative but an organic part of the given traditional mechanism of CMEA cooperation. The cooperation that took place within this framework was an integral part of the system of instruments of CMEA cooperation because it was realized partly through the coordination of five-year plans (in the form of protocols), and partly through medium-term and annual commodity exchange contracts, since the annual deliveries were modified in view of the bilateral balance of trade in the preceding year. This also holds true of investment contribution contracts. After the raw material exporters have paid back the "target credits" granted on the sliding price basis and not yet valorized, further supplies— thus also the delivery of the products of the joint projects—"can be linked" (in accordance with the general conditions evolved in recent years in bilateral trade) "to the counter-delivery of specified products" (Pécsi 1979b, p. 32). In other words, after repayment, the exporter of the raw material could decide what item and how much of it he accepted from the importer country as a counter-delivery of equal hardness. This arrangement did not mean more favourable or more secure procurement possibilities than the general conditions prevailing in CMEA raw material imports.

All this illuminates why the implementation of the target programmes directs attention to the importance of the financial issues of the Comprehensive Programme which is still, for the most part, unimplemented. For commodity (market) and monetary relations have an active effect on the extent of investment cooperation under the target programme in the periods of both planning and implementation. Hence the degree of interestedness of the individual countries depends on the level of contractual prices, on credit conditions, etc. (Brendel 1979 and Karavaev 1978). The individual countries were not interested in the total additional value of the project created through joint effort, but only its part raising the efficiency of their own economic activity (Shiryaev 1981, p. 107). As a matter of fact, granting credits—including investment credits—is a field of the financial system of socialist integration which requires further improvement. As has been discussed in several publications in the economic press of the various CMEA countries, the valorization of credit granted on a sliding price basis is as yet unsolved, because no progress has been made so far in the fields of either preemption at advantageous prices (over a longer period following the repayment of credit), or the use of different methods of valorization, or in operating the productive capacity as a joint enterprise. (The latter would be justified by the investment effort having been joint, and would mean a share in physical terms from the annual output in proportion to the capital contributed.) Here again, a problem arises in connection with the income-redistributing and normative economic functions of interest, in respect of both its rate, its order of settlement, and its actual transferability.

But the relationship between the long-term target programmes of cooperation and the monetary system of the CMEA can be felt not only in the case of the "raw materials and fuels" target programme, but also in other cases. The interrelation of the agricultural target programme with monetary relations is shown by the fact that in consequence of the considerable capital intensity of agricultural production, its poor export efficiency and high content of imports from the West, the interested countries continued to harmonize bilaterally the extent and methods of their cooperation. One of the priority subprogrammes of the target programme was the so far unsolved problem of economically stimulating agricultural exports to the CMEA. The heads of the Bulgarian, Hungarian and Romanian governments separately raised the problem at the 1981 session of the CMEA in Sofia, and at all the following sessions of the 1980s. The joint resolution adopted in 1981 also stresses this to be a major unresolved field of cooperation.

The interrelation between the target programmes and the monetary system is particularly conspicuous in the case of the engineering target programme. In engineering, which is characterized by the mutual relationship of a great number of cooperating partners, physical accounting and incentives inescapably lead to the "end-product-approach" frequently criticized in the literature of the CMEA countries,[30] and to the undesirable phenomena of autarky within the enterprise. Owing to the nature of technological and economic progress, parts have become independent commodities. As a consequence, the production of both mass-produced parts and parts satisfying special demands—high quality items produced either individually or in small series—has become an independent industrial activity. Hence, the cooperation-intensity of the internationally competitive engineering industry has grown to an unheard-of extent. Since for the production of a single end product there can be 100–400 cooperating partners supplying often as many as 5–10,000 different parts, it seems that in this field, direct cooperation among enterprises cannot really be replaced by the initiative of the planning organs, which have but a restricted overview and a limited working capacity.[31] Therefore it seems to be a highly justified and correct standpoint that the engineering target programme, which comprises about 100 tasks of cooperation, should be focused on the key problems. In other words, in engineering the target programme only pointed out the main lines of cooperation. This was manifested also in the fact that the engineering target programme involved the creation of new capacities only in a few cases, and concentrated mainly on the expansion of cooperation (Nagy F. 1978; and Kresák 1978).

When it came to implementation, however, the balance of payments difficulties of the East European countries in both major trading relations were such that even the cooperation agreements of the pre-1980 period could not all be prolonged for the 1981–85 period. An additional factor explaining this development was the deterioration of interfirm relations, due partly to the increased frequency of the central management authorities' unexpected direct interference with microeconomic processes. These developments have become only more pronounced in the 1986–90 period.

All in all, what explains the fate of LTPs? In answering the question, even professional circles are prone to the misunderstanding thoroughly analyzed by I. Friss (1974, p. 7) more than a decade ago, namely, that the contradictions arising from the underdeveloped state of the financial sphere appear on the surface as if they were the results of too great an emphasis on national sovereignty, or even of conflicting national interests. In fact, the opposite is true. It is the underlying common features of the in many ways different domestic economic management systems, i.e. their immanent tendency to autarky, and the self-propelling and self-reproducing overcentralization in their decision-making, that has inevitably resulted in the demonetization and segmentation of the financial system of the CMEA integration (as detailed in the earlier chapters). This is the organic reason for the atrophy of the orientative function of financial instruments at the enterprise level within the domestic systems, and thus also for the resulting low propensity to compromise both at the micro and the macro levels. In the absence of national monetary systems that would make unambiguous international comparisons of costs and benefits possible, i.e. without currency convertibility in the sense detailed earlier, it is hardly possible to prove to each participant in black and white that the integrative option is indeed more to his benefit than the national or the global solution.

REGIONAL INTEGRATION AS AN INSTRUMENT OF EXPORT ORIENTATION

It has been raised in the economic literature[32] and also at the political level that joint implementation of projects resulting in internationally competitive output and cooperation on third markets might be a promising area of regional integration. Clearly, shortage of hard currency makes the thought of reorienting regional efforts from import substitution to easing the common bottlenecks in the CMEA through more exports, i.e. through earning more hard currency, seem attractive. However, it is a somewhat more difficult task to circumscribe the ways this idea could be put into practice.

It goes without saying that large-scale cooperation aiming at third markets presumes a radically improved and more flexible division of labour within the CMEA itself. Otherwise the present problems will only multiply in the face of a more demanding task. The major outlines of a reform of this kind were elaborated back in the late sixties (Ausch 1972), and the changes in the external economic environment have only endorsed this approach. On the other hand, the national economic management systems have evolved in a different direction than was then presumed, and the modifications during the rest of the 80s did not imply such far-reaching changes as would have made a radical overhaul of the intra-CMEA mechanism feasible. The following proposals and analyses attempt to show what had been possible to achieve under the earlier circumstances. They also attempt to show what the consequences of the non-implementation of the radical reform proposals have been for the enterprise sphere, whose continued and simultaneous presence in both the intra and extra regional division of labour is a fact of life.

The joint implementation of large development projects in production aiming at sales for convertible currencies can, under the former set of conditions, play only a minor role in cooperation on third markets. Experience with the intra-CMEA joint ventures as well as with joint investments indicates that, owing mainly to the underdeveloped state of the financial sphere, it is extremely difficult to mobilize and harmonize the endeavours of a large number of interested parties—each quite inflexibly representing his own point of view—unless rational economic calculus rather than administrative arbitrariness is the chief method of coordination.

Moreover, the nineties are likely to continue to see lean years for investments. Since an international investments is—or at least seems to be—more risky than one under national auspicies, it is hardly likely that abundant funds will become available for this particular purpose. Therefore as far as direct export activities are concerned, it is general contracting, finishing, after-sale servicing, occasionally setting up joint (marketing) enterprises and other activities aiming at improving the non-price components of marketability that would be the most promising ways of cooperation. It is common knowledge that no single country competes through undercutting the others' prices of its own will, but only under financial and market pressures. This method can hardly be a prospective practice for the CMEA countries. Their competitors dispose of comparative advantages in terms of resource base, wage costs and commercial policy status which are objectively impossible to offset through cut prices. This situation is only aggravated by increased job protection leading to the proliferation of various forms of neo-protectionist practices in commercial policy. Thus, for the CMEA countries it would be expedient jointly to set up those elements of modern market organization and sales promotion whose maintenance would be too costly for the limited export volume of a single country to bear. For instance, the establishment of a joint market research institute in non-traditional markets like Japan or the ASEAN countries, or the establishment of joint trading houses which better organize the sale of products bought back from the CMEA countries under compensatory deals. The latter could countervail to some degree the destruction of labels and of prices that inherently follow from buy-back agreements. In the given (limited) market segments, competition among enterprises of CMEA countries could also be regulated in a business-centred rather than in an administrative way. It might prove useful to set up common after-sale servicing centres, say in the automotive industry.

The integrational institutions of the CMEA evolved at a time when international mandatory planning on a regional scale did not yet seem impossible. Moreover, owing partly to their sectoral and state-administrative internal setup, the working style and aspirations of these organs are dominated by the earlier-described bureaucratic, state administrative approach. A reflection of this was the elaboration of over-ambitious LTP projects—when physical targets were set without due attention to their financial consequences, targets whose investment costs were beyond any reasonable reach—implying a redistribution of decision-making competence at the expense of national authorities.

In modernizing the CMEA's joint institutions,[33] it would be expedient to set out from two crystal-clear findings of integration theory. 1) The national framework is not going to be subordinate to a higher regional authority. 2) International mandatory planning is infeasible and impracticable both in theory and in practice.

Consequently, the activities of the joint CMEA institutions should be directed to business practice, and their state-administrative nature should be restricted. The present character of the CMEA organs—in virtue of which they resemble an international plan commission or an international sectoral ministry—should be altered to make them into an international chamber of commerce of sorts, a business information and servicing centre.

At the moment, producer enterprises in one CMEA country know precious little about the activities of similar companies in other CMEA states, which in itself is a limit to their better cooperation. By collecting, systematizing and spreading business information that can be applied in daily business decisions at the company level, CMEA organs could make an immediate contribution to fostering direct interfirm relations both within and outside the region, in line with the political initiatives of the Forty-First Council Session and the Twenty-Seventh Party Congress.

In deciding the rationality, cost and size of the CMEA common institutions that are to be maintained, it is necessary to apply a much more stringent economic calculus than in earlier periods. Costs and benefits should be measured against each other anew in the following cases:

—where the jointly set goals have not been attained, or have been attained only at disproportionate costs in terms of time, financial outlays and human efforts as compared to the originally planned magnitudes;

—where the functioning of the joint—mostly coordinatory—organization is formal, and the results of its activity can be attained without maintaining a separate standing organ, e.g. by signing a specialization agreement, or by a once a year meeting, or in the course of working relations;

—where the originally set targets have been successfully realized;

—where practical evidence indicates that the optimal solution to the given problem is achievable by means other than a joint organization, or when in theory this would be the case, but under the present conditions—e.g. the state of the financial sphere—it is impossible to meet the theoretical eventuality;[34]

—where in the significant time span since their establishment, the Hungarian or other party has clearly lost interest in the subject.

In the listed cases, it is well not to hesitate to reorganize common institutions into more suitable forms, or in the case of a general loss of interest, even to dissolve them. Instead, new forms should be promoted that are in keeping with the new situation: the shortage of funds, and the ever more competitive international market conditions that each member state is compelled to face. Common institutions functioning only formally, inefficiently or at high cost in fact do more harm to the objectives of socialist integration than facing the conflicts induced by their reorganization or dissolution. The target is to adjust to a world economic environment that has become incomparably more demanding than it was in the early seventies. The new CMEA institutions must also meet its requirements: flexibility, business orientation, profit-orientation and a non-schematic working style are the maxims for practice, too. Such institutions—notes Rácz (1982, p. 21) quite rightly—must only be established if business practice positively requires them[35] and, let us add, with a much wider and less schematic use of the arsenal of international private law.

In running common economic organs, it is necessary to look for the most profitable and least costly forms of those activities that are actually done jointly. To this end, it would be well to put into practice the thesis unfolded at the 1976 Council Session, that instead of the gratuitous multiplication of common organs, the contents of their activities should be improved (Lázár 1976). Let us add that the forms should also change in time, in compliance with the modifications in the substance, and in the members' common interests.

It is clear that in all forms of international cooperation in the CMEA, a peculiar weakness of the domestic management and control systems, strengthened by the political aspect of the integration, re-emerges. This is the unresolved problem of elaborating methods and mechanisms for the normal establishment and dissolution of institutions, i.e. methods other than acts of the highest political will. The closing down of an enterprise or even of a factory is a rarity even within the national economies. Even more exceptional is the dissolution of non-economic organizations of the state administration. Target programming as a planning concept has already discovered the significance of this issue. However, since it has looked for solutions within the constraints of the mandatory planning model, it could provide a practical solution only in exceptional priority cases such as the space programme, or the comprehensive programme for exploring and developing Western Siberia. Hungarian economic literature supportive of radical economic reform has realized the need for closures, and theoretically, economic policy has accepted this conclusion.

Thus proprietors are required to think in purely monetary terms, and thus be able to make decisions concerning structural readjustment and the concomitant liquidating of one physical form of assets to reinvest in another physical form following the long-term profit maximization motive.[36] It is common knowledge that capital reallocation faces the resistance of vested interests, e.g. the regional authorities whose power position has traditionally been prominent in Central and Eastern Europe. Furthermore, there are those with an interest in maintaining a given place of employment related to a given qualification structure within the labour force. Then there are the branch ministries which still have a dominant interest. On the other hand, if the CMEA countries are to keep pace with the changes in the international economic environment, capital reallocation must become an organic part of business activity, not one requiring political decisions and campaigns in the case of each and every closure. It is time to search for ways of putting into practice in the case of international organs, too, the theorem: "Aims should determine organizational forms, rather than letting the vested interests of the existing institutions mould targetsetting". True, this approach can become dominant only after entrepreneurial independence has evolved in most of the CMEA states. But even before then, certain transitory measures might be considered.

It must be clearly seen that for the time being, two factors determine our possibilities. First, the deeply rooted protectionist economic policies and the inherent autarkic tendencies of the traditional mandatory planning system together limit the possibilities of international trade. Secondly, the regional international mechanism of cooperation reflects parallel disequilibria in an increasingly demonetized manner. These two factors together severely restrict the mutually acceptable—unambiguously definable—sphere of common interests that can be subject to international coordination. This holds *a fortiori* for the enterprise sphere. Analyzing the two sides of this paradox independently, the Czech economist, L. Rusmich (1983), pinpoints the problem the most directly. On the one hand, "No interstate obligation is in the position to substitute for the lack of efficiency incentives in the national management systems". On the other hand—as our own analysis demonstrates elsewhere—"In the absence of realistic prices, it is not possible to allow autonomous enterprise decisions in foreign trade. Instead, the direct individual evaluation of each economic transaction becomes a must. The latter, however, deprives direct interfirm contacts of their substance of entrepreneurial initiative".

This paradox manifests itself most strikingly in cooperation on third markets. It is a proposal frequently voiced by business executives that the regular underbidding practised by the enterprises of CMEA countries also against one another on the world market should be mellowed by CMEA level interstate coordination and/or commercial policy actions. On the other hand, equally frequent are the complaints of undisciplined deliveries in intraregional trade, although obligations here derive from interstate agreements, and deliveries and counterdeliveries are closely tied to one another. This situation has worsened rather than improved during the 80s.

This paradox is a manifestation of one of the underlying contradictions in the mandatory planning model. This is evident in the formal legal fetishism, and the inhibitory effect produced by the plethora of obligatory instructions. Given the simultaneous presence of both of these, the situation is somewhat schizophrenic. It is, thus, expected, on the one hand, that some regulation of international public law will put an end to the unfortunate competition, which is extremely costly also for the "winning" side. In the meantime, it is common knowledge that the strains in the balance of payments *vis-à-vis* the West induce each and every CMEA member state's national economic control system to encourage sales for convertible currencies at nearly any rate. As evidenced by business practice, in this respect there is no difference between the system in the GDR, which formally sanctions breaches of interstate obligations very severely, and that in Hungary, which relies, in principle, on full enterprise autonomy, or that in Poland, with its middle-of-the-road "reform mechanism".

In one typical case—Czechoslovakia, the GDR, and Romania—the foreign trade company's success indicator is a quantitative target, broken down according to geographical relations and product groups. In case of an unexpectedly favourable sales opportunity for convertible currency, the Ministry of Foreign Trade approves a modification in the obligatory targets of the foreign trade plan. Business practice indicates that such modifications occur even if there is an interstate agreement to the contrary, given the general shortage in convertible currency intakes. Coordination at the firm level between the enterprises of these countries and Hungarian companies through economic methods is rendered nearly impossible by the different ways of dovetailing domestic and foreign prices, by the different role of financial instruments, and also by the basically dissimiliar function of money as a success criterion for the economic actors. While in Hungary production costs plus pricing regulations put heavy limits on the discounts companies may give in their exports for convertible currencies,[37] in the other countries losses to firms resulting from their sales in convertible currency according to and beyond the plan are more or less automatically reimbursed by the Budget. Under these circumstances, a discount of nearly any size may be made a part of the plan, and an overfulfilment of the quantitative export target is reason for a bonus rather than for a penalty.[38] Since the enterprises of the CMEA countries do not "speak the same economic language", any attempt to coordinate them on the basis of their material self-interest does not stand a very good chance.

When calling for coordination through administrative means, two circumstances must be reconsidered. a) Due to the above-summarized factors, the efficiency of coordination does not seem to be particularly high. b) If there is a possibility for an enforceable deal, it is determined by the compromise position taken by the partner with the least flexible system or point of view. Coordination of this sort implies that companies in the country with the more flexible management system sacrifice the very advantages provided by the more decentralized decision-making system there.[39] Since the situation is characterized by increased competition to adjust to world economic changes coupled with parallel shortages and parallel oversupplies in all CMEA countries, cooperation on third markets implying sectoral or even overall commercial policy level coordination to divide the markets *ex ante* and to avoid underbidding seems to be both an unjustified and an unrealistic expectation. This follows from the fact that the joint market share of the CMEA suppliers on most product markets is below 2–3 percent.

The above-described consequences of the national economic management systems only confirm this conclusion.

In the prospective model of joint export orientation, it is the voluntary coordination of company strategies through economic methods that seems to be the progressive and efficient solution. This might be organized by an international chamber of commerce.[40]

It seems obvious that cooperation on third markets cannot serve as a substitute for resolving the immanent problems of the intra-CMEA mechanism of cooperation. Moreover, it is something that can follow, rather than precede, the reform of the CMEA system. Unless real enterprise autonomy and interest in profits evolves, the companies of any two CMEA countries will continue to have difficulties in reaching an agreement even over bilateral issues. Under these conditions, cooperation on third markets can only mean an additional burden for them, i.e. additional risk and effort without proportionate material rewards for it. Moreover, a great many administrative difficulties are bound to emerge, which these days often hinder cooperation on third markets even among firms with sales supplies that are complementary to one another.

The peculiar norms of enterprise behaviour that have evolved under intra-CMEA mandatory planning and the interstate quota system—such as long reaction time, lack of punctuality, the mutual acceptance of second-rank performance and the like—have not left the companies untouched. Each enterprise participating in trade with both the East and West is fully aware of the fact that it simply cannot afford in its relations with a Western partner the style of activity it indulges in in business deals with domestic and CMEA partners (where the norms of the sellers' market are universally accepted). Thus a well-established mutual distrust exists among CMEA companies which is not caused, but only aggravated, by the growing frequency of unforeseeable, and from the company's perspective[41] irrational, interference by the central authorities. The impossibility of going bankrupt or even of being cut back, the umbrella of state paternalism, certainly has a debilitating effect even on the initiating party,[42] which is capable of better performance. If a producer can count on state protection even against market pressures to cease existing activities even at the product level, something which unfortunately, has long been the case, then for reasons of convenience, of production organization, of planability and of technology his propensity to specialize and to cooperate will be low. What is needed to change this is a reliable supplier-buyer system, market equilibrium, a compensation system, and above all, a financial and currency system where individual cost-elements can be internationally compared, so that the costs and benefits of trade can be clearly measured also at the product level. Lacking this, it is small wonder that the propensity of the companies of CMEA countries to cooperate with one another on third markets has decreased rather than increased during the 80s. The efficiency of occasional coordination has decreased, i.e. agreements formally achieved are often not implemented.

It is a further problem that the traditional methods of intra-CMEA cooperation, which have often been praised for providing stability and security for producers, slow down change in product innovation and marketing activities, and sometimes even inhibit these. This is a most severe problem when they try to enter third markets. It is clear that a partner who is ideal in intra-CMEA relations might prove to be quite far from it under competitive conditions.

The situation has been aggravated by the increasingly frequent interference of the central authorities in interfirm relations in each and every bilateral contact, a factor which has intensified mistrust among companies. From the enterprise perspective, it is completely indifferent whether it is the partner company or (one of) its superior organs that bears the final responsibility for disrupting a business contact, be it the refusal to supply, or to accept the products supplied on contract. This practice of the central organs inevitably follows from the state of the intra-CMEA mechanism. It exerts a paralyzing influence on interfirm contacts, since hard practical evidence cautions against initiative and encourages restraint, formalism and conservatism in all walks of life. The tried and tested ways always entail the smallest risk, while their modification mostly implies risks without secure or calculable rewards. It is an ever-spreading conviction among business executives with ever-growing justification that intra-CMEA trade as a whole is none of their concern. As far as they can see, all international coordination activities having anything to do with the CMEA are a job for, and in the interest of, the highest government organs and officials. This has become a norm of behaviour that will exert an influence even when it is no longer justified. It is an attitude which puts extreme restrictions on all step-by-step changes in the CMEA system, and certainly influenced the implementation possibilities of the 1985 Comprehensive Programme for Scientific and Technological Progress in the CMEA countries until the year 2000 (Long-term Programme), which was intended to be realized by heavy reliance on direct interfirm contacts (see chapter 10).

A further relevant fact of life is that selling to the West requires special expertise. Those who already possess it are unwilling to share it with those who do not, or at least to share it free of charge. While this is a truism in East—West business contacts—reflected, among other things, in the lower price level of the products that are bought back—it is occasionally still a subject of dispute between the companies of two CMEA countries. On the other hand, even if all accounting is transacted in convertible currency, it is difficult to quantify the contribution made by the factors of "obtaining the deal" and of "commercial activity" as a proportion of the final receipts (profits).

Finally, the Hungarian experience calls attention to a further consideration. For most Hungarian enterprises, the CMEA market meets overheads and provides the basic volume of profits from foreign trade. This often means sales possibilities for mediocre products on the basis of strict mutuality. Since mutuality—i.e. weaknesses and losses resulting from similar quality counterdeliveries—appears mostly at the level of companies other than the exporter, the latter realizes only the advantages of the CMEA markets, i.e. stability and softness. From this it follows that if a company producing truly marketable or innovative items needs a partner, whether in production or in marketing or services, then this probably will not be its traditional intra-CMEA partner,[43] whose function (role) in this company's overall strategy is completely different. The stability of traditional deals is to countervail the risks inherent in any innovatory venture. The aim is to maintain an acceptable level of profits even if the new venture fails (or does not yet bring profits), a serious problem under the annual state pressure to be profitable. Alternatively, the use of productive capacities out of season may provide palpable

in the case of the rest of the turnover, no imbalances are tolerated even within the span of a year.

8 This feature of the cooperation mechanism of the CMEA was already a target of criticism in the debates preceding the adoption of the Comprehensive Programme of 1971. At the conference held in Budapest in November 1970, the head of the Hungarian delegation noted: "Experience shows that more progress in cooperation has been made in the areas where detailed central planning is feasible such as in fuel supply, in the construction of the common system of electric energy supply, or in the joint use of the wagon park. Problems emerge, however, in dynamic industries, where the fast-changing technology, the changing needs and other factors allow for the central planning of the rate and main lines of development only, but the elaboration of details requires more enterprise-level autonomy. The practical results of central deliberation in fostering cooperation in these areas—joint ventures, mutually advantageous specialization and cooperation—are far from satisfactory." (Csikós-Nagy 1973b, p. 181.)

9 It is therefore a one-sided and misleading—yet popular—approach taken by certain authors—e.g. Gavrilov and Leznik 1982, pp. 97–101, and Shiryaev 1983, p. 79—which, even under volatile international economic conditions, puts the emphasis exclusively on the five-year planning period being too short, without weighing just what a 10–15 year plan can deal with, how and with what level of certainty. The authors also fail to consider that in the areas of fast accelerating production and quickly changing product lines, such as electronics, already in the 60s and 70s the system of binding five-year agreement was a factor that hindered attempts to keep pace with international technological development.

10 Cf. Balassa Á. 1979, p. 257 and p. 299.

11 Cf. Knyżiak 1975, p. 1027, and Nyilas J. 1982, pp. 209–210.

12 Similar considerations were voiced at that time by M. Paraluta in 1975, and the point was reiterated at the 1983 Council Session by the then Romanian Premier, Dăscălescu.

13 Cf. Shein 1980.

14 What is said here of Hungarian large enterprises obviously holds for the large industrial organizations (associations) characterizing the industrial organization of CMEA states other than Hungary. There the profit motive is weaker, even formally, and subject to a set of other plan targets (in some countries, profit is not among the success indicators at all).

15 I do not think that in the present state of the CMEA economies and their organization, real convertibility and multilaterality could be introduced. I expounded my related views in Csaba 1981, and Study No. 1 in Csaba, 1985.

16 Given the existence of parallel shortages, for the time being the opposite interest (getting more of the trade turnover specified in physical terms) is stronger, since the value in exchange of a "value-contingent" is more uncertain, to say nothing of the timing of the payments.

17 It is obvious that problems arising from the technological gap, from parallel shortages, and from a historically lower level of development cannot be solved through exclusive reliance on improving the system of management. We can be sure, however, that changing the economic system of "soft-

budget constraint" for one with more "hard-budget constraint"—to use Kornai's terms—would not aggravate, but rather alleviate the currently existing problems.

18 Planning in value terms is a process in which the physical processes of production are not independent variables but dependent ones (dependent on price, value, and market or profitability considerations). This is a method widely applied by large enterprises for marketing and production optimizing decisions, and involves also decisions on the physical processes of production. Its general use in macroeconomic planning would not make physical planning superfluous in some areas. The prognostication of energy needs, for instance, is obviously a task to be planned in physical terms, too.

19 After the change to sliding pricing, the aim of keeping prices stable for 3–5 years was soon formulated, in conformity with centralized planning practices. This idea was reformulated in the course of the 1981–85 plan coordination. Price levels in some bilateral relations remained unchanged for longer periods—usually for 2–3 years—in 1976–90 on the basis of intergovernmental agreements.

20 The modern import-substituting approaches use so-called efficiency arguments, too. In view of the fact that the products of an import-substituting project are usually not actually measured against the real requirements of the world market, and consequently are not directly compared to actual (or potential) import costs, on paper the efficiency of any such project can be "demonstrated" by ignoring precisely the above actually existing conditions. This fact was brought to the author's attention by L. Antal.

21 Cf. Tardos 1972.

22 This is a term used for the "half-monetized" Hungarian system of management, or rather its model, as described by Antal 1979. While formally, a system based on enterprise independence and profitability exists, actually a management practice equivalent to the breaking down of plans and resources takes place. The main difference from the traditional model is that income positions are formulated *ex post*, and not *ex ante* according to the requirements of physically pre-determined plans. Moreover, the means of implementation is not the breaking down of plans, but individual financial regulation. As the bargaining process on regulators resembles plan-bargaining, Antal calls this system breaking down the regulators. The above is a very simplistic summary of Antal's views, to say nothing of the actual management situation in Hungary in the mid- and late 70s.

23 For an exhaustive analysis of the details of the methodologies, objectives, procedures and the ensuing problems of target-programming at the CMEA level, see van Brabant 1981.

24 Cf. Litviakov et al. 1977.

25 Cf. Szita, 1976; Nyers, 1977; Stancu, 1978; and van Brabant, 1981, p. 156.

26 As reflected directly in Yakushin, 1978, and Starzyk, 1977.

27 In fact, this was reminiscent of the 1956–62 situation as described in Kiss 1976, when similar problems emerged in the elaboration of mandatory international physical product balances.

28 This is a notion common in Marxian political economy. In any society producing for the market, a contradiction may emerge between the use value of a given commodity and its social acceptance, which is its value

in exchange. The difference is most palpable in cases of overproduction or of unsaleable goods.

29 Cf. Gavrilov and Motorin 1979, pp. 81—84, and Georgiev 1978.

30 In their high-standard analysis, Schweitzer and Róth (1979) trace the end-product approach to the one-sided interest of producers in economies of scale. Not challenging this statement, I want to add that the centre would hardly make the enterprise interested in a plan specified in tons, a practice frequently criticized even in the central party press of the countries if it had some other way of control than accounting in physical units of measurement.

31 For empirical proof of this point, see Bauer, Patkós, Soós, et al. 1980.

32 Cf. Bognár, 1979.

33 For details of the practical work on this area following the Twenty-Seventh Party Congress of the CPSU, see Csaba 1986.

34 This is obviously the case with joint ventures in production. Various authors have popularized this form—e.g. Kiss, 1974, p. 299 and Zurawicki 1983—advocating the step-by-step evolution of micro-integrative forms. However, practice has not fulfilled this logical expectation, but has simply bypassed the problem.

35 "A separate coordination organ should only emerge on practical grounds, i.e. only traditionally cooperating business partnerships should culminate in such an institutionalized organ". This is how the author sums up her practical experiences, having worked on this subject for a decade in the Hungarian Ministry of Finance.

36 This problem was widely discussed in Hungary in the mid-80s both by professional economic theorists and at the state administration level, in the context of reshaping the ways the state can exercise its proprietary rights. It would maintain its ownership of the nationalized sectors, but would separate its function as a protector of the public interest from its function as the owner of productive assets. In the latter capacity, it is in need of an institution embodying market-oriented long-range entrepreneurial interests. Cf. Antal, 1985 and Tardos, 1986.

37 It is instructive in this context that none of the antidumping processes started against Hungarian exporters could prove underbidding in the period of 1980–88.

38 This is certainly an oversimplified and schematic description of the underlying logic, rather than the detailed account of the current regulation in the given countries, since in Czechoslovakia and the GDR, there are plan indicators for export efficiency too.

39 True, this factor might even be overcompensated by other elements besides better product parameters, for a firm in a more rigidly controlled economy may have other comparative advantages. For example, a better knowledge of languages, better professional qualifications (employing businessmen with two degrees), better personal contacts and their use, better goodwill, traditions, a more reliable supply, quality guarantees, better commercial policy status (e.g. a "developing country"), or better after-sale services.

40 In theory, it might be objected that existing intra-CMEA joint ventures and common interstate associations may perform such functions. Practical evidence indicates (Rácz 1985, p. 15) that these organs are at a disadvan-

tage *vis-à-vis* national foreign trade organizations even in their line of business specialization both in terms of marketing and of business organization. Thus activities of substance are carried out somewhere else.

41 This does not hold for the macroeconomic level for reasons detailed in the first three chapters.

42 True, this behaviour is not characteristic of CMEA producers in their relations with the West either (and even less of foreign trade companies). This is illustrated by the well-known fact that four-fifths of all cooperation deals are initiated by the Western firms.

43 This holds *a fortiori* when CMEA partner companies are not in the position to honour better technological quality or market performance or higher inputs by higher prices, since the latter are centrally set in macro-level bargains, i.e. irrespective of individual product qualities. For practical evidence of this, see Drechsler et al. 1983, and Stoilov 1985, pp. 57–59.

CHAPTER FIVE

The CMEA in a changing world

The regional economic integration of the East European planned economies, the Council for Mutual Economic Assistance, is a major international organization with a crucial influence on the development of the individual member states. And what is true of the individual member states in their relation to the community holds of both the member states and the CMEA as a whole in their relation to the international economic system. The impacts of external disturbances on the CMEA in the last two decades have made it crystal clear that irrespective of their intentions, the individual centrally planned economies as well as their regional grouping are integral parts of the world economy, and the CMEA does not in any way constitute a separate economic "world socialist system" functioning according to its own inherent laws (as it has customarily been maintained). However, the structural interdependences, the common system of regulating intra-regional trade as well as the nature and forms of the regional division of labour which have evolved in the last four decades do add up to what in any theory can be termed an "integration". This highly specific integration of planned economies was on the one hand the extrapolation of the domestic, national systems of (mostly directive) planning, and on the other hand, was itself a factor ossifying the national systems. This means, among other things, that the behavioural norms and success indicators of enterprises formed under domestic conditions more or less hold of a substantial part of the foreign economic activity as well. In other words, the macroeconomic forms of business activity are determining factors when the CMEA countries enter into economic interaction with other parts of the world. In this sense, we can describe the situation as follows. While from the real economic point of view the workings of the CMEA are a function of the world economy, from the systemic point of view it is the other way around. It is the institutional, structural and behavioural characteristics of intra-CMEA relations that determine to a considerable extent the ways and means of the individual member states' joining in world economic interaction.

The literature on the CMEA is practically dominated by what can be called the formalistic, institutionalist approach. It follows from what has been said above that in this chapter I attempt to interpret the CMEA integration mostly as a term describing the specific regional interdependences between Eastern Europe and the Soviet Union, as trade with non-European member states comprises less than 10 per cent of the total CMEA turnover (that being transacted mainly by the USSR, whose share in the total trade of non-European members varies from 75 to 90 per cent).

So instead of dwelling on the details of the institutional setup and its modifications, attention will be focused on the following issues: a) real economic performance, in other words how the CMEA has fared in international competition; b) description and analysis of what may be called an epochal transformation in the conditions of regional economic cooperation; c) a survey of the changes in the setup of the international mechanism of regional cooperation in the light of the documents adopted at the June 1984 Economic Summit of the Council.

REAL ECONOMIC DEVELOPMENTS—TRENDS IN THE CMEA'S PARTICIPATION IN THE GLOBAL DIVISION OF LABOUR

In the following section, the CMEA countries will be divided into two groups: the Soviet Union, and the European member states of the CMEA-Six, the latter—following the practice of the United Nations, whose statistics are being relied upon—being called Eastern Europe.[1] It would be reasonable to presume that the latter group of small and medium-sized countries generally follow a more outward-looking economic policy, given the necessarily greater discrepancy between their resource endowments and economically viable output structures on the one hand, and their demand structures on the other, which latter is no less diversified than that of any large country. One would also postulate the group's constantly growing share in world trade, as the past 40 years were marked mostly by a trend to rapid industrialization and the fast growth of NMP all across the region. Furthermore, political premises would suggest greater East-West economic interaction, hand in hand with the policy of *dètente*, trade relations often being portrayed as byproducts of the former. The successful cutback of their debt burdens in the early 1980s could also be treated as a sign of successful, i.e. export-led, adjustment.

A review of the long-term series presented in Tables 1a and 1b, and Table 2 indicate the following tendencies.

The share in world exports of the CMEA countries as a group was indeed growing till the mid-60s. From 1965 to 1981 a secular trend of losing ground emerged. The 1983 figure shows a significant growth of more than 1.5 percentage points. This is remarkable if we take into account that total world exports decreased by 8.4 percent in 1981–83, and reflects the extraordinary efforts the CMEA countries made in order to maintain their foreign economic equilibrium. However, Soviet exports made up two-thirds of the improvement, which is indicative of the modest gains attained by Eastern Europe—although it was this group of nations, not the USSR, which faced liquidity problems in this period.

The 1985 figure of 8.8. percent is indicative of the temporary nature of the gain registered in the early 80s, and is already somewhat below the level for the mid-70s. The secular trend of losing ground emerges both in the case of Eastern Europe and of the Soviet Union, and indicates two developments. a) The export offensive got "out of breath" for structural reasons, i.e. its concentration on sectors other than the ones whose markets expanded due to the cyclical upswing in the OECD area. b) Owing to the overall sense of being over most of the necessary adjustments, the feeling emerged among economic policy makers with the advent of the new FYP period that it was time to concentrate on growth again. The obsession with growth can be explained by a number of factors inherent in the economic system, as detailed elsewhere (Csaba 1983; and Szamuely 1983). For purposes of the present analysis, let it suffice to note that this approach already determined the elaboration of the five-year plan for 1986–90, and also of the short-term cyclical policies for 1985. The new Soviet leadership's emphasis on acceleration *(uskorenie)* also strengthened the growth orientation deriving basically from domestic sources. Thus, a somewhat expanding domestic market provided a less demanding outlet for a modestly growing production, irrespective of world economic competitiveness. The radically improved financing situation has also helped. As far as the Soviet Union is concerned, the fall in its share of world exports in 1985 was due to three factors: 1) the Western upswing, producing an expanding world demand of a structure differing from the Soviet supplies 2) the slight drop in oil prices already beginning, and the consequent stagnation of gas prices;

3) the secular turn in Soviet oil production, which is accompanied by not very radical savings in the domestic consumption of fuels, resulting in exports under severe supply constraints.

It is also important to note that even the high 1983 figure fell short of the respective 1970 datum, i.e. it does not signify a change in the secular trend. This shows the continued predominance in Eastern exports of primary products, of intermediate products, and also of the products of the declining industries. This pattern is bound to meet further increasing protectionism as well as competition from Third World suppliers. Therefore there has been a clear tendency to devalue EE exports reflected in constantly deteriorating terms of trade.[2] For this reason, the maintenance of the upward trend in the coming years, when the upswing of total international trade could be observed, would have required an exponential expansion of the volume of East European exports to the OECD region. This has not happened, as the CMEA countries faced a period of structural changes rather than of dynamic growth (Fingerland 1984),[3] and the already strained state of the domestic markets rendered the prospect of such an expansion quite dim, even in the case of marked improvements in the export pattern. As two-thirds of the total CMEA improvement between 1980–83 was registered by Soviet exports, and the favourable terms of trade for fuels and raw materials have definitely changed in recent years, the bulk of the growth realized from this most dynamic segment of CMEA exports was bound to be spent on compensating for the unfavourable trends in relative prices. All in all, the continuation of the secular downward trend has been a rather inevitable feature of the CMEA's future share in world export markets.

The secular trend of losing markets is pronounced in the case of East European exports: both the 1981 figure of 4.1 percent and the 1985 figure of 4.3 percent were only marginally above the Cold War level, and the 1983 level is also more than a whole percentage point below the 1960 relative share. Except for 1983, Soviet exports and East European exports alike had their highest share of world markets in 1965, indicating that the 1960s rather than the 1970s were characterized by an opening up to the world economy. It is also worth noting that oil prices—and oil accounted for 45 percent of Soviet exports to the West—increased twentyfold between 1970 and 1981. Nevertheless, the USSR's share of world exports did not grow until 1982, when price movements prompted an expansive Western fuel sales policy.

Turning to imports (Table 2), we can likewise conclude that the 1960s, and not the 1970s were the really dynamic period of world economic opening. The much publicized grandiose projects of the first half of the 70s could only soften, but not turn, the secular trend of the decline. It is worth mentioning that the top Soviet figure of 4.2 percent for 1983 is identical to the 1960 level, and the East European import share of 4.5 percent was only a half percentage point above the figure for the Cold War era. These data obviously show that in the post-1970 period there can be absolutely no talk of an extreme opening to the world economy, as the CMEA market shares in total world imports also decline in a secular manner. Since there is no sign of overtrading, the therapy can hardly be sought in "optimization", i.e. the further restriction of the international trade participation of the CMEA economies. Moreover, the figures also show that the reason for the CMEA's indebtedness will not be found on the import side; on the contrary. The export performance of the CMEA region in the post-1970 period, when it was the "most dynamic region of the world economy" (and was very proud of it), was so poor that even an import volume growing at below world average rate could not be financed through export earnings. This—among others—is a synthetic critique of the development policies and management methods of the 1970s. The major conclusion can be arrived at if we compare Tables 1 a and b and Table 2. This indicates that the good debt servicing performance of the early 1980s was due primarily to restricting imports, i.e. to a foreign trade policy other than the one causing the liquidity troubles. The 1985 figures not only substantiate the above, but make the picture more pronounced. While world imports somewhat expanded, the CMEA countries continued to lose ground also in the area of world imports because they could afford only a marginal easing up of their import controls. The mid-80s is characterized by a peculiar paradox. The indebtedness of the CMEA states grew worse (Table 15) without being accompanied by a similar growth in the real imports of commodities and services. Moreover, unlike in the 70s, growing indebtedness in both the USSR and Eastern Europe was accompanied not by the stagnation of their share in world imports, but its positive decline.

We can account for this paradox by the following factors. First, following the years of liquidity troubles, several Eastern European countries started a policy of building up large reserves for reasons of security. This has meant more debts without more imports. Second, owing to the facts that Poland is not reducing her indebtedness to foreign governments—the talks on formal rescheduling brought about a turn only in early 1990, so she has been unable to meet her interest obligations, the amount of the Polish debt continues to rise for more or less technical reasons. No fresh money was injected into the Polish economy. Third, speeding up growth in itself involved already in its incipient phase more debt, since the very declaration of such objectives enhances the creditors' propensity to extend new loans. Fourth, given the drop in oil prices, accompanied by supply bottlenecks and the very slack Western European demand for natural gas, Soviet hard currency receipts have declined, while the financing needs of the ongoing imports have grown. It is very important to see that the accumulation of debt in 1984–86 preceded the postulated speeding up of growth. Had this growth actually taken place, if would indeed have implied more imports, especially from the West. Since it did not in fact occur, the earlier debt levels put serious constraints on any speeding up of growth, as incomes derived from the given export structure have proved ever more insufficient even for maintaining the former level of imports. It might be interesting to note that the volume of CMEA imports from the West in 1985 was in real terms 45 percent below the top 1979 level (Kádár 1986, p. 4). Given the characteristics of the reproduction processes in the CMEA countries, it is even more evident that further import cuts have had serious repercussions for growth prospects as well as for the capacity of these economies to modernize and adjust themselves to the changing international environment, and in some cases even for their ability to function normally. The imperative of a changeover to an export-led growth needs no further substantiation.

While studies on the commodity pattern of trade in CMEA countries abound, it is much less frequent to find analyses of the dynamics and geographical pattern of this turnover. A survey of the relevant figures may give some further insight into the degree of correlation between economic and political processes and statements of a theoretical nature. Figures in Tables 3–10 may shed some light on the interrelationships of the intra- and extra-CMEA division of labour.

Total Soviet exports between 1970–85 increased 6.8-fold at current prices. Among the different areas, Western exports registered the fastest growth—8.5-fold. Exports to Eastern Europe grew 5.9-fold; to developing countries, 7.3-fold. That is, Soviet exports to the West grew 1.5 times as quickly as to traditional CMEA partners. If we look at the post-1975 period—when adoption of the US Export Administration Act with the Jackson-Vanik Amendment resulted in an inflection point in the uphill side of the life cycle of *détente*--it can be calculated from Table 3 that Soviet exports until 1983 continued to grow faster to the West—3.1-fold—than to Eastern Europe—2.4-fold. By 1985 growth rates evened out at 2.4-fold, reflecting that intra-CMEA prices grew faster than world market prices in this period, with nominal fuel price levels even overstepping wmp's. Accordingly, the share of Western nations in total Soviet exports grew from 21.2 percent in 1970 to 28.8 percent by 1975, then grew further and peaked at 35.3 percent in 1980, falling somewhat to 32.8 percent in 1983. As can be seen from Table 4, between 1970 and 1983 a more than 11.5 percentage point strong reorientation in favour of OECD nations occurred. The 1985 drop to 25.6 percent can be seen as an inflection point in the secular trend, reflecting what was then only a small drop in fuel prices, as well as the constraints on the exportable quantities. This could not be offset by the UN Statistical Department's regrouping Yugoslavia among the developed countries. Since the only way of overcoming the obstacles to expanding Soviet-Western trade is a change in the Soviet export structure, a task requiring years, it is most probable that unlike in the sphere of political relations, a lasting decline is inevitable in trade with the West for the USSR. As the trade share of the developing countries remained more or less stable from 1970 to 1983, the reorientation in this period took place primarily at the cost of trade with the East European countries, who lost nearly ten percentage points, accounting for 42.9 percent of the total Soviet exports.

The dramatic drop in the Western share by 1985 was compensated for primarily by the rapidly expanding share of the Asian socialist countries (i.e. China) and the developing countries. It is remarkable that despite large-scale price movements in the CMEA, the share of the East European partners grew only insignificantly in the 1979–85 period. In other words, a certain reorientation took place in Soviet exports, but it was not primarily in favour of the East European partners, whose significance was bound to decrease following the CMEA price peak of 1986.

In short, even between 1983–85, Eastern Europe accounted for only the smaller half of Soviet trade. Moreover, their import figures from the USSR reflect mostly price effects, not volume. These figures well illustrate the unrealistic nature of the autarkic approach, which would require that the USSR give up the greater part of their foreign trade in favour of certain theoretical aspirations, and that the East European countries put up with minimally growing imports, while at the same time adjusting to world markets and aiming at more growth.

Turning to the import side (Tables 5 and 6) similar tendencies emerge. Total Soviet imports grew 7-fold in current prices between 1970 and 1985: Western imports 7.5-fold, East European imports 5.9-fold, and imports from developing countries 10-fold. In other words, the dynamics of Soviet imports was definitely higher from the West than from Eastern Europe.[7] The geographical pattern of Soviet imports also mirrors this marked reorientation, though somewhat less pronouncedly than in the case of exports. The share of the West went up from 26.2 percent in 1970 to 39.7 in 1981, and then fell somewhat to 35.3 percent, giving way to a nearly 10 percentage point reorientation at the expense of the East European partners, whose share declined from 56 to 46 percent (Table 6). It is again remarkable that the share of imports from Eastern Europe hardly gained in significance between 1983 and 1985. Despite the marked intra-CMEA price effect, it continued to satisfy the smaller half of the Soviet demand for foreign goods and services. While the share of imports from the West fell back to the level of the early 70s—despite the reclassification of Yugoslavia as part of the West in UN statistics— reorientation is observable, primarily towards developing countries and Asian centrally planned economies. The contraction of the share of Western suppliers—accompanied by the sizable growth of gross and net debts—explains why the Twelfth Five Year Plan based technological reconstruction and the speeding up of innovation primarily on domestic resources. This was a change from the policies of most of the earlier modernization periods, which relied more on imported technology. It is certainly conditional on the progress of economic reforms that a favourable systemic environment for endogenous technological change evolve, since the traditional management methods are known to impede innovation.

For further conclusions, it is necessary to compare these very marked changes in Soviet foreign economic activity with developments in Eastern Europe (Tables 7–10). Total East European exports between 1970–85 grew much slower than total Soviet exports, only 4.5-fold in current prices. Most dynamic among the partner regions were the developing countries with an 8.3-fold growth despite the substantial setbacks suffered between 1981–83. Then comes the USSR, and only in third place the West (a 5.1 and a 4.2-fold growth, respectively), the least dynamic being the "small integrational" turnover, i.e. trade among the CMEA-Six (3.6-fold). East European exports to the West grew only at half the rate of the Soviet exports to the OECD; i.e. there can be absolutely no talk of the redistribution of East European export funds in favour of Western sales[8] and to the detriment of meeting Soviet-related obligations. The poor overall dynamics of East European exports to the West, their virtual stagnation in the post-1979 period, and the 8 percent drop in 1985 as compared to 1981 are also indicative of the results of the development policy of the 70s, and of the adjustment policies of the first half of the 80s. The decline in the intensity of trade with other smaller countries in the region is in line with the general tendencies in the world economy and results from the strong similarities among these countries. Parallel surpluses and parallel shortages provide the explanation for this trend both in general and in this particular case.

If we look at the geographical pattern of trade, the most striking aspect is that the reorientation of commercial relations in favour of the OECD area during the 70s that might have been expected in fact failed to take place. Contrary to what is frequently claimed, the most important change in the export pattern of the East European states is the 8 percentage point increase of the Soviet share in their markets, to no less than 44.2 percent in 1983. The share of Third World markets also grew, but that of the West declined in 1983 after a decade of virtual stagnation. By 1984–85, however, in an effort to balance payments in convertible currencies, the earlier proportions were restored. A certain reorientation in favour of developing countries may be observed, without the Soviet market's losing its traditional role. The stagnation of exports to the USSR reflects also the structural discrepancies between the East European export supply, and the reformulated Soviet demand priorities, an issue to be detailed later in this chapter. These developments are in sharp contrast to the tendencies observed in Soviet exports, the "great losers" being again the East European small socialist partners.

Turning to imports, we see that total East European imports between 1970 and 1985 grew 4.8-fold in current prices. Western imports grew on a par with the overall figures—4.9-fold, i.e. three-quarters of the Soviet Union's import dynamics (8.5-fold). Imports from the Soviet Union grew even somewhat faster than Western purchases: 5.2-fold. This means that East European imports from the West cannot be termed excessive in any comparison, this being a further proof that their indebtedness is not a product of their allegedly extravagant import policies. Accordingly, unlike in the case of the Soviet Union, we find no significant reorientation, or world economic opening, in the East European nations. Trade with the West increased only temporarily, and even then partly for statistical reasons, since nominal intra-

CMEA prices underestimated the role of this trade. The 1983 figure of 25.1 percent was just somewhat higher than the 1970 datum, while the Soviet market share regained its earlier prominence, and reached 40.4 percent in 1983, and again in 1985. In other relations, a major feature of the 70s was a modest reorientation from small socialist countries to developing partners. However, their role stagnated due to financial problems in the 80s. Since imports from the South are anything but strategic for Eastern Europe, this is the easiest to restrict at times of difficulties. It is remarkable that in exports the share of developing markets could grow by 3.6 percentage points by 1985, regaining its previous relative position without the value of sales overstepping the 1981 level—a further indication of the extremely poor performance of the region in trade with other areas. In the meantime, through restricted imports, the South continued to play a "currency earning role" for the East European states during the first half of the 80s. With the drop in oil prices, this role may change for reasons of the shaky liquidity of the East European claims.

From the world economic point of view, but also in connection with discussions of intra-CMEA trade, it is relevant to compare how the industrial development of the CMEA countries fared in international competition. This set of issues is treated here only from a single aspect, i.e. export performance. This is measured by the share of machines and transport equipment (SITC 7 category) in the total exports, as well as by the dynamics of total and machinery exports to the world at large, and separately to the developed market economies. This measure—a single digit statistical category—is very crude, and the method of evaluating export performance by the share of a certain commodity group in the total foreign sales is also subject to justified criticism. However, as the development of the engineering industry has been a priority task in all CMEA countries in the last decades, and the aim of increasing the share of machinery in the total export has also been a constant preference of national commercial policies in the period under scrutiny, it is instructive to look at the computations in Tables 11 and 12.

The total export of developing countries between 1970–84 grew 8.5-fold in current prices. Exports of machinery and transport equipment grew 34.6-fold; thus, the share of machinery in total developing country exports grew fourfold. The figures well reflect the very low initial level as well as the impressive dynamism of this commodity group, where export growth was unaffected by the world recession and increasing West-European protectionism.[9] For the East European countries, we find that the increase in total exports shows just over half the dynamism of the developing nations—a 4.7-fold growth— which is completely unwarranted given the higher level of development and the poor resource endowments of Eastern Europe. Machinery exports grew somewhat faster—a 7.2-fold growth—that is, at a rate close to a fifth of what we saw for the developing countries. Eastern Europe's higher level of development, as well as regional protectionism, is reflected by the high share of machine exports. It would, of course, make no sense to expect growth in shares to have been comparable to the developing nations' performance, but the stagnation of both total and machinery exports in 1983–84 was already a warning sign.

Total Soviet exports grew faster than machinery exports (7.1-fold and 4.2-fold, respectively). This is a phenomenon worthy of attention, even if it was rational for the USSR to make use of the favourable changes in relative prices between 1973 and 1982. It is common knowledge that Soviet efforts to increase the share of machinery exports date back well into the early 60s. Soviet economists have constantly been demanding changes in the export pattern. In this context the continued decrease in the share and recently also in the absolute value of machinery exports is cause for concern, even if in the last decade it was precisely this lack of change that brought enormous windfall profits,[10] especially since *total* machinery sales have been stagnating since 1978.

It is also interesting to compare these figures with similar data calculated for exports to developed market economies. In this case, the figures of the three columns in Table 12 are directly comparable, since the need as well as the will to increase machinery exports was equally strong in each seller under scrutiny.

The overall exports of the developing countries to the OECD grew 7.7-fold, while between 1970–84 their machinery exports increased 41.4-fold! While the developing countries' total sales in 1984 were *below* the 1981 maximum by 16.8 percent, their machinery sales nearly doubled in those very same 3 years on the same markets! This means that if a "Southern" (developing) exporter country is able to market its machines, it is able to make sales even under the most competitive conditions. This conclusion is supported by the following figures, calculated from the UN statistics (Table 13). While the machinery exports of the developing countries grew 34.5-fold between 1970 and 1984, their sale to the OECD expanded 41.4-fold. In just the 1980–84 period, the share of Western markets in all "Southern" machinery sales grew from 51.1 to 63.4 percent. The US as a market took 27.8 percent of the developing countries' machines in 1980, and 41.7 percent in 1984. In absolute terms, this has meant no less than a 2.7-fold expansion of the American market for Southern machine exporters ! This interrelationship would be even more pronounced if we compared the CMEA states not to the extremely broad category of "developing countries", but to the more appropriate, directly competitive group of newly industrializing countries.[11]

Looking at Eastern Europe, it is striking that the dynamics of overall exports already lags behind the developing countries' sales, and this goes *a fortiori* for machinery exports. While developing countries increased their machinery exports to developed market economies 41.4-fold, Eastern Europe could expand its sales only at somewhat more than a tenth of this rate between 1970–84, i.e. 4.8-fold. Between 1981 and 1984, they registered a drop of more than 20 percent, and the export level in absolute dollar terms was on a par with that for 1978. While developing countries increased their machinery exports continuously, with the share of machinery in all exports growing from 1.9 to 10.5 percent between 1970–84, improvements in the East European export structure came to a halt in 1975, so that in the 1980s, there was in fact, a deterioriation: the share of machinery exports grew from 11.3 to 15.5 percent between 1970–75, then declined in 1982 to 13.9 percent, and in 1984 to 11.3 percent, i.e. fell back to the level of the late 60s. It is remarkable that already in 1970–75, the East European countries were lagging behind the developing nations: "Southern" exports grew 4.8-fold, Eastern machinery sales only 3.4-fold. In the 1975–84 period—as can be calculated from Table 12—East European machinery exports grew by a mere 42 percent, while that of the developing countries expanded 8.6-fold. The relative figures might also be of some interest. While in 1970 East European countries exported 4.8 times more machines to the world than the developing nations, by 1983 this ratio had changed, and in 1984 the developing nations had an edge of 34 percent. But if we take only exports to the most competitive OECD markets, then as early as 1970 the developing countries already had an edge (already then exporting half of their foreign sales to the OECD) of 56 percent. By 1984, this advantage had grown into a gap: the developing nations were exporting 13.4 times more machinery to the West than the East European industrialized states ! While the relative share of Western markets among all sales during the difficult years of 1980–84 grew by 12.5

percent in the total machinery sales of Southern producers, for Eastern Europe Western markets contracted both in share and volume: OECD buyers took 8.9 percent of East European machinery sales in 1980, and 6.3 per cent in 1984—a drop of 22.4 percent in dollar terms. The American market, which grew 2.7-fold for Southern exporters, contracted for Eastern Europe nearly by half, i.e. to the negligible amount of 144 million US dollars distributed among six East European countries (cf. Table 13). Table 13 also demonstrates that it is not lack of markets and the increasing protectionist barriers that are the main causes of the poor East European export performance in machinery sales. Three-fourths of the developing countries' machinery exports are realized by those newly industrializing countries which are not preferred by the international tariff concessions of the EC. Looking at the Soviet Union it becomes clear that her machinery exports grew at a significantly lower rate than overall exports to the West. The share of the product group grew from 5.3 to 5.7 percent between 1970 and 1975 (i.e. the process continued also after the first oil price hike), but then decreased to less than half, to 2.3 percent. In volume terms, this meant a mere 28 percent increase in nine years, including a drop in 1984 to below the 1978 level. This is clearly indicative of the presence of other factors than just making good use of the windfall profits. The strongly deteriorating international competitiveness of Soviet machinery exports is underlined by the fact that total machinery exports have also been more or less stagnating since 1978.

It might be of interest to compare in greater detail the market performance of the traditionally priority engineering sector of the CMEA countries with that of the developing countries in the adjustment period, and also over a longer period. The comparisons are available in Table 13. The figures indicate the intensification of the well-known processes of the CMEA countries' losing ground. They also give a value judgement on the adjustment policies of the early 1980s. As it is known, besides growing investments to substitute fuel imports, all five-year plans for 1981–85 allotted a priority role to the engineering sector in restoring the balance of payments equilibrium, or in further reducing debt. In principle, world market demand should already have played a role in development and company strategies. True, overall conditions were far from favourable for sellers, as indicated by the absolute drop in the total and the OECD exports of Southern countries (cf. Tables 11 and 12) by 10.5 and 16.8 percent in the 1981–84 period, respectively.

In fact, in the "adjustment" period, the unfavourable tendencies intensified, reflecting a continued inward looking in investment policy, a slowdown in systemic changes, and the practice of short-term, enforced adjustment. This policy equilibrated the balance of payments by exporting everything that was possible, and by cutting back imports. Since structural and quality considerations were pushed to the background, the balance of payments equilibrium could only be restored by a crude redistribution of the national product produced in favour of foreign use. This policy was inevitable as a short-run therapy. It could, however, hardly sustain its results since it has not been accompanied by appropriate systemic and structural policy measures, because the crude methods of forced adjustment centring on quantitative targets in themselves hinder true structural adaptation to changing market demands. The figures in Tables 13–14 indicate the consequences of policies that did not go beyond mere redistributory steps. The sales of non-priority branches had to be forced at nearly any cost, while the priority sectors fare even worse than they did in the 1970s. In the case of engineering, it is a novel fact that not only Western exports have declined (they have always been under 10 percent of all foreign sales), but there is also a drop of 5.4 percent in Soviet sales, and a growth of a mere 9.1 percent in 4 years in the East European case. In the case of the Soviet Union, the loss is not only the traditional relative one but is also a loss in absolute terms, which is new. While the total East European exports of machines grew by 9 percent, Southern exports grew by 80 percent. In the longer run, between 1970 and 1984, East European machinery exports grew 5.4-fold, while developing exports grew 34.6-fold. Thus, in 1983 the *total* machinery export of the developing nations surpassed that of the industrialized East European countries. While in 1970 Eastern Europe exported nearly five times as much machinery as the whole developing world, by 1984 Southern exporters had an edge of 33.6 percent (Table 11). These figures, however, were arrived at using a different measure, for they take exports to the protected regional markets to be of equal value to sales under competitive conditions. When no such allowances are made, the CMEA's performance is seen to be even worse. In 1984, the absolute value of both Soviet and East European machinery sales to the West was less than in 1978! Not only the market shares of the CMEA countries are seen to have shrunk, but the share of machinery in the total Western export and the exportable part of the produced output as well, the latter in sharp contradiction to the economic policy considerations which at least in theory favoured export orientation. In fact, we find the share of the Western market in all East European foreign sales to have dropped to the level attained by the Soviet engineering industry, a sector not exactly famous for its export orientation.

Can these developments be attributed to the lack of markets, as is commonly maintained by many business executives in the CMEA countries? On the basis of the statistics, the answer is a definite "No". All the more so as the bulk of the machinery sales registered in Table 13 by developing countries fall to NIC's not enjoying any special commercial policy preference. While the share of machinery sales from Eastern Europe dropped, and their Western exports in the SITC-7 category fell by 22.4 percent between 1980 and 1984, the developing nations more than doubled their exports to the very same markets. This holds *a fortiori* of the US market: while East European machinery exports fell by nearly half in 1980–84, the developing countries' sales nearly trebled, achieving no less than 143 times the level of the East European exports in 1984! Table 13 underlines a fact already noted: if a developing producer is able to sell its output abroad, it is mostly —and growingly—able to do so under the most competitive conditions! While developing countries proved the established thesis that manufacturing exports may still grow on a depressed market, the East European sellers could not make use of this opportunity. On the contrary: their decade-old position of being "crowded out" of the market grew worse instead of improving in this period of "adjustment". Thus it seems legitimate to ask whether it is at all appropriate to use this term for the years 1981–83. Or was it rather only a period of the short-term consolidation of liquidity problems? As the latter was in fact, the case, the market constraints on a more dynamic growth policy preceding structural and policy adjustment are more than obvious for 1986–90.

If we look at comparative performances, the extent and dynamics of the growing edge that the developing countries have on Eastern Europe given cause for concern and refute the "lack of markets" argument. Moreover the growing share that the most competitive markets have of their machinery sales is also indicative of the size of the foregone gains and efficiency losses implied by the East European countries' maintaining the patriarchal structure of the East–South division of labour.

This fact, rather than the absolute size of the CMEA debts, raised questions about the future of East–West trade, and also about the ways the 1986–90 growth ambitions of the FYPs could be financed. In the early 80s, the high fuel prices favoured Soviet exports and enabled the energy-intensive intermediate product sales of Eastern Europe to earn hard currency. With the drop in fuel prices, not only the liquidity position of the traditional sources of the East European surpluses became shaky, but the structural weaknesses of a sales pattern based on primary and intermediate products became reflected in the terms of trade—a development that proved to be characteristic for the 90s as well. Since neither agriculture, nor the intermediate product fabricating sectors could earn enough extra hard currency to enable Eastern Europe and now also the Soviet Union to service their growing debts, this task fell more or less inevitably on the engineering sector. All the more so as the service sector, including transportation, tourism and banking, is still in a rather backward state. Incomes from these activities may grow, but not to such an extent that they could evolve into a substitute for manufacturing, primarily engineering, exports. These interrelationships may justify the space and weight devoted to this segment of the CMEA's exports in this section. A change in past trends is strongly conditional on systemic and policy reforms, whose chances will be discussed in some detail in the last chapter.

The above findings are also of direct significance for discussions on the prospective model of the intra-CMEA division of labour. Soviet economists (e.g. Shmelyov 1979a) have long been advocating a change in the basic pattern of the intra-regional division of labour. Instead of the traditional interbranch cooperation—which entails the exchange of Soviet raw materials and fuels for East European finished products—they proposed a more up-to-date pattern of intra-industrial division of labour. This suggestion was in line not only with a long-standing Soviet commercial policy decision to improve their export structure *vis-à-vis* Eastern Europe by increasing the share of machinery, but also with overall world economic trends, and the theory of economic integration. The well-known and irreversible supply constraints on the Soviet energy and raw materials sector would have made such change imperative if the overall geographical distribution of trade with the East European countries was to be maintained, in other words, if the dynamism of intraregional trade were to be preserved to some extent. Subscribing to the theoretical feasibility of the proposal. I shall not detail, at this point, the problems arising from the over-centralized bilateral trade mechanisms of the CMEA for cooperation in the manufacturing branches. One thing, however, is certain. For the implementation of this idea, it would have been absolutely necessary from the real economic point of view to have Soviet machinery that is qualitatively more competitive on the international market. Since the unfavourable trends of the years 1975–84 have not been reversed in the second half of the 80s this in itself precluded a meaningful increase in the intraindustrial division of labour within the CMEA. Both overall Soviet machinery exports and sales to the West fell back in absolute terms durng 1980–84. Yet even without Most Favoured Nation treatment, the second largest industry in the world should be capable of selling more machinery to the USA than the seven million (!) US dollars worth that was the average value of the years 1980–84, as compared to the 21 billions' worth of the developing exporters.

The Soviet plan to increase machinery sales to Eastern Europe is much more than abstract theorizing. It brings us to the very nub of the discussions on integration policy within the CMEA. These focus on the ways and means of coping with the evolving new situation, which we can well call epochal transformations within the CMEA region.

RADICAL CHANGES IN THE TERMS OF REGIONAL COOPERATION IN THE 1980S

The substance of this issue can best be illustrated by contrasting two typical official statements. The first is from a Hungarian brochure on the CMEA written in 1973, which describes the main advantage of the socialist integration as follows: " . . . Through mutual supplies of energy and raw materials it has enabled the individual member states to develop the most progressive industries, those that play a determining role in technico-technological development, irrespective of their domestic resource base". Furthermore, "It has contributed to the industrialization of the less developed member countries as well as to the high per capita consumption of fuels and industrial materials such as cement and steel" (Pálfai 1974, pp. 35–36). A decade later, two semi-official Soviet commentators writing in a monthly close to the Soviet Ministry of Foreign Affairs noted the stand taken at the June 1984 Economic Summit Meeting, i.e. that countries lacking appropriate resource endowments should concentrate on energy and raw material saving industries. As far as the energy and fuel complex is concerned, they speak of "qualitatively new" tasks. "The point in this context is not the further increase of fuel extraction, but a radical improvement in use in order to maximize its efficacy. There are enormous possibilities left for enhancing the efficiency of energy utilization" (Rybakov and Shiryaev 1984, pp. 23–24).

The basic reasons for this change are the following:

Factor One is that with the exception of natural gas, Soviet raw material and fuel production was no longer growing in any significant area for a number of economic, technological, geological, georgaphical, organizational, infrastructural and other reasons. This is not the place to elaborate this point again;[12] let it suffice to recall that the reasons are objective and the process is irreversible.

Factor Two is that during the period of socialist industrialization, for reasons of copying the Soviet practice, and following the principle that "socialism equals freeing industrialization from the factor endowment constraints" (the idea reflected in the official publication quoted above) (Pálfai 1974), the industrial structures developed in Eastern Europe were highly material and energy intensive. Although the dramatic and unexpected changes in intra-CMEA pricing have made East European governments more than aware of the fact that the period of cheap raw materials and fuels is over, as late as 1975–79 nothing was done that reflected this realization.

This gives us Factor Three, which translates into nearly a decade having been wasted in arriving at decisions to save energy and raw materials through structural policy changes and qualitative changes in the economic mechanism. (For a clear-cut formulation of this problem in time, see Goldmann 1975.) It is quite obviously an independent factor, as years of delaying decisions, continuing economic policies and maintaining structures as if nothing had happened was in itself a serious mistake. I wish to stress at this point that the intra-CMEA energy problem was not the transmission of world economic changes. It was the emergence of this very problem that resulted in large-scale investment crediting in this sector (the credits being granted to the USSR by the East Europeans) already in the early 60s. The issue clearly dominated the practical, disposing part of the 1971 Comprehensive Programme. Fitting the "energy problem" into the logic of physical planning practised in the CMEA states itself constitutes a physical disproportion (between extracting and manufacturing industries). In other words, a serious, ever-growing shortage was realized at the level of central planning in the form of deficits in the centrally set material balances that are the main instruments of physical planning from the input side. The shortage evolves when, in the course of iteration, i.e. the international dovetailing of medium-term plans in the CMEA, the offers lists and demand lists do not meet even after several rounds of talks, and there are systematic discrepancies between them.[13] In other words, it is a physical shortage, not (implicit) profiteering by one side or the other by keeping an eye on world market prices, that is involved. All major joint investments were decided upon before 1975. (Prior to that year no one admitted that the oil shock had had an impact.) On the other hand, reference to world market prices turned out to be a potent windfall argument in coping with the growth of shortage. Since what is, in fact, involved is an internal, non-monetary and long perceived (and discussed) intra-regional disproportion,[14] the East European decision-makers' failure to act emerges as much more serious a mistake than their failure to correctly calculate "opportunity costs" or "implicit subsidies" according to the alien logic of the world market.

Factor Four is the growing Soviet need to reorient increasing amounts of exportable funds in favour of convertible currency areas, coupled with the lack of effective demand-constraining means in the mechanism of the USSR and of the CMEA. This was the most serious problem: the combination of a new and unforeseen task with a persistent old shortcoming of the management system. It is quite obvious that in the given international situation the Soviet leadership has decided not to let the country's indebtedness grow beyond the easily manageable magnitudes of the mid-80s. Since Soviet import needs were given, export had to be pushed to attain the not-higher-than-planned indebtedness level. Exports can be increased either through radical positive structural changes in the commodity composition (which seemed unlikely, judging by previous trends) or through a cut-back in consumption, as it could be forecast, no new windfall profits or even terms of trade improvements were to be expected. Although the very high level of domestic consumption within the Soviet economy is frequently criticized—a cutback was also the object of a long-term state target programme for energy saving—despite some local results, no overall change in macroeconomic indicators occurred. This has to do primarily with the economic management methods, the use of gross-type physical indices—such as the volume and structure of sales and commodity production—as success indicators, which, given the former concepts, remained the practice till the end of the 1980s.[15] This also means that while the reserves inherent in economizing were indeed great, the results that could be realistically expected at the macro-level were modest. It is also a historical fact that in a large and thus by definition inward-looking country like the Soviet Union, if there is a choice or a conflict between domestic and foreign (economic) objectives, the former usually takes precedence. This means that in a period which countless reports published in the Soviet daily press see as one in which supplier–customer relations have been particularly poor and unstable in the field of material-technical supply, Soviet decision-makers do not have the alternative of giving preference to expanding (or even maintaining) supplies to Eastern Europe. On the contrary. The required additional exports to be sold for convertible currency can only be made available —besides domestic economizing—at the cost of reorientation. I wish to stress at this point that it is not the growing intra-CMEA prices that put constraints on the demand of the CMEA countries. These prices went up considerably between 1975–81, but not until the Soviet decision to reorient supplies was made in October 1981 was the demand of the East European countries set limits to. It is important to realize that this has absolutely nothing to do with the "lack of purchasing power" of the East European countries, as some analysts (Betkenhagen 1984, and 1985, pp. 185–187) maintain. On the contrary: when instead of in accounting units calculation is in real money terms, i.e. in intra-CMEA convertible currency trade, Hungary, for instance, has always proved to be very potent, and has earned a surplus for more than a decade. This illustrates the established fact that in the case of a bilateral accounting unit—which the TR is, in essence[16]— it is hardly worth speaking of purchasing power, and that prices denominated in this clearing unit do not influence the expansion or contraction of trade. And this precisely is the crux of the problem. The dynamic growth of contractual prices has been unable to suppress demand for Soviet raw materials and fuels. Investment contributions could do the job, but—for a number of reasons unfolded in Chapter 2—they could be applied but to a small segment of the fuel–raw material sector. In the course of the international coordination of medium-term plans, the conflicting interests of producers and buyers have indeed had to be confronted from time to time. However, since scarcities are reflected in the somewhat subjective categories of "hard" and "soft" commodities, and since plan coordination took place mostly at a high political level, there has been no efficient (and objective) means of constraining demand at the USSR's disposal.

Factor Five is one of the by-products of the change in CMEA pricing. While—basically—"everything" in the mechanism of the CMEA has remained unchanged, pricing has been modified. This has brought about a number of inconsistencies within the regional financial system, which has also influenced real economic developments.[17] The most conspicuous among them has been the accumulation of several billions' worth of TR indebtedness by the East European countries *vis-à-vis* the USSR. This was a result of the partial nature of the 1975 changes: annual pricing was introduced, but its complement in the monetary mechanism—i.e. long-term crediting other than one granted exceptionally at government level—remained among "the forms to be developed" (Bartha 1984, pp. 141–142). As a consequence, although the East European member states have paid for 80 percent of the approximately 30 billion TR that the Soviets gained from changes in the terms of trade between 1973–85, only around 5 billion, i.e. one-fifth, of their terms-of-trade losses has been credited by the USSR (Dietz 1984, pp. 32–36), and this problem is far from being solved at the time of writing.

From the economic point of view, the clearing nature of the TR would discount any attempt to interpret the above indebtedness in convertible currencies. This indebtedness was a byproduct of an incomplete, partial modification of the monetary mechanism of the CMEA by the visible hand, rather than the reflection of a higher-than-justified domestic use. The domestic utilization of national incomes in the CMEA countries is based on macroeconomic balances, the latter relying on the reception of those volumes of commodities and natural resources that have been agreed upon during the coordination of plans. In this sense, the East European countries' use was completely justified (in terms of plan coordination), and not a matter of over-consumption. For in coordination, the fixed volumes were the independent variables, and monetary flows the dependent variables. The problem arises from the fact that the coordination system was kept, but with a pricing formula—which is inconsistent with its very essence—inserted in it.

One theoretical possibility would be to return to prices fixed over several years.[18] The other would be the elaboration of a mechanism to recycle petrorubles in the banking sphere. This was advocated by an economist years ago (Pécsi 1979c), but practically nothing has happened in practice, nor is there any action in sight. With no consistent theoretical solutions being put forward either, it follows from the above that an economically sound medium-term solution could only lie in a more or less automatic "rescheduling" of the remaining 20 percent of the terms of trade losses. This, in my judgement, should be considered a logical by-product of the decision to maintain an inconsistent set of economic regulators and planning instruments. As the theoretical inconsistency was in practice the result of a compromise among the interested parties, it should be clear that the "rescheduling" was not a modification, but a part of the compromise embodied in the maintenance in its earlier form of the CMEA's economic mechanism of cooperation. However, at the time of writing, this question is far from being generally resolved.

Factor Six is the radical change in the structure of Soviet needs. While traditionally, the "Soviet fuels and raw materials for East European finished products" model was the basis of the CMEA division of labour, this situation began to change at the end of the 1970s. In a book originally published in 1979, a Soviet author usually close to the official line voiced the new priorities, putting emphasis on items of the East European offers structure which previously did not have top priority, such as foodstuffs and industrial consumer goods (Shiryaev 1981, p. 31). This priority intensified considerably during the following round of plan coordination talks for 1986–90, which started after the 1982 Budapest Session of the Council. Following numerous publications by researchers, the new priority has been emphatically put in an article by the then Deputy Chairman of Gosplan (the Soviet State Planning Commission). He formulated (Inozemtsev 1984, pp. 6–7) the requirement that raw material suppliers be "compensated"[19] both in material and financial forms (which he described as an "internationalist obligation of the socialist commonwealth"). Among a number of interesting details, he explained: "The production of oil and other shortage items necessitates large volumes of investment. Therefore the Soviet partner is justified in expecting an efficient compensation for these. As the development of industrial sector B[20] is lagging behind, we expect to perform a manoeuvre. In exchange for continuing our raw material and fuel supplies, we should obtain increased quantities of those products which are of equal macroeconomic significance, such as foodstuffs, industrial consumer goods, pharmaceutical items, metallurgical products and technologically advanced machinery." Furthermore "the Soviet Union is interested in the modernization of its own enterprises in the food, light and local industries as well as in services, relying on the support and active participation of the other CMEA countries". This was cold turkey, especially if one knows that two-thirds of East European exports consist of machinery and equipment. The Soviet official also noted a number of new priorities as compared to the established machinery product pattern, priorities requiring a change from investment goods to machinery for consumer-related industries, high-tech products, mining equipment and material-saving technologies. He emphatically stressed the need for change in the industrial substructural pattern of the division of labour in engineering. This is complemented by raising the issue of "economically sound prices for components and spare parts". This last point is not further elaborated in his article, but it usually means the traditional demand voiced by Soviet economists (e.g. Silvestrov 1982) that prices in cooperation be established on the basis of—usually quite low—domestic Soviet prices, and those for spare parts as a percentage of the price of the finished product.

It is quite obvious that both requirements were economically unjustified. Prices for spare parts are usually 2.5–3 times higher than the proportional part of the end-product on the world markets. Furthermore, for reasons elaborated in Chapters 1 to 3, domestic and foreign prices cannot be compared within the CMEA. Thus the pricing proposal was also absurd. Knowing nominal price relations in the CMEA, it may be assumed with a degree of certainty that the proposal was a tactical argument trying to depress nominal manufactured product prices within the integration. All in all, as has been clearly formulated by competent Soviet specialists (Rybakov 1984, pp. 80–81), the crux of the intra-CMEA trade's "structural" problem is that the Soviet Union requires Eastern Europe to supply those items the shortages of which are viewed to be of a structural, long-term, rather than of an occasional, nature. That is why the Soviets think precisely the above-surveyed substantial change in EE export structure to be an adequate counterweight to Soviet efforts at maintaining the raw material and fuel supplies to Eastern Europe on the 1985 level.[21] It is important to underscore that it was the USSR's objective national economic interest stemming from the country's domestic proportions of development, and not from pure foreign policy or ideological considerations that is formulated in these analyses. This means that it could neither be interpreted nor coped with in these latler terms. The East European countries, thus, should have found adequate economic answers to the challenge, which only increases the need to multiply national economic efficiency and adjustment capacities, as well as to increase international competitiveness, all of which could have been achieved only through radical reform. According to N. Inozemtsev (1984, pp. 6–7) all the objective conditions for the above-outlined structural change were given in the CMEA countries: the material-technological base, the qualified personnel, the traditions and the capacities of production. Others noted that the applied traditional planning techniques and centralist management methods were suitable only in the energy and raw materials sector. They contrasted this to the requirements of integration in the manufacturing industries, which would rely primarily on direct interfirm relations (Vazin and Bibil 1984, p. 72). It is a contrast that implies the establishment of a whole set of nonexistent pre-conditions both in the economic and in the legislative spheres.

This latter proposition was not at all self-evident. There was a debate among Soviet economists as to whether or not the conditions for direct interfirm relations did, in fact, exist (which of course implies fundamental differences as to what interfirm contacts actually are). Some Soviet economists firmly maintained that "the substance of direct interfirm relations lies obviously not in the freedom of individual enterprises, combines and associations to sell and buy at will" but in "the further development of the planned methods of cooperation" (Bautina and Shiryaev 1984). Supporters of this conviction main-tained that—given the 1983 Soviet decree on joint enterprises—the economic and legal conditions were already present for this form of activity (Sitnin 1984, p. 11, and Inozemtsev 1984, p. 6). Others were definitely of the opinion that these conditions were still to be created (Konstantinov 1984, p. 7; and Tybakov 1984, p. 84). This latter view was shared by Hungarian economists and also by the then Czecho-slovak Premier (Štrougal 1984a).

THE PRE-GORBACHEV OPTIONS

The answer was to be given in trying to find an adequate long-term (rather than perfunctory) solution to the new stage of development in Eastern Europe as summed up in the six factors in the previous section. The solutions elaborated must also help to change the secular trend of losing ground in the world economy described in the first section. In other words, the economic policy and management changes suggested should contribute to strengthening the CMEA's position in international economic competition. This requirement was formulated —among others—also in those joint Documents (1984), that were made public after the Economic Summit of the CMEA. These Docu-ments established the framework for the rest of the 80s in many re-spects. As I have had the opportunity to elaborate on my understand-ing of these decisions elsewhere,[22] let a general statement suffice here. From the Documents, it appears that "it would be a mistaken con-clusion to state that we already have the solutions for all concrete issues of our further development. The Documents accepted at the Economic Summit outline the main path of future development, but they also require further common search for solutions" (Rusakov 1984, p. 6).[23]

It would be unreasonable and also scientifically unsound either to expect or to offer a universal prescription for the solution of all the comprehensive and interrelated difficulties outlined earlier. Comprehensive solutions can only be arrived at through concentrated, strenuous interdisciplinary efforts by scholars in the different social sciences, in close cooperation with (but not subordinated to) practical people of different qualifications in the various branches of the state apparatus and the business sphere.

As a point of departure, we can accept the theoretical premise that the CMEA economic mechanism is in need of being transformed so that it might solve the practical problems that have evolved in the integration process, with a view to enhancing, in due time, the interest the individual member countries show in integration (Rybakov and Shiryaev 1984, p. 85). The need to introduce more flexibility and orientation in day-to-day practice is also clearly formulated in the following Council Sessions' critique of the currently formalistic and bureaucratic practices of the integration institutions.

In the search for improvement, two contradictory considerations must be kept in mind. On the one hand, it is beyond doubt that the main instrument of cooperation, the regional coordination of medium-term plans, was more than 90 percent confined to the bilateral dovetailing and specification of the volumes and structures of mutual deliveries. This, clearly, implied simply taking over inherently microeconomic functions, and results in the end in there being no time and energy left for realizing the basic theoretical advantages of a planned economy: the possibility of a rational, voluntary *ex ante* harmonization of divergent national priorities. So I find justified those criticisms (Shiryaev 1984, p. 85) which attack this practice as the relegation of inherent national economic functions in favour of petty business activities (even if this is enforced upon planners by circumstances, i.e. by the demonetization of the cooperation mechanism).

Just as clearly, on the other hand, "If we spend an excessive amount of our economic resources on solving the long-term 'strategic' tasks of cooperation, or if we artificially speed up the transformation of the structure of mutual deliveries along with the resolute alteration of the established set of interests within the CMEA, then the maintenance of equilibrium and of growth will be endangered. It is also known, however, that these significantly influence longer-term prospects, and that is why it is impossible to give up the better supplying of the (East European—L. Cs.) populations—for this is a precondition of improved productivity—or the improvement of living standards, or the necessary decrease of hard currency debt servicing, which also constitutes a serious burden" (Bartha 1984, p. 136). This, in other words, means that there was a need to reconcile short-term national economic interests with the side effects of the Soviet conceptual constructs.

In this context, it was easier, at least in theory, to find a compass for the short-term issues. In his above-quoted analysis, one of the leading Hungarian authorities on the subject formulated three main strategic tasks: finding new areas for regional cooperation, reforming and perfecting the regional cooperation mechanism, and securing the long-term supply of the most important fuels and raw materials. It seems to me that of these points it is especially the third that deserved some further meditation. The long-term tendencies I tried to outline in an earlier study (Csaba 1980) as well as the interrelationships surveyed in the previous section should have made it reasonable at least to contemplate an alternative approach, one that would prepare for the impact of the inevitably evolving long-term tendencies in East European commercial and development target setting. New tendencies in the world economy—generally speaking—devalue all considerations of stability and security, and revalue the qualities of flexibility, competitiveness, innovation, and market orientation. In order to acquire these qualities, it is even worth making certain short-term material sacrifices. On the other hand, eschewing short-term shocks could result in sacrificing all prospect of a longer-term upswing. This is far from saying that the inevitable structural change in the intra-CMEA division of labour could occur overnight, or might automatically follow those new, dynamically formulated commercial policy deliberations that were documented earlier. The change will inevitably come, as the East European countries have subscribed to the objective nature of the new requirements, as was reflected in the economic document of the CMEA Summit. On the other hand, since then, there have been signs in all CMEA countries indicating an understanding that inter-industrial division of labour would not be replaced by a very different pattern of cooperation in the foreseeable future. This is because the traditional structure of mutual deliveries is based on factor endowments, decades-long cooperation patterns and structural interdependences, specialization patterns develped *ab ovo* for the partners' needs. And last but not least, strong economic and extraeconomic interests contributed to the preservation of the interindustry pattern (Šedivý 1984, p. 110; Marjai 1984; and Rybakov 1984, pp. 84–85).

The increasing share of the intraindustrial division of labour—also expressed in priority joint programmes in electronics, computers, and microprocessors—would obviously have required changes in the traditional methods of cooperation. This would have implied primarily a less formalistic and more flexible approach to the whole arsenal of cooperation mechanisms. In planning it would be necessary to have a clear idea not only of the differing planability of the individual sectors but also of the constraints of five-year planning. The latter reflects a dualism of the modern economy which at once shortens and lengthens foresight. While the development of the infrastructure, of education, ecology and several social aspects of socio-economic development require longer-term strategies, in innovative branches and also in foreign economic relations a plethora of reasons make prediction in the traditional sense and in the traditionally accustomed detail next to impossible. So instead of the recurring attempts (e.g. Kuznetzov 1984) at one-sidedly lengthening the horizon of planning, and extending it to areas that are objectively beyond the control of national planners, it would be more efficient to concede the objective limits of medium-term physical planning. In other words, instead of the former practice of planning volumes, output structures and demand structures in detail, it would be more efficient to plan in the market sense of the notion. Namely: prognoses should have taken as their starting point the tendencies in effective world market demand, rather than the existing domestic production capacities. Foreign economic orientation should have embraced the whole planning methodology, instead of being one of its subchapters, i.e. it should have become the determining factor of planning. The quality of prognoses could have been improved a lot if they had been based on the international market evaluation of applied research and development instead of on the aspirations and verbal statements of technicians. In this respect, in several priority CMEA programmes it would have been of great use if in one way or the other the commodity substance of intellectual products (e.g. software) could have been institutionalized and rewarded according to market criteria. This—of course—leads to the traditionally unresolved state of the financial sphere.[24]

It would be a tangible sign of understanding the need to change from collective import-substitution to coordinated export orientation (Bognár 1979) if, instead of the traditional efforts to launch production in nearly every dynamic industry, joint regional projects would centre on the application and implementation (rather than re-invention) of the newest technological achievements. In this way, regional

11 These comparisons have been made by several researchers. Among Hungarian analyses see Inotai 1983; Palócz-Németh 1981; and Inotai 1986.
12 For details see Hewett 1984, Chapters 2 and 4; Csaba 1980; and Vozniak 1984.
13 A detailed description of the procedures involved may shed light on it. See Kiss 1976, written well before the change in intra-CMEA pricing, and stating the problem clearly.
14 That is why it is a complete misunderstanding for certain theoreticians to try to interpret intra-CMEA energy problems in monetary terms, using concepts of "opportunity cost" and "profit maximization", neither of which applies in reality. The USSR did not increase investments in oil production in 1973–77; she did not reorient her oil sales to world markets when prices peaked (e.g. 1979–81), i.e. when opportunity cost logic would have indicated; but she did do so when she should have done the contrary, at falling prices in 1982–84. For a further elaboration of these issues, see Köves 1983a; Dietz, 1984, pp. 45–58; and Bergson 1980. On the oil market—unlike on the gold market—the USSR does not even pursue partial profit maximizing, i.e. restricting sales at low prices and increasing them at high prices; coordinating output volumes with other major price determining producers, etc. As actual sales policies have long been running counted to what would be logical, in terms of profit maximizing, reference to the latter is misleading. The afterthought, supplementary, nature of the Soviet references to world market prices is quite obvious.
15 For a description of the system of plan indicators see Starodubrovskii 1983. For a look at the "experimental mechanism" to be applied in all the country's industries from 1987, see Ekonomicheskii 1984. That the Soviet economy is a shortage economy—i.e. that in the largest raw material producing country of the world there are raw material shortages—is, of course, independent of the type of obligatory indicators in force, and has systemic causes (Kornai 1980).
16 Cf. Ausch 1972; Vincze 1984; Chvoika 1980; Špaček 1984.
17 For details of this point, see Chapter 1.
18 This has been formulated both directly (Totu 1984, pp. 21–24), and indirectly, with reference to the inconsistencies of the physical and value aspects of plan coordination (Doichev 1984, pp. 2–6).
19 Competent Soviet economists usually close to the official point of view repeatedly stressed that CMEA trade is mutually advantageous, and they specifically elaborated why it is so for the Soviet Union. Cf. Rybakov 1984, pp. 83–84; Konstantinov 1984, pp. 4–5; Progress 1984; Rybakov and Shiryaev 1984, p. 22.
20 Consumer-related industries in Soviet parlance.
21 It is worth remembering that all the quoted Soviet sources continued to lay emphasis on the better "in kind" imports countervailing the further increasing extraction costs of the Soviet deliveries. The monetary logic of the opportunity cost concept is not even mentioned. This, by the way, is also true of other recent Soviet publications not quoted here. None of them want higher prices, but they do want harder commodities.
22 Cf. Study No. 3 in Csaba 1985.
23 Author's translation from the Hungarian edition of the journal.
24 For some suggestions, see Chapter 1 and Study No. 1 in Csaba 1985.

CHAPTER SIX

The strategic options of integrational policies

THE THEORETICAL DEBATES PRECEDING THE SUMMIT OF 1984

Following the second oil price hike in 1979 and the resulting international economic disturbances, conditions for regional cooperation within the CMEA also became more difficult for the small East European countries. This situation makes it unnecessary for this author to add further pages to the already existing voluminous literature describing in detail all the achievements of socialist integration. Instead, I shall attempt to describe some of the major new questions and trends of CMEA cooperation in the 1980s without, however, aiming at an exhaustive study of all the details concerning this comprehensive set of issues. This enquiry is made relevant by the fact that in the early 1980s it was asserted with increasing frequency both in scientific and political fora that the whole concept of existing CMEA cooperation was in need of a comprehensive overhaul.

The above conviction was based on three major development 1) Possibilities of increasing or, in some important cases, even of maintaining already existing levels of Soviet fuel and raw materials supply to Eastern Europe have become objectively limited.[1] 2) The cooling down of general East–West (and especially of Soviet–U.S.) relations after December, 1979, but especially in the months following the declaration of martial law in Poland, were indications of growing international tension. 3) Last but not least, according to the pre-Summit proposals, the policy options of individual CMEA countries were intended to be synchronized on a much wider scale than it had been customary up to the 1980s. In other words, the number of questions decided upon on the basis of regional international coordination was to grow considerably at the expense of formerly individually determined ones (Bogomolov 1983b).

Already preceding the evolution of the above processes—which we may call an epochal transformation within the CMEA international economy—it was established in economic literature that the East

European countries were faced with "developments that could not be foreseen by the means currently at the disposal of science". Not only in their relations *vis-à-vis* Western nations, but also "in the relations among socialist countries, in many respects it has proved impossible to secure macroeconomic consciousness, the planned development of their ties" (Nyilas J. 1982, p. 190).

This feature became even more pronounced in the 1980s, with the resurgence of the parallel development of industries. Nearly fifteen years after the adoption of the Comprehensive Programme, the CMEA has remained an integration based on the physical planning model, comprised of bilateral sets of relations, maintaining a low key approach to monetary and market relations. In this light it is paradoxical that despite the predominance of centralized physical planning, a fourth wave of parallel industrialization evolved in the 1980s. What is more, actual coordination of national development projects has remained slow (occasionally even symbolic) even in fields—such as electronics—earmarked for joint CMEA programmes. It seems quite obvious that the major cause for this lies in the underdeveloped state of the monetary system of the regional economic cooperation. This is the prime reason for the impossibility of proving unambiguously the efficiency of any international cooperation that would also include ending certain already existing activities within individual states. What's more, the growing instability and insecurity of the intra-CMEA trade flows is also directly related to the backward state of the monetary sphere. As a consequence, the avenues towards direct inter-enterprise relations, primarily for specialization in the mutual supply of spare parts and components, i.e. relations having an immediate influence on the process of plant-level production ("production integration") are severely constrained. Specialization in spare parts, actual interfirm cooperation in production, is hardly possible according to international experience unless relations among suppliers and buyers are absolutely reliable. Otherwise, a delay of supplies disrupts the production process of the buyer relying on the regular supplies of the other company.

As early as at the turn of the 80s it could be forecast with a considerable degree of certainty that a comprehensive reform of the economic mechanism of international cooperation in the CMEA would not occur in the course of the 1980s. What is more, proposals in the early 1980s aiming at a complete overhaul of the former concept of division of labour within the CMEA did not deem such a comprehensive change in the management methods of international cooperation necessary. (They rather put up with modifications that did not reach beyond the lines of the traditional framework.) So it was not only understandable but also completely justified that practical planners, who have to rely on actually existing—rather than ideal or desirable—conditions of cooperation when deciding on actual problems, tried to secure the stability and planability of supply relations by developing their own, national productive capacities. It might well incur a higher cost, but would bring about more reliability than the frequently irregular international (CMEA) supplier-buyer relations could provide.[2]

CHANGES IN REAL ECONOMIC CONDITIONS IN THE 1980S

It became clear already in the very first phase of the international coordination of macroeconomic plans for 1981–85 that substantial changes were bound to occur in those traditional conditions which were in force also in the course of the coordination of plans for 1976–80. In this tradition, volumes of commercial exchanges actually transacted in the preceding five-year-plan period were taken for granted, and the subject of actual bargaining was solely the volume and composition of incremental sales (including their financial conditions). This situation changed first during the coordination of plans for 1981–85, especially in trade among the small East European countries, as lengthy, tough bargaining went on about the conditions of balancing the supplies of frequently decreasing volumes of fuels, raw materials and agricultural produce. Bargaining went on not so much about the adequate "hardness" of counter-deliveries, as it has become common practice to balance the supplies of certain products within the same commodity group, or even within the same commodity class. This means that in order to obtain the traditional, priority import items that used to be available under "normal" conditions of structural bilateralism, a different assortment of the very same commodity had to be supplied in exchange (as e.g. coking coal for brown coal briquets; tone type of petrochemical intermediate product for another type, etc.).

As a sign of the further hardening of the conditions of exchange, for the period 1986–90 fuel and raw material exporting countries formulated the requrement that investment contributions be provided even for the maintenance of the decreased 1981–85 level of supplies (Tikhonov 1983; and Dudinskii 1983, p. 181). With all that, the volume, the timing and also the quality of internationally co-ordinated supplies have become increasingly uncertain.

All this boils down to a basic change in two major characteristics of the CMEA cooperation of the 1970s. In the mid-70s, the CMEA was regarded by central planners primarily as an institution cushioning the Hungarian economy from the unfavourable impact of international economic disturbances, one stabilizing the environment for the activities of Hungarian firms. Furthermore, CMEA cooperation played a major role in the consolidation of the position of those large industrial enterprises whose liquidity and development possibilities were shaken by the 1968–72 processes of economic reform (Kővári 1976, p. 8 and 10). Hungarian central planners then were of the opinion that the prime factor embodying the advantages derived from the CMEA was that it established—in the sense of macroeconomic physical balancing—the basis for all those central development programmes that determined the dynamics of Hungarian industry, both from the input and the output (market) sides (Mosóczy 1976).

A major change took place by the 1980s in both of the above mentioned fields. The "consolidating" policy of the mid-70s was not very highly rated by international markets, including the CMEA markets, although the latter played a substantial role in shaping the industrial policies of those days. The CMEA partners were less and less willing to supply the raw materials and fuels necessary for the production of those manufactures which were developed just for their needs. This phenomenon is described by Soviet economists as a structural constraint on the continuation of the intra-CMEA division of labour along the traditional lines, one that "can't be solved simply by an increase in Soviet raw material supplies" (Dudinskii 1983, pp. 180–181). The point is that the traditional inward-looking, import-substituting policies of the East European countries were becoming less and less sustainable, primarily from the CMEA side, as fuel and raw material producers no longer took any interest in maintaining the traditional CMEA division of labour, exchanging raw materials for manufactured products. This was the most obvious sign of the failure of regional import-substituting industrialization policies, and this factor makes export-orientation an imperative for East European countries in the most tangible manner. Not only considerations of security of supply and of market, but also daily commercial experience seem to substantiate the applicability, for the CMEA, of an important finding of general integration theory (Inotai 1978), that under the epochal transformation of the world economy, the traditional logic of Friedrich

List has been inverted. No longer is the presumption valid that it is in the protected national and regional markets that internationally competitive industries and products can evolve, which—having developed their abilities on a sheltered training ground—can later prove their qualities on the world market. In fact—as CMEA experiences demonstrate—the opposite is the case. The failure of the inward-looking policies itself is an indirect proof that the way out is the adoption of an outward-looking, export-led growth strategy.

An East European economist hardly needs any proof that if a product is indeed competitive on the world market, it can in fact be exchanged for goods of the same quality within the CMEA as well, and if not, the wanted product can be bought for the hard currency that is earned from the sale of one's own product in the world market. For everyday practice this makes palpable the theorem that in fact it is the acquisition of general competitiveness on international markets that has increasingly become a prerequisite for being successful in the longer run in intra-CMEA division of labour, rather than the other way around. (Nevertheless, this latter conviction, reflecting the economic *Weltanschauung* of an earlier period, is still frequently voiced by theoretical economists, planners and businessmen in Eastern Europe.)

These tendencies could clearly be spotted by the mid-70s. A leading official of the Hungarian National Planning Office expounded prior to the finalization of the coordination of plans for 1976–80 the view that the increasing raw material and fuel supply constraints, coupled with the phenomena of more and more rigid structural bilateralism, have put severe limits on capitalizing on a basic potential gain from international trade in the CMEA, namely the possibility of obtaining via exports those natural resources whose domestic production is uneconomical (Mosóczy 1975, p. 915). It seems a sobering evaluation of the industrial policies followed by several East European states in the course of the 1970s that the economic performance resulting from their priorities and management methods has not been valued by precisely those markets whose requirements were to be served by the inward-looking adjustment policies of the period under scrutiny. This thesis can also be inverted. The overcentralized mechanism of economic cooperation within the CMEA can also be judged by the fact that it transmitted requirements, preferences and priorities that were incongruous with the real economic processes taking place in the respective national economies. By the same token, instead of exerting pressure to adjust existing structures to the radically changed external conditions, it has led to policies postponing rather than implementing adjustment processes.

Some analysts still tend to interpret the above as an achievement, rather than a shortcoming. In this concept the actual priorities and methods of CMEA cooperation and the related defensive foreign economic policies made it possible for the CMEA to avoid the immediate and drastic transmission of external shocks to the population and also to avoid crises of entire East European industries. This line of thought was not devoid of reason, especially in the months following the first oil price hike, when the size and nature of world economic changes were not even perceptible. Somewhat later, too, it seemed to be a possible, though not quite convincing, position. In principle any subvention or loss-compensation granted by both national governments and regional economic organizations to industries and enterprises lagging behind in the competition for international markets serves only to buy time in order to prepare for readjustment and to soften its social and economic costs.

In theory, protectionist solutions, *ipso facto,* should not necessarily and directly be followed by unsuccessful results. In practice, however, similarly to the experiences of the developing countries (Balassa B. 1977), protectionist measures—any form of subvention, or defence of a national market—do tend to stabilize and even ossify in the CMEA region. Particularistic vested interests are often successful in lengthening the validity of even temporarily granted benefits, whereas automatic reductions are far from being a general method of managing them. What is more, subventions and market protection are more often than not granted *ab ovo* without steady reductions and without time limits. Since the overall restriction of imports (coupled with the shortage-economy character of the domestic markets), producers have a good chance to stabilize their favoured position through the well-known mechanisms of plan-bargaining and bargaining about financial regulators. In other words, given that the national economies of the CMEA states have developed for decades in a non-competitive climate, it was nearly inevitable that defensive economic measures be used for the postponement, rather than the preparation for or the speeding up, of the adjustment to the changed external environment. The cumulative financial and social costs of deferred adjustment, however, can reach intolerable levels. Accordingly, instead of a very painful radical therapy they are conducive to further automatic defensive steps that lead to further lagging behind in world economic competition. In Eastern Europe the policy of opening up to the world economy is "a policy of change and transformation" (Köves 1981). This policy faces serious difficulties despite the renewed good intentions of several East European governments, because the earlier-described automatisms started to operate already in the mid-70s. In the absence of a central initiative—more precisely, of radical action—they lead in the opposite direction automatically, unless there is a resolute turn in economic policy. As it can be seen from the growing significance of import restrictions in all CMEA states, this may well happen as a result of daily improvisations, quite independently of the aims of an officially formulated strategy. As we all know, "Practical men, who believe themselves to be quite exempt from any intellectual influence, are usually slaves of some defunct economist . . . In the field of economic and social philosophy there are not many, who are influenced by new theories after they are 25 or 30 years of age, so that the ideas which civil servants and politicians and even agitators apply to current events are not likely to be the newest" (Keynes 1973, pp. 383–384). This is particularly dangerous if an epochal change takes place (as in the world economy now), i.e. when the trends of the earlier period dramatically change. Furthermore, it is also very dangerous in the event of a general international recession, when a daily economic policy void of long-term strategy, and so reacting with short-term therapies only to phenomena appearing on the surface, might itself lead to a deterioration of the situation.[3]

A detailed analysis could substantiate the thesis that it is impossible to elaborate such feasible proposals that would simultaneously conform to the logic of the traditional model of CMEA international cooperation, would add up to a radical therapy for today's ills, and would also result in a contribution to a long-term solution. That's why it is certain that in defining an ideal long-term target-model of CMEA cooperation one has to set out not from the present model of the basic principles and functioning of socialist integration, or from the requirement of conformity to these, but from the necessities of the future, determined by epochal transformations in international economic relations. As the probability of a far-reaching institutional reform of the international mechanism of economic cooperation during the 1980s was low, it was necessary to develop those partial solutions whose implementation had been feasible within the old framework, without forgetting, however, their inherent limits as reform-substitutes. They could, however, have provided some remedies which had not been without value in themselves, or in view of the deteriorating real economic situation. It can be assumed with near certainty that the gradual and mutual opening of national markets in Eastern Europe advocated by reform-minded Hungarians in the late 1960s (cf. Ausch 1972; and Nyers 1970), reasonable and even lucrative as it might sound as a concept even today, will hardly come about during the 1980s. On the other hand, a concept of international regional cooperation which adopts competitiveness on the world markets as a point of orientation, and concentrates on the development of just this bottleneck of the East European economies among other things by channelling joint regional efforts into this direction, can be acceptable on the CMEA level.

THE INITIATIVES OF THE TWENTY-SIXTH PARTY CONGRESS OF THE CPSU AND THE REVITALIZATION OF THE COMPREHENSIVE PROGRAMME

Far-reaching strategic concepts of CMEA international division of labour gained new political momentum following the 1981 Party Congress of the CPSU. In the preceding decade debates concerning these issues had been put to an end on the political level by the joint adoption of the Comprehensive Programme in the year 1971. The Programme, however, was itself a non-homogeneous document both in form and in substance, reflecting the compromise solutions it embodied.

This relates both to its implementation and to the macroeconomic significance of the individual problems raised by the Programme. A leading Hungarian authority on the topic, Tibor Kiss, correctly drew attention to this already then: "The Comprehensive Programme contains a number of tasks whose solution is already under way; but it also includes a number of tasks that are only to be worked out later, because they are related to the most important and also the most difficult questions of integration"[4], i.e. those which concern primarily the desirable extent of liberalization of intra-Comecon trade. "In order to develop methods applied in foreign trade, an agreement has been reached to make the system of quotas more flexible, but only to a minor extent. The differences in views concerning the development of intra-trade free of quotas boils down to the fact that representatives of some member states consider this merely as a very moderate additional form of division of labour, as they deem it to be irreconcilable with their system of planning, or they find this form of trade very hard to fit into it" (Kiss 1972, pp. 51–54).[5] This, and other contradictions in the Programme, have become a major drawback. Moreover the

Programme contained "a number of concrete tasks for joint action". This basically meant that a fairly large number of the usual end-products of international coordination of medium-term macroeconomic plans (in this case for the years 1971–75) figured with equal weight as fundamental strategic and functional issues of international integration. For instance, the principles of preserving national sovereignty, developing integration and taking into account opportunities of global division of labour (i.e. the straight and explicit rejection of cyclically recurring isolationist endeavours) are mixed with lengthy enumerations of day-to-day agrotechnical and business administration tasks. This heterogeneity itself reflects the conceptual disagreements. From the Hungarian point of view, it was also a substitute for a break-through. Such fundamental principles of cooperation as the preservation of national sovereignty, the open character of the East European integration, the priority of medium-term international coordination of macroeconomic plans in determining the volume, structure and dynamism of intra-CMEA trade, or reassertion of the state monopoly on foreign trade, profound and all-important as they were, had already figured among the "Basic Principles of Socialist International Division of Labour", adopted in 1962.[6]

Looking back, it is quite difficult not only to share, but also to understand, the optimism and the liberal interpretations that were characteristic of the Hungarian economic literature after the adoption of the Comprehensive Programme. In his above-quoted book, Tibor Kiss voiced a then generally shared view in Hungary when he argued that the Programme was not a final timetable for socialist integration, just the beginning of it, and was to be continuously supplemented. "The Comprehensive Programme has got to be interpreted as a minimal programme for the realization of CMEA integration. This, however, is also a process in which constant progress is to be achieved in perfecting the set of instruments of CMEA integration." This approach, which has been applied to both the CMEA as a whole and to its individual fields (primarily the financial one), was in the early 1970s already incongruent with the centralizing tendencies that had already gained ground by then in the majority of the East European countries, to say nothing of the priorities of "rush growth" and the prevailing unchanged bilateralism in planning and trade alike. The economic scenario transforming the bilateral physical planning model of the CMEA of the 1950s and 1960s into a sort of East European common market would indeed have required exactly those measures which were detailed at length in the works of Ausch, Nyers and Kiss quoted above. The crux of the problem was the lack of the political feasibility of the correct economic programme in the 1970s.[7] This fact was also reflected in the general decline in the scientific level of East European economic literature dealing with the CMEA. It can be demonstrated that with the exception of a minority of publications, the bulk of the literature on the subject is a repetition of the Comprehensive Programme, of statements made at the different annual sessions of the Council, rather than something addressing itself to the economic (theoretical) questions still unresolved after interstate talks, or to elaboration of the alternatives brought about by the radical changes that took place during the 1970s. An important group of writers confined themselves to the formulation of day-to-day foreign trade interests, and supplied "theoretical" ammunition for the fight for the international redistribution of national incomes.

Summing up, it can be established that the adoption of the Comprehensive Programme marked an end, rather than the dawn of a period characterized by attempts to institute marketizing reforms at the political level. The following appropriate remark was made by Shiryaev (1981, p. 123): "As a result of the adoption and implementation of the Comprehensive Programme, a concept of cooperation prevailed, and was scientifically and also practically substantiated in the firmest manner, which interpreted the use of commodity and monetary relations as an instrument of plan-based management as opposed to a mixed-economy or plan-and-market concept, which presumes the parallel functioning of two, relatively independent regulatory mechanisms of planning and of monetary-commodity (market) relations." In a correct interpretation of the Programme, "The role of the price and monetary mechanism used in the cooperation of socialist states cannot be translated as a parallel coordinating mechanism acting independently of the harmonization of economic strategies. On the contrary, they are tools of management which can orient the synchronization of economic strategies and promote the implementation of its results in detail in the course of daily practice" (Kozma F. 1974, p. 321). However, the model of the reforms of the 1960s implied precisely this, i.e. that economic automatisms guided by universally applied (normative) financial regulators would act as a form of social feedback controlling *ex post facto* the reality of national economic plans.

It was a direct consequence of the concept of regional cooperation adopted in the Comprehensive Programme and implemented during the 1970s that trade liberalizing and monetary measures envisaged (or sometimes not completely excluded) by the Programme could not be realized. Instead, intra-CMEA cooperation, which was insufficiently monetized already in the 1960s, was gradually and increasingly demonetized in the 1970s and 1980s. Reacting to this phenomenon and a host of others resulting from it, as well as tackling the challenge of the deterioration of Soviet–US relations (which became especially marked from late 1979), the Twenty-Sixth Soviet Party Congress gave an answer at the political level. It again put on the agenda some of the progressive ideas of the Comprehensive Programme, and also formulated a number of new requirements. As a critique of the practice of intra-CMEA cooperation in the 1970s, it stressed the need for supplementing the coordination of plans with the harmonization of the national economic policies of the CMEA states as a whole, and for a convergence of the different structures of national economic management systems *(sblizhenie)*. It also stressed the need for the development of direct interfirm, inter-association, inter-institutional and inter-ministerial contacts. In order to elaborate ways and means to implement these goals, it supported the earlier raised Romanian idea of convening a CMEA summit meeting (the previous one had been held in 1969).

As it was a political-level initiative, it had to be expected that the general formulations should leave room for various alternative interpretations. This fact was also reflected in the length of the preparation for the Summit, which was definitely justified from the point of view of substance, as both national economic interests and the alternative interpretations and proposals were quite divergent on a great number of points.

What was the point of further developing the provisions of the Comprehensive Programme along the lines of the Soviet suggestions? The first idea—the need to supplement coordination of plans with coordination of economic policies in their entirety—aimed at overcoming a deficiency in the practice of the previous fifteen years, when coordination of medium-term economic plans had to a decisive extent been confined to bargaining about the volume, structure and final delivery conditions of intra-regional trade flows. This left little room and energy to capitalize on the abstract potentials of the centrally planned economies' coordinating their structural policies and harmonizing their interests *ex ante* in order to avoid competition among each other both in the regional and on the world markets. Yet such measures could have been ever more warranted in the light of the growing competition from developing countries.

The interpretation of the concept of the harmonization of economic policy would be misleading without due attention to the fact that this initiative—unlike some formulations of the debate preceding the Comprehensive Programme[8]—was not followed by a theoretical campaign explaining the "obsoleteness" of the framework of the national economy. On the contrary: the new initiatives were compounded with statements not only allowing for, but even appreciating the values of the national framework (also for the longer run). Writing on the coordination of the foreign policies of socialist countries, a spring 1983 editorial of *Izvestiya* noted that it "aims at the fraternal countries helping each other in the realization of their national interests in the international arena, in order to enhance their authority". Convergence among socialist states does go on. However, "this process naturally does not overshadow national characteristics, the historically developed specific features of fraternal states ... There is nothing more remote from reality than the picture of a monolithic socialist community" (Moguchaya 1983). In other words, the endeavour to extend the sphere of coordination of economic policies did not modify the Soviet standpoint that the "cooperation of the socialist countries for the time being and also in the foreseeable future will not lead to the withering away of national economic complexes". Moreover, this view directly contrasted developments in East Europe with those in the European Community, where "multinationals forcibly break through national frontiers". There are "aggressive attempts" to enhance the authority of the Commission in Brussels, whereas "the favourable experience gained in the CMEA integration in solving the problems emerging from the preservation of socialist (national) statehood is of immense international significance" (Shiryaev 1979). Commenting on the same issue, an official of the Czechoslovak State Planning Commission noted that "participation in the international coordination of plans must be subordinated to the endeavours of national economic policy" (Holeček 1982, p. 72).

How then to interpret the coordination of economic policies as an act reaching beyond the former practice of the coordination of macroeconomic plans, and consultations on economic policy priorities? In one—rather extreme—judgement, coordination of policy options should have been extended to the whole process of social reproduction, from science, research and development to marketing (Henyš 1983, p. 58). Soviet authors have viewed structural and foreign economic policies as prime new subjects to be added to the traditionally coordinated areas of defence, foreign policy and planning, as they have found the CMEA's dependence on the West excessive (and largely a product of the 1970s) (Kheifetz 1983, p. 71).

Among a number of other sources, Bogomolov (1983a) also defined the objectives of such harmonization as the attainment of the technological and economic independence of the CMEA from the West, and an increase in the share of intra-trade in the total foreign turnover of the individual CMEA member-states. A further purpose was to bring intra-CMEA trade and financial flows into equilibrium (!), as well as to replace the parallel industrial structures with complementary ones, especially in the fields of chemical industry, metallurgy and engineering. On the one hand, he found the whole complex of relations with the non-socialist world to be an area that is "ripe for regional coordination"; on the other hand, "the program of development of scientific, technical and economic cooperation within the CMEA has obviously (!) got to be oriented to enhance exports to advanced capitalist countries. This is a precondition for putting an end to indebtedness incurred in convertible currencies."[9] It is worth mentioning that the latter idea did not reappear in another text (Bogomolov 1983b) where the Soviet author developed the whole subject in detail. Reflecting the thinking of earlier-quoted Soviet sources, and in accordance with the Soviet official statement made at the Thirty-Seventh (Berlin) Session of the Council (Tikhonov 1983) he laid great emphasis on the description of the dangers of excessive reliance on relations with the West, which, in his view, have become unreliable. He even advocated a general overhaul of the former CMEA policy of intensive borrowing from the West, and proposed a common, unified *(edinaya)* policy in imports from advanced capitalist states. He also suggested that the more coordinated the economic policies and economic management of individual CMEA countries, the more efficient they were. He found coordination desirable in the fields of investment and technology, and in the structural and foreign economic policies of the CMEA states. However, he noted: "Today as yet it is, of course, impossible to settle conclusively the exact character of this activity." Others (Gavrilov and Bagudin 1983) have emphasized the need to take the objective nature of the constraints on the Soviet ability to expand fuel and raw material exports to the CMEA countries as a starting point. In this concept, the substance of the coordination of economic policies would have lain precisely in the exploration and implementation of joint regional solutions to this problem, through greater reliance on domestic natural resources, on energy saving measures, and on joint technological developments, as well as on a harmonized change in national structural policies in tackling the basic problem. More or less implicitly discussing this approach, others (Butenko 1982; and Belovič 1983) have underscored that it is not the entire investment fund of a given national economy that was to become subject to coordination.[10] Furthermore, investment harmonization also in the longer run was not intended to result in the co-ordination of the indicators of long-term development projects in the usual way i.e., by means of the physical balances used in macroeconomic planning. Some of the adherents to this line of thinking—as e.g. the Slovak and Soviet sources quoted above—believed, however, that the elaboration of a planning model or regional allocation of production forces gradually approximating to a CMEA-level optimum is both feasible and desirable. Disagreeing with this approach, Romania has emphasized that such a harmonization could occur only after the practical problems facing the international coordination of medium-term plans for the 1986–90 period (such as the supply of East European states with energy, with agricultural produce, the introduction of price incentives for intra-CMEA agro-exports) had been solved. Moreover, they subscribed to this concept as a function of overcoming these and other short-term problems, provided that such regional coordination did not diminish the role of the nation-state (Badrus 1983).

To sum up, endeavours formulated in the individual CMEA states differed as to the methods as well as to the scope of economic policy problems that were to be coordinated. Moreover, they also disagreed as far as the motives for closer coordination were concerned. A common feature of these views was, however, that—with the exception of the (standard) Romanian standpoint—they were for the institutionalization of a significantly more far-reaching coordination of various economic policy issues at a regional level than had been customary in the previous three and a half decades of CMEA history. This held for both an extensive and intensive interpretation, as formerly not coordinated (or only informally consulted on) topics were to become subject to interstate agreements (especially the choice of national development projects and foreign economic policy). The obligatory nature of some CMEA agreements was to be strengthened, to the detriment of the earlier predominant forms of recommendation. The character, formulations and fora of these proposals hardly permit one, in the view of this author, to shrug them off as "wishful thinking". It would also be wrong to attribute them to the jointly accepted final wording of the Comprehensive Programme. Consequently they mean far more and are far different from a mere reiteration of the formulations of this fundamental joint document, as some Western analysts (Lavigne 1983, pp. 148–149) suggested at that time.

The endeavours under scrutiny fit into a long-term tendency where, on one hand, the terms of trade for the small East European countries are becoming tougher, and on the other hand, as an extrapolation of the logic of the directive system of planning prevailing in the majority of CMEA states, difficulties in international economic relations were to be overcome by means of increased centralization and by enhancing the compulsory character of formal regulators. It is also a noteworthy feature that some of their proponents have tried to depict as a new course precisely that economic strategy which has traditionally characterized CMEA intentions (though not real economic flows). It would be difficult to state that the plans to reduce and substitute "undesirable" Western imports both in general and in individual fields (e.g. raw material supply, agriculture, engineering, high technology) were brand new plans, ones that have not even been formulated in the preceding thirty-five years. So we need to face the results of the markedly import-substituting, inward-looking policies of the 1970s in all the CMEA countries, which have led to an increase rather than a decrease in reliance on Western imports both at national and regional levels (Köves 1982; and Csaba 1983). In reality only competitiveness on the world markets, and a set of mutual interests related to this, can provide a sound economic basis for the evolution of real interdependence replacing asymmetric relationships. This seems to be the safest and only feasible way for the CMEA to achieve those policy goals which have, in my judgement, been mistakenly approached by the proposals discussed above: i.e. to transform East Europe's somewhat vulnerable state *vis-à-vis* the ups and downs in international trade and finance into a balanced set of economic interdependences. Coordination of national structural policies with an eye on global competitiveness in order to implement a joint regional export-oriented strategy would indeed add up to a break with the value judgements and with the majority conviction characterizing the past decades. However, such a new approach could better and more efficiently serve the frequently reasserted common aims of integration, namely to become more successful in the ever-growing international competition both at national economic and CMEA levels.

The practical experiences of several decades have shown that without a mechanism of currency convertibility and in the absence of a jointly accepted regional compensation mechanism, the room for feasible and efficient coordination of national structural policies is

limited. This statement should by no means be interpreted as a denial
of the urgent need to achieve some actual international coordination
of structural policies within the CMEA even under unreformed conditions. With growing competition from the developing countries, it
was in the elementary interest especially of the small East European
countries to avoid, or at least to soften the impact of, the re-emer-
gence of old and also newly created[11] parallelisms in industrial development (such as in car, bus and truck production, steel industry,
pharmaceuticals, electronics, etc.) through international macroeconomic coordination. It deserves attention anyway that a leading
Czech Marxist theorist, the late Josef Tauchmann (1983a), while considering a regional-level structural policy as an urgent, immediate
task for economic policy, and expounding this conviction on a generalized theoretical level, also stressed that in the earlier international
economic mechanism of the CMEA it is impossible to determine
the final gains from international division of labour at the national
economic level. The basis for such a regional cooperation model—primarily internationally applicable long-term efficiency and optimum
criteria—is lacking. Without having such criteria, the feasibility of
even technically absolutely justified coordination (including investments) seems questionable. What has been said for structural policy
coordination, of course, can automatically be applied to foreign economic policies and their coordination.

The second set of issues raised by the Twenty-Sixth Congress of
the CPSU was the requirement for a convergence of the structures of
the national systems of economic management. This thesis has traditionally been advocated by Hungarian and other economists, who had
deemed the monetization of CMEA cooperation desirable already at
the time the international reform discussions started in preparation
for the Comprehensive Programme. The need to find convergence on
new grounds springs from the underlying fact that although the
directive systems of economic control, being more or less copies of the
Soviet model of planning, are all structured and function basically
in the same manner, this similarity is embodied primarily in their
inherent autarky and disregard for the requirements of international
trade (Friss 1974, p. 7). That is why it has traditionally been an official
Hungarian endeavour to achieve some convergence in national economic mechanisms, first of all in pricing, in the way of establishing
an organic link between external and internal markets, and also in the
active use of some financial regulators of prime importance from the
foreign trade point of view (such as the exchange rate). Without a

certain degree of uniformity in these areas, it is hardly possible to construct a workable international monetary system of regional integration.[12]

The role of money, however, is a function of the type of economic mechanism. It is a condensed expression of actually existing relations of production (the economic environment). If we repudiate the theoretically eclectic and practically non-feasible concept of step by step transformation (proved erroneous by numerous analysts and practical experiences of the last decades), we must realize that a qualitative change in the methods of international cooperation that would result in a qualitative change in the role of money in CMEA trade presumes reform decisions instituted in parallel in a number of member states. Unless this is done, it is inevitable that even uniformly denominated or formally similar management solutions or regulators will continue to exert substantially different impacts on real economic processes, and to involve a different economic substance in the various countries.

Soviet economists attached a different interpretation to the idea of convergence *(sblizhenie)* in the early 1980s since the economic thinking of the Twenty-Sixth Congress of the CPSU followed a logic different from that of the Hungarian economic mechanism (the regulated market). This interpretation was closely related to the significant, then new idea of the mutual study of economic methods by the socialist countries, indicating that it was not only a one-way flow of experiences that was seen to be desirable. It is the Soviet economy which has the longest history and thus the greatest experience in macroeconomic planning. When deciding upon changes in the economic mechanism of the USSR, however, Soviet decision-makers were to take into account the experiences of other CMEA states. Moreover, they seemed inclined to adopt the successful elements of these (after having tested them experimentally under Soviet conditions).

What would the necessity of a convergence of national economic mechanisms and of their structures have implied in this context? There were several interpretations.

In one approach, the need for national economic control systems to convergence emerged from the fundamental features of the socialist relations of production, "as they require the application of system-inherent management methods". As a consequence, the emphasis was laid upon circumscribing and diminishing the role of specifically national solutions. Representatives of this reasoning were the Soviet professors Bautina and Shiryaev (1982) who pointed out: "There are objective limits to the national character of the economic mechanism, stemming from the very substance of the new social order". Furthermore, "It would be hard to subscribe to the view, argued for by some economists, that cost accounting *(khozraschet)* should be replaced by commercial accounting, as the economic mechanism is also required to ensure the reproduction of socialist relations of production". That is why in their view "It is impossible to exchange experiences concerning just any economic method abstracted from their theoretical substance and practical implications".[13] Bogomolov (1983b), too, maintained that a major shortcoming of the 1970s had been the uncoordinated state of even those elements of economic reforms which directly concerned the development of integration. He was of the opinion that not only studying the various experiences, but their joint evaluation, had also been necessary, and could serve as a basis for individual countries using the solutions of others.

In an alternative concept, the point of the idea of advanced socialism was the switch from predominantly administrative methods to economic ones. From this it follows that a basic feature of coordination of economic policies was the introduction of international market relations. The main task in making the structures of national mechanisms converge was to elaborate, with joint international effort, a detailed and feasible long-term target model of a regulated market, and the concomitant changes in integration methods. In an article setting forth this idea in detail, the Czech economist, L. Rusmich (1983), clearly indicated that such a target model would by no means be identical with any of the management models then actually applied in various CMEA states. Convergence in this sense would preclude, even in theory, implementing changes in one CMEA country so that they would gradually approach the contemporary practice of any other East European state (or to use the degree of conformity with the latter as a measure, which this concept was frequently misinterpreted to involve). A basic feature of this model was the establishment of unified and parametric (external) optimum and success criteria for independent enterprise decisions. Another one was that what was then the general rule, i.e. that government bodies individually decide on conditions of international economic intercourse, would become an exception. As a consequence, the terms, the volume and the structure of intra-Comecon trade would have resulted from the economic self-interest of enterprises. This development presupposes the monetization of individual CMEA economies and the final abandonment of the autarkic approach to theory, which has been haunting socialist economics since the 1930s.[14]

A third main line of reasoning has considered as a main task in the convergence process of national economic mechanisms the wider use of economic levers along with administrative methods. According to this conviction, the operative independence of "prime" economic units would already gain ground by limiting the scope of centrally determined compulsory indicators and increasing the role of intermediate-level control organs (associations, combines, but significantly, not enterprises). These measures would free the central planning organs from the woes of dealing with a plethora of minuscule details. Unfolding this more moderate and essentially different approach, Knyazev and Bakovetzkii (1982) were of the opinion that in this sense a considerable degree of convergence had already taken place among the CMEA states. It is noteworthy that in substantiating their position they also considered contemporary Hungary, which, in my judgement, was quite right.[15] They pointed out the similarity of the centralized organizational structure of Hungarian industry to that of the quasimonopolies of other CMEA states, the general tendency to create more direct links between domestic and world market prices, the general increase in the role of the small-scale sector, etc. They correctly underlined the inadequate impact of economic regulators in restoring foreign trade equilibrium, which had brought about an increase in direct governmental control of foreign trade flows in each CMEA country. They emphasized that there was no need even to attempt the unification of the whole system of economic management or of its specific elements. The point was to orient them towards efficient solutions of the practical tasks of the intensive type of development and of socialist integration.[16]

In my view, this third approach contained the most realistic elements as far as actual (feasible) possibilities for the convergence of national economic mechanisms in the 1980s were concerned. It can be proven by a thorough analysis of the economic models then applied in the individual CMEA countries, and by a comparative study of the details of the modifications in regulation, in planning techniques, and in the institutional and enterprise organization sphere, that those underlying historical causes which brought about the differentiation of the traditional physical planning model from the mid-1950s on have not ceased to exist. As its causes continue to be present, the diversity of national economic management methods which appeared then have stayed with us during the 1980s. Further elaboration of this point would go far beyond the scope of the present analysis, but the earlier discussion which surveyed widely divergent views among even those authors who were close to the then official position of their respective countries may serve as an indirect proof of this finding. This is especially so when the views within individual states also differed on such basic issues as the reasons for, the scope, and methods of, convergence.[17]

A third set of problems raised by the Twenty-Sixth Congress of the CPSU and discussed widely in CMEA countries was the institutionalization of direct relations among the ministries, institutions, associations and finally also among the enterprises of the CMEA countries. This, in fact, was a reassertion of a provision of the Comprehensive Programme. In Hungary this has always been a popular theme, and some typical misinterpretations were given right after the adoption of the Programme. At the time, Szita (1971, p. 34) suggested that the main emphasis in this form of contact is to be laid on interfirm dimensions, since channels of continuous intercommunication between planning organs, ministries and research institutes have already been established for a long time. In his view, the slogan of direct relations signified a turning point, "as this concept starts drawing the line in general between the authorities and entrepreneurship, implying an incipient acknowledgement of the dissimilar rules of the game in the respective categories". The quotation formulates a correct economic thesis, or to be more precise, a correct requirement, which—in the manner frequently to be observed in those days—was presented as an accomplished fact.

In reality, however, in the 1970s the sweeping merger campaign in the industry and agriculture of the CMEA states resulted precisely in the nearly complete abolition of the enterprise sphere as a prime subject of microeconomic decision-making. The evolving intermediate control organs (associations, combines, VHJs, and WOGs) gained more rights (even independence) not so much from the supervising ministries as from their member enterprises as far as redistribution of financial funds, setting plan-targets, control of activities, granting bonuses or other fields were concerned (Bauer and Szamuely 1978). These intermediate-level organs are much more of an authority (part of the ministerial hierarchy) than an entrepreneurship of any sort. Indeed, their international direct relations are different from an actual or textbook interfirm contact. Even when an association incorporates the foreign trade enterprise, its relation to a member-company of a trust based in another CMEA state is far from being "interfirm" in substance, as this contact is usually void of micro-level initiative. Moreover, former legislation in most CMEA states strictly limited the scope of possible agents of international economic intercourse. In addition, the demonetization of intraregional trade made the promotion of this type of contact less and less possible, even if, in principle, a national economic policy is strongly in favour of such developments.

Authoritative Soviet sources of the early 1980s have never concealed their intention to develop a combination of inter-ministerial, inter-association, inter-institutional and inter-enterprise contacts, rather than merely (or primarily) interfirm relations. The role of these was meant to be an exchange of experience in planning techniques and in plant-level organizational methods, as well as the elaboration of proposals for scientific and technological cooperation under the auspices of a macro-level coordination of plans (Bakovetzkii and Grinev 1982, as well as Bakovetzkii and Gavrilov 1983, p. 103). These authors considered, for instance, the direct contacts established among branch ministries and also among other national control organs the most promising and progressive forms of this new field of CMEA cooperation.[18] A professor of the Academy of Social Sciences under the Central Committee of the CPSU (Oleynik 1982, pp. 129–136), listed among the effective and prospective forms of direct contact the exchange of information between local and regional party and trade union organizations, as well as the traditional exchange of visits by factory delegations. All in all, he visualized a mutual flow of those forms and methods of (primarily plant-level) industrial organization which usually do not alter the mode of functioning of the economic mechanism as a whole, i.e. which can be applied under any system of management (e.g. restricting the use of fuels, imposing fines and penalties on companies that fail to meet their contractual obligations, etc.). The extent to which contemporary official blessing was gained by this interpretation of direct contacts was well mirrored in an autumn 1983 editorial of the Soviet government daily, which explained the practical significance of the problem in much the same terms (Sovmestnyi 1983).

As far as enhancing the role of sectoral ministries is concerned, as was proved in Chapter 4, in the absence of objective criteria for local decisions, and without a "hard budget constraint" for those concerned, this could only have led to a process of international plan-bargaining in the course of coordinating medium-term plans, and could have exerted a disequilibrating impact on the respective economies. As a consequence, no central decision-making body of any CMEA state was in a position to allow a development of this peculiar form of direct relations for a time longer than the technically inevitable minimum level.

Some extreme proposals have been formulated on the issue of direct contacts, which defined it as a means to elaborate in detail joint technological concepts that were to be implemented two or three five-year-plan periods. These were to serve as the basis for specialization programmes adopted for ten-year periods. The actual contractual prices resulting from the final agreements would have affected the financial results of industrial enterprises as well (Gavrilov and Leznik 1982). The earlier discussed interrelationships should be sufficient to prove the abstract and practically infeasible nature of such proposals. Interestingly enough, this holds true especially for those elements which seem to be the most progressive ones (such as the impact of CMEA foreign trade prices on the financial results of industrial producers).

There was absolutely no sign in the early 1980s that micro-integrational forms would gradually gain ground in the CMEA, as some analysts suggested. A deputy head of the International Department of the Central Committee of the CPSU formulated the Soviet initiative quite clearly: "The establishment of direct interfirm and inter-association contacts is not meant to substitute, but to supplement, cooperation among the central management organs of the CMEA countries. They will develop in the framework of joint planning, under the scrutiny of central planning agencies and foreign trade ministries" (Chukanov 1982). This concept was embodied in the contemporary Soviet regulation, effective from 1981, and also in its renewed edition of 1984 allowing for the establishment of direct interfirm contacts conditional on discretionary approval by the Soviet branch ministry concerned. The purpose of such contacts was "to promote reaching the existing compulsory plan targets, to help find the operative solutions to problems emerging in the course of meeting interstate agreements, and to exchange experiences, to widen existing cooperation agreements, to utilize (unused) capacities and to enlarge the range of the products exchanged".

It is quite obvious that in promoting the concept of direct relations, Soviet sources in the early 1980s did not even think of the role of enterprise initiative, which is what Hungarian economists usually mean by the term. If they had thought of it, however, only a supplementary role would have been allotted to enterprise initiative, strictly in order to meet national and international plan targets, which, all in all, was a justified position under existing conditions. This is further demonstrated by the fact that one of the conditions for a Soviet firm starting any additional international cooperation has been all over the 80s that this be done without its applying for extra material (i.e. the material needs arising from the new contact are to be filled from the preplanned quantity of materials allotted, and without exerting extra pressure on the Soviet supply organs).

FEASIBLE ALTERNATIVES FOR DEVELOPMENT: CONDITIONS AND CONSTRAINTS

It follows from what has been stated above that in the 1980s it was by improving the techniques of international plan coordination that one could have brought about some positive change. The earlier practice of cooperation in planning is characterized by a considerable discrepancy between formal potentialities and eventual outcomes.

This feature was probably most conspicuous in the contradiction between the traditionally strong endeavours to coordinate national structural policies (supported by a number of institutional forms of CMEA integration) on the one hand, and the moderate results achieved, on the other. This could be attributed to a number of factors, including a comparatively inadequate knowledge of the real economic situation of the individual CMEA states, partly due to the insufficiency of the information obtainable from public sources, and partly to the not infrequent confusion of the declarative, with the factual, elements of statements and publications. Former international agreements on information policies among CMEA countries, promoted the more or less successful filtering out of pronouncements which might be onesided, perhaps offensive to national or other sentiments, or might be interpreted as interference with the internal affairs of another socialist state. Meanwhile they also contributed to the comparatively backward state of the scientific knowledge of the socialist world economy. The resulting losses in information could only partly be made up by experiences gained through regular working contacts by management organs. That is why it proved to be so difficult to assess the real position and prospects of the partner states, which would have been of prime importance especially in the phase of preparation of national plans and international cooperation proposals, when the need to differentiate between desires, presentations and realities was probably the greatest.

This situation was particularly unfavourable when the traditional priority of trade policy, the unconditional promotion of increases in intra-regional trade flows at any cost, proved to be unsustainable because of foreign economic equilibrium and efficiency considerations or supply constraints of certain partners. The organization and the institutional setup of the international coordination of medium-term plans has remained much the same as it was under the conditions of a dynamic and extensive model of growth, when problems of efficiency, equilibrium and, more generally, the value aspect of CMEA trade, could be treated less meticulously. It was just these formerly neglected considerations that obtained high priority, so it was paradoxical that cooperation in planning continued to be insensitive to the value aspect of international exchanges, as it still formulated its aims in tons, metres and Kwh, while costs remained secondary for their inherent logic.

While the volatility of conditions outside and in the 1980s also inside Comecon has turned alternative planning into practice in a growing number of member states, the much criticized one-sided commercial bargaining character of cooperation in planning has not decreased. Rather, it has been on the increase as a result of the demonetization of integrational mechanisms. This was inevitable since demonetization leads to a growing number of decisions being made at ever higher levels. The self-propelling process of further centralization implied not only a more consistent and immediate implementation of the central will and of the public purpose, as it was frequently asserted, but also involved a forced takeover of inherently microeconomic responsibilities by the national central management organs. This was detrimental to their basic macroeconomic planning functions. And if a central planning organ is overburdened with looking after elementary microeconomic tasks, time and energy are bound to be short for the elaboration of alternative variants for macroeconomic cooperation. However, while business administration requires the greatest possible concreteness and maximum attention to small details, alternative macroeconomic planning needs distancing onself from the *status quo*, preparation for unusual, unconventional but discernible future developments, abstraction and even free imagination. This is not just a matter of mentality, but also of organization. In alternative planning (especially if it is in value rather than physical terms) the degree of long-term predetermination expressed in physical terms is comparatively small so as to maintain room for manoeuvring and for flexible adjustment to changing conditions. Under former CMEA conditions, however, it was useful to attain maximum predetermination in physical terms, to aim at the meticulous elaboration of all the details of the complex set of interdependent deliveries and counterdeliveries, and, if possible, to conclude the maximum number of detailed, compulsory interstate agreements. The aim was to minimize insecurity of supplies as well as to attain equivalence in exchange even in the absence of real convertible currency.

It is obvious that the realities of the tendencies to increasingly rigid and insecure intra-CMEA supply ran counter to the theoretical requirements of a more open, more flexible, monetized approach to national economic planning, one that would be oriented to improving the adjustment performance of the East European countries. On the one hand, the practice of cooperation in planning "overdetermined" some economic processes which, optimally, should be decided upon at the given moment. On the other hand, it supplied a false feeling of security—through the existence of formally binding agreements—even in those cases when objective preconditions for such security simply did not exist. That is why any disruption of supplies caused so many problems. From the point of view of a comprehensive reform, these processes adversely influenced the qualification and also the skills of specialists employed in central planning. Skills in business administration and knowledge of technicalities have been appreciated, while abilities to forecast, analyze, and comprehend macroeconomic and general interrelationships have been undervalued, and so was receptiveness to new ideas and solutions. This has developed into an independent barrier to major change.

The above processes have been adverse influences also on the soundness of the earlier cooperation in planning, as they discounted any attempt to see the projects of CMEA partners in another context that of a business offer (e.g. in its reality as a macroeconomic prognosis). One consequence of this has been the inability of the planning cooperation to adjust flexibly and organically to any prompt or major change among the factors presumed when drawing up the plans. Adaptation could be instituted only through invoking government-level-operative interference, i.e. in a sluggish manner, just in a period when the frequency of such changes was on the increase.

Since cooperation in planning remained insensitive to changes in the financial sphere, the probability that bilateral trade policy considerations will overtake priorities of general economic policy is growing. This could disequilibrate any given economy. A deficit in the foreign economic sphere had to bring about adjustment measures, the latter thwarting earlier coordinated plans (based upon bilateral trade policy considerations).

From this it follows that it is underdeveloped state of market relations, the resulting lags, and the hidden or distorted forms of reconciling conflicting interests that has brought about the increased insecurity in national planning and also in the planned foreign trade turnover.[19] This was the prime cause of the growing suspicion among national management organs, who have increasingly had to cope with daily business problems. This has led to a level of international coordination of major structural decisions which is even below the level justified by restraining conditions.

This boils down to the finding that it is the typical shortcomings of physical directive planning that have been recurring on the international level. Decisions following from its inherent logic, however incontestable as they are "in themselves", run increasingly counter to the tendencies and requirements of the world markets.

In his thought-provoking article the Soviet economist Sheinin (1982) raised the idea of the CMEA countries' subjecting their relations with the world market to the regional coordination of medium-term plans. In my judgement, it could have been the inversion of this idea that might have brought about results. What is needed is the reforming of the organization and methods of regional planning cooperation in accordance with the requirements of the transformations in the world economy. Until it does come about, cooperation in planning should have taken the tendencies and results of CMEA participation in the global division of labour as a starting point, and concentrated its efforts on activities resulting in a tangible improvement in this position. This could mean primarily joint export-oriented projects, harmonization of structural policies according to the requirement of adjustment to the world market rather than other criteria, and finally, modifications aiming at a restitution of the inherent macroeconomic functions of planning. There could be a great many possibilities. Strengthening the role of analyses of trends of development at the expense of detailed accounts of individual activities and of the surveillance of the production of a large number of products. An improvement of the quality, and a parallel decrease of the quantity, of information supplied for the preparation of macroeconomic plans. Exchange of more substantial information on economic policy priorities. A better preparation for consultations on economic policy. The development of all institutional forms that can promote microeconomic contacts, such as the better organization of technical documentation, a more active role for trade and diplomatic representatives in the organization of business deals and the supplying of relevant business information. Finally a radical improvement of information concerning the state of the economy in individual CMEA countries, which is also a general common policy objective.

These and a number of similar measures could bring about palpable results. However, they do not allow the circumvention of the basic issues. In an international mechanism of regional cooperation based on the physical planning model, it is impossible to create an inherent enterprise interest in technological change, in product innovation, in the spread of the marketing approach. In the process of adjustment to the world economy—partly as a result of new trends in technological progress, and reflecting decentralized rather than centralized forms of enterprise organization—the role of local initiative is on the increase, and this cannot be replaced by anything else. As the national systems of economic management of individual CMEA states did not realize this requirement in institutional reform, the unreformed, traditional model of CMEA cooperation—itself a product of the period of extensive growth, embargo and isolationalism—was confined to patterns which were alien to the needs of these countries. This regional system of cooperation can only become more successful and more competitive than it was in the 1970s if it undergoes a thorough reform. Reform is also urged by the radical transformation of the internal set of conditions of East European cooperation, as the preservation of insufficient export performance brought about continued restriction and shrinking reproduction. Only a renewed CMEA could have efficiently served the institution's main declared objective, i.e. to contribute to the growth and competitiveness of the member states.

This brings us to our conclusion. The problem of the market could not be circumvented in regional international cooperation either. Development of regional international market relations is a precondition for a qualitative improvement of cooperation in planning and also for the harmonization of structural policies. It had been the introduction of the regulated market which could enable the CMEA to become a truly integral part of the world economy and enable its members to be more successful than their growing number of competitors have been.

NOTES

1 For elaboration of this point, see Csaba 1980.
2 This was met with pressure from protectionist interest groups, as could be seen from the successful attempts to launch colour T.V. production separately in the GDR, Poland, Czechoslovakia and Hungary in the early

1980s, although it was obvious from the very outset that none of these could aspire for success in international competition.

3 This is a lesson learned also from the economic history of the 1930s.

4 In the quotation, instead of "because" the word "although" would be justified in my view.

5 As is known, Hungarians deemed a 25–30 percent share desirable (Nyers 1975, pp. 14 and 17).

6 However, it is of major significance that these provisions were re-stated in a different international environment, despite endeavours to the contrary.

7 In the context of economic reforms it was logical that the idea of switching the CMEA over to a regulated market model was formulated in a number of East European states, as mirrored in the proceedings of an international conference on price theory held in Budapest in 1967 (Földi and Kiss 1969). Although only a few years passed from this conference to 1971, a series of major events took place in Eastern Europe. For instance, beside the Hungarian reform, the Polish riots of March 1968 and December 1970; the collapse of the "structural policy" and economic reform concept of the GDR by mid-1970; and last but not least, the Czechoslovak events, leading to a change in the leadership of the CPC in December 1967 and April 1969. The 23th Session of the CMEA was also convened in late April 1969, in the declining phase of the life-cycle of the reforms. The May, 1968 Plenum of the CC of the CPSU made the end of support by the Brezhnev leadership for internal economic reforms in the USSR obvious. So in 1971, the majority of the signatories to the Comprehensive Programme were trying to find alternatives to the reforms of the 1960s.

8 See the much disputed article by Sorokin 1969.

9 Author's translation from the Russian original.

10 The contemporary official Bulgarian position was that the range of the problems to become subject to regional coordination should be even narrower, and encompass only the most important of those projects that were directly related to intraregional cooperation (Stoyanov 1983).

11 For a detailed list of some of the new (post-1980) parallel developments, see Mosóczy 1983.

12 This was far from being an attempt to "export" Hungarian solutions, as it is sometimes misrepresented to have been. Analyzing Bulgarian and Soviet literature, Lányi 1976 correctly pointed out that several Soviet economists favouring the concept of converging national mechanisms, in fact, wanted to provide an additional "international" argument for supporting the monetization of the Soviet economy, which they deemed necessary anyway.

13 Author's translation from the original Russian edition of the article.

14 The eminent Czech economist unambiguously implied that the contemporary Hungarian practice fell short of the conditions of his model; so it would have been completely unsound to consider the extension of the Hungarian model of planning.

15 This point may provoke a great deal of justified discussion. For my views, see Csaba 1983 and 1987.

16 The interpretation of convergence as even a partial unification of national management methods was flatly rejected also by a leading expert of the

GDR, Professor Christa Luft, speaking at an international seminar devoted to the topic. For a review of the seminar, see Kogan 1983, pp. 158–159.

17 Romanian authors repeatedly rejected any concept of convergence of the national mechanisms, emphasizing that the choice of a planning model is an integral part of economic sovereignty. For this decision "the party of the respective nation is responsible exclusively to its own working class" (Ionescu 1983). Instead, they advocate top-level discussion and the solution of the practical problems of CMEA cooperation which have been raised by the Romanians in May 1980.

18 It is not without interest to note that the Soviet foreign trade regulations in force from January 1987, still contained similar practical provisions. Cf. O merakh 1986a.

19 Sometimes the existence of parallel shortages is suggested as a prime cause. From the very concept of a plan as a picture of the future, however, foresight of these and so the possibility of timely action would follow. As it is possible to prepare for foreseen difficulties, insecurity should decrease rather than increase.

CHAPTER SEVEN

Economic policy and planning in the CMEA

The general theory of regional economic integration draws heavily on the experience of market integration within the European Communities. This one-sidedness has become conspicuous for developing countries, when living under fundamentally different historical, social and economic conditions, they attempted forming integrational groupings of their own, relying on generally accepted theses.

From the basic systemic point of view, the CMEA was an integration based more or less on opposite principles to those of the EC. Primacy of macroeconomic planning, integration through coordination of the foreign trade section of national plans, maintenance of economic sovereignty, inclusion of the largest political power of the military alliance to which most of the members belong, continued attempts at self-reliance within the nation states and also within the region—these have been the major characteristics of this alternative type of integration. Since the concept of planned versus free market economy has always been an important subject of controversy, it is probably inevitable that a predominant part of the professional literature on the CMEA has been directly ideological, trying to prove the superiorty or conversely the inferiority of integration through planning. In the following chapter attention will be focussed on how national economic policies have been coordinated, and what the role of planning in dovetailing divergent interests was. It might also be instructive to contemplate what state economic and political activity is able to deliver and what not, and under what conditions. Last but not least, obviously a number of problems similar to the ones in the EC have also emerged. The differences in the ways of articulating interests and in the ways of solving conflicts might draw attention to similar issues in and outside the region.

PLANNED DEVELOPMENT ON A REGIONAL SCALE,
OR THE LACK OF INTEGRATIONAL STRATEGY?

Coordination of economic policies with the Soviet Union has always been a determining feature in the development of the integration of the East European countries over that last four decades. This followed from a number of factors. The common structural characteristics of the economic and political systems; the hegemony of Marxism—Leninism as the established official ideology in each of these states;[1] the similar or—at times—even identical structural policies aiming at catching up with the-most advanced industrial powers of the world; and last but not least, the regularly concerted activities in extra-economic areas, such as defence, information policy, foreign policy and state security.[2] Harmonization of the latter took place partly in the framework of the Cominform from 1947 to 1956, when this institution was abolished, but primarily at bilateral meetings of the Communist Party of the Soviet Union with other ruling communist parties. Since 1955, besides the continued dominance of the bilateral fora it has been the Warsaw Treaty Organization (WTO) that has provided a multilaterial framework for coordinating strategies and action.[3] All this has obviously led to a high degree of similarity in, and interdependence among, economic strategies, irrespective of the formal institutional framework of the synchronization of planning-and economic policy decisions. As is well known, the Council for Mutual Economic Assistance as a multilateral organ for cooperation played a pretty marginal role till 1956. These were the very years, however, when that specific, radial interdependence evolved between the Soviet economy and the East European ones, which still forms the underlying structure of their integration. Exchanging Soviet fuels and raw materials for East European manufactures and other finished products has been the determining factor in the economic development of the small CMEA states over the last forty years.

Coordinated paths of development were demonstrably present in the investment policy priorities of the East European countries in the 1950s and 1960s (Bauer 1981). Similarly parallel features can be seen in their lagging adjustment to the epochal transformations in the world economy, and in their defensiveness throughout the 1970s and also in the first half of the 1980s. With detailed analysis it can be proven (Csaba 1983) that this is not mere coincidence. In setting national priorities, in trends of macroeconomic management methods, and also in the ways economic policy choices were made in individual

CMEA countries, professed similarities have been present. In explaining these, however, it would be inexpedient to abstract from the common features of the institutional system of the respective countries. On the other hand, the thesis that not only systemic, but policy-making similarities and even coordination have been present is easy to substantiate by a mere survey of the milestones of the postwar economic history of the East European countries. At the end of the 1940s, the reorientation of commercial relations and the introduction of mandatory planning. In 1949–53, the Stalinist policy of forced (heavy) industrialization. Renewed similarities between 1953–57 in launching the Malenkovian "New Course" and later its termination in more or less open reform discussion. The Great Leap Forward in Eastern Europe,[4] as expressed in the Seven-Year Plans for 1958–65 and their collapse between 1961–63. The experiments with overhauling the economic mechanism went parallel between 1963–69, though admittedly with significant national differences. In the 1970s, each country followed reform-substituting policies, increasing the rate of investments to maintain growth and recentralizing economic decision-making. But, as shown in Chapter 5, the existence of a world economic opening can be statistically proved only in the Soviet Union (over and above the processes of the 1960s). Finally, striking similarities were present in their defensive reaction to world economic changes in the 1980s: the dominant role of import restrictions, slowing down growth; and further centralization combined with limited new possibilities for the small-scale sector, in the hope of managing the country's shaken liquidity position and domestic disequilibria. It is, naturally, beyond the scope of the present analysis to produce empirical evidence and detailed substantiation for the above conclusions. However, the mere enumeration of the most important points may sufficiently illustrate that what has been going on in the East European economies is far more than a series of occasional or random coincidences. To put it directly, similarities are based on the (in many ways) parallel features, of their real economic situations ensuing in similar pressures and challenges, and on the parallel features of their economic and political systems, which have led to similar decisions, despite the dissimilarities in their natural conditions, factor endowments, historical background, etc.[5] This has been supplemented and reinforced by direct regional coordination, whose form and intensity can and does vary.

The above recapitulation of these basic interrelationships might seem a commonplace to many, still it is not entirely unwarranted.

Discussing a narrower, but very topical issue, the coordination of the economic policies of the East European countries with the Soviet Union in the framework of various institutions of the CMEA in the 1980s, even leading scientific authorities and practising experts have voiced the opinion[6] that in fact, we could not speak of a proper integrational policy within the CMEA. This statement was substantiated by referring to regularly recurring parallel priority development projects in industry that have been complemented by the less frequently mentioned but no less important national endeavours at self-reliance in agriculture from the mid-1970s on. Uncoordinated, parallel industrial development in the nations of the region was first subject to criticism at the 1956 Session of the CMEA. Since then, there has hardly been a Council Session that did not have this question on its agenda.

The choice of parallel industrial priorities again evident in the fourth wave of industrialization in the 1980s was paradoxical, as the CMEA was an integration primarily in planning—not in production or of markets, as is sometimes erroneously maintained. The basic method of connecting individual national economies used to be the determination of intraregional trade flows through the compulsory dovetailing of the socialist (regional) foreign trade sections of the macroeconomic plans. Compared to this, direct relations among producers and even more among national markets have been secondary, dependent variables (depending on coordination of plans). The concept of planning, historically and also logically, involves negating *ex post* market regulation by the invisible hand, and by definition means the *ex ante* formulation of the major trends and proportions of future development. Thus integration in planning should, at least in theory, lead to a much closer *ex ante* synchronization of national development paths than in previous decades. However, the moment we look at planning as it is in reality rather than as an abstract idea, in place of a transcendental omnipotent centre—itself the embodiment of the public purpose—we find a process of harmonizing the conflicting interests of a large number of participants. Even within a small country like Hungary, in the course of planning continuous conflict goes on among institutional, territorial, sectoral, local, social and other particular group interests. Among the plethora of hierarchically and vertically dependent and interdependent actors, more or less open and continuous parallel bargains were reached about plans, about overall and special financial conditions, about state regulation of prices, about income redistribution and about investment possibilities. It follows from the very nature of this practice that contrary to the majority conviction in socialist planning theory, the presence and the significant role of *ex post* regulatory processes is not only possible, but also inevitable. Practical experience in CMEA countries over the past four decades provides more empirical evidence for this conclusion than any abstract theorizing could. If the process of planning is in fact a form of continuous coordination of conflicting interests even within a small nation state, then this must hold *a fortiori* in a regional grouping of sovereign states. The presence—and even the occasional predominance—of *ex post* regulation that is easily demonstrable with the long-term comparison of planned and actual figures of the CMEA countries (Bauer 1981; and Csaba 1983), does not, however, invalidate the theoretical distinctiveness of a planned economy from a market economy. From the practical point of view, these two systemic models continue to denote in a condensed form two characteristically different modes of the economy's functioning. The validity of this thesis is not discounted by the fact that the empirical *modus operandi* of any planned or of any market economy bears very little resemblance to the simplistic textbook models, and occasionally not much more to detailed scientific theories.

Analogously, the obvious fact that the CMEA countries have not managed to avoid recurring parallel priorities through the international coordination of their plans does not disprove the presence of synchronization. Lack of success in this area is due to the chronically weak elaboration of foreign economic strategies, as well as to the subordinate role of the foreign trade sector in overall macroeconomic planning. (It is subservient to national structural policy concepts and relegated to filling the bottlenecks in physical balances.) Within an individual national economy, regular and significant discrepancies, between planned and actual values of investments or of other macroeconomic indicators may reflect either arbitrary ways of setting priorities, or the limits of the existing concrete methods of central regulation in the given area. Or, they might simply be the reflection of the limits of central intervention as such, (a possibility insistently denied not so much by theorists as by practising planners). Whenever discrepancies tend to grow and/or to stabilize in the longer run, some combination of the following alternative conclusions is drawn concerning the methods of planning and regulation:

—either their technique of implementation or their area of application is inadequate;

—individual plan objectives or elements of financial regulation are not in tune with the overall policies of the centre, or with its priorities followed in a related area;

—they get subordinated to other, more important regulations or priorities, or to some by-products of these (as in practice it does not happen that all compulsory indicators were obligatory to the same degree, i.e. involved the same sanctions);

—the deal between conflicting interests struck during the elaboration and finalization of the plan document (or of the regulatory system) has been invalidated by a significant change in the original balance of forces, and this has resulted in a radically different course of implementation;

—during the elaboration of the plan only a formal rather than substantial coordination of interests had taken place. Interests that were considered non-existent or had been unilaterally suppressed by the centre later exerted a hidden but efficient influence on the course of implementation, so that the central organs were unable to counteract them.

These and other possible conclusions do not mean at all that central regulation exists only as an intention. In a system of interdependent institutions and (economic) management tiers, of rulers and ruled, bargaining is not conducted among equal partners, and cannot be modelled along the rules of game theory.

It is the hierarchical subordination among the different management levels that dominates horizontal relations, behavioural norms, and so the bargains themselves. Economic self-regulatory processes are not separated from the ruling (political) hierarchy. Rather, all people in the higher echelons of enterprise and the entire ministerial management are constituent parts of the ruling state and party hierarchy at the lower levels as well. This formally total—practically the only significant—dependency also dominates horizontal self-regulatory processes. It creates specific behavioural norms and specific possibilities for the attainment of particular interests, and leads to a peculiar *modus operandi* even outside the direct scope of hierarchical control.

From the above it also follows that any "really existing" socialist planned economy differs not only from a (postulated) free market economy, but also from a mixed one. Its mode of functioning is basically dissimilar even from that of the most *dirigiste* welfare state. In the latter, the principles of market regulation prevail in the majority non-state sector, whose distributional effects are mitigated through income regulation, and in the nationalized sectors. In the planned economies of the CMEA, the role of the market has remained supplementary even after the reforms, and the basic success indicator for economic agents has remained the satisfaction of the higher control organs, not that of the customer.

The recurring parallel priorities in the industrial structural policies of the CMEA countries are indicative only of the inadequacy of the methods, the institutions, or the objectives of regional cooperation. It is absolutely no proof of the alleged lack of attempts at coordination, or of the lack of an overall coordinating strategy (Bialer 1984, p. 150). Still less is it evidence of lack of political-level endeavours at expanding the scope of regional coordination, even before its purposes, ways, instruments and conditions have been unambiguously clarified in scientific and regional political fora. Nevertheless, it is a widespread conviction that the divergence of national priorities (Götz 1983), and/or the lasting differences in national economic management systems (Bautina et al. 1983), *ab ovo* preclude, or at least seriously limit, any earnest measure to harmonize national economic policies.

National economic priorities are naturally dissimilar in the CMEA just as they differ in the EC, or in any other regional grouping. It would, however, be erroneous to blame this factor for parallel structural priorities. It has been proven long ago in the economic literature (Ausch 1972) that it is the common, rather than the different, features of the national economic mechanisms of the CMEA countries—e.g. their inward-looking, autarkic and demonetized character and the consequent frequent subjective differences in the national tax, subsidy and price systems—that hinder more intensive regional cooperation. It has also been demonstrated in the previous chapter that it is the lack of a well functioning international market that is the major obstacle to the efficient harmonization of the priorities of the various nations. In other words, it is the inherent logic of mandatory planning, i.e. trying to cure every ill through increased centralization and through proliferating obligatory instructions, that time and again comes up against the political and economic realities of the region, and national sovereignty. The latter takes the form of national economic interests expressed mostly in national monetary categories. With the national currencies being inconvertible, however, the possibility of comparing these, and subsequently the propensity to reach a compromise, is limited. On the one hand, the mandatory planning model used to prevail in the great majority of the Comecon states, which *ab ovo* precluded the introduction of the market model of integration and thus the use of a convertible currency of any kind. On the other hand, the same national decision-making authorities that opposed the monetization and marketization of the domestic economic systems vetoed time and again all attempts at the administrative streamlining of regional cooperation according to the needs of the directive model. For obvious reasons, they were the staunchest adversaries of the recurring concepts of supranational planning, joint planning and "international economic policy". The more centralized the national decision-making system is the greater the number of prerogatives they stand to lose. It is not by chance that in the last twenty years the GDR and Romania have been most heavily engaged in fighting both the marketization and the joint planning concepts.

International economic policy, planned development on a regional scale and even joint planning exist as an exception rather than as a rule.[7] However, the two-tier national and regional level import-substituting policy (Köves 1985) that has been followed in an internationally coordinated way for decades has produced production capacities, skills, behavioural norms, motivations and standards that could not have developed either with the continuation of the interwar period, or with a world market oriented, export-led growth concept. Regular and lasting participation in CMEA cooperation has moulded technological, organizational and marketing skills, and the attitudes, knowledge, and connections of enterprises that still exert a determining influence on the vast majority of East-European managers.

These skills and motivations are valid only in the national monopolistic markets and within the CMEA. They are mostly inconvertible to the competitive world markets, as they enable enterprise targets to be met even if performance lags behind international standards. From this it follows that there is a strong pressure at enterprise level to maintain, reproduce and expand the existing structures that have evolved under the umbrella of double protection. This tendency has become even more pronounced in the last decade, i.e. at a time when growing disequilibria in the convertible currency balance of payments should have induced most East-European economic policy makers to more intensive export-orientation. In the 1970s, when large enterprises, associations and combines already actively participated in the interstate synchronization of medium-term plans, for reasons detailed in Chapter 4, interfirm coordination "from below" frequently prevailed even over general economic or over national commercial policy deliberations. This is hardly a surprise from a systems theory point of view, since it is an established fact that in the course of plan bargains commands are, as a rule, elaborated by those who are to implement them.[8]

Thus it can be taken for granted that economic policies in the CMEA countries have developed as a result of multi-dimensional and multi-level immediate and indirect coordinating activity. True, the ways and means, the motives and results of this coordination bear little resemblance to the textbook view of how in a block of command economies, or in a commonwealth of selfless, ideally planned altruistic nations, things are or ought to be.

REGIONAL-LEVEL AUTARKY, OR SOMETHING ELSE?

Direct regional coordination had a decisive say in shaping the concrete paths and priorities of industrialization in Eastern Europe. This coordination moulded the basic structure of the intra-CMEA division of labour. Whole industries have been developed from the outset and more or less exclusively on the basis of Soviet fuels and raw materials, and manufacturing similarly exclusively for Soviet markets (over and above the all-out national import substitution). This fact dominates —although not exclusively, and together with systemic similarities— the technological level, orientation, plant organization and commercial techniques of the East-European industries. Major development projects of the GDR, Czechoslovakia, Poland, Hungary and Bulgaria provided ample evidence for this point. Moreover from 1976 on, the economies of Romania—despite the continuation of its specific foreign policy line—and also that of Yugoslavia, which is not a subject of the present book, have turned increasingly towards the CMEA. Trade with Comecon partners surpassed the 50 percent mark in the total trade of both nations in 1984 (the traditional norm of the late 60s being scarcely 30 percent). It is not without interest, especially in the post-1979 period when the second oil price hike and the war between its two main suppliers, Iraq and Iran, have drastically narrowed Romania's ability to import crude, to note that an even faster reintegration of the Romanian economy into the CMEA than actually took place was forestalled by factors other than the lack of political will on the part of the country's leadership. These factors are: the energy bottleneck in intra-CMEA trade coupled with a lull in the demand for mediocre manufactures; the falling international competitiveness of Romanian industrial output; and the market restriction of its main element, i.e. investment goods, by the overall recession of (planned) demand across the whole region. With the radically changing structure of the demand of the largest regional buyer, the Soviet Union, in 1986–90 this trend only intensified.

It is also worth mentioning that Romanian economic diplomacy, having played an initiatory role in convening the June, 1984 Moscow Summit Meeting of the CMEA, has been aiming at regional self-sufficiency on a much wider scale than any other member state, including the Soviet Union. According to the former Romanian concept (Dăscălescu 1983), regional self-sufficiency should not have been confined to those strategically sensitive areas that were stressed by all Soviet sources. It should also have included the whole agriculture and food complex, all high-tech industries, the whole of machine-building, industrial consumer goods as well as the entire fuel and raw materials sector. In the Soviet view, as has been repeatedly voiced, it is not feasible and thus not desirable to attempt regional self-reliance in the energy and raw materials sector. The Romanian standpoint was the reflection of the autarkic concepts that economic policy-making followed in that country. On the other hand, it is quite commonplace in the world economy for lagging behind countries to try and compensate for competitive losses with successes in a "softer" regional market.

This marked change in Romanian foreign economic policy since 1979 that was in contrast to the more or less unchanged overall foreign policy line is indicative of endeavours to coordinate the economic policies of the CMEA countries much more closely than before. The abundant literature of the 1980s is divided as to the beginning, the motives for, as well as the substance of, this closer coordination. A good deal of misunderstanding has evolved from the misinterpretation of three different types of Comecon documents. There are decisions reached at the community level; the official standpoint of the individual member states; and the personal views and individual proposals published in the specialized and daily press of the various countries. Only those documents can be considered as CMEA integration documents which have been unanimously approved by all the member states. Speeches by Prime Ministers at the Council Sessions, and the various commentaries on these, express the different interests, approaches and standpoints of the respective states. These are obviously dissimilar both from one another and from the "compromise" joint document that represents the common body of the various opinions—although without a considerable overlap it would hardly be possible to come to a mutually acceptable conclusion. Such national statements, however, must not be interpreted as the views of the entire grouping (although the press habitually acts as if they were). Finally, publications in the third group are written by authors of different competence, position and convictions, who unfold their understanding of the past and their proposals for the future with varying degrees of official blessing. The scope of these varies in time and also by country, but despite the bad habits fuelled by the daily press, these—even in case of the Soviet Union—can never be considered as an official position taken by a member state (let alone the community). Official standpoints are stated in documents of the second category or other suitable forms such as communiqués, official bulletins, and those agency dispatches that bear the appropriate sign of direct officialdom. Further verbal information is provided by the authorized representatives of the member states at bilateral and multilateral fora of consultation. It might well be useful to note that this book falls into the third category.

As far as the first group of documents is concerned, it seems appropriate to remember that none of the joint documents approved since 1978 (contained anything in favour of an overall inward-looking integration policy. On the contrary. Each of them contain explicit pledges in the interest of expanding extraregional trade contacts, specifically referring to East—West trade. This feature was the most pronounced in the documents published after the 1984 Economic Summit (Documents, 1984): the declaration on international affairs contains this position no less than four times. This supports the conclusion that in integration policy as defined above in the narrower sense, there was not a single overall inward-looking CMEA decision, and even less any talk about an overall seclusive line. This thesis is not weakened by the fact that apart from a large number of publications advocating defensive adjustment strategies, at the Council Sessions of 1982 and 1983, some regional import-substituting programmes were adopted, and that at the 1984 Havana and 1985 Warsaw Sessions further projects of the same type were discussed.[9] Among the common industrial programmes the most publicized ones were the extension of a longstanding computer programme, the project on microelectronics and on robots, i.e. areas that seemed most prone to be embargoed on political and military grounds. It is worth noting that Soviet analysts writing on this subject almost never tried to make a virtue out of necessity. Rather, they stressed that the import-substituting projects were forced on the community by outside developments (Goryunov 1984), and that such projects touched not the entire economy, but only the areas that appeared directly endangered by Western embargo practices (Ultanbaev 1984). It is also remarkable that even those Soviet analyses that were published after December 1979, but before the announcement of the 1985 US—Soviet Summit in Geneva, have never denied the absolute necessity of expanding East—West relations in the economic sphere (unlike in some other areas).

Besides the approval of East—West economic relations, an important qualifying notion started spreading after the 1984 Economic Summit: the concept of technological and economic invulnerability *(neuyazvimost')*. This parlance—in contrast to the earlier talk of "independence" *(nezavisimost')*—reflects clearly that the aim was not autarky, but the promotion of that certain level of development that is the minimum requirement for technological exchanges based on the equality of the partners. More exactly, development is a technical requirement for the efficient use of the most advanced technologies. "Invulnerability must be increased", noted a group of officials and researchers commissioned by the CMEA Secretariat. "Not as if the share of East—West trade were excessive in the total trade of some member states, but because the present one-sided dependence on imports of raw materials, agricultural products and semi-finished products reflects the weaknesses of the domestic economic structures" (Stoilov et al. 1984, p. 108). Accordingly already in 1983–84, several publications appeared in the Soviet professional literature, which analyzed the international debt situation in a sober way, elaborated practical possibilities of how to expand East—West credit relations, and vigorously countered the then fashionable misconceptions of "credit dependence", "credit-pressure" and "one-way credit relations". An article that appeared in the monthly usually reflecting the views of the Soviet Ministry of Foreign Affairs argued as follows: Instead of voicing apocalyptic visions of the fate of the international monetary system, CMEA countries should concentrate on finding further financing for their development projects, as they do have that prerogative since their indebtedness was far from dramatic by international comparison (Shmelyov 1984). It is noteworthy that authoritative economists of the GDR voiced similar ideas, arguing with unprecedented vigour in favour of overall export-orientation; instead of the usual reservations they depicted this course as a must (Nötzold 1983). The Poles rejoined the IMF in August 1986. No further comment is thus needed on the 1982–83 concepts of reorienting Polish trade to the CMEA. Thus, despite statements by certain

Soviet public figures frequently appearing in international fora and/or drawing disproportionate media coverage, both the analyses of the trends in Soviet—Western trade in the post-1979 period and the authoritative joint CMEA programmes equally disprove all statements which purport to establish a change in the CMEA countries' commitment to maintaining and expanding extraregional economic relations, in fact at a rate which surpasses intraregional turnover. The ideological warfare notwithstanding, there are ever-growing indications that most of the East European countries continue to be reliable partners to all realistic and balanced Western and Southern concepts of economic cooperation.

True, unexpected drastic turnabouts in international politics —much less probable these days than in the 1981–84 period when daily confrontations persisted and kept intensifying—may bring about a somewhat inward-looking CMEA development. This, however, would run counter to the interests of all European nations. True, the international competitiveness cyclical prospects of the East European economy remained less than promising for the second half of the 1980s, and this puts a constraint on the national and integrational outward-looking strategies. It is also true that the maintenance of obsolete institutional forms and planning methods has resulted in the insufficient development (and occasionally, as in the case of the GDR, USSR and Czechoslovakia, in the explicit deterioration) of the international competitiveness of CMEA industrial exports, primarily of manufacturing. This reinforced the defensive adjustment policies of import-restriction which followed in the 1978–84 period. This is all the more important, as these objective economic processes and the improvised, reflex-like reaction to them have actually lead spontaneously to further decreasing the already low international trade participation of the CMEA countries, without any central decision.[10]

A closer examination of the harmonization of economic policies within the CMEA will show that the process of harmonization began during the debates preceding the annual Council Sessions. Political level final decisions were reached here and at the bilateral talks among party leaders. In these discussions, a continuous and long-term synchronization of interests took place at various bilateral and multilateral fora, and new decisions were based on sets of earlier concluded agreements. For the evolution in the 1980s, it was the 1978 Bucharest Session that constituted a milestone. The decisions at this session did away with the extreme proposals aiming at a ten to fifteenfold multiplication of the sums earmarked for joint CMEA projects between 1973–76. Such proposals—as shown in Chapter 4, unresolved technical and financial issues notwithstanding—would have led to partial supranational mandatory planning in the five priority areas of the Long-Term Target Programmes.

As Long-Term Target Programmes, as a rule, have not led to increased Soviet supplies of fuels and raw materials to East Europe —except for natural gas[11]— and could not even secure the maintenance of the supply level of the late 1970s in respect of essential items such as crude oil, they have left no doubt of the need for significant structural changes in the East European economies. Energy saving has become imperative both at enterprise and at national levels. On the one hand, the use of energy and material saving technologies has somewhat intensified; on the other hand, such formerly prestige sectors as petrochemistry and metallurgy have had to be restricted as part of the defensive adjustment in all small CMEA countries. This factor was also the driving force behind the expensive and inefficient large national (CMEA) import-substituting projects aiming at the better utilization of domestic natural resources, sometimes at any cost (i.e. serious environmental damages and efficiency losses notwithstanding). These have accounted for 40–45 percent of all industrial investments between 1981–85, and this ratio grew closer to 55 percent in the rest of the decade. (Its stagnation would already mean a great victory for macroeconomic efficiency.) Much smaller amounts were being spent on the development of less material and energy-intensive branches. In these areas national self-reliance and the concomitant parallel developments prevailed rather than regionally harmonized evolution.

In the resolution of the 1977 Council Session, two of the five long-term target programmes (LTP's) received priority treatment: energy and agriculture. Despite repeated appeals by the Bulgarian, Romanian and Hungarian delegations, measures to provide additional incentives for intraregional agricultural exports were not agreed upon,[12] although net importer countries pledged to do so in 1978. Thus the LTP for agriculture also set out from the primacy of national self-reliance. As the possible exports were determined by the surpluses of Bulgaria, Romania and Hungary, the demand was much greater than the potential supply, since the demand is a function of primarily the Soviet and Polish shortages.[13] It is, however, striking that details of this LTP were confined to agrotechnical and plant-organizational measures, to fish-processing and packaging, and there was hardly a word about expanding intraregional sales and its appropriate economic preconditions (Dolgosrochnaya ... 1982). So the Berlin Session of 1983 approved additional measures. These envisaged incremental supplies of fruits and vegetables, a better utilization of agricultural raw materials, the expansion of fishing, the modernization and wider use of up-to-date agrotechnology (Goryunov 1984), in other words constituted no change in the basic issues. The economic document approved by the 1984 Summit, however, took the position that energy and agricultural supplies are of equal "hardness", so incremental sales in one area are a function of similar increments in the other. The acceptance of agricultural exports being of equal hardness was a sign of a change in the attitude of the net importing countries. What exactly this meant in practice was to be elaborated at the coordination of plans for 1986–90.

Experience, including the two Council Sessions following the Summit, indicated that there have been certain attitudinal changes in evaluating the agrosector in general: each member state was in favour of increasing intraregional supplies. However, the communiqués issued after the Havana and Warsaw Sessions reflect a change in emphasis: the equal evaluation of energy with agricultural sales had been modified. Similarly to the post-1977 period, questions of (the security of) energy supplies have come to the fore, while agricultural sales have been relegated to the background. For instance, at the Havana Session, several cooperation projects were proposed, including joint investments whose costs would have ranged between 45 to 55 billion transferable rubles (Štrougal 1985), ten times the nominal sum spent between 1981–85 for the same purposes. Each of the proposed investments involved the raw materials and energy sector, and none the agricultural. In the communiqué issued from the Warsaw Session, the problem of agricultural incentives was not even mentioned (although the subject was raised in the debates). Accordingly, in the course of coordination of plans it turned out that, e.g., Hungarian agricultural sales would be accepted as counterdeliveries for energy less and less (Kovács Gy. 1985).

It also has become clear that net importers were supportive of neither the idea of joint investments in agriculture for incremental intraregional exports (the idea of the Summit document), nor of the idea of a preferential agro-price system which has been raised several times with reference to EC practice. Moreover, the possibilities of sales for convertible currency were also on the decrease because of the overall hard currency shortage in the region. Consequently new investments in the agriculture of net exporting countries could not be substantiated with a general reference to intraregional shortages in these products, and regional exports for transferable rubles should not have been increased without creating the appropriate additional economic incentives. The macroeconomic efficiency of East European agriculture is on a very low level, and the high proportion of convertible currency inputs is also a factor to be compensated for.

ALTERNATIVE IDEAS FOR INTEGRATION IN THE SECOND HALF OF THE 1980S

The above summarized fate of the priority LTPs, unfavourable developments in the international arena, and the growing and in many respects common difficulties of the member states induced CMEA countries to search for new ways and methods of harmonizing their economic policies in the early 1980s. They linked this with the idea of convening an Economic Summit, the first since 1969. I have surveyed these far-reaching political and professional initiatives and their possible outcomes in the preceding chapter, so let me confine myself here to some basic interrelationships.

It will be clear from the above why it was Romania that had shown the greatest dissatisfaction with the working of the integration process. Romania has not succeeded in obtaining a resolute change in the functioning of the CMEA. What is more, in its three priority areas —agriculture, energy and finding new markets for manufactures—the situation within the country has further deteriorated. The paradoxical situation of the 1981–85 period was well reflected by the coexistence of the austerity policy—constructed and rigorously controlled by the IMF in the interest of maintaining the international solvency of the country—with the very ambitious Five Year Plan, which envisaged the repetition of the 7 percent per annum NMP growth performance of the 1976–80 period (despite drastically deteriorating financing possibilities). The conflicting goals could not, of course, be simultaneously achieved, despite the jumbo loan of 1.5 billion US dollars extended by the IMF in July 1981, as a then unprecedented gesture towards a socialist debtor. However, the reluctant implementation of the adjustment policies, and the spillover effects of the Polish debt crisis, forced the country to reschedule in 1982 and also in 1983. International financing conditions thus took precedence over the extremely ambitious growth objectives of the Five Year Plan, whose fulfilment had proved impossible already by late 1982.[14] In 1980–85,

Romania reacted to these developments with a radical cutback in her Western trade relations. It had been planned, for instance, to pay back all debts by 1987, a target whose feasibility had been doubted by international bankers, but efforts at whose attainment were intensified in 1983–85 even at incredibly high costs. Despite the efforts, a new rescheduling in September 1986 could not be avoided (although the sum of gross debts had fallen significantly). Thus it is understandable that in Bucharest, a radical improvement of the functioning of the CMEA was considered as a basic condition of the restoration of the growth dynamics of the Romanian economy. No wonder that this country had been very active both in criticizing and in making new proposals for the overhaul of integration practice.

While in Romania attention had been focussed on the above-noted three commercial policy issues, the Soviet approach had been quite dissimilar. For a change, the difference did not extend to the question of national sovereignty, as the former Soviet concept placed a high value on national sovereignty. As far as ends and means were concerned, they proposed an opposite order to the Romanians. In Romania the basic restructuring of the institutional system of the CMEA, and the introduction of principally new integration methods, was seen to be possible only as a function of solving the practical problems they have raised (Badrus 1983). Soviet authors, however approached the issue the other way around. They interpreted the coordination of structural policies as a community-level joint answer to the challenge posed by the shortage of Soviet fuels and raw materials. In other words, as the specific East European adjustment process to the new Soviet real economic conditions. In their view (Shiryaev 1983), coordination would have enabled these nations to pay back their debts incurred in transferable rubles (TR), and safeguard them from American attempts to implant ideological controversies into technological and commercial relations. Every Soviet author attached prime importance to the technological and economic "independence" that was supposed to be achieved in all embargoed high-tech industries. In the pre-Summit preparatory discussions most Soviet authors were of the opinion that major institutional overhauls were needed to achieve a qualitative change in coordinating new investment priorities. The choice of foreign trade partners, sometimes even the domestic economic mechanisms, were to be harmonized or even converged (Bautina et al. 1983). True, the idea of converging national economic management systems *(sblizhenie)* was dropped from the agenda after the May 1983 Moscow meeting of the CC Secretaries in charge of the economy. Occasionally reappearing publications of this proposal[15] supported the idea only in general terms, promoted harmonization *"grosso modo"*, and criticized particular details of individual national practices only implicitly. To overcome what they found to be erroneous practices in some CMEA countries, the acceptance of common norms of socialist planning and of the multiplicity of national experimentation was proposed. In the Soviet Union—unlike in Romania—various concepts had been published as far as the intensity, the methods, the areas and even the purposes of economic policy coordination was concerned, implying significantly different consequences for practical policy making. A common feature of the Soviet positions was that in their view, the solution of practical problems was conditional on mastering theoretical issues, issues of principle. This would have entailed a radical overhaul of the model of intra-CMEA division of labour. In the evaluation of East—West relations, the differences have developed along new lines. While the issue of self reliance received similar treatment from the Bulgarians, the Romanians and the Soviets, their approach was not shared by the GDR and Hungary, nor by the majority of the Polish economists. It is also noteworthy that the furthest going (sometimes extreme) proposals to extend coordination, as well as to enhance the obligatory, binding character of joint decisions were voiced not by Soviet, but by some Bulgarian (Angelov 1982) and Czechoslovak (Henyš 1983) authors. Besides the earlier-mentioned duality of the Soviet view (which also included some support for expanding East—West ties), it is noteworthy that the Bulgarian earlier official view was that the economic policies of the CMEA countries had been in a state of coordination for years (Penchev 1984). This position was very critical of the major direct coordinative instrument of the 1970s, joint investments, which hardly implies unconditional enthusiasm for proposals to dramatically multiply the sums earmarked for this purpose. While besides Romania, it was the GDR that allotted absolute priority to securing the stability of energy supplies for TRs (Stoph 1984), there was a significant difference in the ways the two countries wanted to attain this objective. In Romania the earlier categorical refusal to grant investment contributions had been revised, and now the country was willing to extend investment credits for incremental fuel supplies (Dăscălescu 1984). However, well-informed GDR authors have been very critical of the practice of investment contributions. They emphasized that increasing the efficiency of national investments (in production and also in saving energy) rather than their increased international redistribution is most conducive to mastering the energy problem in Eastern Europe.[16]

What were the major issues for the harmonization of economic policy priorities of CMEA member state in the mid-80s? Two areas seem to be of major importance in this context: investments and foreign trade. In judging former proposals to coordinate national structural policy priorities through obligatory agreements and/or plan instructions, we must set out from the fact that it was not in the 1980s that these ideas were first raised. The institutional and economic barriers that had hindered development in this area in the past were by no means done away with. Until the establishment of the complicated set of preconditions for the functioning of a truly convertible currency on the international CMEA market, the real question is the very feasibility of a closer, more "rigorous" synchronization procedure than the one practised previously. Inevitably, under the earlier conditions there was no economically sound exchange rate either between the national currencies of the CMEA countries, nor between the respective national currencies and the TR, or between the TR and convertible currencies. Furthermore, national pricing, taxation, subsidy and monetary systems differed structurally from one another, and having no common denominator they did not allow for direct international comparison among them. In practice, however, there was a number of cases when conversion of one national currency into another cannot be evaded. For this purpose, two common methodologies have been invented, one for joint investments and the other for non-commercial (mainly tourist) settlements. Without my dwelling on the technical and practical difficulties of their implementation described in Chapter 1, suffice it to recall that there was no universally acceptable way of finding out the real efficiency of the cooperation variants. If the divergences from planned values were regularly no more significant than average, in the investment sphere the joint projects could be planned with no greater uncertainty than national ones. Even in this case, it could not be established whether the nominal profitability of a given project is a result of comparative advantages, or is an accidental product of the largely subjective differences in the national financial systems. As the international mechanism of CMEA cooperation has got increasingly demonetized in the post-1975 period, it was not possible to delegate these tasks to enterprises either. They possessed no better compass in their microeconomic decisions than the centre does. (They lack even the limited rationality of structural bilateralism that planners have as a means of measuring.) From this it also follows that unlike in market economies, in the CMEA there existed no company initiative to change existing structures radically. If such endeavours were nevertheless made, they were by no means better founded than the central planning decisions. The more a company knows about product-specific and microeconomic aspects, the less it knows about, and the less it is interested in, such vital national economic criteria as balance of trade and payments in the given bilateral relation, the quality of counter-deliveries and their timing, and so on. Since the CMEA was an integration in planning, advantages and disadvantages of international economic intercourse could only be judged at the macroeconomic level. Individual prices are derivatives of bargains among bilateral monopolies (monopsonies). They were not related to product quality or to scarcities, thus cannot be evaluated in their individuality, only as part of a structure established in this bargain. This is why more microeconomic knowledge provided no tradeoff for sacrificing the national economic point of evaluation. Consequently, intra-CMEA interfirm contacts can develop only after the monetary problems of the integration have been solved, but not parallel with this, and even less preceding (substituting) the overall reform process.

Enhancing the obligatory character of CMEA agreements used to be a frequent proposal. However, this step could hardly bring about results for two reasons. One is analogous with the practical evidence of the domestic economies having for decades proved unable to master the recurring serious difficulties in interfirm relations through "strengthening contractual discipline". Practically enforceable legal norms are unable, and not even meant to, countervail the chronic lack of economic self-interest in certain types of deals among horizontally related partners.[17] The other cause is related to the nature of international relations. Lack or loss of interest in a given deal, if it is reflected in a decision by a national organ of the executive, usually cannot be counteracted either by means of international civil law or of international public law for lack of enforceable sanctions (Balásházy 1984). (Supranationalism is not a viable option in the foreseeable future.) In the practice of interstate trade, problems of a lower level also still need to be solved. For instance, the issues of responsibility and sanctions have remained unresolved when interfirm contractual relations—themselves the derivatives of intergovernmental agreements—are disrupted by an operative intervention of the national administration in one of the countries (Meisel 1979, p. 165). Demonetization of the international mechanism of cooperation itself has become an independent cause of the growth of operative governmental interventions in trade relations, as there were no alternative means at hand to efficaciously secure equality in exchange. From this it follows that solving this practical problem should have been much more urgent than abstract theorizing about harmonized—certain authors say uniform—structural policies. The practical impact of the latter will continue to be negligible in the 1990s.

The other major area of synchronizing activities should have been foreign trade. Two aspects seem to be the determining factors in this comprehensive issue. On the one hand, it is not at all so obvious as is occasionally maintained (Bogomolov 1983b) that the more coordinated, the more efficacious the foreign trade policies of the CMEA states were. This would imply that joint action was always able to produce more results than separate national activities relying on the nation-specific opportunities in given areas. For instance not every CMEA country could aspire to get the preferential treatment the GDR enjoyed in the EC. Czechoslovakia could hardly attempt to get the status and benefits of a developing country that produces tangible customs preferences for Romania in the EC.

For methods of administrative coordination among national foreign trade policies both at micro and at macro levels, the points elaborated for structural policies are directly applicable. Moreover it is common knowledge that interstate harmonization is by definition based on the bottleneck principle, so the jointly acceptable platform is always determined by the party taking the most rigid position in the given question.

Coordinating foreign trade activities of national CMEA commercial organs on third (extraregional) markets is frequently advocated primarily by business executives, with reference to cartel agreements in the Western world. However, an elementary familiarity with the basics of economics should suffice for accepting the following proposition. A monopolistic *ex ante* segmentation of the market is feasible only if those party to the agreement together are in a price-making position. Otherwise such an agreement would only bring losses to all participants, until competitive rules break the "monopolistic" agreement. Since the joint market share of the CMEA countries amounts only to a few percent in the case of the vast majority of products, it is obvious that they will not in the future either be in a position to provide the comfort of monopolistic deals for their companies.

Harmonization among companies through purely economic means may indeed be hampered by the differences in national economic management systems. A Hungarian enterprise, working under the rules of "competitive" pricing[18] is likely to be deterred from giving in to the "temptation" of dumping its products at or below cost by pressures of profitability, which is not the case for a GDR or Romanian enterprise. In the traditional system of control, the producer is either ignorant of export prices, or the specialized foreign trade company automatically gets reimbursed from the Budget for its losses, provided it met quantitative export plan targets. Bonuses of enterprise management both in production and in trade are dependent on fulfilment of plan-targets, not on profits, so planned losses do not really matter. In harmonizing the activities of enterprises of two equally mandatorily planned economies, however, rigidities also are added together. Using the same type of "economic language", however, does not make up for the lack of interest in, and flexibility of, profitable foreign sales activities.

It is, in fact, in cooperation on third markets that CMEA countries could coordinate their foreign economic policies. As all member states are interested in activities resulting in convertible currency earnings, this is a promising field both in itself and as a transitory step towards a more outward-looking, export-oriented, integration model. This concept is closely related to the overall reform of the domestic economic mechanisms (the necessity of which is not a byproduct of the integration concept). Reforms would be necessary to enhance the overall competitiveness of the grouping—especially in manufacturing. A further promising area would be a joint offensive in the East-South division of labour. To this end, East European countries could implement coordinated measures to diminish their national and regional protectionism as well as to phase out their lagging behind industries, thus opening up their markets to the manufacturing exports of developing countries (Csaba 1983a). This could promote their joint adjustment to the world economy and would enable them to change the present patriarchal pattern of the East-South division of labour. In this context, Eastern Europe has yet to catch up to the North American states.

Elaborating more flexible forms of cooperation and their successful implementation would require more intensive cooperation from the CMEA member countries, which at present follow various priorities and various management methods. It was precisely because of the inevitable, but in any case lasting, nature of these differences that the idea of coordinating national economic policies in the late 1980s and beyond made sense.

SOME FEATURES OF THE POST-SUMMIT INTEGRATION PRACTICE

Documents approved by the June 1984 Moscow Summit of the CMEA countries contain those political decisions that circumscribed the concrete ways and means of harmonization.[19] The Economic Summit was an event of great political significance. It expressed a fact that has frequently been called into question by the various extremes of political journalism: the dialectics of unity and differences. The Summit served primarily as a demonstration of the political togetherness of the CMEA members. This, however, bears little—resemblance to the monolithism of the 1950s. This was a unity of a new type (even if not of a new quality), based on the common body of interest among the CMEA members rather than on artificial uniformity. On this basis, the Documents outlined areas and methods of cooperation. It is noteworthy in this context that economic policy coordination at the level of integration comprised only issues of regional trade, of joint investments, and of joint companies and their regulation. The interested countries could develop closer forms and methods of cooperation. Ways, means and methods were to be determined by the interested countries themselves. This means that different speeds and forms of cooperation may develop in various individual bilateral relations. There is no obligation to extend these terms to other bilateral contacts, which might well be characterized by an entirely different set of conditions (bargains). This means an extension and political-level generalization of the "principle of the interested party", which had been the earlier practice in decision making in the CMEA. To the extent that it reflects and institutionalizes the new approach to unity, this seems to be a most important conclusion of the Summit.

CMEA countries have been characterized—besides certain basic similarities in economic policies and institutional systems—by a growing diversity. This is rooted in the enlargement of the grouping with non-European members, which led to a secularr trend of divergence in the levels of economic development, and in the consequent diversity of the economic management methods. On the other hand, even in the East-European countries, which are more or less in similar positions, a period of experimentation took place. Therefore both in economic policy and in management methods there have been a lot of improvised elements that are applied under specific short-term pressures, and that are not considered even by their inventors to be of cardinal importance on matters of principle. In the nucleus of the CMEA, the Soviet Union, there has been a political-level recognition since spring

1985 that without a qualitative overhaul of the entire economic mechanism it is impossible to speed up technological progress, which is also a central element in the defence capabilities of the country. It is a subject of another chapter to sum up and forecast how this concept has been translated into practical measures. Conceptually opposite ideas have been voiced in the professional literature, and current management practice is also dominated by sometimes conflicting partial measures. From the above it follows that in the 1980s there was little room left for those—recurring—out-of-date proposals that try to promote integration through the unification of national economic policy priorities and management methods. It seems certain, however, that these views will continue to be voiced in the future, too. It is, however, equally certain that this is not the way that the CMEA countries should seriously contemplate if they really want to attain a better regional division of labour.

From the above and also from the extrapolation of secular trends it follows that increased bilateralism and an increasingly radial integration development is evolving in 1986–90. This means first of all a further growth in the share of the Soviet market in the total trade of CMEA member countries. For the non-European members, trade with their CMEA partners has accounted for 75–90 percent of their total trade, of which 90 percent is accounted for by the USSR. For the East-European countries the 1970s was characterized by a growing share of the Soviet market both in their total and in their intra-CMEA trade. It increased to over 40 percent in the former, and to half to two thirds of the latter. Rising intra-CMEA contractual prices, coupled with the need to equilibrate payments in convertible currencies (through import cuts), has led to a drop in the share of East—West and partly also to that of the East—South trade, and thus to a certain "reorientation" of the total trade of the CMEA countries in the first half of the 1980s. Also in this—geographical—sense, not only in the traditional meaning of trade and payments, a process of increased bilateralism was to be observed. In the larger programnes of the CMEA, it is characteristic that the "driving force" is the Soviet Union, and cooperation among the small countries is much less intensive.

How should we interpret the coordination of economic policies in practice in the light of the Summit Documents? In the well-known formula of the Summit (Documents 1984) synchronization means those joint activities in which interested member states determine the tasks that are to be solved through regional cooperation, and elaborate the methods of implementation in those cases and forms that are considered appropriate by these countries. Furthermore, any two or more countries that find it reasonable can cooperate in different areas, or through different—e.g. closer—forms, or on wider sets of issues. Commeting on this resolution of the Summit, an authoritative Soviet source (Chukanov 1985) has noted that in this sense, the economic policies of the CMEA countries have been subject to coordination for years now. Over and above this, newly instituted regular meetings of leading party personalities became characteristic of 1985–88, to elaborate agreements in principle and perspective guidelines for regional economic cooperation (Rybakov 1984, p. 82). A good example of this new regular and also less formal method of harmonization was the May 1985 Moscow meeting of the CC Secretaries of the ruling parties in charge of the economy. Its subject was an exchange of national experiences about the control of the economy by the party organs. This was considered a major event by the Soviet side according to the statement made at the 1985 Council Session inWarsaw (Tikhonov 1985). This was not only because it familiarized all of them with one another's experiences, but also because they felt that increased party control would be able to speed up integration processes considerably.

Economic policy coordination thus consisted in the better elaboration of information supplied for decison-making with respect to integration, in the provision of regular information flows for planning and exchanges of experiences, and in turning the coordination of interests into a continuous process. Its basic method remained the dovetailing of the regional foreign trade sections of medium-term macroeconomic plans, but it was not confined to plan coordination. The emphasis was laid on continuity, i.e. on overcoming the somewhat formal and rigid limits set by the five-year planning system. In fact it means that similarly to national planning practices, the possibility of the modification of medium-term plans which—unlike in theory—has long been established in practice has received formal, *ex ante* acceptance in integration planning as well. On the other hand, new cooperation possibilities or reserves that appeared in the course of the plan period could, in theory be "planified" without waiting for the first year of the following medium-term plan period. The point is not to multiply jointly approved decisions for their own sake. It is, after all, common knowledge that the number of decisions is frequently an inverse function of their significance and efficiency. It is not that a return to the somewhat extensive practices of the 1970s in establishing joint organizations would be desirable. The loss of interest or the lack of

financial or other economic conditions cannot be offset by a formal
extension of the institutional framework. Therefore it is only welcome
that with the exception of Summit or near-to-Summit meetings, both
information flows and decision making on concrete joint development
projects or on practical commercial issues will take place in existing
CMEA fora such as the Committee on Cooperation in Planning—the
Executive Committee and the Council Sessions (Kovács 1984; Dlugos
1984).

For the existing fora to be able to deliver better results than before,
two matters had to be settled. One of them has been raised at the
June 1985 Warsaw meeting of the Executive Committee: it has to
be examined on what issues a decision requires consideration at such
high (Deputy-Premier) level. The demonetization of the international
mechanism of cooperation has resulted in an increasing share of cases
being decided upon at a level that was disproportionately high compared to the substance of the issue. This also explains why central
decision making organs proved to be unable to benefit from the new
potentialities opened up by the above-mentioned new forms of economic policy coordination. They continued to be overburdened with
petty details. The other precondition would have been a radical change
in the approach to macroeconomic planning.

It is known that traditional central planning and thus also intra-
CMEA cooperation in planning were oriented to growth and stability.
The steady growth of intra-regional trade as well as the ability to
see 5 to 8 years ahead seem to have been unchallenged, even trivial,
underlying assumptions among planners. It goes without saying that
several aspects of economic development, e.g. infrastructure, education
and social processes, require even longer-range planning. On the other
hand, we must also face the fact that foresight in the detail and with
the certainty required for traditional planning and also for coordinative practices has become objectively impossible as concerns the majority of tradeables. This has to do not so much with the allegedly
unexpected changes in the world economy and its instability, as is frequently argued, as with the radical acceleration of the pace of technological progress and of product innovation. These exert a macro-
economically measurable impact on such traditional variables in central planning as optimal plant size, input—output ratios, capital, material and energy intensity of production and the elasticity of these, not
to speak of the size and the geographical location of solvent markets.

Income-generating ability and its processes get increasingly separated from the physical commodity flows. Thus the impact of tradi-

tionally planned items of physical units of production on the decisive proportions, and on the income processes, of the national economy has been decreasing. While the sphere of influence of traditional planning was getting narrower, the dominant new factors tended to get regulated by current cyclical and fiscal policies. But their means were traditionally restrained in planned economies. That is why coordination of plans within the CMEA should indeed have been supplemented by continuous economic policy harmonization.

Trade flows within the CMEA have been increasingly determined by the practically unchanged traditional methods of dovetailing medium-term plans. Unlike in previous decades, however, its two earlier mentioned preconditions, i.e. overall growth and stability of turnover, were not present in the 1981–85 period. In the coming periods it would not be realistic to count on their return. Even before the last phase of coordinatory talks for 1986–90 it became clear that for reasons of international competitiveness, of technological level and of economic conditions it was not realistic to expect other than a very minor growth in CMEA trade (Kővári 1985). In the meantime, the methodology of dovetailing plans continued to disregard the above-mentioned constraints on foresight. Instead it tried to implant stability into the objective processes by its own means. It was hardly a surprise that in the 80s this has worked to an even smaller extent than usual. Coordination of plans for 1986–90 was late not only as compared to the timetable approved at the 1982 Council Session, but also as compared to its own norms of delays. Not even after the Summit, when bargaining should have concentrated on the details of mutual deliveries, were the final version of the economic policy proposals—which serve as the basis for the preliminary plans that are then subject to coordination work—worked out (Faluvégi 1984, p. 9).

From the above it should be obvious what shallow reasoning it would be for somebody to blame incompetence, laziness, or a lack of discipline or of devotion on the part of the central planners for the delays. Delays are mere reflections of deeper objective processes. It is not my purpose to analyse the coordination of plans for 1986–90 in this theoretical work. It is obvious, however, that at a time when there were developments both internationally and within the individual national economies that were outside the scope and methodology of traditional central planning, an attempt to mould reality according to the needs of traditional planning techniques was in vain. An opposite approach would have yielded better results. In the methodology of planning and of coordination, the new trends in economic reality should have been taken proper account of, and corresponding changes should have been instituted.

Coordination of economic policies, as approved by the CMEA Summit, remained within the boundaries of the traditional model of CMEA cooperation, but it may alleviate the above problem of dovetailing plans. If the conditions necessary for the continuous harmonization of interests could be created, this could enable CMEA members to face the fact that the shortage economy character of the respective domestic economies has increased rather than decreased between 1980–85, and this trend is likely to continue till 1990. This is due to continuously straining for foreign economic equilibrium. This effort has two facets. a) In trade with the West, easy-to-mobilize reserves have been exhausted, and as the present export structure, which has been subject to devaluation, has not improved (but rather deteriorated), it must be compensated for by corresponding increases in the quantity of sales. b) The potentialities of the raw-materials-for-finished-products type of integration between the Soviet Union and the East European states have also been exhausted. Intraindustry trade, for reasons of low competitiveness and the inadequate economic mechanism, is in no position to assume a dynamic role. The change in the Soviet demand structure also implies other priorities. Under these conditions equilibrating trade (if not payments) in TR is a serious additional task for the East European economies, a new one added to the ones of the previous decade.

Strong shortage-economy elements and the basically unchanged, traditional mechanism of international cooperation have together inevitably led to a decrease in the stability of intra-CMEA trade relations. The concept of coordination of economic policies and of continuous harmonization of interests took this circumstance into account. If due attention is paid to the two conditions of implementation, as described above, the decisions of the 1984 Summit could have provided an opportunity for the better use of the traditional framework. In reality, however, nothing significant happened. Thus the ossified arrangements could not prevent the collapse when confronted with the open politico-economic crisis of the late 80s.

NOTES

1 It has been observed for the fourth decade now that, as a rule development of the same industrial sectors were deemed desirable in each CMEA state. This was an outcome partly of the similar objective position of the individual countries, partly of identical concepts of what a "proper", "ideal" or "desirable" industrial structure is. This approach was based on a unilinear concept of world development, presuming a functional interrelationship between the overall level of economic development and a definite economic (and industrial) structure. In this reasoning it is inconceivable to reach a higher stage of development without the establishment of certain "basic structures" (e.g. heavy industry), so these must be created at any cost, in each individual country, to attain this particular stage of development.

2 The system of mandatory planning, however, was definitely not one of these factors. True, it was indeed a common feature for the majority of the member states. Its basic feature, however, used to be its inward-looking, autarkic essence, which was a serious constraint on intensified division of labour within the CMEA.

3 The relatively subordinate role of this multilateral forum is easy to see if one takes into account the bilateral (military) agreements between the USSR and other members (which—among others—provide the legal basis for stationing Soviet troops in several WTO member states). Moreover, the WTO has only a small apparatus of its own, engaged chiefly in technical organizational work. Attempts at expanding and institutionalizing the apparatus of the Political Consultative Committee along the lines of the CMEA Secretariat and Standing Committees were not considered to be necessary, especially by the small member states. For the latter point, see Thürmer 1985.

4 Yugoslavia did not participate in this, but China, the originator of the whole concept, did. The East European Great Leap Forward can only be interpreted as a last attempt by the Soviet Union and its allies to avoid an open schism with Maoist China (in other words: with the most populous party of the world communist movement, aspiring for an avant-garde role in the post-colonial Third World social transformations). This is a conclusion that follows directly and inevitably from the pronounced parallel features in the details of the developments, although a documentation meeting the requirements of historiography is impossible to produce for the time being. Later explicit statements by some leading politicians of the era, however, tend to support this conviction. Cf. Friss 1976; Nyers 1983b, p. 302.

5 The decisive role of this factor is well illustrated by the fact that Yugoslavia, which constitutes in many ways an exception, has been showing an increasing convergence in her economic development to other Eastern European countries in the last decade. Cf. Richter 1984 and Soós 1986.

6 Lectures delivered at the 1983 annual meeting of the German Association for Eastern European Studies are surveyed in *Neue Zürcher Zeitung*, 1–2, January 1984 and *Osteuropa Wirtschaft*, 1984/1.

7 The exception being the Multilaterally Concerted Plan of Integration Measures, containing the joint investment projects of CMEA states.

8 Since it is only the enterprise level that possesses the information input needed for planning in sufficient detail, the plan-proposal approved by the ministry and the Central Planning Board, but prepared in detail by the respective enterprises themselves, is decisive in shaping the essential points of the mandatory state plan. Given the exponentially growing quantity of information required for detailed planning, central organs tend to get lost in the course of processing them, and the act of approval and/or command is frequently a mere formality.

9 Approval of these projects is conditional on the elaboration of the financial, and some further economic, aspects. Only then will it be possible to determine which country is interested in what project. Cf. Communiqué 1985.

10 For details of this scenario, see Csaba 1984.

11 Incremental natural gas deliveries of the 1980s result from a joint investment agreement, signed several years before the LTP agreement was concluded. It was only later incorporated in the final Target Programme.

12 The only exception being the deals transacted in hard currency. This useful device has also been elaborated outside the multilateral framework; moreover, the LTP for agriculture has neither institutionalized nor guaranteed this form of mutually advantageous deals.

13 It is also not without interest to note that even net agroexporters of the region depend on extraregional imports of protein fodder.

14 This has been announced by Chairman Ceauşescu at the December 1982 session of the Central Committee of the Communist Party of Romania, noting that "even if we are unable to meet the demanding targets of the five-year plan, we must not spare any effort in attempting to approach them". *Scînteia*, December 18, 1982. — Speeches made at CC plenums are made available in English by the foreign language edition of the Romanian political weekly, *Lumea*.

15 Borisov 1984. The issue was raised in a similar form, reminding one of earlier approaches also by Vladimirov 1985. For a contemporary critique of the simplistic approach in the Soviet literature see Bogomolov 1985a.

16 Thede 1982, pp. 67–69. Relying on this concept Stoph (1984) urged the solution of the accounting problems of joint investments, i.e. the determination of the exact quantity, timing and price of counterdeliveries.

17 For a detailed proof of the statement from the point of legal science cf. Vörös 1981.

18 This is a regulation that relates domestic profitability directly and administratively to profitability of sales for convertible currency.

19 For this author's view on the details, cf. Study No. 3 in Csaba 1985.

a half million tons of the previous five-year-plan period.[1] The crisis of confidence and the attendant credit squeeze of the 1980–83 period appeared to be a thing of the past. Every CMEA country received substantial new loans between 1984 and 1986. Moreover, as the Baker plan indicated, creditor nations were also beginning to recognize that the debtor countries cannot follow austerity policies indefinitely without this having deleterious consequences. Therefore creditors, too, have an interest in easing the terms of repayment, provided the debtors undertake the appropriate institutional reform measures and institute a policy of export-orientation. The possibilities for increased sales were to be worked out at the new round of GATT talks, where steps were to be taken—not only in industry, but in agriculture and in the service sector as well—to remove or ease the proliferating neoprotectionist measures that "protect jobs" or "safeguard domestic production" by impeding the marketing opportunities of the debtors. A new round of talks has begun between the CMEA and the EC, and finally successful attempts were made to work out a contractual settlement between the various CMEA countries and the EC Commission. The CMEA countries' share in world trade again grew between 1981 and 1983, and this has served to relativize the macrostructural and microstructural problems so often referred to in previous years.

In the determining part of the external environment of the East European countries, i.e. within the CMEA, too, things started moving. The sweeping changes that began to take place in the largest member state, the Soviet Union, were formulated as a programme at the Twenty-Seventh Party Congress, outlining the guidelines for future development as well as the means to achieve it. There was a new tone of critical self-evaluation at the Forty-First session of the CMEA held in Moscow. Following the critique voiced by the head of the Soviet delegation, the activities aimed at modernizing the system of multilateral cooperation have become more vigorous within the joint organs. These had started after the Economic Summit of 1984, but progress was slow and confined primarily to formal measures. In sharp contrast to previous years, when a more or less permanent sense of self-congratulation pervaded the activities of the CMEA's joint organs, there was a more self-critical, businesslike attitude in the making. How far this was so was indicated by the fact that the Secretary of the CMEA himself has called for qualitative changes in the work of agencies for multilateral cooperation, requiring major organizational overhauls as well as fundamental changes in the methods and style of operation (Sychov 1986, p. 19). Having concluded the talks on plan coordination in the summer of 1985, the Council held an extraordinary session at the end of the same year, adopting a document under the heading "The Comprehensive Programme for Scientific and Technological Progress in the CMEA Member Countries until the Year 2000" (Long-term Programme 1985; hereafter: Programme). The Programme detailed areas of cooperation for the long run, whereas on issues of principle, it was the compromise decisions approved at the Moscow Summit of 1984 that represented the common denominator in the medium-range perspective. There seemed to be nothing left than to see to the disciplined implementation of all the ambitious targets that figured in the FYP's and in the jointly-adopted CMEA plan documents.

In view of the facts, however, it was already then clear that certain unplanned, but nevertheless foreseeable, circumstances should also have been taken into consideration.

First, a basic feature of the Programme—reflected also in its official commentaries (Antonov 1986)—was that it attempted to promote technological progress, which is by definition unpredictable. Some basic qualities of the conventional planning methodology were called into question thereby. Thus what would have been needed were self-correcting plan targets coupled with flexible, changeable organization and financing. The traditional desideratum of "correct targets—disciplined implementation" is, thus, seen to have lost its meaning. So has the ritual homage conventionally paid to stability in cooperation something it would be well for the mass media, too, to keep in mind, as well as for those engaged in the political evaluation of economic performance.

Second, the structural and qualitative characteristics of the East European economies, the insufficient level of their technological development (reflected in part II of the Programme), and the fact that even the planned rates of growth in their sales for convertible currency lag behind the world average (this export being composed primarily and to a growing extent of products of the lagging sectors) all indicated that there had been a very real chance that the region's continued marginalization in the world economy would take historic proportions.

Third, the region continued to suffer the tensions that have accumulated during the post-1973 period, when structural adjustment was, by and large, postponed. No real structural adaptation has taken place to date, and attempts to consolidate the balance of payments have mostly been confined to cutting back convertible currency im-

ports and investments. A further factor in the very relative success of
the first half of the 1980s was a permanent balance of payments deficit
in the TR trade. All in all, the predominance of a series of short-term
measures was more than obvious, while more far-reaching decisions
have been eschewed. Therefore, it must have seemed probable—even
abstracting from the clear indications of the 1985–86 performance—
that the reserves which could be mobilized by such measures were
already tapped in the years 1979–84. They have, in fact, been exhausted, without, however, new reserves having been created for the latter
part of the decade. Thus, while the social and political expectations
of the mid-80s called for the easing of the restrictions that had, by
then, lasted for several years, and also for a higher rate of growth
(in the GDR, for maintaining the high rates of the officially reported
NMP growth) the structural, qualitative, technological and especially
institutional and economic-policy preconditions for a policy of expansion were, for the most part, missing. The real question, thus, is to
what extent the changes that can be expected to take place are
likely to alter this situation.

The CMEA's Programme explicitly called for an overhaul of the
former system of cooperation. In other words, it did not give itself
much of a chance of succeeding under the existing arrangements. In
all of the CMEA countries, only the improvement of the former
systems of economic management was on the agenda. Nevertheless,
with the exception of the Soviet Union—which we shall discuss later—
the impetus to real change has slackened everywhere. The "adjustment" measures and policies of the previous years were seen in the
mid-eighties to suffice to overcome immediate difficulties, since they
proved—in the official understanding of most countries—that serious
challenges could, indeed, be mastered without initiating major reforms. Even in the case of *Hungary*, where political decisions and
the general atmosphere were for far-reaching changes between
1984–86, the pace of actually implemented reform measures remained
slow; their scope and the actual legal and regulatory arrangements
were limited and lagging far behind the reform rhetoric,[2] for more or
less similar reasons/considerations as overrode policy making in other
East European countries. In *Romania* and in the *GDR*, the party
congresses held in 1985 and 1986, respectively, explicitly repudiated
every suggestion that might have involved the weakening of immediate and operative party control over the economy. At the Eleventh
Congress of the SUPG, no proposal to this effect was even discussed.
Instead, the congress expressed satisfaction with the success of the

steps that had, in fact, been taken in previous years. In *Romania*, speakers at the congress came out strongly against the attempts at decentralization going on in some of the neighbouring countries. The Seventeenth Congress of the CPCz laid emphasis on increased reliance on the economic, rather than administrative, means of management. As for the concrete steps, the period to 1990 was declared to be an experimental stage, with farther-reaching economic changes planned for the 1991–95 period. Neither the timing, nor the issues of substance seem to have changed (as certain quarters tended to speculate) following the Soviet-Czechoslovak summit of 1987.

In *Poland*, the party favoured reform in principle, but has found that the practice of the past four years called for certain modifications. For one thing, self-management in enterprises continued to fail to have the role envisioned by the framers of the laws passed in 1982. For another, it has proved to be unrealistic to expect imports to compete with Polish producers, given their limited availability from both intra- and extra-CMEA relations. The liberalization of domestic prices was further restricted by the popular hostility to inflation, something that was partly related to a lack of confidence in the government's ability to restore the equilibrium of the consumer goods markets by other than fiscal measures. These factors—along with political considerations—have put severe constraints on the efforts to liquidate insolvent firms and apply the law on bankruptcy, measures that have been preconditions of the tight monetary policies making sense at all. For this reason, what were originally considered to be temporary measures taken under the force of circumstances—e.g. large-scale budgetary redistribution in favour of companies with a loss, widespread use of administrative price controls, the prolonged presence of administratively created "associations" in large segments of industry, the continued application of a below-marginal exchange rate, and the placing of state orders for a third of all industrial products—have all come to be stable features of the Polish economic system of the second half of the 80s. In fact, under the slogan of accelerating technological progress, the role of the medium-level control organs, the associations grew even stronger (Szalajda 1986). Under these circumstances, it was also inevitable that operative state interventions increased. Interpreted as part of the process of normalization, these processes has been no longer given the negative rating they originally had, and were becoming permanent features of the Polish economic system.

In *Bulgaria*, the transformation of the economic mechanism in the spirit of what was officially termed "the new economic approach" was completed according to plan by 1986. With the reorganization of state administration and the Planning Office in January 1986, an institutional system adequate to this concept came into being. Auxiliary small industries are being developed in keeping with the decisions of the party congress. However, there has been no talk of breaking up the extremely centralized system of industrial organization based on medium-level control organs (DSO), or of the liberalization of the price system. Rather, the idea of self-management has been repeatedly raised recently, with the aim of increasing the role of the workers' councils in discussing issues of plant organization and in controlling the implementation of plan targets. Self-management functioned parallel to the compulsory indicators, among which those aiming at quality and technological development were to gain in significance in the control organs' evaluating company performance.

Thus, ongoing, continuous small modifications in the system of economic management of all the East European countries remained on the agenda. However, the economic programmes adopted by the East European party congresses in the mid-80s all concentrated on the issue of accelerated technological development, with no serious attention being paid to decentralization and monetization.

A significant feature of the East European *structural policies* of the mid-80s was that though more theoretical attention was being paid to the issue of technological development, investment practice still concentrated on securing raw material and energy supplies from domestic resources. Nearly half of all industrial investments go into this sector, where effectiveness falls short of the national average (which is itself not very high). Endeavours to attain self-reliance in agriculture (despite structurally weak world market prices) have been proving to be ever more costly. The pressing need for reversing the decline in infrastructure and for countering environmental decay, as well as the requirements of defence and state security all involved sizeable expenditures from already strained state budgets. On the borderline between two FYPs, Eastern Europe in the mid-1980s was, thus, finding itself in a paradoxical situation. On the one hand, it had recovered from an economic nadir, had regained its international credit-worthiness, had won less stringent terms within the CMEA than was expected, and had entered a period of relative domestic political consolidation. On the other hand, it was beset by cumulating tensions that originate primarily from the postponement of structural adjustment to the world economy (though these tensions are not yet always directly perceptible). Among the further adverse factors of development, the remarkable degree of continuity of the structural policy priorities and institutional arrangements of the seventies, and the renewed one-sided emphasis on rates of growth, deserve attention.

All in all, the temporary easing of foreign economic constraints has presented these countries with greater room to manoeuvre. Clearly, the way each evaluated the international situation, their divergent past histories, and the specifics of the domestic power relations within each individual country predisposed each of them to give its own specific response to what are fundamentally similar circumstances. Still, without wishing to suggest solutions, I should like to examine the external conditions which delimit the options that Hungary and the other small countries of the region have in the 1980s. First we must reiterate an axiom of the practice of "open planning", namely, that evolution in several of the factors of decisive importance is unpredictable. Thus neither national nor international plans are in a position to predetermine them. Even when everything is formally "settled" as best it can be at a given time, the passing of time calls for ever new decisions that have to be taken at later periods. The question, thus, is *how the countries of Eastern Europe have made use of their temporarily enlarged elbow room* in the mid-80s, and what consequences their decisions—or their failure to make decisions—will have on their ability to adjust to the world economy (something which most of them have already accepted as imperative at least in principle), and also on their freedom of decision in the future.

In what follows, I shall be discussing East Europe's possibilities in the context of its two major trade relations, the CMEA and the OECD, for its trade with the developing countries continued to be residual, though from time to time it might be significant. Nevertheless, Eastern Europe's trade with the developing countries remained a function of domestic economic decisions and of its two major trade relations. Though it might have repercussions on these latter spheres, it has no formative influence as such. Of equally slight significance was the "small-integrational" trade among the Eastern European countries. For the time being, it implies no closer a tie than any set of similarly developed neighbouring nations maintain in their mutual trade with one another. Parallel shortages and parallel surpluses also serve to make this "small integration" trade seem nearly irrelevant when compared to the challenges and pressures which trade with the Soviet Union, and with the OECD, implied for their balance payments. Hence in what follows, I shall be discussing intra-CMEA trade from two aspects: a) from the real economic point of view, focusing on East Europe's trade with its major partner, the Soviet Union; b) from the institutional point of view, interpreting the multi-lateral integration arrangements as the external determinant of East Europe's international environment. The subject of trade with OECD countries I shall discuss in both its political and economic aspects.

CONDITIONS WITHIN THE CMEA

The Eastern European countries' largest trading partner in the mid-80s was the Soviet Union, accounting, on an average, for over 40 percent of their foreign turnover. This, too, warrants an examination of what the process of renewal taking place in the Soviet leadership involved for these small nations' foreign trade policies in the medium run. At the time of writing, not much time has elapsed since the Twenty-Seventh Party Congress. Nevertheless, the need to take some practical steps in response enjoins on us the responsibility of trying to give a partial, perhaps mistaken, but for the time being applicable, analysis.

The outlines of the changes became apparent already at the April, June and October 1985 sessions of the Central Committee of the Communist Party of the Soviet Union. Following a public debate on the guidelines of the Fifteen-Year Plan and on the draft of the new edition of the party programme, the new policy was summed up in the political report of the Central Committee. It was translated into terms of economic management by the Prime Minister's report *(Materiali . . . 1986)*. The documents adopted by the Congress have more or less reflected a synthesis of these novelties, and contained some theses important for later developments—e.g. that socialism is inherently a commodity-producing social system. They left sufficient room for further changes (which actually took place at the January and June 1987 Sessions of the Central Committee of the CPSU). What were the most relevant elements of the economic programme of the Twenty-Seventh Congress from the point of view of our topic?

The new Soviet leadership has shown remarkable sensitivity in its evaluation of the gravity of the problems and in identifying their causes. Its main aim was to introduce a new leadership corps, one whose ability to analyze the situation and come up with proposals was not impeded by the inevitable side-effects of uninterrupted decades of tenure, by the need to justify what had or had not happened during those years, and one not fettered by the great variety of ties and interdependencies that accrue to any group that long holds office. The chief concern of the new leadership was the imminent danger of the country's falling conclusively behind, something which—unless there is more than just the semblance of taking action, more than "somehow improving matters without changing anything"—is a very real danger. Unlike previous leaderships, the Gorbachev team saw the *belatedness* of the attempt at renewal as the main difficulty, not its obvious concomitant costs. Another radical departure was the new importance of the speed factor, and the new prestige of expertise as opposed to the old practice, best summed up by an old Russian proverb: "Measure seven times before cutting once". All this has been given clear expression by the rejection of the proposed Five Year Plan, and the Twenty-Seventh Party Congress's stand being summed up as a policy of acceleration.

Whence this great impatience? In the debates preceding the Congress and while it was on, the various difficulties which Soviet society and the Soviet economy has been facing in previous years were discussed with a publicity that was in sharp contrast to the extremely tactful (if any) reporting of earlier years.

Along with the self-critical reappraisal, the new analysis which the political report gave of capitalism as a system was most significant in shaping the new leadership's overall concept. Besides providing a ruthless critique of capitalism, the report noted: capitalism will not fall of its own weight, its contradictions will not lead to its disintegration; it shall continue to endure for quite some time, posing a challenge to the Soviet Union, a challenge to a race which the Soviet Union can, in fact, lose. Fraught with contradictions as capitalism is, it is in Western countries that the revolution in technology and electronics goes on, a revolution that transforms society, the economy, the relationship of man to his environment, and even defence. The basically new Soviet military doctrine, that military supremacy is impossible, that mutual dependence is a fact of life, and that "the only security possible is mutual security" was not only a strategy for peaceful coexistence, but also implied the inevitable resurgence of ever more stiff ideological and economic competition. In both these spheres, however, the Soviet Union seemed to stand a chance of success only if it undergoes a fundamental renewal, and is able to develop at a much faster rate than before. Qualitative change, not only quantitative growth, are involved here: primarily, things must be done better; however—as the plan figures indicate, and the criticism levelled at previous years shows—*more* should have been produced as well.[3] This presupposes "a thorough renewal in political and economic institutions, more far-reaching socialist democratization, and resolute end to indifference, passivity and conservatism". The essence of the analysis, as presented in the report to the Congress, was, nevertheless, not this, but the acceleration of scientific and technological development, considered to be the chief material means to achieving better quality and higher productivity. Though institutional changes were considered instrumental in all this, the General Secretary emphasized changing the country's investment policy as the first and foremost task. In this context, a reversal of emphasis took place only at the January 1987 Session of the CC. The major priorities of the Twelfth Soviet FYP, such as the primacy of the machine industry, particularly of engineering and electronics, on which the national economy's technological level depends, logically follow from this. Investments in engineering were planned to grow by 80 percent. The Bureau for Engineering has been set up by the presidium of the Council of Ministers of the USSR in order to coordinate the activities of the eleven subsectoral ministries of the area. The Bureau functioned in a way reminiscent of the late Economic Commission of the Hungarian Government (dissolved in 1987): it had a small apparatus, but the right to give instructions and even to pass law-decrees (Silaev 1986).

We should note here that concentrating on engineering has traditionally been a priority in Soviet economic policy. One of the most salient features of the industrial policy of the post-1965 period was the preference of the machine industry over the raw material and fuel industries, with a resultant 10 percent advantage for the former by 1977 (Köves 1980, pp. 233–234). From 1978 on, emphasis did shift to the raw materials sector—mostly to the petroleum and natural gas industries. Nevertheless, the foreign trade picture of the years 1978–85, as presented in Chapter 5, bears out a well-known truism of economics, namely, that there is no direct correlation between investments and growth, and even less is there a direct correlation between investments and international competitiveness. True, there had been no qualitative changes in the mechanism during those years; in the mid-80s, however, plans have been made for its restructuring (how, we shall discuss later).

No less important, however, was the other priority set by the 1986 Congress of the CPSU: the modernization of agriculture. Mikhail Gorbachev had been the Central Committee's Secretary for Agriculture from 1979 to 1984, and had had no small part in working out the food programme adopted in May 1982. Initially, the programme had set itself moderate goals: reorganizing the management of Soviet agriculture, the setting up of a top-level coordinative organ by the presidium of the Council of Ministers, and eliminating shortages in most of the basic staples, thereby increasing self-sufficiency by 1990. Originally, the programme was a rationalization of the centralized model of agriculture along the lines reminiscent of the Bulgarian endeavours of the time. There was to be better coordination of the various branches, greater independence for the medium-level control organs, and increased opportunities for those with household plots. A later added, but consistent feature, was the experimentally introduced limited collective incentive scheme called "brigade undertaking" *(brigadnyi podryad)*. Subsequently, and especially following the CPSU Central Committee's October 1984 session, the food programme was reevaluated in the spirit of the—none too successful—Soviet traditions. Instead of fostering local initiatives, attention focused on the big central melioration projects, and reinvigorated age-old Utopian projects of transforming nature (including the reversion of rivers); the measures introduced to encourage household farming fell by the wayside. It hardly came as a surprise, thus, when the Congress passed some new measures giving primary producers a greater interest in production. These did not involve following the Hungarian and Chinese practice of to a large extent doing away with the meticulous central direction of agriculture. Staying within the framework of the mandatory planning model, however, they did call for a more generous system of economic incentives and a more effective system of sanctions, with greater earning opportunities for "brigade undertakings" and the household plots. Following the Congress, the decrees containing the concrete measures have been promulgated. Some of these detailed the measures and incentives introduced under the auspices of *Gosagroprom*, the State Committee for Agriculture, others contained measures aimed at preventing the illegal trade in state-produced goods using state-owned transportation facilities, and at eradicating the corruption that attends these practices (O merakh ... 1986a, b).

The essence of the first set of measures was to cut down on the bureaucracy involved in the elaboration of plans and in checking up on how far they were kept. Stable plan targets have been promised for five years for the same set quantities with those producing more assured of a 100 per cent premium/surcharge, and of the goods —necessary for agricultural production. Workers and managers achieving production that surpasses the actually achieved average of the previous five-year period were to receive substantial benefits— a year-end bonus amounting to three months' salary over and above the quarterly bonuses. Smaller investments were to be decentralized, and entrusted to the competence of a variety of lower-level decision-making bodies, depending on the amounts involved. The regulations aimed at increasing production at practically any price. Even a short-term fall off in production was heavily penalized within the given year, and the shortfall has to be made up for in the following year. The produce of household farming was also integrated into the state plan of purchases (following the practice of the GDR). It was encouraged to play a greater role in supplying the local population and in contributing to the state's produce fund, with only what was left going to the kolkhoz market. The kolkhoz market was to be regulated by the disciplinary and control measures mentioned above.

The third main topic at the congress was economic management. A great deal was said about the need for radical reform, about the concept of full or real economic accounting *(polnyilpodlinnyi khozvaschet)*.[4] Let us, thus, look at some of the practical consequences of these considerations. Of the theoretical guidelines, the most significant instructions called for less operative intervention, for decreasing income redistribution in favour of those lagging behind by the state budget, for a more efficient use of financial levers, for greater recognition for the small and medium-size enterprises, for correlating wages to profits, and for equal rights for the cooperative sector. Concrete regulations aimed at flexible prices reflecting the use value of products and at a securely-delivering, stable material and technological supply system *(snabzhenie)*. Plans were to be stable and well-coordinated with the financial regulators stabilized for the entire plan period.

The economic report to the Congress—besides giving the specifics of the plans and evaluating the results of the previous plan period— gave a good picture of what radical reform involved in practice in the short and in the medium runs. Economic management was primarily meant to be an instrument for accelerating economic growth. For acceleration was to be accomplished with a more economical use of resources than to date. In other words, a radically new trend is needed in resource utilization and in the capital output ratio. The technological development already mentioned and a somewhat increasing rate of investment were the envisioned means. Technological development was to be accelerated primarily relying on domestic research results; for understandable reasons, technology was to be imported as little as possible. The plans call for doing away with what were then considered the two main impediments to effective technological progress: the bureacracy of the ministries, and the levelling of wages (at the expense of the better-qualified strata). The earlier often praised, but little used system of target programmes, the setting up of supra-branch ministries, and giving greater independence to large scientific production associations of enterprises and R + D institutes *(nauchno-proizvodstvennoe obedinenie)* were held to be the most effective means of   macroeconomic management. All-union associations that actually functioned as medium-level control organs *(glavki)* were to be dissolved. The State Committee for Agriculture *(Gosagroprom)* had been set up to exercise supreme control over the entire agricultural sector and the food industry, where cutting down on expenses, greater work discipline, better planning, and building up the infrastructure—primarily storage and transportation facilities—have been specified as the major goals.

It was generally accepted that the application of sectorally differentiated financial regulators remains a lasting feature of the Soviet economic mechanism. In the mid-80s, regulators tended to be differentiated by companies/associations. Various experiments were going on in the service sector and in the construction industry. The "large-scale experiment" of the previous years has been subjected to severe criticism by Soviet economists. As early as 1985, at a round-table discussion of mostly practising economists jointly organized by two leading economic journals, *Voprosy Ekonomiki* and *Planovoe Khozyaistvo*, the consensus of opinion was that the basic theoretical expectations attached to the experiment had not been fulfilled (Ekonomicheskii . . . 1985). Technological progress had not speeded up and innovation and the marketing of new products was as slow as it had previously been. Short-term regulation tended to overwhelm general rules, and though theory dictated stable five-year planning, in practice the plans were modified a number of times a year. Gerasimchuk, the Deputy Director of the Institute of Economics of the Ukraine, presented a number of case studies to prove that the experiment had brought absolutely no change in the conduct of the enterprises, neither *vis-à-vis* the planning organs, nor in interenterprise relations. As for the oft-mentioned production-regulating function of interenterprise contracts, it remained completely formal. The case studies written up at the Novosibirsk Institute for Industrial Economics (Karagedov 1985) called attention to the fact that the management methods of the branch ministries and of the associations have not changed at all, and the conduct of the enterprises has likewise remained unchanged as a consequence. They have also shown that the gradual preponderance of the extra-experimental economic mechanisms illustrates the inadequacy of the changes that the experiment has conceptualized.

The same critical spirit was reflected in the call for an end to experimentation, and for a full-fledged changeover to new methods of economic management. The Party Congress took no stand on the issue of content related to the experiment as a whole: certain of its elements were endorsed, while different solutions (and experiments) were recommended to replace others. The proposed system of flexible prices reflecting technological parameters and quality could be an improvement over the earlier practice of fixed (cost-plus) pricing. Still, there can be no doubt that it differs significantly from the Hungarian approach, in that it refuses to recognize that demand has a major price-forming role, except perhaps in the case of services. The wish to soak up solvent demand was also new. It is, however, primarily the specialized large-scale service enterprises that were expected to do so. Sanctions, quality control *(Gospriyomka)*, and reducing prices for obsolete goods were considered to be prime instruments of economic management, as was a party line that is daring in its cadre policy when penalizing those responsible for shortcomings.

There can be no doubt that the new Soviet line on economic management was rather vague at the time of the 27th Congress. For an interim progress report, however, we can subscribe to an opinion expressed in an article on the details of the radical reform published in the economic weekly of the Central Committee of the CPSU (Milyukov 1986). According to this, every officially evaluated recommendation made to date calls for retaining at least some of the compulsory indicators as well as the planning in physical terms of at least the major items of output and stipulated that investment sums and extended reproduction must be centrally directed. Giving greater independence to the large organizations is thought to be the best management method. However, until the price system comes to orient production about scarcities properly, operative direction was, of necessity, to be restored (in the case of the experimental enterprises, the centrally predetermined part of their output choice has even grown). This proved to be indicative of the actual evolution of the Soviet economic system during the second half of the 80s.

The fall in oil prices has made for fundamentally new circumstances in Soviet foreign trade. While in the 1970s the Soviet Union benefited from a 20 billion dollar terms of trade gain, and using the credits thus becoming available to it was able to bring in 30 billion dollars' worth of additional imports (thus between 1979 and 1981, for instance, the windfall profits alone proved sufficient for covering the agricultural import bill—Hewett 1984, p. 17), by 1985 the situation had changed. Even before oil prices collapsed, at the time of the 3 percent fall in prices, production declines in 1985 and the winter hardships led to a 30 percent drop in Soviet oil exports to Western Europe, resulting in a 7 to 8 billion dollar loss of income. As for the 1986 fall in oil prices, it is estimated that this cut by half the Soviet Union's income from the export of fuels and energy (Müller 1988; Bogomolov 1986b), which, as is well known, accounts for four-fifths of its export to the OECD. Another way of putting all this is that in the 1970s, financing the Soviet Union's growing import orientation caused no particular problems even with a stagnant foreign trade mechanism. In fact, the backwardness of the Soviet export structure, much criticized by economists already in the early 1970s, proved to be a positive advantage after the two oil-price explosions. Now that the price trends have so radically turned, this decade-long immobility has had to be reconsidered. The economic report delivered to the Twenty-Seventh Party Congress specified changing the one-sided export structure and switching to the sale of manufactures as primary—though not immediately achievable—tasks, and ones that require changes in the Soviet Union's foreign trade mechanism, and altered producer–exporter relations. It is important to note that the desiderata apply to Western and CMEA trade relations alike. As yet, there is no telling what concrete form "full cost-accounting" (as distinct from the current transitory measures) will take in the future radical reform of the Soviet foreign trade mechanism in the early 90s. There can be no doubt, however, that the thought of a more flexible Soviet foreign trade mechanism has gone beyond the theoretical plane to become an urgent need, and that this, in the medium term, can mean radically new possibilities for change in the CMEA mechanism as well. The growing solvency problems foreseeably involved in the Soviet Union's trade with the West have already objectively increased the reliance of the Soviet economy on East European supplies. The problems—as the economic report pointed out—stem partly from the fact that switching from a one-sided dependence on raw-material exports to that on finished goods is a time-consuming process, one that can be but started in the 1986–90 period. The difficulties were but compounded by the new trends in Soviet trade relations with the developing countries—where the Soviet Union has traditionally had a 6 billion dollar annual trade surplus just from the export of goods not detailed in statistics—since it is precisely the group of developing countries which have been the Soviet Union's regular trading partners that faces liquidity problems due to low prices for fuels. For this reason, even with substantially increased Soviet indebtedness to the West, trade with the developing countries had a decreasing role in the Soviet attempts to compensate for the structural deficits in its trade with the developed market economies.

Some analysts claim that the Soviet Union's convertible currency trade with developing countries has shown deficits for the past two years. This, while it can be ascribed to the usual credit operations, still aggravates her liquidity problems. There is little hope that increased productivity and greater foreign demand will lead to the growth of Soviet exports. On the other hand, the Soviet Union's net national debt practically doubled in 1985–86, before the programme to step up Western exports was as much as formulated. Consequently, there is a very real likelihood that her credit rating will deteriorate in the not-too-distant future—at least to the extent that she will not have access to low-interest and unconditional credit to bridge her domestic trade deficits. This, of course, would considerably restrict the range of the Soviet Union's programme of economic acceleration. But it would also be prejudicial to the other CMEA countries, especially if their foreign trade performance continues to be less than satisfactory.

The Soviet Union's reevaluation of her trade with Eastern Europe brought about a reexamination of the division of labour within the CMEA. Signs of this could be observed already during Yurii Andropov's General Secretaryship, and became pronounced in the course of the debates that preceded the CMEA Economic Summit of 1984. As documented in detail in Chapter 6, they were also evident during the coordination of the medium-term plans for 1986–90. As an analyst generally close to the official line has pointed out, in the past the Soviet Union had regarded the division of labour within the CMEA as a means of promoting industrialization in the East European countries, with the Soviet Union assuming the role both of raw-material exporter, and a market. By the 80s that industrialization in these countries was an accomplished fact the Soviet Union expected "with justification" that they cease to treat the USSR as nothing but a soft market (an attitude not really in the interest of the East European countries either). Since the Soviet Union continued to accept the role of supplier of primary products—which, in the view of the above-quoted source, was not in her trade interest—then it was "only right to expect its partners to contribute to solving the current problems of the Soviet economy by supplying—among other things— up-to-date machines, agricultural produce and consumer durables" (Kormnov 1985). It is an equally important, but perhaps less well known, fact that it is not only for the East European economies that the Soviet supplies are vital. The counter-deliveries play a role in covering Soviet needs that is far from negligible. For instance, in the case of industrial consumer goods, East Europe provides 16 percent of the Soviet domestic consumption. In productive investments its share is 17 percent, but in the case of machinery and equipment investments, it is 35 percent (Dyakin and Medvedev 1986, pp. 22–23; Bogomolov 1986a, p. 46). This is far from being a *quantité négligeable*, especially if we take into account that these deliveries, whose quality is often subject to Soviet complaints, still satisfy the upper segments of the country's demand, and are usually much more popular among Soviet consumers than their domestic equivalents.

When the difficulties of the Soviet extractive industries, as well as the country's pressing need to sell for convertible currency, are added to this picture, it becomes evident that "hardening" the terms of intra-CMEA trade is an objectively inevitable fact of life for the East European states. It is not in their power to do anything about this. In the longer run, even with stagnant or declining intraregional trade, it is certain that intraindustrial trade will gain while interindustry trade, primarily supplies of primary products, will lose in significance in the intraregional division of labour. This would have required that a qualitatively new mechanism of intra-CMEA cooperation evolve, one which—is in compliance with the nature of exchanges in finished products. True, since this theoretical condition was not fulfilled in practice, there was an objective contradiction between the newly-formulated Soviet commercial policy deliberations on the one hand, and the inherent features of the intact traditional mechanism of intra-CMEA cooperation on the other (its being an impediment to produce innovation and technological change, for instance). It was also evident that the structure of Soviet demand, as reflected in the plan-based mechanism of cooperation, differs both in its forms and motivations from that of the West, at micro-, meso- and macro-economic levels alike, if for no other reason then because it is a transmission of current domestic Soviet shortages.

A further problem that emerged for East Europe is that the direction of the net flow of capital, which has implied extra resources in most of the previous 15 years, would be reversed. To be able to service their debts, these nations had to run regular current account surpluses *vis-à-vis* the West, whereas the arithmetics of sliding pricing has brought them into surplus positions in trade transacted in TR without their really wanting it. This means that the process of adjustment that was postponed at the time when their domestically disposable national income regularly exceeded the NMP produced ought to have been undertaken in the inverse situation, when the domestically disposable NMP was far less than the NMP produced. That alone—if nothing else—was an indication of the seriousness of this task, as well as of the social and income distributional costs that such a process involves.

The criticism of the activities of the CMEA voiced by the Soviet side was, therefore, the result of a paradox. The former system of multilateral cooperation that used to be so strongly supported by the Soviet Union proved clearly unable to induce and enforce the extra performances that would have been required for the modernization of the largest member's economy. Better performance, and thus the requirement that they give better performance is, in my judgement, quite in keeping with the best interest of the small East European countries in the longer run. In the medium run, however, the need for restructuring, for finding alternative markets for old products, and for penetrating, new markets with new products, as well as the concomitant need to redeploy the work force entails serious costs. It is, however, far from indifferent, motivational and punitive system transmits these higher requirements to the companies.

Soviet endeavours to modernize the multilateral framework of cooperation in the CMEA have been formulated on two levels. In *commercial policy*, the target has been to enhance the share of hard commodities and quality items in Soviet imports as well as to tighten delivery discipline. In the *multilateral organizational and institutional system*, the objective of streamlining has been parallel to the measures (to be) instituted in the Soviet industrial administration. This implied cutting back formal and bureaucratic activities, as well as devising better-organized and more efficient means of implementing political-level decisions without delay. Without going into the details of what may well be a subject for separate analysis, it should be clear already from what has been said that when they spoke of changes in the mechanism of cooperation, which includes planning, trading, accounting, and organizational and institutional elements, it was change in the latter two, rather than in all areas that was being put on the agenda.

In specifying concrete tasks for the long run, it is of some help to look at the *bilateral cooperation programmes* signed by the East European countries *with the Soviet Union*.[5] Similar agreements had been signed already for the 1971–85 and 1976–90 periods. What was involved here is continuous, long-term planning as part of the process of cooperation, plannaing which provides some general orientation but is primarily of political significance. These documents, besides dealing with the principal issue of cooperation, involve a lengthy list of concrete tasks and measures. It should be clear, however, that these, too, were plan-preparatory documents, traditional, constituent parts of intra-CMEA practice. The orientations of these long-term programmes were usually translated into cooperation deals or inter-state delivery obligations during the coordination of medium-term and annual plans. It is an exception rather than a rule that long-term international obligations were derived immediately from the bilateral framework-programmes. Among the areas covered by the 15 year bilateral cooperation agreements, a major share falls to the manufacturing subsectors, where for inherent reasons it is neither appropriate nor possible to set quantities, choice, and the financial and delivery conditions of supplies 15 years in advance. Taking this fact of life into due account is a basic feature of the Long-term Programme for Scientific and Technological Progress until the year 2000 (Long-term Programme 1985). The detailed analysis of this *Programme* is the subject of the following chapter; let us, thus, here survey only some of those of its aspects that were of *immediate relevance for Soviet-East European commercial policy issues.*

By definition, the Programme is also a pre-plan document containing a political-level pledge to cooperate, and setting the major lines, objectives and requirements of future development. It thus includes no delivery obligations, since the conditions for these are to be elaborated only by the bilateral agreements that specify the material contents of the sub-programmes. Not every CMEA country participates in each of the 93 sub-programmes. Joining any of these or not was a function of "interestedness" and also of the availability of financing. Thus it was completely misleading to assume that the Programme in fact has externally predetermined the investment structure, or even a considerable part of the investment structure, of the East-European countries for the coming 10 to 15 years. As is common knowledge (Lozanov 1984, pp. 110–112), the conditions for such far-reaching administrative coordination of investments were simply missing from the CMEA, and the suggestion that it be undertaken—occasionally voiced by some theoreticians—was out of touch with reality. Moreover, the member states of the CMEA passed a decision already at the 1984 Havana Session of the Council that this multilateral Programme would be built on the analogous national programmes, summarizing and harmonizing these. This harmony is complete in the case of the Soviet Union, which follows from the very fact that each of the 93 sub-programmes were elaborated by a Soviet coordinative head organization *(golovnaya organizatsiya)*; therefore the final (summary) version of the multilateral Programme is also a brainchild of the Soviet party (which produced this document in about two months) (Chukanov 1986, pp. 12, 14, and 17; Antonov 1986a). All this took place parallel to the elaboration of the Soviet Fifteen-Year Plan. It was an advantage of the Programme over the Multilaterally Concreted Integrational Measures that the international plan is the result of adding up the national projects, instead of the latter being derivatives of the former. Moreover, the financing of the joint plans is not a linear function of the objectives commonly set in physical terms. Instead, the sums already earmarked for technological development by the sovereign national plan decisions are spent in a regionally coordinated manner, rather than for autarkic purposes. Commenting on this peculiarity, a leading economist of the GDR has emphasized that the choice of areas for cooperation originates in the national economic structures (and the changes in them), rather than the other way around (Kunz 1985, p. 66).

Clarifying this point has a direct bearing on the concrete organizational and economic measures implementing the Programme. During its preparation, some Polish experts on the CMEA proposed, for instance, that the most important areas of this programme be "exempted" from the overall CMEA mechanism of cooperation, and form a special *enclave* under the direction of a joint staff in order to promote their speedy implementation (Iskra 1985, p. 70; Pasienczny 1985, p. 70). Others were of the opinion that regional integration implies the internationalization of production inasmuch and to the degree that it results in spending a growing share of national investments on common purposes. A major practical consequence of this thesis was the view that along with, but not replacing the joint investments into the extractive industries, a similar grandiose regional concentration of capital should promote technological progress in the dynamic priority sectors (Shiryaev 1986a, pp. 133–134).

The jointly adopted Programme does not follow this extremist approach, which aimed at a substantial rearrangement of the balance of compromises struck at the 1984 Summit and in other CMEA fora, though under the guise of technical modifications. It is clear that when the common political decision favours the maintenance of the existing polycentric model of regional cooperation with uniform mechanism in every country. It was not only infeasible, but even theoretically unjustified to raise proposals involving a conceptually different integration even in a partial sphere. Any measure, therefore, that rejects the uniform rules of the integrational mechanism, or tries to "transcend" national interests in the name of a postulated (but non-existent) separate "international" or "community" interest is out of place. Two major ways have, thus, evolved for implementing the Programme: a) the interested parties sign specialization and cooperation agreements at the state administration level, specifying delivery conditions under the traditional intra-CMEA arrangements; b) the interested companies and research institutes concluded a comprehensive frame-agreement, and established joint ventures, temporary work teams, or construction bureaux, or chose another form that is appropriate to the nature of the given project (Sychov 1986, p. 17).

How all this fits into the overall CMEA mechanism will be detailed in the following chapter; therefore it seems sufficient to recall here the evergreen problem of "interestedness". It should be stressed that this aspect of technological and scientific cooperation is anything but new for the CMEA. Although the number of measures, of progress reports and of appraising articles has never been small, this area has been characterized by an especially high degree of formalism. Eighty-five percent of what passes for cooperation is confined to coordination, which is not only its simplest form, but also one usually involving no financial consequences. The Soviet deliberations thus called for replacing the large number of moderately practical measures with fewer, but more relevant activities, ones that are of tangible profit (Bogomolov 1985, p. 44). This would have required qualitative changes in the CMEA, both in its organizational setup and in the economic conditions prevailing there. As this requirement continues to remain a slogan, a set of empty words, some earlier shortcomings was inevitably reproduced, with a direct bearing on the Programme. To give one example. While member states had declared their interest in micro-electronics, robotics, flexible modules, and the production of trucks, none of them took on the responsibility at the ordinary Council Session of 1985 where the coordination of plans was concluded of organizing cooperation. Since later signed agreements could hardly be incorporated into the protocols of plan-coordination, they lacked material coverage as well (Key field . . . 1986).

A further area where the Programme was closely related to Soviet–East European commercial policy issues was the *energy sector*. As is known, the traditional East European quest for additional energy supplies dominated the coordination of plans for 1986–90 too. In compliance with the documents of the Economic Summit of 1984, East European member states managed to preserve the 1985 delivery levels of Soviet primary products by "hardening" their export pattern as well as by granting substantial new investment contributions. The interpretation of this development in East Europe is well reflected in the writing of a leading Bulgarian economist, Nesho Tzarevski (1985, p. 97), when he puts the method of investment contributions fifth among the options possible for easing the "energy problem". That saving was the only feasible way for the East European countries to solve this problem was first declared at the Economic Summit, and later reiterated by the 1985 Warsaw Council Session as a reflection of trade agreements. The Programme translates first as priority for nuclear engineering; second, as the subprogrammes for the elaboration and use of energy-saving technologies, and third as the ones for developing new synthetic materials. It seems clear that cuts in imports, coupled with domestic development and the promotion of its application, would, indeed, save the CMEA countries substantial quantities of energy and raw materials. After all, this would be the point of less factor-intensive growth, an idea that has been worn out by frequent reiteration in theory, without at all influencing the type of growth of the last two decades. Unless this is changed, only an irrational type of growth can come about in the CMEA countries, and even that only for a very short period.

It is an open question yet at the time of writing how the *modernization endeavours in the CMEA* will be related to the implementation of the Programme. In theory, there is no doubt that the modernization of organization should promote the goals set by the 1984 and 1986 Summits, as well as by the Programme. Every organ that is a remnant of earlier approaches, has proved inefficient or is simply superfluous for meeting the new demands, should be dissolved without delay.

This is not the only reason why the personnel of the common organs, especially of the Secretariat, should be cut back to the size justified by the present intensity of the trade which is actually transacted in a multilateral fashion. It is inexpedient to run interstate and interfirm coordination organs with a permanent staff, since experience shows that those interested are able to harmonize their activities in direct business contacts and through occasional meetings. Activities that have been under way for years without, however, producing any tangible results whatever should be terminated (these have proliferated in standardization as well as in R + D cooperation). Following the new Soviet approach, a very limited number of intersectoral organs should replace the large number of standing committees composed of organs at a subsectoral level. Their activities are, at any rate, interrelated and therefore overlap. In this respect, the decisions of the 43rd Session of the Council in October, 1987 are but a very modest start. On the other hand, we must note that the establishment of the Committee for Cooperation in Engineering, called into existence partly to promote the Programme's tasks, means that in fact an organ parallel to the Executive Committee and the Committee for Cooperation in Planning has come into being. Its level —Deputy Premiers—as well as the domestic competences of the representatives to this body—significantly overlap with the other two top-level standing organs. Moreover, as is known (Kirpichnikov 1985, p. 18), within the Committee for Cooperation in Engineering sixteen sectoral bureaus have been set up, which equals the number of the "working groups" of the former Standing Committee. What is more, at the first meeting of the Executive Committee following the adoption of the Programme in January 1986, two new Standing Committees were called into being, one to deal with the developing of new materials and one with biotechnology. This was not complemented either by mergers in other areas, or by a detailed study of whether or not these activities were feasible within the framework of some existing organization. This development is worth mentioning precisely because cooperation in science and technology has traditionally been quite prone to formalism, a feature that was to be conclusively done away with in the spirit of the recent resolutions. It is, thus, especially important that success in the realization of the Programme be measured by performance on the world market, rather than by the number of joint organizations, measures and conferences.

Until now, intra-CMEA cooperation has been discussed partly *per se*, partly from the point of view of the policy choices of the

Soviet Union. The question naturally arises whether East European policy choices existed at all *vis-à-vis* the USSR? There is no single answer to this, owing to the growing institutional and policy plurality in the East European region. The various national concepts of CMEA integration are, understandably, more or less an extrapolation of the real economic situation and domestic problems of the respective states, as well as of the dominant economic philosophy of each. The causes of the lasting nature of this plurality have been discussed in Chapters 4 and 7. Suffice it to recall that these approaches are as diverse as the various nations' interests and economic philosophies. Differences over immediate commercial interests and over the very general issues of economic philosophy apart, the core of the disagreements was whether or not a feasible alternative to the earlier functioning arrangements existed at all (both in general terms, and in relation to concrete issues). Since changes in the national systems of economic management have not been very radical, their impact has not been particularly impressive either. In the light of this experience, and also as a theoretical reflection of the "adjustment" policies of the first half of the 80s, when short-term considerations tended to overwhelm everything else, there was a growing and seemingly irreversible inner conviction among practical policymakers that there were no feasible alternatives. This is true for both the short-term policies of "crisis management", and of the general systemic issues as well. The constant reiteration of fashionable policy slogans which, at that time emphasized restructuring and renewal did not really penetrate either to the existing management practices, or to the inner conviction of the lack of alternatives.

By the mid-80s, nobody seriously cherishes any illusions about the size of those incremental efficiency and performance gains which the traditional arsenal of integration and its improved versions were able to deliver. Still, it was precisely this conviction of the lack of alternatives—or various other considerations that add up to the same conclusion—that has led each East European country to adopt what András Köves (1985a) has properly termed a *policy of import-maximizing* in their intra-CMEA trade. From the point of view of policy analysis, it is hardly sufficient to allude to this being an inevitable by-product of the shortage economy, where demand is by definition close to infinite. The limits to any significant growth in imports from the CMEA deriving from objective economic and interest factors have by the early 80s become conspicuously evident even to laymen in Eastern Europe. It thus seems a trivial requirement of any economic policy—but particularly of one legitimating itself as having a scientifically elaborated project for the future at its disposal—that it adjust itself to foreseeable future developments rather than try to escape the inevitable. What, then, explains a commercial policy practice which in the course of coordinating medium-term plans regularly continues to restate objectives whose attainment so evidently runs counter to the interests and the oft-revealed policy preferences of by far the largest trading partner? However, odd it sounds, the answer was: the pragmatism of the planners (or their "realism", as they tended to call it).

The central planning organs calculated—with justification—that actual and feasible changes in the national economic management systems would not lead to those efficiency breakthroughs that have already been produced on paper in several preceding FYP periods. Therefore they were equally right in not expecting major penetration in any of the competitive world markets, nor major improvements in the export patterns and in the resultant convertible currency earnings. This being so, the plan targets of accelerated growth for 1986–90 which originated primarily from socio-political expectations could be made credible even on paper only if at least the input side was secured. Due to domestic resource constraints, this seemed possible only if additional imports from the Soviet Union were made available. For contemplating imports of primary products from developing nations, or for a major import of Western technology that would permit substantial savings in the raw material and energy intensity of production, the acceptance of at least one (or both) of those basic assumptions is necessary, whose rejection is the very foundation of the above-described, implicit, official way of thinking.[6] Thus, there remained nothing left for the East European central planning organs but to try to attain the impossible. While they were the ones best aware of the earlier-described real economic situation and the resulting interest relations within the CMEA, including their foreseeable consequences, planners felt they have got to make it, at least on paper. It is important to see that it was the domestic balance of forces, implying a hardening of the priorities that the central plan had to serve, that have pushed planners into a corner, rather than "unforeseeable" developments in the international economic processes. This vicious circle could have been broken only if the duality of the policy of import substitution and of mandatory planning had been given up, as has been suggested in the economic literature of several CMEA countries, and not only in recent years. (Cf. Jánossy 1970; Goldmann 1975; Winiecki 1983; Daianu 1984.) However, several factors impelled in the opposite direction in the 80s.

There is the problem of adjustment to a net outflow of capital due to surpluses *vis-à-vis* the Soviet Union and the West alike, which enhances the propensity/need to use administrative measures to keep the process under control. The cost of structural changes has significantly increased due to the long delays in adjustment. The political motivation for radical systemic change has decreased rather than increased in the eighties for reasons explained at the beginning of this chapter. All these together made the East European governments' heeding this type of advice not only more difficult, but also less probable. Within the vicious circle, however, even the real questions cannot be raised properly. The "energy problem" cannot be solved by staying within the framework of the raw materials and energy policy, i.e. the sectoral approach. From the sectoral point of view, it might well seem in the interest of East Europe to decrease reliance on Soviet imports while at the same time maximizing its imports of primary products (Wettig 1986). This is a highly infeasible proposition for a number of reasons. On the other hand, very few would doubt that structural, technological and systemic changes could bring about substantial cuts in the energy and raw material intensity of the East European economies, which would thus approach the parameters achieved by market economies of a similar size and at a comparable level of development. In this case, of course, there would be no need for those primary commodities that otherwise do have to be imported "at any cost" from somewhere (preferably in quantities pre-fixed for at least a decade).

Looked at the other way, it is again clear that the prime Soviet interest no longer lies in preserving the stability of the existing structures and the related performance, but in contributing to their change. In the case of immobility, the economic and technological performance of the region was by the mid-80s already significantly lagging behind even those Soviet needs that were formulated prior to the conception of the ambitious modernization drive, i.e. at the Economic Summit of 1984 and the coordinating plans for 1986–90. It is not very difficult to prognosticate with a fair degree of certainty that in the context of the policy of acceleration taking place while deficits in the Soviet current account were bound to grow, this discrepancy was only be aggravated, without the East European countries' being able to make up for their economic weakness with top performance in other areas. Thus, contrary to the idea forwarded by Rácz (1985), the national foreign trade mechanisms definitely play a subordinate role in the manufacturing sectors' being devalued not only on the OECD, but also on the Soviet market. Since Soviet ability to reject major items of the country's purchases from the West, i.e. raw materials, intermediate products, spare parts and agricultural produce, will continue to be limited in the medium run, it is probable that imports of machinery and equipment will be restricted to ease trade imbalances. In this case, in a development that is by no means historically unprecedented, imports of manufactures from Eastern Europe will objectively become substitutes for Western imports to the USSR, despite their very limited capacity and efficiency to do so. It is for this reason that Soviet commercial policy has explicitly formulated the stand that the sole criterion in evaluating imports from East Europe is their performance relative to that on the world markets (Bogomolov 1986a, p. 48). This policy line is not comparable to the short-lived "quality and efficiency" campaign of the mid-seventies; it marks the beginning of a trend. This does not mean that commodities not reaching world-market standards will eventually be eliminated from intra-CMEA trade, as advocated at the Warsaw Session of the Council by N. Tikhonov (1985). What it does imply is that East European manufacturing industries, having evolved for decades under the double umbrella of national and regional protectionism, were bound to have difficult years ahead. Their excessive cost levels, which have never been accepted by Western markets, will be covered less and less by the declining TR prices. The pressure from the monopsonist buyer, i.e. from cost-based ruble prices, was bound to intensify. Hence it was naive to assume that the drop in oil prices would benefit East Europe. As we have tried to prove all along in this section, precisely the opposite is the case. And it would be difficult to put the blame for this on the Soviets or on some other external factor, since structural change and adjustment is a task to be mastered domestically in East and West alike.

REFLECTIONS ON THE CONDITIONS OF ADJUSTMENT TO THE WEST

The nature of the structural changes going on in the developed and developing market economies as well as the ways of adjusting to these changes have been adequately elaborated in Hungarian economic literature. It thus seems sufficient simply to complete the previous line of thought.

The import restrictions of the early eighties, which in Hungary for several years have meant only that the "normal" growth of imports did not take place, have made economic actors and policy-makers conscious of the degree to which trade with the West has become an integral part of the functioning of the East European economies (given that they want to maintain the socially tolerated minimum of rationality, which has not been the case in some of the other countries of the region). East European attempts to cut back economic ties with the West, or the exigency of doing so, have had serious repercussions. In some cases, it was the complete disorganization of the domestic market. In others, the entire increment of the NMP produced had to be used to service the debts in measures to manage the external finances of the region. All this constituted an important warning. Unless each of the recently declared policy goals of growth, technological progress and structural change is to be given up irreversibly, unless shrinking reproduction and lasting decay of domestic economic relations is taken for an acceptable alternative, relations with the West cannot significantly be cut back in the economies of East Europe. The developments of the eighties have demonstrated the infeasibility of the inward-looking variant. Inward looking, or development—this is the message of the region. No wonder, then, that the discussions of the early eighties on the rationality and feasibiliy of an inward versus an outward-looking integration have ebbed in the relevant literature.[7] By the mid-80s, it was only some political authorities of the traditional breed (e.g. Obzina 1985) and the new left of the American universities (e.g. Bunce 1985, pp. 2, 38) who cautioned against the East European countries' stronger integration into the world economy, blaming the policy of opening (rather than its half-hearted implementation) for the region's marginalization.

It is common knowledge that the Economic Summit of 1984 opted for an outward-looking policy, which was supported by the Soviet initiatives to normalize relations with the EC and to convene a conference on world economic development. Still, it is important to see that it is one thing to set appealing objectives, and another to work out the set of conditions for successful integration into the world economy. In order to contribute to the latter task, let us, for the sake of analysis, separate the political from the economic factors.

From the *political* point of view, the intensification of Soviet-American rivalry in 1979–84 was of decisive importance. This led to a strain with spillover effects on the small states, especially in technology and credit relations. By way of reaction, the subject of invulnerability and the search for ways to avoid unilateral dependence on credits and their repercussions became fashionable topics in CMEA fora. In this period, ample evidence substantiated the traditional thesis of large countries' being prone to use trade as a political weapon, which is just the inverse of the position of small countries. This was only aggravated by the strong ideological orientation of the first Reagan Administration, which postulated the imminent collapse of the "evil empire" from the sheer weight of its inner economic contradictions. The collapse was to be helped along by the "policy of denial", i.e. by refusing the Soviets credit, trade and technology. At the same time, the Soviet Union was hindered by a number of factors in its renewal, and thus in adjusting to the post-détente climate; accordingly its propensity to compromise was not particularly great. This situation hardly favoured new conceptual initiatives, and tended to promote the old reflexes of antagonism. This period was a test case of the thesis that the small and medium size countries are able to assert their interests and maintain and even expand East-West ties. Convincing analyses were produced in both camps[8] proving that the politically most contested areas, such as *credits and technology, are not very useful means of attaining immediate political objectives.* As such, their exchange constitutes no threat to any social system; thus there is no good reason for either side to hinder their trade for extra-economic reasons. Put another way, there are no political side-effects to credits and technology to limit the East European countries' integration into the world economy.

In the granting of credits, the earlier practice of regional risk assessment has given way to the rating of the individual countries. To see how far technology relations have been politically overemphasized it is sufficient to recall that machines have only a one-fifth share in Eastern imports. The Soviet Union, a prime target of the politically-motivated technology embargoes between 1970–82, had only 7 to 14 percent of its total imports in technology-related items (according to the analysis conducted by the OECD). More detailed studies proved that the Soviet Union had a much smaller international trade involvement in the exchange of technologies than the East European countries. This feature became only more pronounced with the deterioration of the political climate. While in 1970 the highly technology-intensive items constituted 3.20 percent of the East European and 1.97 percent of the Soviet imports from OECD countries, in 1982 the respective figures (representing the long-term trend) were 4.32 percent for East Europe and 1.47 percent for the Soviet Union (Bornstein 1985, p. 21; and

OECD 1984, p. 270). And we may add: with the exception of the
Soviet Union and the GDR, at the present level of their development,
what the CMEA countries usually need is not the highest technology,
since that is not appropriate to the technological and economic
tasks they face. It is clear that small countries at a medium level of
development cannot, as a rule, compete in the absolutely highest
technology branches; it is not the most R + D intensive and the
usually concomitant capital-intensive sectors where their comparative
advantage lies. Consequently, their international economic competitiveness is only very loosely related to the international flow of high
tech and its political constraints. An indirect proof of this point is the
experience of the liberal 1970s, when, though generally available, new
technologies did not penetrate the East European economies and
modernize their export structures. The reason for this — besides the
mistaken methods of technology imports—we will find in the well-
known endogenous constraints on technological change inherent in
the mandatory planning system.

The enlargement of the EC, its agricultural and budget crisis and
growing neo-protectionism do, however, pose serious problems for
East Europe. This is aggravated by the national market barriers
increasingly erected by non-tariff means. The common external
trade policy of the EC is shaped by the slow growth of the domestic
markets coupled with the advances made by Japan and a number of
developing nations, by the influential trade unions, by regional and
industrial lobbies, and by a defensive integrational industrial policy.
All this has led to a major *devaluation of the traditional ties to East
Europe among the Community's priorities.* If something escaped the
consequences of this growing inward-looking at the EC level, it was
the issue of the non-developing countries, which was kept on the
agenda by the social democratic parties (whose power base is often
strongly related to, and even coincides with, the protectionist lobbies).
Third World problems are often discussed in contraposition to relations with the CMEA countries. This has led several East European
countries to reexamine their former one-sided orientation towards
West European social democracy, both in geographical and political
terms. This, however, has proved insufficient to counter their growing
devaluation as trade partners. True, hesitation on the side of the
East European countries also contributed to their missing the opportunity for a contractual regulation of relations to the EC Commission when the conditions for this were given from the latter's point
of view between 1975 and 1979. In the post-1979 period, the stronger

partner had neither a political nor an economic interest in such a deal succeeding. Although Hungary has been conducting talks since 1980 (Marjai 1984b), the EC Commission has invented artificial and secondary hindrances to signing an agreement, due to lack of interest by most of the EC member states, and an unwillingness to compromise, primarily on the part of France. In a typical procedure, the EC Commission called into question Hungary's contractual GATT rights which it had already recognized in 1973. In another ploy, the competence of the CMEA delegation composed of representatives of the 9 member states plus the Secretariat was declared moot. An efficient way of eschewing a contract was to present the Hungarian partner agreement projects offering virtually no advantage over existing practices, or even to refuse to guarantee some of those conditions of market access that are integral parts of the multilaterally valid GATT agreements to which both Hungary and the EC are signatories. In 1985–86, the new Soviet foreign policy initiatives brought about improved political conditions for an agreement. On the EC side, however, the accession of Spain and Portugal meant two new full voting members which have no traditional cultural and political links to Hungary, but which do have a supply pattern that competes with Hungary's in a great many ways. All this took place without the Community's having found solutions to the acute and intertwined problems of the EC budget and EC agriculture. By the mid-80s competent analysts of the EC states had themselves produced analyses demonstrating that the CAP was contrary to the interests of the vast majority of EC citizens, and that the preceding years' commercial policy practices were inappropriately discriminatory against the East European countries (Hanson 1985, pp. 20–23). Nevertheless, there are no grounds for expecting favourable changes in the above-summarized gloomy interplay of interests.

If there are some bright spots, they come from the *US*. The experiences of the 1980–84 period proved that politically-motivated economic sanctions in a number of cases violated the interests of the allies of the US more than those of the Soviet Union. The limits to extraterritorial law enforcement have become clearer. What is more, the easing of superpower strains have led to a number of measures and proposals that were beneficial already prior to the 1987 Soviet-American summit. Already in early 1985, the Department of Commerce liberalized the sale of every commodity that was clearly available to the CMEA countries from other suppliers. Initiatives to grant the Soviets MFN status and Exim Bank credits started as early as 1985, and well-informed sources saw a good chance for these two narrowly missed objectives of détente to succeed, provided Soviet-US political relations improved (Hardt and Gold 1986; Farnsworth 1985). Such a development could open a whole new chapter in the history of East-West trade and finances. Since US foreign (economic) policy has always evolved cyclically between liberalization and trade restrictions, after a decade of rather restrictive practices and following the collapse of state socialism in Eastern Europe there are no grounds to reject out of hand the stabilization of a more cordial *Ostpolitik* in the US for the 1990s.

Turning to the *economics of East-West relations*, it can be taken as proven that the principal constraint on East European adjustment to the world economy is the unfavourable export pattern of the region. This is the prime reason for their sales meeting ever stiffer competition, and the growing barriers of market protection. These latter phenomena are not the causes but the results of the region's structural problems. Only a production pattern which sets its goals "autonomously", i.e. which disregards the international market signals, and fails to prepare for the foreseeable, suffers standard terms of trade losses in international economic intercourse, whatever the change in relative prices might be.

In the years 1981–83, most East European countries managed to overcome their liquidity troubles, and restored their credit-worthiness. Besides the increased liquidity of the markets, this is why the channels of credit supply opened up again in 1984–88. The indebtedness of the CMEA countries started to grow again, surpassing the previous record levels already in 1986. Still, it would be self-deceptive if anyone seriously considered this as a return to the "normalcy" of the 70s. The situation in the mid-80s was very different, for several reasons. In the first place, in the 1970s, it was the first time in their economic history that the CMEA countries had applied for major credits to Western banks. Their reputation and debtor's rating was, thus, exceptionally favourable, which is no longer the case after the experiences of 1980–83. Secondly, the post-1973 period was one of extraordinary international liquidity, leading to even negative real rates of interest—a phenomenon that will not repeat itself in the foreseeable future. Thirdly, the international debt problem has been managed by the IMF and the governments of the major OECD nations in such a way as to bail out the largest debtors whose prolonged insolvency would shake the whole international banking system. An important method of doing this is for the IMF and the creditor governments to induce the major banks to extend fresh loans to precisely the largest debtors, even if it runs counter to their immediate business considerations. As a by-product of this practice, the not-largest and not-yet-insolvent mediocre debtors are forced out of the markets, since the rest of the money at the commercial banks' disposal must be lent out at very good margins and to first-rate debtors, since nearly each of the banks engaged in international business has already got its share of writeoffs (Bogdanowicz-Bindert 1985). These features apply also to the Baker Plan; in other words, the East European debtors had little chance of benefitting from it. Fourthly, one should realise that debts rescheduled in 1982–83 matured in 1986–87, increased by front fees, spreads, cumulative interest, and other expenses. This is reflected in the new Polish, Romanian and Yugoslav reschedulings. In other countries, the expensive credits raised in 1982–83 have matured at a time when the drop in nominal interest rates was mostly neutralized by inflation, with the weak dollar inflating the nominal terms of new indebtedness. But while large financial reserves do provide invulnerability and room to manoeuvre, they also involve economic costs. The point is not the frequently overstated losses due to interest (this, in reality, is small given the differences in rates of interest). The real trouble in the second half of the 80s was that reserves, by definition, cannot be invested. Their repayment must be earned by other segments of the economy. A credit used for reserve-building is never self-liquidating. By giving the illusion of solvency, reserves contributed to the aggravation of a situation, since the pressure for adjustment could be warded off precisely with their help. Reserves, thus, bought time and could be spent unwisely. This brings me to the fifth point. A growth in debts involved a growth in debt-servicing requirements (paid on gross, rather than net debts). This has become increasingly difficult to secure through the traditional ways of making up with quantities for what has been lost in terms of prices, as effective demand for the traditional East European export products is becoming ever more limited. And this brings us back to our starting point of export patterns.

The other dynamizing factor in the upswing of East-West trade in the 70s was the energy sector, primarily of the Soviet Union. The world economic role of this area has become reversed, probably for quite some time. Due to this factor and also to problems of increasing output and domestic utilization, the Soviet energy sector will not be in a position to repeat its performance of the 1970s in any of its major trading relations. In fact, for reasons explained in Chapter 5, East

European economic policies could have foreseen this sector's play-ing a diminishing role also in intra-CMEA exchanges in the 90s but certainly in international trade at large. This implies that *each* CMEA country faces financing possibilities in the 1990s quite different from those they had in the 1970s. Thus, it would be a mistake to judge the financing possibilities of the CMEA countries' plans for restoring growth by extrapolating from the trends of the 70s, in disregard of the six new secular factors determining the 80s, though cyclical currents on money markets may temporarily overshadow the lasting features for some time.

IN LIEU OF A SUMMARY

Unlike some twenty years ago, nobody in Eastern Europe really doubts the need for adjustment to the changes in the world economy. Still, transitional improvements in perfunctory indicators, short-term successes and the pressure of socio-political expectations, coupled with an underestimation of the real significance of qualitative and structural factors led to a false sense of security by the mid-80s. It seemed to policy makers that thorough institutional reforms were not all that urgent. From what has been said above, it should be clear that the reality of the situation was just the opposite. There was no justification for the lack of performance on any of the major markets of Eastern Europe. The possibilities of non-economic instru-ments compensating for lack of progress/performance were getting slimmer by the day. The feeling of security was out of place. Their widening elbowroom by no means implied the easing up of economic requirements for the region's countries. The costs of immobility are soaring. The possibilities still open to it were becoming drastically limited, primarily owing to the intra-CMEA changes. Step by step improvements proved obviously insufficient for keeping pace with the deterioration of the external conditions. Gradualism could only lead to renewed loss of the freedom of action, and to an even greater marginali-zation within a dynamically changing world economy. Although radical reforms are costly ventures, in the mid-80s this option was objectively still open to the East European countries in their attempt to escape from the vicious circle of stagnation and decay. Had they instituted radical reforms, their room to manoeuvre would have in-creased in keeping with the interests of their major trading partners. The alternative was the exchange of inefficiencies.[9] It was naive to pretend that this has no political repercussions, including international ones. The open politico-economic crises in each of the member states, the collapse of the old political and regional cooperation systems in the late 80s were therefore anything but unexpected. It was an inevitable outcome of inaction of missing even the last chance to reform during the mid-80s.

NOTES

1 Admittedly, no practical steps have been taken in the other two areas specified in the target programmes—agriculture and transportation—in spite of the growing acuteness of the problems involved. Though this failure to follow up on the theoretical decision was far from being a matter of indifference to the East European member states, it had no real bearing on the programmes' political evaluation.

2 Cf. Csaba 1986 and 1987.

3 This was pointedly noted by Nikolai Ryzhkov.

4 Full economic accounting *(polnyi khozvaschet)* is used in a number of senses by Soviet economists. For some, it means that the system of financial incentives have been extended to areas hitherto financed by the budget; i.e. the old mechanism extended to new areas. For others—the majority—it is a substitute for what Hungarian, Polish, Czechoslovak and GDR economists term "regulated market economy". (The use of the term "market economy", as is known, was carefully avoided in the reports to the Twenty-Seventh Congress.)

5 These programmes were published in the 1985 volume of the economic weekly of the Soviet party, *Ekonomicheskaya Gazeta*. For the Hungarian–Soviet programme, cf. *Figyelő*, 9 May 1985.

6 This notwithstanding, it still is astonishing that none of the East European countries has elaborated a FYP variant that seriously considers the consequences of a secular drop in fuel, raw material and agricultural prices in the 1986–90 period.

7 Cf. Kozma F. 1978b; Betkenhagen 1984 and 1985; Köves 1981 and 1982; Csaba 1984, and the literature quoted in these writings.

8 Cf. among Western sources Vogel 1984; Hardt 1984, Hanson 1984; Schröder 1984; Bornstein 1984; and Schiavone 1985. Of the Eastern literature, cf. Shmelyov 1984; Kulka-Fiedler 1985; Nötzold 1983; and Köves 1985b.

9 This expression was first applied, to my knowledge, by Zbigniew Fallenbuchl (1977).

CHAPTER NINE

Perestroika[1]. The restructuring of the Soviet economy

Though in what follows I shall be presenting the changes in Soviet economic policy from a Hungarian point of view, I wish to look at the new developments as having an immanent logic of their own. It is in this vein that I shall be analysing the Twenty-Seventh Party Congress and the changes that followed.

THE ANTECEDENTS. RENEWAL—OF WHAT AND AS COMPARED TO WHAT?

The state of the Soviet economy and of Soviet society that we shall take as our point of departure developed during the eighteen years that Leonid Brezhnev was General Secretary. His policies as such may be considered to have been a negative reaction to the continuous series of shocks that the half a century between 1914 and 1964 had been. The constant stress of the preceding period, the policy shifts, contradictions and personal insecurity weighed heavily on the masses and leaders alike, and had brought about a genuine social demand for a normalized, predictable and stable state of affairs. In the aftermath of wars, revolutions, campaigns and organizations, the Khrushchev era had indeed put an end to the Stalinist regime, to the rampant lawlessness that had fettered all political and intellectual activity. Nevertheless, implementing a myriad of constantly changing and often inadequately thought through innovations, unexpected shifts and turnabouts in both internal and foreign policy, and the excesses of an obviously utopian ideology became the trademarks of Khrushchev's political rule. While these irritating, though in retrospect less relevant practices do not diminish the historic merits of either the Twentieth or the Twenty-Second Party Congress or of their leading personality, they did come to determine the overall consciousness of Soviet society and of its more influential groups. Undoubtedly, the precariousness of his standing in the hierarchy, as much as his own personality, inclined Khrushchev to follow this indecisive path of haphazard changes in political direction. In retrospect, it may be considered the price that had to be paid for lasting historic achievements; but it also precipitated a genuine and, as it turned out, determinative, popular demand for permanent consolidation and stability. When Brezhnev made this stability-orientation his platform and achieved it, he clearly represented the interests and aspirations of the entire Soviet society, but first and foremost, those of the absolute majority of its politically dominant groups and strata. Unlike the Czechoslovak policies of the seventies, Brezhnev's programme of preserving the political *status quo* was not a defensive one. Its three characteristics were: a) It consistently allowed the politically dominant strata to satisfy their own interests and became, in effect, the embodiment of their common interest at that particular time, as Western observers have frequently emphasized (Nove 1977 and Brus 1985). b) It achieved economic results that brought the Soviet Union into a position of relative parity of power with the United States. This was done along with solving a number of bread and butter issues, such as housing. c) In foreign affairs, it resulted in a significant geographical extension of Soviet influence. This, of course, won Brezhnev domestic support as well.

Just as decisive for shaping the policies of the Brezhnev years was the "Prague Spring". The Soviet leadership understood this combination of political changes and economic reforms as a process undermining the leading role of the party as well as the basic structure of the Warsaw Pact. This further strengthened from both an ideological and an economic standpont their fundamental belief in adhering to the tried and tested solutions. The views of the 1977–82-period, which rather than searching for new alternatives concentrated on lauding what had been achieved, were the results of what was seen as a decade of well-founded success.

In the above context, the socio-political malaise that mushroomed as the by-product of the consolidation appeared to be of secondary importance. And when Yurii Andropov, his ill health notwithstanding, set about trying to tackle the problem, a massive resistance swung into action, determined to preserve the 'proven ways' at any cost. Resisting were the people threatened by Andropov's energetic moves to make personnel changes at all levels, by the effects of his campaigns for the rule of law and order, and by the emphasis on productivity and on the inadequacy of the economy's output in the light of worldwide competition. When the personification of this resistance, K. U. Chernenko, L. I. Brezhnev's former personal secretary, took the helm, the campaign for law and order slowed down and once again the Suslovian ideology began to dictate policy moves. Although in March 1985 the self-proclaimed heir to the "November plenum", i.e. to Yurii Andropov, M. S. Gorbachev was elected General Secretary, Chernenko's short tenure and his achievement of a quick and trouble-free return to "business as usual" indicated that the practices of the two decades following 1964 have become very deeply rooted by virtue of their capacity to satisfy a great variety of particularistic interests. Certainly, they are far more deeply rooted than one would ever suppose from the criticism so often levelled at the time at "the prevailing attitudes", at "leading cadres" and at "political mistakes", in the Soviet Union as well as in Hungary. It was much more than sheer eloquence when in Khabarovsk Mikhail Gorbachev called the programme of acceleration and *perestroika* a revolutionary task involving the whole of society, and embracing education, ideology and the political system as well.[2]

The fundamentally political nature of *perestroika* and what cross-section of society it is that supports it has to be borne in mind throughout its analysis. Gorbachev and the recently appointed or elected officials belong to a generation different from those who filled the positions that were made available by the great purge of the thirties. Their qualities for leadership are based on experiences other than the Second World War. In setting their goals they take for granted the restoration of the rule of law, and the existence of a consolidated state of affairs in which the Soviet Union's international political and strategic position as a superpower is what it is. They tailor their targets not with the past, but with the challenges of the world at large in mind. Challenges like the third industrial revolution. Challenges like the strategic defence initiative based primarily on the participation of a decentralized private sector. Challenges like the enormous success of the Chinese reform policy, or the structural realignment of the world economy. And challenges like the growing differentiation within the Third World (the failure of the non-capitalist orientation, and the problems of the Eastern European integration stemming from the economic weaknesses of the CMEA countries). All this means that it is more and more expensive and dangerous to stay out of those international organizations and mechanisms of cooperation which determine matters of international trade and finance along with the conditions of credit.

The external challenges coincided in time with the objective, immanent challenge that the Soviet economy and Soviet society face in the 80s. It is a crisis that has been in the making and has been forecast for the past two decades as the logical conclusion of the factor-intensive type of economic growth. By the 80s, however, it has become a short-term reality.

In essence, the Soviet Union's taking an active part in international politics, maintaining the former level of her defence budget and of her standard-of-living, keeping up with world technology, dealing with acute, heretofore neglected, ecological problems, and improving on her alarmingly backward infrastructure especially in the area of transportation is all possible only with the complete revamping of her entire economy. In other words, if the Soviet Union wants to maintain her present status as a superpower she has to solve concurrently all the problems that are the result of earlier procrastinations and neglect (Kornai 1972). The economy has become the all-encompassing political task, and a new factor-saving type of economic growth has by then become a categorical imperative. This is not merely a slogan, but a fact.

We must realize, however, that economic production at the level attainable within the earlier-developed structure will not satisfy the demands set by the new Soviet self-interpretation and the drastically changed circumstances. The difficulty is only compounded by the fact that these demands are in no way consistent with the kind of motivation and functioning of the economic and social mechanism that has become the norm within the past two decades. (These mechanisms have operated as part of a system of institutional interest representation enjoying the support of all or the majority of the affected social groups.) "Under the prevailing circumstances we cannot put up with partial solutions. Radical reforms are needed", stated the often-quoted official position taken by the Twenty-Seventh Congress.[3] True reform is a social process, and as such, it is by nature contradictory. The leadership has to take steps overriding its earlier power base in order to achieve long-range objectives. However, it also acquires a new group of supporters along the way. This is what constitutes the unique dichotomy of the process. On the one hand, the coherence of the economic reform is necessarily subordinated to the very different logic of political reasoning, at least in its present stage. On the other, one has to realize that, even in the midst of the social and political turmoils of the eighties, the Soviet policy of economic "reforms" has been consistent. It followed the principles of the July 1979 decisions and gradually expanded on them in the course of the "large scale experiment" (Csaba 1989a; and Bauer and Soós 1981). As I shall substantiate it later, all the major economic "reform" measures implemented from 1986 to 1988 fall into the category of being up-to-date without overstepping the boundaries of the system of mandatory planning. Yet, the fact that today never-before-sanctioned reform ideas and personalities are published on the most prominent pages of *Kommunist*, of *Izvestia* and on occasion even of *Pravda*, while the responsible ministers publish their defence only in the professional journals, plays a determining role in shaping current economic climate. In the 80s, this "switching of roles" influenced the day-to-day workings of companies and governmental bodies only very indirectly. However, this may change in the future. The political thinking behind the reforms initiated from above sees economically contradictory steps and rulings as forming an organic whole. Decentralization is lauded while a disciplinary and anti-corruption campaign is going on. They encourage personal initiative while waging war against "unearned income". The much-heralded "openness" runs head on into the airtight borders. Companies are encouraged to develop direct international relations, to take advantage of proven business procedures, yet they are held to rigorous performance schedules. What is, or would be needed is the complete restructuring of the now obsolete system of institutions and of interest protection. The reevaluation of the *modus operandi* and of the economic influence of the party and particularly of the local/territorial party cells is also part of this process. M. Gorbachev has dealt with this problem on a number of occasions. He was most critical in his addresses to the June 1986 and the January 1987 meetings of the central committee. He pointed out many examples of how the party cells were entrenched in the old ways and how they stood staunchly against new policies. The General Secretary concluded that there would be no *perestroika* without the reorganization of the party.[4]

To group these measures taken under the headings of "like it" and "don't like it" as some of the Hungarian and Western media does is both useless and unwarranted. The Soviet press is not seeking sensationalism when it gives full coverage to organized corruption and other syndicated crimes, as in the case of the trial and conviction of practically the entire Uzbeg ministry of the cotton industry, the minister included (Khbanov 1986), or the trial in the summer of 1988 of Brezhnev's son-in-law, formerly first Deputy Minister of the Interior, for corruption. This type of reporting is part of the all-out war against *de facto* unearned income and corruption, is part of the campaign for a healthy social environment in which a healthy economy can function, an environment which is devoid of all undue privileges and which fosters an all-encompassing atmosphere of "openness".

Although in the past this was not a topic to be publicized, everyone even slightly familiar with the Soviet Union has noted the proliferation of socio-pathological phenomena. The Chief Public Prosecutor of the mid-eighties (Rekunkov 1986) referred to the seventies as a period when, in the absence of openness and public control, the abuse of official power, the practice of using power to amass personal wealth, and the intertwining of personal relationships to safeguard this system of corruption became so widespread as to pose a positive threat to the economy. The few voices that were raised were quickly silenced by those who had everything to lose by the disclosures. The principle that the law applies to everyone equally was regularly violated, with select individuals and organizations being beyond its reach. In his above-cited article, the then Chief Public Prosecutor took extremely strong stand against the attempt made by party organizations to have their members exempted from lawful investigations, and even more outrageously, to make any action by the courts subject to the prior approval of the party. The fight against this system of privileges goes on. It is in this vein that customs regulations and inspection procedures are being tightened, that former foreign trade and customs officials are being arrested and put on trial. The one-time Soviet Ambassador to Hungary, N. Bazovskii, the head of the new national customs office reorganized as a bureau of the Presidium of the Council of Ministers, stated in an interview that all this is part of the war against corruption and those involved in it, "regardless of title, position or previous achievement" (Shmiganovskii 1986).

The spontaneous meetings of the Soviet writers' association, the constant scrutiny directed towards the performance of the ministries and the generally prevailling critical atmosphere are other aspects of this openness. *Glasnost* has affected the vested interests of a great many people in very sensitive ways. This is responsible for the fact that along with the practice of constant self-criticism which has extended even to the means and the speed of *perestroika*, there has also developed a not-so-positive tendency to self-justification. Signs of this attitude became quite evident in the fall of 1986 and again in the fall of 1987. A publicity campaign was launched to explain the failure of the Reykjavik summit. Then, the modest results of the 1986 interim economic acceleration were played up in a political analysis of the recorded results of only ten months. (This unjustified optimism was corrected in the party press (Latsis 1987) a few months later.) It should be quite clear, without belabouring these events, that it is much more important to understand *the processes* of the Soviet reform in their context of social change than to scrutinize the letter of the new laws and regulations, or to cite statistical data pertaining to the achievements of the acceleration. The latter acquire significance and meaning only as a function of the former.

From the speeches delivered since the April 1985 meeting of the Central Committee, from the documentation and opening arguments of the guidelines of the 1986–90 Five Year Plan, and from the material covering the Twenty-Seventh Party Congress we could glean that a new strategy was being formulated, one which was built on a deeper and more realistic evaluation of the facts, and one which forms a politically[5] logical whole, a possible solution. Looking at the economic policy, it might well appear that there is some master plan, lacking nothing but some rather minor details as to its execution. This, however, is not the case. The General Secretary himself has denied the existence of such a plan in his speech at Khabarovsk. To the party-activists of Krasnodar he approvingly quoted the famous novelist, Gelman: Rather than asking where the great programme is, people should try to make what has been achieved irreversible, and help the process of *perestroika* crystallize in the war against conservatism and bureaucracy, a struggle that will no doubt go on for several years to come.[6]

At this point we are left with a relevant question. Is *perestroika*, and especially, acceleration *(uskorenie)* to be understood in a quantitative or a qualitative sense? There is no definite answer. Based on the speeches given by the General Secretary, it appears that the emphasis is on the means through which growth is to be achieved — the interpretation reflected in what has been termed as "the new growth path" in Hungary. Yet at the Twenty-Seventh Party Congress, and at the November 1986 meeting of the CMEA, the Soviet Prime Minister ascribed great importance to the actual figures, to the rate of growth in the conventional sense of the term. Chances are that in the future, too, the emphasis will shift from one interpretation to the other. The difference, however, seems a semantic quibble if we consider that there is certainly no way to achieve the quantitative plan targets if there is no break with the old patterns and means of promoting growth. The calculations for the first plan-alternative worked out under Baibakov and rejected in June 1985 bear this out indirectly. According to the approved five-year plan, technological advances were to produce two-thirds of the industrial growth, and one-fourth of the increase in the gross national income was to derive from raw material and energy savings.[7]

The economic strategies of the Twenty-Seventh Party Congress and the approved Twelfth Five-Year Plan have been dealt with in the preceding chapter examining the conditions for Eastern Europe's adjustment to the world economy. There we shall focus on the changes in Soviet leadership practices, comparing them with the acceleration plans of the other CMEA member states.[8] In the present chapter we wish to examine two principal questions: What has actually changed in the years 1985 to 1988, i.e. in a period of strong reform rhetoric? What kind of changes can be projected in the long run, in what direction, and how dynamic will they be?

HALF-MEASURES: EFFECTIVE REAR-GUARD ACTION BY THE INSTITUTIONS

The developments of 1986 and 1987 seem to warrant a reminder that the decades-old gap between the practice of economic management and the suggestions that economic theorists publish in connection with the long-range targets of the reform has widened, rather than narrowed. The gap keeps widening proportionately to the growing role of open criticism, the greater honesty in the search for alternatives, and the leadership's heightening susceptibility to change. Less than ever can something that appears in the Soviet press be taken as the basis for automatic projections as to the actual policies of the authorities.

How, then, can we come to know the *dynamics* of the system of management in effect? One has to start by examining the new regulations and the partial measures that have been attempted in the form of various experiments. For unlike the opinions to be found in the press, these are official enough to warrant our expecting their more widespread implementation in a year or two. Committees of experts, with some independent members, now work side by side with those within the central committee of the communist party. This is a novel practice in the Soviet Union. Their theoretical counselling efforts notwithstanding, the actual work is being done by a new top-level committee attached to the Council of Ministers. As part of its task, this committee is called upon to finalize the practical approach that, in fact, was taken to bring the suggestions of the various administrative branches into harmony, to check on the implementation of the regulations, to help along in the transition to the new economic practices, and to supervise the reform efforts of the ministries and other high authorities.[9] The economic press reports regularly on the activities of the "reform-committee", which incidentally also has a scientific council attached to it. It is the "reform-committee" that is working out the prototype regulations *(tipovoe polozhenie)* that provide the framework for the new economic system. While this diminished the role of the sectoral ministries and of the planning board, it seemed more likely to result in the centrally approved changes finding their way into practice, at least in the stage of promulgating regulations.

The basis of the modernization all throughout the 80s was still that "large-scale economic experiment" which has been going on in the whole of Soviet industry since January 1983. Detailed analysis of this experiment (Bornstein 1985) proves that, in essence, it is much of a rehash of the 1979 regulations. These regulations were based not on the age-old lessons to be drawn from the experiences with command planning, but on the illusions and self-justifying promises connected with it. They did not touch the interrelationship between the various management levels of the economy, nor affect the interaction between the hierarchy and the enterprises. Thus it is hardly surprising that, as the evidence from recent years indicates, they did not produce any significant change in the functioning of the Soviet economy. They were but a part of the ongoing effort to make command planning a viable system. However, the dual challenge that the Soviet economy faces today demands something radically different. Soviet economist agree that, even within the context of its own target- and value-system, the experimental mechanism has been a positive failure.

Space not permitting detailed documentation, I will cite only a few telling examples. Academician Bunich, basically always in tune with the official platform, was—as always—somewhat critical. Writing for the general public, he discussed "the large-scale experiment" in no uncertain terms as one that obviously does not alleviate tune with the official platform, was—as always—somewhat critical. and moreover it does nothing to accelerate scientific and technological progress, to ameliorate interfirm relations or to curtail interference by the sectoral authorities (Bunich 1986). (To do so would have been the prime objectives of the experiment.) Business executives write about the fact that even those main physical indicators that were purportedly to remain stable for the duration of the entire

Five-Year Plan, and also purportedly serving as a base for the equally stable financial regulations, get out-dated so fast that they cannot be, and in fact are not, even seriously considered in the elaboration of the annual plan targets. Reliance on the normative net output *(uslovnaya chistaya produktsiya)*, which is something like value added (with built-in projected cost-reduction factors) as the basic indicator in the experimental system, implied a further proliferation of bureaucracy. Moreover, the very concept of measuring and managing the "own contribution" of constituent factors could not, of course, be made operational on the plant level, since the target function that is to be maximized exists by definition only at the level of the entire company. The chief indicator, therefore, was not, in practice, incorporated in the plan, neither was it used as a basis for setting wages. Rather, it tended to be replaced by other primitive indexes measuring direct manual labour input (Khlistov 1986). Nor did that decrease in the number of plan indicators targeted by the experiment take place. Indeed, the novel indicators introduced "for accounting purposes only", for all their uncertain legal force, were nothing but the old plan indicators by another name, and it was these that the sectoral ministry took into consideration in setting the bonus conditions.[10]

Speaking for the "other side", one of the leading experts attached to the Ministry of Finance, Bazarova, noted that far from remaining stable for the entire five-year plan period, the financial regulators kept on being modified several times a year. Sometimes this was made necessary by the modifications of the plans themselves. The current practice of drawing off residual profits *(svobodniy ostatok pribyli)* differed from the conventional one only formally. Companies had no way of projecting the amount of their compulsory year-end contribution to the budget. Economic incentive funds were still not disbursed on the basis of operating profits, but were contingent upon a number of stipulations having nothing to do with profit. In other words, the role which finances actually played in the large-scale experiment was still more consistent with the earlier practice than with the new approaches voiced at political fora since the Twenty-Seventh Party Congress.[11] Others have pointed out that the financial funds, the experiment envisioned as being allocated by the companies themselves as often as not existed only on paper; the companies' enhanced discretionary power was, thus, only theoretical (Kolesnikov and Lapidis 1986). Meeting the contractual plan obligations in terms of detailed assortment or formulating the plans on previously contracted delivery obligations was supposed to become the primary criterion in evaluating performance. Management bonuses were to be contingent upon this factor, considered to be of major importance by the framers of the experiment at all levels. Meeting the contractual plan-obligations in terms of detailed assortment was seen as the final macroeconomic result (*konechni narodnokhozyaistvenii rezultat*).

It is well known that one of the major problems in Soviet industry is the poor selection both of consumer goods and of means of production. This is what precipitated the above noted regulatory measures focusing on assortment. However, one has to consider that even this rather limited selection means twenty-four million articles that appear in the price lists. These are approximated in the practice of macroeconomic planning by three hundred thousand to three hundred and fifty thousand items figuring in the macroeconomic balance of the Five-Year Plan, and into three thousand to thirty-five hundred in the annual plans; the latter will be broken down further to forty-fifty thousand instructions at the company or association level (Ivanchenko 1986). This makes the above-quoted author and most of the managers believe that what is needed is an even tighter and more detailed assortment-planning. Since even this cannot be detailed enough, they feel that basing the plans on previously contracted interfirm obligations would be the way to fill consumer needs.

Economic theorists point out that it is rather simplistic to infer the need for more detailed physical assortment planning from the theoretically postulated primacy of use-value under socialism. The usefulness of a given product cannot be reflected by a series of physical indicators alone. It is also subject to its scarcity (Borozdin 1986). Even more important are two practical observations. a) Contracts continue to serve as a means for cementing the physical indicators in the plan. The large-scale experiment has not led to contracts assuming their role of moulding decisions on the structure of production (output). This idea would imply that under this form of mandatory planning it would be the concrete choice stemming from the decisions of companies that would constitute the basis for setting up the plans. b) The sellers, taking advantage of their monopoly position, contracted within the framework of the experiment, too, for only a part (at times forty- to seventy percent) of their output, thereby disclaiming even formal responsibility for shipments. This, of course, may be judged justifiable self-defence in a situation where the producer's premium is a direct function of his meeting the requirements of the planned assortment-contract, while he is fully at the mercy of the organizations providing him materials and technology (*snabzhencheskiye organiv*, Shokhin 1986).

The large-scale experiment has been seen with increasing scepticism by Soviet economists and business executives alike. Still, the political leadership has not rejected the experiment in 1986 and 1987, though it has fallen short of its own expectations, and short of producing even a minimal change in the functioning of the mechanism. The 1979 ideology still governs the attitude of the state apparatus, and circumscribes what it can envision as possible alternatives. Convictions held by the majority in the state administration—as evidenced by the history of the Hungarian, Polish, Chinese and Yugoslav reform efforts—have much more influence on government practices than writings of economists or statements made by leading politicians. The force of the old habits of thought remain considerable even if there are committees of experts, capable of setting clear, long-range programmes, ones that the political leadership would wholeheartedly embrace.

Here we are faced with two simultaneous constraints: the one of theory, and the other, the government apparatus itself. To both, there have accrued a number of often uncoordinated economic influences originating in various elements of the political scene. The constraint of theory is itself twofold: internal and external. It is internal in the sense that the conservatism of ideology and management has led to the stagnation of the relevant scientific debates between 1970 and 1985. Otto Latsis states in his strikingly honest and pointed article that what goes on in the mid-80s was much of a rehash of the debates of two decades ago, while the events—or the lack of events—of the interim period, the suspended reform efforts and the causes of stagnation, even in matters of theory, were not being discussed and/or analyzed (Latsis 1986). This train of thought is also supported by a Western observer in an analysis which took into consideration the views of unofficial Soviet publications as well. Surveying the latter he concluded that even the *samizdat* literature either lacked expert economic analyses altogether or, if there were any, they dealt with generalities rather than the feasibility of alternate programmes. They did not address themselves to the question of setting the way from the problems of today to a desirable tomorrow (Hanson 1985). The essence, therefore, of the internal constraint of theory is that since the experience of the past two decades has proved the persistence of the earlier mistakes, the same old criticisms and analyses kept being reiterated. As for the political leadership, it tolerated but certainly did not encourage any efforts to go beyond what had been achieved in the sixties. Instead, it supported the sanctimonious exponents of the "theory of advanced socialism". All this was coupled with the superficiality of the information available to Soviet reformers about the experiences of the countries that had gone through economic reforms. What is even more deplorable from a sociological point of view is the practically wholesale ignorance of the results achieved in these countries on the theoretical plane. Under these circumstances, mistakes already made elsewhere in trying to put reform ideas into practice are likely to repeat themselves in the Soviet Union.

While a great deal more could be said about all this, I feel that from the point of view of the near future, it is more important to talk about the external constraints of theory. Just how receptive is the political leadership to all-encompassing reform proposals? Even after the Twenty-Seventh Congress, professional journals such as *Planovoe Khozyaistvo* and *Voprosy Ekonomiki* kept on advocating the introduction of measures improving the efficiency of the set of compulsory indicators, measures such as financial incentives. This, then, was what the established segment of "science" had to offer the political leadership by way of the options available to them! Due to the efforts of their new managing editors, *Ekonomicheskaia Gazeta* and *Kommunist* as well now contain current radical analyses. Examples of this are the above-cited writing of Latsis (1986), and an article by Shatalin and Gaidar (1986) highlighting—with no direct reference—a reform procedure identical in essence to the target model of the as yet unrealized third stage of the Hungarian reform. Even more revealing is the fact that this very different practical programme had gone totally unnoticed by the official organs in 1985–86, precipitating never an argument or debate. This seems to indicate that a reform proposal as radical as Shatalin's and Gaidar's was not seen as posing a real threat to the establishment before the January 1987 session of the Central Committee. (Since then, the voices of conservatism have become louder, and there is more talk about the evils of self-righteous criticism, not only in the ideological but also in the literary sphere.)

The proposals to replace one set of indicators by another, or to increase the flexibility of pricing—regulations that in the past have been implemented by the stroke of a pen—have always provoked energetic response from the press. (Unlike the historic and obviously utopian proposals to turn the Planning Board into a scientific center.)

For a long time, thus, the commitment of the press to reform ideas did not strike officialdom as presenting a threat serious enough to have to defend themselves against it.

The political report of the Party Congress came out strongly against the practice of pushing finances into the background, of trivializing the role played by money. It is, thus, a matter of no small interest what the new financial managers infer from the new political ideas, how they interpret the activization of commodity- and monetary relations. The then president of the State Bank, V. V. Dementsev, has dealt with this matter in several of his articles (Dementsev 1986a and 1986b). According to him, the bank will: simplify its credit policies; substantially reduce the number of the legal grounds on which credit can be applied for, and the subdivision of credit contingencies; restrict the financing of non-planned losses and overruns on operating expenses; take steps against the lack of financial discipline and for the tightening of discipline in keeping to the terms of payment schedules; restrict the launching of new projects, and initiate a differentiated approach towards companies in establishing their credit status. All of this seems to indicate the Bank's intentions to upgrade its traditional role in financing and in policing the "Plan".

The experiments introduced in the construction sector, in domestic trade, in sea freight and in railway transportation all have a common denominator. They tend to cut the number of centrally-established performance indicators and accounting regulations to give companies (or cooperatives) the responsibility for deciding on certain operational matters, while at the same time maintaining the upper hand of the centre in respect of decisions on major investments, production output, or assortment makeup. Furthermore, efforts have been made to have certain forms of strictly individual labour activity in the second economy brought under official supervision and legalized. The "result" of these efforts is the much discussed Law on Individual Labour Activities.[12]

This law, often overrated by the Hungarian and Western mass media alike, is not at all devoted to private enterprise. This type of activity was prohibited by the May 1986 Law on Unearned Incomes. From the economic point of view, entrepreneurship means the investing and the risking of one's own wealth, a practice which simply does not exist in the Soviet Union. In fact, both laws specifically prohibit intermediation and, perhaps with added emphasis, the intertwining of state-owned assets and private initiative, a form of association that has been dominating the flourishing second economy in Hungary. Ivan Gladkii, the president of the *Goskomtrud,* and one of the legislators of the law on "private" work, emphatically stated that association of private individuals, the private hiring of wage-earners, and the marketing of these "entrepreneurs' " products is out of question. He added that their prices shall be set by the Ministry of Finance and by the State Price Committee.[13] This net income allows the employment of part-time, split-time or seasonal workers, and in exceptional cases the setting-up of leasehold operations, mainly in remote areas and resorts. The performance of management, however, is still evaluated on how well the company meets its contractual plan-obligations in terms of detailed assortment. This feeds this subsystem back into the mainstream of the overall "improved" experimental mechanism, although regulations specific to this sector have the potential to operate under much looser central control than some other areas. Here, too, all major investments remain in the hands of the central authorities, and until 1988 there was no talk about modifying the price-system or the methods of price calculation. The establishment—as in the GDR—of a separate network of specialty shops with separate high prices for highly fashionable and sought-after merchandise is a relatively novel phenomenon.

On the theoretical plane, the salient features of the "improved experimental system" are the following: limited decentralization, applying only to matters of minor importance, generally simplified procedures, and the illusion of the five-year stability of plans and financial conditions carried over from the July 1979 regulations. For the practising economist looking at either the company-level or the central direction, the absurdity of assuming such stability even given the inflexibility and slow reactions under mandatory planning is perfectly clear. It is precisely through the oft-criticized plan-modifications that the economy can adjust to the realities. Without the *post facto* harmonization of the uncoordinated plan indicators and financial and production indices, the economy would simply stop functioning.

There are plenty of valid arguments for a more "enlightened" centralism. Still, it seems a bit far-fetched to subscribe unconditionally to the thesis of Hans-Hermann Höhmann (1985), which has enjoyed such wide acceptance among the more realistic of the Western authors, namely that the leadership practices of Ryzhkhov imply a major reliance on East German experience. The GDR was a much smaller country. Its size was determinative of the way its administratively decentralized system functioned. There were a hundred and thirty centrally managed industrial combines (plant complexes) in the country. They were independent from an operations-standpoint only, but very much centrally directed in every other respect. Since there were only a hundred and thirty of them, their rigid central direction notwithstanding, they had a relatively flexible mode of functioning and an informal correcting mechanism based on vertical and horizontal personal relationships. This was what, in effect, lent flexibility to the East German economy. The Soviet Union, given its size and its historic make-up, could not develop this basic criterion of the East German economic mechanism even if it were to install a system far more centralized than the present one. It is hardly surprising therefore that despite the new regulations and despite the constant political criticism levelled at petty official interference, Soviet economic management has not become more liberal in the course of 1985–90. With the continued insistence on performance according to continuously modified central indicators and plans, the centrally-initiated devolution of authority has mostly remained a formality. What is more, a number of branch-ministries have vindicated additional competences for themselves in the course of the 1986 reorganizations (Shilov 1986). In the area of finance, for example, where, according to the president of the *Gosbank* the emphasis is on simplification and on reducing paperwork, the number of instructions and circulars has even been growing, and local branches are at a loss as to what procedures they are to follow under the present circumstances.[15] These developments indicate quite unambiguously what the continuation of the experiment held for the future.

1987—YEAR OF THE TURN

The year 1987 brought with it the acceleration of Soviet political development and its conflicts. The significant changes which were promulgated in June-July 1987 have added relevant elements of novelty to the picture as it has developed so far. They even warrant a change in the emphasis of its overall evaluation, especially in terms of the long-range trends.

How can one be certain that the Soviet Union has, in fact, made a move, and it is not just the rhetoric that has changed in Moscow? Gorbachev himself has stated[16] that in his first two years in office the modifications have affected only the highest authorities, and practically nothing has changed on the company level. No radical measures have yet been taken, and the directives formulating the new goals are so sketchy and ambiguous that they never reach the companies, for the central organs continue to function the old way. Might there be something to the widespread conclusion that *perestroika* is nothing but the old wine in a new skin?

The answer to this, of course, depends largely on what we consider to be a genuine change. If the existence of democratic pluralism and the dominance of private enterprise are the sole criteria (Ströhm 1987), then the *perestroika*, too, will be found to fall short. For it is an attempt to reform the *Soviet* power system. As such, it embodies the basic interests of Soviet Union as a great power, interests which can only be realized through a fundamental change. It is not merely an attempt by certain groups of the intelligentsia to assert their self-interests, as some conservative commentators and authors of the new left (and the old right) seem to think. This underlying interest in survival through adjustment gives the *perestroika* a chance of success against the vested interests of a government apparatus of eighteen million *apparatchiks*.

Slogans are important in every society. This is especially true where public information is a state monopoly, and the style and tone of the mass-media, the values they represent have a serious impact on the behaviour of the people, and as a consequence, on the relationship between the people and the leadership. Slogans and practice cannot differ substantially for any length of time without serious repercussions. One or the other has to adjust itself. Gorbachev (1987a) emphasized often that openness is not a tactic, but the fundamental means of eliminating public apathy and corruption.[17] Doing away with *glasnost'* would mean doing away with the new Soviet leadership, who can't assert themselves with the traditional subservient role of the mass media.

The degree to which there is freedom of expression largely determines the degree to which competence will have its due in any debate. Debates in the social sciences are no exception. Having competent people speaking their mind in turn makes for the kind of social awareness which is the prerequisite of setting realistic goals, and realistic means to attain them. All of these factors have great significance in reform-type changes originated and directed from above. The traditional Stalinist supposition that once you have the formula, the execution is merely a function of ample propaganda and discipline, is mistaken. Yet it is on these very premises and by emphasizing the contradictions in the new measures that *perestroika* is being disparaged primarily by the German-language scientific journals and press. It should be obvious that no reform can ever be introduced as a neat package of contradiction-free measures. It is reminiscent of the simple-minded schematism of some grade-school textbooks when a set of measures which were adopted and can only be understood and interpreted as part and parcel of a political process is often taken out of context in static analysis. Moreover, its potential success or failure, and even its political value, is judged by how far a few of its documents are unambiguous. This allegedly scientific approach, which is currently very much in vogue also in retrospective analyses of the 1966 Hungarian reform programme is the utmost oversimplification of the interrelations between society and the reform programme.

The Soviet leadership does not seem to share the above static approach. The General Secretary stated in his closing address to the June 1987 meeting of the Central Committee that there were at the time and there would be for some years to come two mechanisms running in parallel: the old and the new. It is the prime task and responsibility of the political leadership to overcome the opposition to the new, manage and effectuate the transition to it.[18] The vested interests' quiet opposition to the reforms can become an "inevitable" majority stand only if society remains indifferent and the political leadership remains uncommitted to change, thus observing resistance to change. However, if the opposite happens—as it did in China, for example—the reform line can win even from a losing position. There is, of course, a distinct difference between the approaches of the two countries. True to its traditions, China changed its practice first, and modified legislation later. The Soviet Union, also in the spirit of its traditions, proceeds in reverse order. Thus, while it can indeed make a great deal of difference what laws are in effect, this—as the example of China shows—is not decisive in itself, and certainly should not be interpreted *per se*, i.e. abstracting from the dynamics of the given socio-political environment.

Perhaps the most important mistakes from the point of view of these dynamics were the over-zealous execution of the Law on Unearned Income, and the wide reliance on police methods to which the relatively favourable yields in centrally registered stocks in 1986 and 1987 were, in part, due. What, in fact, happened was that the fight against unearned income did not stop at bribery, the cheating in statistical and performance reports and at other socio-pathological symptoms. It extended also to the rural population's free marketing activities and individuals' taking odd jobs on the side, and thereby restricted the expansion of the officially unrecognized but until then condoned "grey area" of the economy, an area essential for the reform's social acceptance. The matter became a political issue because it touched on a vital area of the Gorbachevian line. The immediate improvement in the population's provisioning with basic staples has repeatedly been pronounced a chief priority, a precondition of the functioning of *perestroika*. Thus, any encroachment in this area had to evoke a political response.

It was probably the new leadership's need to give some immediate proof of having the situation well in hand that precipitated its introducing in the agro-industry new incentives that were formally in line with the stipulations of the Law on Unearned Income. Although these relative liberalizing measures—described in detail in Chapter Eight—implied more freedoms and less controls, practice has been dominated by the political need to improve the gross indicators of overall agricultural performance, practically at any rate. Therefore local authorities replaced the earlier-described mechanism of incentives with the system of compulsory deliveries *(prodrazviorstka)*, and ruthlessly enforced it (Shmelyov 1987). Furthermore, reliance on methods which Shmelyov has described as a "pogrom" on the household farmers has been widely accepted to fill the central produce stores. These obvious abuses of power had two implications. On the one hand, they prompted political action (Latsis 1987) calling for reassessing agricultural policies and management practices alike. This theme figures high on the agenda of both the professional and the daily press. A special Central Committee session—postponed several times in 1986–88—discussed an alternative programme. However, documents adopted at the All Union Party Conference in June 1988 seem to indicate that the issue seems to have been considered as resolved by the new statute of and Law on Agricultural Cooperatives, fitting the agricultural policies set in 1986 (despite frustrating outcomes). The other result, as Shmelyov (1988a) has pointed out in his penetrating analysis, is that instead of support there's growing scepticism against *perestroika* all across the provinces. This may become the source of even more serious supply problems in townships unless political authorities disapprove all these practices publicly and punish those responsible.

A further by-product of these developments was that the law on individual labour activity and the 1987–88 regulations stipulating the establishment of small service cooperatives have remained dead letter, due primarily to a lack of public interest. For example, of the eight million inhabitants of Moscow, only a few thousand have asked the

Executive Committee of the City Council for a licence. (This is required prior to forming and registering these cooperatives. The authorities have discretionary rights.) A separate Politburo resolution has dealt with the question of tax-incentives for potential applicants, and has also condemned the administration of a number of the constituent republics for hindering the process by putting up bureaucratic obstacles.[19] This makes it clear that had the leadership been a cautiously passive one with a "wait and see" attitude, the social dynamism of the reform process would have come again to a standstill at the previous years' level by 1987.

In view of this, the political leadership adopted a much harsher tone in their criticism, extending it to many more areas, and many more people than before. At the January and June 1987 meetings of the Central Committee, they instituted a plan of action more concrete and more far-reaching than the programme worked out by the Twenty-Seventh Party Congress. All this went far beyond being a self-serving exercise in party rhetoric. A forward thrust was the only way to counter the threat to the entire reform process's falling apart; not to do so would have been equivalent to a retreat. The political and economic price of such a retrogression was only too well known from the experience of the past ten to fifteen years, especially in its international ramifications. It was no longer a viable political alternative. It would call into question the very legitimacy of the entire programme of *perestroika*.

Certain Western analysts take the view that the January 1987 Central Committee report and decision were based on the principle: "If it doesn't work in the economy, let's switch to politics." This is clearly a misunderstanding. Anyone familiar with not only the condensed excerpts and media commentaries but with the entire material of the Central Committee meeting will come to a different conclusion. In reality it was at this meeting that the new platform was formulated and the new phase of development was launched. When the Twenty-Seventh Party Congress was convened, there was a strong need for continuity. Consequently, it had been content with merely skirting, rather than taking a stand on what was a fundamentally novel political approach (Meissner 1987).

The communiqué of the January 1987 Central Committee meeting, on the other hand, did no less than re-formulate, in the light of the current approach, the entire official dogma of the day—known to all East Europeans from their college textbooks—the entire view of socialism as it has, in fact, turned out to be. A detailed analysis of the report and of what it conveyed is beyond the scope of a book devoted to economic issues. However, for the sake of clarity, certain observations deserve reiteration.

Economic breakthrough can be achieved neither by changes in the techniques of regulation, nor by comprehensive modifications that remain strictly within the realm of the economy. Economic management is a function of the entire socio-political environment, which depends on the degree of democracy within the system. This, in turn, is subject to the arrangements prevailing in the party. Only greater democracy within the party can break this vicious circle. However, this requires radical reforms in the field of education and information, and a dissolution of the sectoral authorities. Elite recruitment has to be altered accordingly, without regard for the years spent serving the party and other similar considerations.

The economic reform programme was approved by the June 1987 session, where certain steps were also taken with regard to elite recruitment. Further conclusions, as far-reaching as the circumstances permit, can be drawn from an analysis of the June 1988 All-Union Party Conference (see below). Thus, with the mere declaration that change was under way, the January plenum provided the impetus for the reform forces' political offensive for at least a year and a half. This, of course, does not mean that since January 1987 the forces of reform alone have played the lead on the political scene, but it does mean that the entire process has got over the first dangerous deadlock. What seems to be quite important is that political self-criticism and the modest evaluation given of the results of the previous two years has robbed the bureaucrats and the conservative forces of one of their strong suits. They can no longer stop meaningful change by presenting the fundamentally unchanged *status quo* as the new, post-reform reality. The INF Agreement on the reduction of intermediate missiles, the solution of the Afghan question and even the Mathias Rust airplane incident were lending added impetus to the reform.

The more detailed reform blueprint was adopted by the Central Committee in June and by the Supreme Soviet in July 1987. I have undertaken their textual analysis in a separate article (Csaba 1989a). From the standpoint of our present argument what is of importance is that in his programmatic speech to the Central Committee Mr. Gorbachev clearly stated that the aim is to *entirely do away with the system of mandatory planning in the Soviet Union by 1991.*[20] Thus the experimental solutions—including the self-financing of some more sectors from 1988 on—are to be considered as solutions not of the

new mechanism, but of the interim period. However, it is important
to pinpoint: what is targeted is a model of indirect state planning rather
than a market mechanism, of any sort.

This goal goes far beyond the conventional playing around with
regulators and organizations, as it often is the case under such re-
arrangements. If it were only that, they would not precipitate the kind
of strong opposition they do. Mr. N. Slyunkov (1988b), Politburo
member and secretary to the Central Committee for economic affairs
since 1987, pointedly emphasized the need for the total restructuring
of such central organs as the *Gosplan*, the *Gosbak* and the Ministry of
Finance not only through significant reductions in their staff and
sphere of competence, but through internal reorganization, i.e. the
elimination of the effective production-controlling departments.[21]
Major changes are contemplated in the interrelations between plan
targets and monetary categories. Most importantly, this is an open-
ended programme. In his speech to the Supreme Soviet, the Premier
emphatically stated the need for continuous development even after
1991.[22] At that time, judging by the arguments advanced in the economic literature, not even the emergence of a full-fledged regulated
market model along Central European lines of thinking could be
ruled out (although this would have required a further political decision even in a continuously prevailing climate of reform).

To get back to realities, the official reform blueprint in its palpable
form, the Law on the State Owned Enterprise[23] in fact in many instances reflects the circumstances that obtain in 1987 rather than the
vision of the future. Not only does it treat companies and their associations and also their medium-level control organs as one, but it does
not apply to agricultural cooperatives or to the private sector. Its
wording, probably reflecting the compromises between the various
vested interests, is quite ambiguous. The June 1987 party resolution
on the centralized system of material-technical supply *(snabzheniye)*
states expressly that it is ripe for elimination. The Law on the State
Enterprise, however, still contains quite detailed regulations on how
the organs of material-technical supply should properly function (both
at central and at local levels). Both the place and the role of sectoral
direction seem to be more secure as reflected in the Law than in the
relevant party-resolution. Unlike in Hungary, in the Soviet Union
the sectoral portfolios are left with significant financial funds and
their role in foreign trade is even growing. This hardly reflects the
point made by the general manager of the Leningrad Elektrosila
Association at the July 1987 Central Committee meeting, i.e. that if

the sectoral ministry continues to be responsible for every step the companies take, it will keep interfering even if it has been instructed not to.[24] A positive development, however, is that unlike the Law on the State Owned Enterprise, the party resolution of June 1987 addresses itself to anti-trust legislation and to the complete overhaul of the entire legal system in the spirit of the new political decisions.

Both the Law on the State Owned Enterprise and the party resolution of June 1987 left plenty of questions unanswered. For instance the determination of the tasks of the workers' council and how to delineate these from that of other social organs, and the extent of mandatory state commissioning *(goszakazy)* imply qualitatively different things, depending on whether they cover 5 or 70 percent of the post-1991 output. Among further issues yet to be tackled more specifically are the nature of the new pricing system and price mechanism, not to mention the system for deciding on major investments and capital flows. All this implies that a great many issues will require close scrutiny and evaluation in the coming years in the Soviet Union. Along with the topics needing further theoretical clarification and political decisions, we must not lose sight of the fact that the conflicts of interest within the Soviet Union are manifold. [Quality control *(Gospriemka)* and increasing productivity was bound to meet resistance from the producers as well, and there is no country where raising the rents and cutting subsidies is received with popular enthusiasm.]

At the same time, as two leading British scholars (Wallace and Clarke 1986) have pointed out, Eastern Europe does have an interest in the success of the *perestroika*. An alternative scenario implies a further weakening of the Soviet economic performance, a growing East-West animosity in the political, military and ideological arenas alike, all of which will certainly restrict the East European countries' own elbow room as well.

1988—THE ALL-UNION PARTY CONFERENCE

As could be expected, the radicalization of the reformist policies induced the growing and open opposition of the established structures still embodying the Brezhnevite consensus. On the surface, this conflict cumulated in such political headlines as the Yeltsin affair and the controversy about Soviet history. It is partly this that accounts for the moderation with which Gorbachev expressed himself in the speech given on the seventieth anniversary of the October revolution. As is usual in the Soviet Union, the conspicuous events tended to overshadow the more imminent, and incommensurably more real "other danger" (Shmelyov 1988b) of silent sabotage by the bureaucracy, which has managed to undermine all the post-Stalin attempts at reform, while paying ritual lip-service to the radical slogans. In political terms, the newly discovered danger of *avant-gardisme* as well as the obvious impact of the manifest nationality conflicts have, beyond doubt, created a tendency towards centralization. The economic benefits of the first three years of restructuring have definitely been meagre both in terms of overall macroeconomic indicators and even more in terms of bread and butter issues. The discrepancy that the man in the street perceives between the radical vocabulary and the limited palpable results raises questions as to the feasibility of the reformist policies and weakens societal support for them. This realization figures high in the keynote speech of Gorbachev (1988) to the All-Union Party Conference. Cataloguing the achievements of his three years of tenure, he enumerated all but the economic areas. Listing the most urgent tasks yet to be solved, he spoke in detail of the various aspects of everyday life like the scarcity of food supplies, the limited availability of consumer durables, insufficient housing[25] and inadequate services.

In a way, the resistance of the inherited structures to the attempts at their restructuring was quite successful. First, at the political level, it proved to be infeasible and inexpedient to carry out major personnel changes at the All-Union Party Conference, as originally envisaged in January 1987. This was due to the publicly discussed fact that the local and medium level party aparatuses dominated the selection of delegates to the Conference. On the other hand the strategy of watering down grandiose reform projects worked a bit too well. For the policy of economic reform this turned out to be advantageous as it revealed—earlier than expected—the conceptual and also the political impediments to implementing the June 1987 decisions. Thus, relevant improvements have become possible within a relatively short period of time, in both areas.

As far as professional economic arguments are concerned the most obvious weak points of the June-July 1987 blueprint have become evident. The system of state orders, for instance, has led to even tighter centralization and to the even more detailed physical planning of the output of enterprises by 1988 than before (Smirnov and Nesterovich 1988). The expansion of the various cooperatives in services and elsewhere have been severely curtailed by the very restrictive income tax regulations (cf. *Izvestitya*, 20 March, 1988). These regulations flatly disregard the need to reward risk-taking and try to set the incomes of the members of the cooperatives at par with the state-run wage system, whose lack of incentive is one of the commonplaces of Soviet economics. The new tax regulations—noted several speakers at the Conference—reflect the attempt of the bureaucracy to deter those willing to put in extra effort from launching something unconventional. The use of "control figures" so vaguely defined in the Law on the State Owned Enterprise turned out to be a further way of justifying the ministries' additional breaking down of the detailed plan instructions. Thus, the control figures have become "a new form for the unchanged old substance"—as two observers (Sukhotin and Dementsev 1988) have noted. These "advances" have been well reflected in the 1988 Law on Cooperatives. The independence of the farms and even of their associations remains subject to "state interests" and their due observance (secured, of course, by some uncontrolled organ of the state administration). The scope of the state orders—exceeding in some cases 100 percent of the capacities of the industrial enterprises—is not limited at all, and the issue of financial incentives—the obvious weak point of the 1986 regulation of agriculture—remains ambiguous (Voskresenskii 1988). This is a very serious problem indeed, as the relatively good harvests of 1986 and 1987 have not led to improved supplies in urban areas.

In sum, the remarkable ability of the old structures to integrate any new initiative and to make most changes merely formal just about succeeded in bringing the process of reform to a standstill again —for the third time in three years. Therefore it was legitimate for the Gorbachevian reform to become even more political, and to draw the practical conclusions from the January 1987 analysis: without a thorough overhaul of the political system that had evolved under Stalin, no relevant economic reform could come into being—let alone succeed. Translating this finding into deeds required a detailed draft and timetable. By promulgating these, the All-Union Party Conference of June 1988 gave new impetus to the process of the Soviet reform.

The analysis of mostly economic issues led Central Committee Secretary and Politburo member N. Slyunkov to conclude already in early 1988: the major reason why the bureaucracy has the upper hand in state administration and thus in socio-economic affairs is the fact that there is a similar style of bureaucratic rule by the *apparatchiks*

within the party itself (Slyunkov 1988a). Thus it is no surprise that
the keynote of the Gorbachev report approved at the Conference was
the need for finding ways and means of de-bureaucratizing the party
and de-étatizing society by calling into existence a system of "checks
and balances" aimed at avoiding the recurrence of previous mistakes.

Considering earlier Soviet economic reality, one could hardly
imagine a more daring idea than the Gorbachevian vision of the Party
giving up its prerogatives to decide over everyday affairs, the core of
the set of measures approved by the All-Union Party Conference in
June 1988. Although it will certainly take a long time for this idea
to become practice, the crux of the conceptual framework is definitely
a new redistribution of powers. Accordingly, the Party is to be entrusted with the conceptual and theoretical issues, while *de facto* decision-
making is to rest partly with the parliament-controlled government,
and partly with the presidential system. It is worth noting that the
very idea of a continuously functioning elected parliament (only
one third of whose members are to be the members of centrally control-
lable national organizations), the wide publicity attending decision-
making and the limitation of tenures to a maximum of 10 years inevitably involves a fair degree of spontaneity and a loosening of
controls, even at its most formalistic implementation. It is also very
relevant to Soviet conditions that a fair degree of devolution to elected local bodies, as well as the redefinition of the economic rights of
the member-republics is under consideration—issues that might
overcome a series of bottlenecks resulting from over-centralization.
Nota bene, devolution also means the decentralization of frictions and
conflicts, and would make local/national authorities the target of a
plethora of grievances and of opposition traditionally directed against
the authorities in Moscow. Thus, more enlightened, and by definition,
less meticulous regulation may, in fact, enhance the efficacy of central
control. Moreover general international experience shows that a
more pluralistic, i.e. more elaborate set of mutually controlling and
balancing authorities is more conducive to efficient central management than the formally overcentralized "oriental" regimes, which
will be absurdly out-of-date by the turn of the millennium. Therefore
if we try to define the interests of the ruling strata in a less narrow-
minded manner than was done during the Brezhnev period[26] it is not
at all as obvious as is traditionally maintained that the only way of
monopolizing power is to enforce direct controls through a single
bureaucratically centralized party machinery. Conditions today disfavour monocentric "white elephants" in all walks of life. One should

not reject out of hand the idea that the Soviets are able to cognize their own interest, and adjust to the changed conditions—a *conditio sine qua non* for the viability of any complicated organism.

All in all, despite the continuous and demonstrable presence of a vast number of vested counter-interests, one cannot help but see that the ruling strata have an elementary interest in keeping the system functioning through continuous changes. This interest is embodied in the Gorbachevian draft for political reform, and was approved by the All-Union Party Conference in June 1988. It is important to remember that it is a new division of powers that is at stake: it is not just a matter of trying to find a new institutional *façade* for the "dictatorship of the proletariat". The proposed Law on Publicity—if taken seriously—and the concept of *Rechts-Staatlichkeit* can be extremely important factors in promoting decentralizing economic reforms.

Significant among the economic issues of the Conference was the fact that a thorough overhaul of the system of state orders was envisaged for 1989. The urgency of a price reform—limited to the correction of the price relatives, without being specific about the function of prices—has been reiterated and politically endorsed. The need to introduce wholesale trade in place of the system of material-technical supply has been voiced, and 1990 was set as the deadline for achieving this goal. It is striking, however, how vague the Conference documents were on the issues of agriculture and foreign trade. In the former area, nothing specifically new has been decided, although the General Secretary did speak about the need to abolish mandatory targets. Moreover he talked about the need "to introduce new relations of production in rural areas". These formulae foreshadowed decisions which did not have sufficient political backing at the time of the Conference, such as abolishing the *Gosagroprom* system, for example. The foreign trade issue might also receive some new impetus—although the single sentence on the convertible ruble may or may not imply the introduction of serious changes, as a function of domestic Soviet developments. The statement on the need to restructure finances, banking and prices as a package could be very relevant in the medium run.

All in all, the political dynamism of the reform process has once again been secured for another year or so. The Conference has created a more lasting framework, one that may serve as a point of reference at least, for another five years—especially, if the foreseeable resistance to, and setbacks in, the process are taken, *ex ante*, into account. However, it would be difficult not to share the "new concerns" of Nikolai

Shmelyov (1988a) that have proved to be valid for the post-Conference period as well. Without tangible economic improvement in the living conditions of the masses in the next two to three years, societal support for any meaningful reform was bound to vanish earlier than the relatively slow organic evolution of the established politico-economic arrangements reached the point where no return is possible to the Brezhnevite core. In fact, the Soviet analyst is quite right in pinpointing: the discrepancy between the dynamics of political and of economic changes/reforms cannot go on forever. In order to stabilize *perestroika*, he has proposed the abolition of the *Gosagroprom*—and even of the *kolkhoz* system—and advocated doing away with all mandatory planning in agriculture. He urged open support for urban cooperatives, the massive imports of consumer durables from the West, and direct political punitive measures against ministerial and local party leaders sabotaging reforms.

It is obvious that the All-Union Party Conference has fallen short of this programme. Still, it has left the door open to such decisions in the future. If these will actually materialize, the Conference's demonstrative and political roles may be similar to that of the Twenty-Seventh Party Congress at the initial stage of *perestroika*—provided that future decisions do follow the trend of the 1986–88 period. At any rate, the then postponed decisions—including those on personnel issues—will have to be taken in the not very distant future.

The historical fate of the Soviet policy of restructuring is an open-ended story at the time of the final updating of the present book. The inevitable question one faces after having surveyed so many paradoxes and dilemmas of past and present developments is: Why should we maintain an optimistic *scenario* at a time of growing scepticism in East and West alike? Over and above the remarkable skills and intellectual capacity of the General Secretary, it seems decisive to me that the major reason has, in fact, been publicly pointed out in January 1988: this is the last chance the Soviet Union has to modernize herself, and maintain her role as a great power.[27]

THE IMPACT OF EXTERNAL DISTURBANCES ON THE SOVIET
REFORM POLICY

Perhaps the most incredible aspect of Soviet economic policy—given the predominance of gas, oil and oil derivatives in her exports to the West—is the fact that neither the post-1982 stagnation of oil prices nor even their collapse in the post-1985 period has provoked any major Soviet policy reaction. Not that there is any shortage of resolutions or of decisions to contract more loans and to restrict Western imports (while trying to import more and more from the CMEA). Soviet manufacturing, too, is getting plenty of encouragement to increase its share in total exports. Still, not even in the preambles to the measures regulating the implementation of the 12th Five-Year Plan, or those specifying the rate of growth in various sectors, or those aimed at improving the system of management even mention the truly radical changes in the post-1985 world market, and the new challenge that this poses to the Soviet economy. Foreign trade is still discussed in the traditional terms of being just one of the arenas in which the competition between the two world systems takes place. And yet, any look at the trend of trade between the Soviet Union and the West for the years 1982 to 1986 (Hanson 1986) clearly indicates that this is a whole new ball game. For the second time in its economic history, the Soviet Union faces the need to make a major adjusment to the world economy. What is more, the form of this adjustment will determine the overall direction that economic policy and management can take. As in the years 1929–32, the conventional inter-relationship between domestic and external factors of development —implying the priority of the former in large countries—has been reversed. It is again no longer the country's domestic endowments that determine its foreign trade relations, but the other way round: it is the Soviet Union's foreign trade performance that will determine how far its economic policy can go. If this performance is inadequate, no amount of modification will salvage the plan: it will fall apart. Opting for autarky would, naturally, have immediate repercussions on the system of economic management, though the example of China has shown that decentralization is still an option even without any real change in the macro-economic function of foreign trade. That this should happen in the Soviet Union seems unlikely, in view of the political setup reflected in the Twenty-Seventh Party Congress, but it is not impossible.

Chapter Eight goes into some detail in showing the size and severity of the change in the world economy, and the challenge it poses for Soviet economic development. The same ideas shed some light on the causes for increased Soviet reliance on Eastern Europe. Taking Soviet reform policies for granted, a logical follow-up would be their implementation by the CMEA, an institution having been moulded to a fairly large degree by traditional Soviet preferences and priorities.

In theory, a reformed Soviet trade policy could have been the first step to the genuine reform of the mechanism of CMEA cooperation. In practice, however, this is not how matters stand. The resolution the Politburo adopted in August 1986 and published in September of the same year[28] means by and large that as of 1987, Soviet foreign trade policy has become part of the "improved" large-scale experimental system.[29] The State Foreign Trade Committee, with powers extending to every foreign trade organ, was set under the immediate jurisdiction of the Presidium of the Council of Ministers. There was some attempt made at decentralization, but these were half-hearted measures that did not affect the competences to import. On the export side, some seventy associations and some twenty sectoral ministries received foreign trade rights. This was an odd measure, inasmuch as sectoral ministries possess neither the macro-economic overview of *Gosplan*, nor the kind of detailed knowledge of products and their markets which is specific to enterprises (and here we have not even mentioned the ministries' personnel problems and their traditional seclusion from the outside world). It was only manufacturing industries that were given autonomous export rights, i.e. industries whose Western exports have hardly been significant. The organizations which had won export rights could establish a separate convertible currency fund for importing non-consumer goods. However, in order to qualify for actual imports these companies must also register and incorporate their needs in the all-union import plan. Their requests will be "considered in order of priority"—an expression that hardly leaves room for illusions in those familiar with the procedures. The above organizations were to operate as autonomous partners to the implementation of the multilateral interstate agreements designed to help realize the CMEA's Long-term Programme for technological progress: make cooperation agreements on the delivery of components and spare parts, themselves negotiating the prices, and establish other types of direct contacts—other than trade deals—with companies in the other CMEA countries. The CMEA joint companies enjoy autonomy in setting their prices and signing contracts. Profits are shared proportionate to the capital invested. If located in the Soviet Union, such joint ventures are also integrated to the overall Soviet management system. Every item of macroeconomic importance, exports as well as imports, continues to fall under the immediate control of the *Gosplan* and the Ministry of Foreign Economic Relations.[30] The Soviet companies operating within the framework of cooperation agreements or as part of multinational companies do not enjoy priority in the allocation neither of materials, goods, nor of technologies, and are set as many plan targets as before. What remains decisive is the fact that usually three, or at most four percent of a Soviet company's products will be sold on a foreign market (Konstantinov 1986). Even when there are incentives to export, it is the domestic market that continues to be crucial for a Soviet company. Competing on foreign markets is a burden that brings few advantages to compensate for the extra work it requires. In this sense, the interest of Soviet companies' involvement in foreign trade is not even primarily a matter of adequate legislation, it is a function of the overall socio-economic environment.

BILATERAL IMPLICATIONS

It is something of a commonplace that its multilateral structure notwithstanding, the CMEA is becoming more and more an institutional system of bilateral contacts between the Soviet Union and the small member states. The Long-term Programme for technological development was initiated by the Soviet Union; the plans were elaborated by the Soviet partner, and every one of the ninety-three coordinative head organizations *(golovnaya organizatsiya)* is Soviet based. In the same way, most of the intra-CMEA joint ventures function bilaterally, with the Soviet Union being one of the partners.

Both within the framework of the Long-term Technological Programme and in general, it is the Soviet partner who professes most interest in direct interfirm cooperation. In theory, this is a good thing. In practice, however, it is clear that the Soviet economic mechanism being what it is, such general endeavours cannot in most cases lead to genuine interfirm cooperation. The Soviet enterprises are in no position to establish real production or trade relations with companies of other nations, nor, presumably, will they be in such a position for some time to come. Given that this is so, it is unrealistic to try to increase the role played by the Hungarian companies within the CMEA, as some economists suggest (Rácz 1985; Bautina and Samovol 1986, p. 93; and Vladimirov 1987). What is more, such a step is hardly consonant with the interests of any small country of the integration. For it would leave Hungary, for instance, open to the Soviet partner's taking advantage of the more liberal central controls and of the greater latitude open to companies operating here, resulting in an unplanned surplus compared to what has been achieved through bilateral bargaining at the macroeconomic level.

The Soviet leadership is critical of the CMEA as an institution. The Soviet commercial policy *vis-à-vis* Eastern Europe, which focuses on additional purchases of agricultural produce, consumer goods, materials and high technology and devalues manufactured goods, is not something the new Soviet leadership has invented, but reflects the objective shortages in the Soviet economy. If a small CMEA country adjusted to these short-term trade policy goals directly and unconditionally, this would imply giving up the aim of adjustment to the world market.[31] But independently of the success or failure of the Soviet policy of acceleration, Hungary stood in danger of being drawn into following the line of least resistance. The more successful the policy of acceleration is, in fact, and the more energetic are the attempts to implement it whether successfully or not, the more there was a suction on the Soviet market towards the short-term priorities, as described above.

The Soviet leadership's radical reform programme deserves strong support for both political and economic reasons. However, we must have a clear understanding of the nature of this programme. It is a fact of history that often different things are meant by the same concepts in Hungary and in the Soviet Union. Reform in the Soviet Union is intended to be an open-ended process that has started a few years ago and, as Mikhail Gorbachev has repeatedly pointed out, is likely to go on for a generation's lifetime. Thus, without losing sight of the process as a whole, it is to the situation given at any particular time that Hungarian policy making should adjust its expectations. Running ahead of the times can be a costly mistake.

One cannot help but share the Soviet leadership's disaffection with CMEA institutions. It should be borne in mind, however, that the issues of intra-CMEA cooperation are far less relevant from the overall Soviet policy point of view than they are from Hungary's angle. It is hardly a surprise thus, that the Soviet ideas for reforming the CMEA do not follow from the abstract needs of promoting regional integration as such. They, too, have developed their views on the CMEA from the actual needs of the Soviet economy at this particular time. Thus, from the wide ranging criticism of the CMEA institutions voiced in the mid- and late 80s follow proposals, mostly reflecting the logic of the domestic Soviet "experimental mechanism", and aimed at strengthening the Soviet Union's bargaining position in bilateral trade. Except where the CMEA bureaucracy can frustrate it, this meant further cuts in the number of committees and cutbacks in staff. The insistence on direct contacts was aimed at strengthening the bargaining position of coordinative head organizations *vis-à-vis* their subcontractors; further, it aims at improving the access of Soviet firms to additional East European supplies. In principle, one must support these aims as attempts to do away with central omnipotence. In practice, however, considerations of reciprocity and the principle of a balanced bilateral trade should not fall victim to one-sided endeavours. Since the Soviet Union's policy on CMEA integration is the function and extension of her actual domestic economic mechanism, no amount of dissatisfaction with the integration's institutions and no political slogan, however apt, will result in any thoroughgoing market type reform of the CMEA in the near future. In the short run, thus, we cannot expect that economic principles rather than the commercial considerations of the moment will give rise to a concept that challenges the coordination of plans and the bilateral quota system. For what should be considered a point of departure is not a decision of principle, but the degree of autonomy the Soviet companies have. This applies to the interstate, joint ventures as well, thus it does not seem expedient to establish new giant joint firms by political *fiat* alone.

The Soviet leadership wants to see a practical, bureaucracy-free cooperation take shape. One can only applaud this goal. At the same time we must keep in mind the following:

a) Personnel reductions notwithstanding, the number of management tiers in Soviet management and control has grown between 1985 and 1987, rather than declined. The Soviet companies' foreign relations have been made even more difficult by the steps taken to tighten the controls over the country's borders, and by other disciplinary measures. It still takes five months to get the papers necessary for someone to make a five-day trip to a CMEA country (Zhuravlyov and Kalasnikov 1986). Those seeking to enter the Soviet Union are often subjected to rigorous customs checks. It is unlikely that we will see the day when a prospective buyer or seller can visit any plant of his prospective Soviet partner.

b) During the 80s it was the state-level coordination of interests that remained decisive within the CMEA. Major decisions on integration measures were taken at the political level, prior to—rather than following—meaningful endeavours to harmonize conflicting interests of substance. Given the demonetization of the intra-CMEA mechanism of cooperation, the companies themselves lack a proper compass in making their decisions. Therefore in essence, synchronization of actual national standpoints was left to the respective bodies of state

administrations in negotiating even the most petty details of a transaction; furthermore it was precisely this bureaucratic procedure by
which equivalence of exchange was by and large secured. Nor could
the state apparatus, purely in the name of quick businesslike decisions
(operativnost'), be divested of these functions as there was no alternative way of fulfilling them.

A more businesslike functioning of the multilateral CMEA organs
has been urged primarily by the Romanians since 1976. It is no
surprise that it is Romania that is most frustrated by the comprehensive and somewhat tedious decision-making process within the CMEA,
which effectively prevents the multilateral fora from foisting unilateral political decisions on the entire integration. This, however, must be
seen as something on the credit side of the CMEA "bureaucracy",
and as an element that should not and cannot be abandoned without
fundamentally overhauling what the entire system of CMEA cooperations for the market type coordination of various interests within the
integration are unlikely to be realized for some time to come, the
most we can subscribe to is the novel slogan of quick, businesslike
decisions *(operativnost')*, the elimination of self-serving projects and
organization.

In the late 80s the changes going on in the Soviet Union tended to
exert favourable ideological and foreign policy implications on Hungary. From the point of view of Hungarian economic and trade policy,
however, the new Soviet approach implied new structural priorities
against the Hungarian economy, demands that were fundamentally
incongruous with the secular trends in the world market. One cannot
realistically expect a thoroughgoing change in the mechanism of
CMEA cooperation in the near future, primarily because the radical
reform of the Soviet system of management is bound to be a lengthy
process. Nor should we underestimate the tenacity of old structures
and old ways of doing things. The modifications in the management
and control of Soviet foreign trade effective January 1987 and the
subsequent partial measures introduced from January 1988 on are
important but small steps forward. Therefore the growing demands
(in quality etc.) of the external market does not automatically
imply increased performance criteria in terms of the competitive
norms. In fact, for the reasons elaborated above, exactly the opposite
is the case.

The Soviet programme of growth acceleration has already brought
with it a growing demand for Hungarian deliveries. The "radical
reform" of the Soviet economy, however, has not resulted and will not

yet result in such major improvements on performance and competitiveness that would permit Soviet imports to play a more significant role in the Hungarian economy. What is more, it cannot even reverse a trend of the past decade, namely, that the intra-CMEA division of labour is a diminishing source of growth. Hungary can count on the Soviet Union's maintaining its level of energy deliveries only in terms of a five-year average, and only with recourse to investment contributions, primarily the natural gas coming through the Yamburg pipeline. As for oil and electricity, Hungary must count on seasonal fluctuations, and even a decrease in absolute quantities. Given that the policy of growth acceleration could but compound the domestic shortages within the Soviet Union, the sanctions on non-delivery built into the interstate agreements were bound to be ineffective. Thus, intra-CMEA availability of primary products did not substantiate the growth dynamizing policies implicit in the Hungarian and other East European five-year plans for 1986–90, let alone for the 1991–95 period.

Having surveyed the 1985–87 measures to improve the Soviet mechanism of agriculture in a different chapter we must harbour a fair degree of scepticism as to whether or not the country will be in a position to cut back her reliance on imports in the medium run. With the cutbacks in the Soviet convertible currency income, and given that, for all practical purposes, the CMEA functions as a dominant market for Hungarian agricultural produce, there is a decreasing possibility for Hungary's earning convertible currency surpluses via intra-CMEA special agreements (cf. Chapter 1) whose economic efficiency is questionable, considering the secular fall in world agricultural prices (cf. Lányi 1984). And though the Soviet policy of acceleration also calls for imports of engineering products, this is true only of those that will effectively substitute for Western imports. Though the Soviets will continue to accept mediocre manufactured products, it will be at prices that are less than satisfactory, considering their high production costs.

There can be no doubt that the line of accelerated technological development embodied in the multilateral CMEA Programme (discussed in the following chapter) is a step in the right direction. Under the Soviet economic arsenal, however, it is not at all that clear how these ambitious goals can be realized. Given that the original deadlines for the Programme's elaboration have been substantially moved up the soundness of the hazily improvised projects is subject to doubt from the very outset. Thus, the tardiness with which the

CMEA's Longterm Programme is being implemented must be seen as a blessing rather than a shortcoming. In the light of the uncertainty surrounding the very existence of the preconditions for technological progress, one cannot help but wonder what sense it makes to speak of any kind of reform going on in the CMEA. This issue will be dealt with in the chapter "The CMEA Under Restructuring", and in the closing chapter detailing the October 1987 Council Session and its decisions on the *perestroika* of the CMEA.

NOTES

1 Updated version of the author's December 1986 Hungarian-language analysis. Completed in July 1988.

2 Mikhail Gorbachev's speech in Khabarovsk, *Ekonomicheskaya Gazeta* 1986, 33.

3 Mikhail Gorbachev's opening speech at the Twenty-Seventh Party Congress, *Pravda*, 26 February 1986.

4 Mikhail Gorbachev's speech at the Central Committee meeting on the guidelines of the Five Year Plan, *Ekonomicheskaya Gazeta* 1986, 26.

5 Contrary to the views of Levcik (1986) and other analysts, my opinion is that this was not yet formulated in economic terms at the time of the party congress. As it is borne out by what follows, real reform ideas were conceptualized only at the June 1987 Central Committee session; and, according to Gorbachev's evaluation at the June 1988 party conference, the details were still to be worked out.

6 Mikhail Gorbachev's speech in Krasnodar, *Pravda*, 20 September 1986.

7 Nikolai Ryzhkov's opening speech to the Supreme Soviet about the Twelfth Five Year Plan, *Ekonomicheskaya Gazeta* 1986, 26.

8 The two key issues—the growth and acceleration strategy and the reform—are two very different things. I will not elaborate on this, as several first-rate analyses of the conclusions to be drawn from their contradictions have been published by others (cf. Hewett 1986 and Shmelyov 1988a).

9 Organizatsiya Komissii po sovershenstvovaniyu upravleniya, planirovaniya i khozyaistvennovo mekhanizma. *Izvestiya*, 23 January 1986.

10 G. Deshalit: Plyusy i minusy normativov. *Ekonomicheskaya Gazeta* 1986, 39. (The author is economic director of one of the associations of the Ministry of Precision Engineering.)

11 G. Bazarova: Normativnyi metod raspredeleniya pribyli. *Ekonomicheskaya Gazeta* 1986, 28. (The author is deputy director of the Monetary Research Institute of the Ministry of Finance.)

12 O proekte Zakona SSSR ob individual'noi trudovoi deyatel'nosti. Opening speeches by Ivan Gladkii, chairman of the National Committee on Labour and Social Affairs of the Soviet Union and by I. Titarenko, chairman of the legislative committees of the two houses of the Supreme Soviet, *Izvestiya*, 21 November 1986. For the text of the law, see *Izvestiya*, 22 November 1986.

13 The new Soviet Law on Individual Labour activities (Ivan Gladkii interviewed by Ferenc Szaniszló), *Magyar Hírlap*, 21 November 1986.

14 O sovershenstvovanii planirovaniya, ekonomicheskogo stimulirovaniya i upravleniya v gosudarstvennoi torgovle i potrebitel'skoi kooperatsii. *Ekonomicheskaya Gazeta* 1986, 33.

15 Ustroit' perestroiku (editorial discussion). *Den'gi i Kredit* 1986, 10.

16 Korennoi vopros perestroiki (soveshchanie v TSK KPSS) *Pravda*, June 13 1986.

17 Mikhail Gorbachev's speech to the leadership of the central press, *Ekonomicheskaya Gazeta* 1987, 31, and Mikhail Gorbachev's speech at the KOMSOMOL Congress, *Ekonomicheskaya Gazeta* 1987, 17.

18 Mikhail Gorbachev Closing address at the Central Committee session. In *Az SZKP 1987. júniusi ülésének anyagai* (Topics at the June 1987 session of the Soviet Communist Party). Budapest: Kossuth, 1987.

19 Politbyuro TSK KPSS. *Ekonomicheskaya Gazeta* 1987, 4.

20 Mikhail Gorbachev's speech at the Central Committee session. In *Az SZKP 1987. júniusi ülésének anyagai* (Topics at the June 1987 session of the Soviet Communist Party). Budapest: Kossuth, 1987.

21 N. Slyun'kov's comments at the Central Committee session referred to in footnote 16.

22 Nikolai Ryzhkov's speech to the Supreme Soviet, *Ekonomicheskaya Gazeta* 1987, 28.

23 Zakon SSSR O gosudarstvennom predpriyatii (obedinenii). *Pravda*, 7 July 1987.

24 B. I. Fomin's comments at the Central Committee session referred to in footnote 16.

25 The measure here, of course, differs from that of the early Brezhnev years, when the abolition of the previously quite widespread system of shared communal flats in townships was considered the great achievement.

26 For a good description of the contemporary Soviet reasoning, see Nove 1977.

27 The point was made by the Secretary of the Writers' Union, G. Baklanov, and was supported openly by Gorbachev, as reported in Demokratizatsiya sut' perestroiki, sut' sotsializma (Soveshchaniye v TsK KPSS). *Pravda*, 13 January 1988.

28 O merakh po korennomu sovershenstvovaniyu vneshneekonomicheskoi deyatel'nosti. *Ekonomicheskaya Gazeta* 1986, 40.

29 For a detailed analysis of the October 1987 amplification on this legislation and its implications for direct interfirm relations—both in an East-East and in an East-West context—see Csaba 1988a.

30 This feature has been reinforced by the 5 May 1988 decree of the Soviet Government on the procedures of coordinating plans with other CMEA countries.

31 On this point, cf. Chapter 5.

CHAPTER TEN

The CMEA under restructuring

"Restructuring" is the closest English equivalent for the Russian word *"perestroika"* which has become a catchword for the concept of the far-reaching changes that have been under way in the Soviet Union since the April 1985 Central Committee Session that elected Mikhail Gorbachev to the post of General Secretary. New winds have been blowing and the period that has passed enables observers to tentatively evaluate the significance, the scope and speed of, as well as the constraints put on, the process which the CC's political report to the Twenty-Seventh Party Congress of the CPSU called "radical reform". Speaking to the Krasnodar party cell, Gorbachev noted that restructuring is a process of many years, one which requires a thorough revamping of the current ways of thinking and acting, and will, thus, inevitably meet resistance. He criticized the unchanged attitudes and practices of the central management organs and spoke of the active and passive resistance to restructuring, noting that only a small initial part of it has so far been implemented (Gorbachev 1986c).

The dynamic renewal process in the Soviet Union has not left the Council for Mutual Economic Assistance untouched. Numerous changes of personnel have taken place in the Soviet organs dealing with CMEA affairs. Since many of these changes involved delegate chairmen of various CMEA organs, the effects on this multilateral organization were immediate. Moreover, every time a new Premier, a new chief of the *Gosplan,* a new foreign trade, finance or other minister, a new permanent representative of the USSR to the Council (in the rank of Deputy Premier) appears, or a new Secretary to the Council is nominated, the event exerts a refreshing and mobilizing influence on this institution, where stability used to be a matter of first priority. If nothing else it is quite certain that these hard decisions have left no doubt about the way the new Soviet leadership will evaluate previous results. On the other hand, the retiring of such exponents of immobility as Baibakov, Patolichev, Garbuzov and Faddeyev have opened the way for relevant changes in working style. More businesslike and critical ways of analysis and a multivocal search for new solutions have emerged to replace the ritual self-appraisal and enumeration of achievements. What Gorbachev said of the Soviet Union certainly holds true for this multilateral organization as well. This might well afford an insight into the ongoing modernization and possibly provide for more effective measures. According to the Soviet evaluation, the earlier forms of intra-CMEA cooperation, having evolved in the period of "extensive" (i.e. factor-intensive) growth, are no longer adequate to the new tasks; thus, nothing less than a brand new economic mechanism can effectively secure multilateral division of labour (Antonov 1986a).

It is conspicuous that the impetus for modifications came from outside the integration, and was determined on the political level. Conceptual debates and the usual wrangling about quantities, prices and delivery conditions ebbed in the course of the coordination of medium-term plans. The former were concluded by the Economic Summit of 1984, the latter by the June 1985 Council Session in Warsaw. As I have already had the opportunity to unfold my understanding of these processes in Chapters 6 and 7, let me confine myself here to those changes that have come about in the second half of the 80s in the integration arrangements among the planned economies of Eastern Europe.

One of the most pronounced priorities of the emerging new Soviet leadership was the improved coordination of activities in the Eastern alliance. This was not restricted to economics, but included the military, political, ideological, diplomatic and other spheres as well. While convening the Economic Summit required more than three years of preparation, a similarly high-level meeting took place at the Political Consultative Board of the Warsaw Treaty Organization in Sofia already in October, 1985; an extraordinary CMEA Session was convened in December, and the CC Secretaries in charge of the economy met in May of the following year. Secretaries in charge of ideology and foreign affairs also met; the meetings of the Deputy Foreign Ministers of the WTO became more frequent, along with the multilateral meetings of lower ranking officials—e.g. the Department Heads of the CC. The Soviets held unprecedented multilateral briefings of their allies following the Geneva Meeting of President Reagan and General Secretary Gorbachev, and also in connection with the subsequent arms control talks, and informed them of the preparations for the Twenty-Seventh Party Congress of the CPSU. All in all it seems remarkable that endeavours at closer coordination embraced a great many areas, and the economy, by the same token, was just a secondary matter. In other words, the CMEA seems to be considered not as an economic institution, but as a segment of a wider context. This is reflected in the stand taken by the WTO PCB meeting, where for the first time, some major criticism of the CMEA's functioning was made public and more effective division of labour among the various multilateral organizations was advocated (Communiqué Oct. 1985).

The new dynamism of the Soviet leadership has also left its imprint on the CMEA itself. In 1984–85, four Council Sessions were convened. Besides the regular Sessions in Havana and Warsaw, the Economic Summit and the nearly equivalent-level December 1985 extraordinary Session were held (the General Secretaries did not attend; instead, they had met seven weeks earlier at the WTO PCB talks, although such gatherings were planned to be held only once every five years). The purpose of the Moscow meeting was to approve the Comprehensive Programme for Scientific and Technological Progress in the CMEA member states to the year 2000, a subject I will return to later. The Programme (Long-term Programme 1985) was to be elaborated according to the Economic Summit decisions of June 1984 and the original deadline for completion was to be the regular 1986 autumn Session of the Council. This deadline was substantially shortened at the new Soviet leadership's initiative in September 1985, and as the then Deputy Premier Antonov noted with satisfaction, two months proved sufficient for the Programme's finalization (Antonov 1986b). The upspeeding to the work proved to be exemplary. The 12th five-year plan, whose guidelines—true to the new spirit—were submitted for public discussion, was also conceptualized as part of the acceleration platform. This was subsequent to the Politburo's rejection, in early summer of 1985, of the earlier draft of the Twelfth Five-Year Plan on the grounds that it was not sufficiently dynamic, and to the Party Congress's pronouncing acceleration *(uskoreniye)* the cornerstone of the CPSU's economic strategy. The new Soviet Premier, Nikolai Ryzhkov, who took office in September, made a remarkable debut at the extraordinary Council Session, delivering his speech (Ryzhkov 1985) in a tone so critical as to be unprecedented in CMEA circles. What he criticized about the Council as a multilateral organ was its sluggishness, its bureaucratic practices, its self-satisfaction and less than businesslike activities. He stated that a

major change in the workings and practices of the Council's organs
was inevitable. The Programme adopted at that Session also calls for
the improvement of the integration's planning, organizational, legal,
institutional and financial arrangements. Direct interfirm relations
were to play a major role. It follows logically that the joint institutions
and the legal regulations are also to be adjusted to meet the new
requirements. The Czechoslovak, Bulgarian and GDR Party Congresses have followed suit, and practical legislation has started to trans-
late the decisions of the Soviet Party Congress into actions. These
developments are very instructive as they provide some indication
of the extent, the ways, the means and the timing of the implementation of the large number of new tasks which have been set
within a relatively short time. In the following, I will make an
attempt to scrutinize each of these issues in order to pinpoint the
new elements and tendencies, before suggesting the conclusions
which might be drawn.

THE PROGRAMME

Scientific and technological progress have been key issues for the
Soviet leadership. Acceleration in these areas was the major objective,
and this gives some clues to an understanding of the new approach.
As it is well known, on the supply side, the Twelfth Five-Year Plan
envisaged a modest acceleration of the growth of the GNP despite
growing constraints, and the Fifteen-Year Plan envisaged a substantially accelerating rate of development from 1990 on. In other words,
the Twelfth Five-Year Plan had a double task: a) to change the so far
dominant trend of extremely factor-intensive growth; and b) to bring
about the conditions of a radical breakthrough in efficiency. The latter
task was exemplified by a major indicator of the plan, that of capital
productivity, where the declining trend of the preceding 15 years was
to be reversed. This target was envisaged, although the share of
sectors with below-average yields, such as energy, transport or agriculture, was not shrunk within the total sum of investments. The
new growth pattern presupposed radical savings in the use of energy,
raw materials and manpower, and all this was to be brought about by
improved productivity. The latter was to be induced by technological
changes, i.e. better machines and a more strongly motivated (rewarded
or penalized) intelligentsia. Some improvements were to be introduced in the economic system to eliminate the hindrances to technological progress.

It is in this context that the CMEA Programme should be understood. Although envisaged by a Summit convened in the atmosphere of an earlier period, the new interpretation was certainly a departure from the era when intra-Comecon trade was most pronouncedly distinguished by the inverse ratio of formal measures to substantial results. The whole document—its wording as well as its approach to the main substantive issues—was already indicative of the new period.

The Programme is basically a pre-plan document (Kapitonov 1985). As is reflected in Section III, par. 3, it is a political-level declaration of cooperation, a summary of objectives and an outline of the most important priorities that are to be translated into action in future bilateral agreements. As Section I, par. 1 explicitly states, the Programme is based on national programmes, and par. 2 repeatedly refers to the priority of intensifying national undertakings, which are to be implemented in a regionally coordinated manner. (The latter point reemerges in the introductory part of Section II.) As far as financing is concerned, Section III, par. 4 contains a pledge that the signatories will establish both the material and the financial conditions for the Programme's realization. In other words the December 1985 Council Session had not yet mastered this task. Paragraph 6 in the same Section also stresses the importance of national-level financing, coupled with the availability of credits from the CMEA banks and, if necessary, the establishment of joint funding. In other words: a) financing, as a rule, would not require convertible currency outlays, b) other expenditures would be covered from within, and by traditional CMEA financing techniques and transferable rubles. Conspicuously there is no mention of any joint CMEA programme that would be "imposed" upon the individual member states. Moreover, no major capital flows are envisaged, and not even the form of the Multilaterally Concreted Integrational Measures, i.e. the joint and obligatory plan document, is outlined. As par. 10 of Section I states, "the CMEA member countries . . . will take into account the obligations originating from the Programme, and will include them into their plans for socio-economic development". This means that the formerly much-heralded "special chapter on integration" is definitely an optional method, rather than a regionally concerted overall practice. This follows from the new approach embodied in the Programme; as Part Five of Section III states this will be implemented primarily through extending direct contacts between national firms. On these grounds, it would be difficult to subscribe to interpretations depicting the

Programme as a step towards joint planning (Hošková 1986) or as one that involves major capital flows such as are customary in the energy sector (Shiryaev 1986, p. 188).

There are five pronounced priority areas: electronics, automation, nuclear engineering, the elaboration and use of new materials and raw-material processing technologies, and biotechnology. The concrete areas of cooperation include 93 sub-programmes. Participation follows the "interested party" principle, since the member states are at different levels of technological and overall development. Thus, their tasks also have to be differentiated. In other words, full-scale participation, especially for the small countries, was an exception rather than the rule. Then there is the Soviet Union. Since the Soviets drafted the Programme, and their priorities are those of the simultaneously elaborated Soviet Fifteen-Year Plan (Chukanov 1986, pp. 14, 17)- it is hardly surprising that they were keenly interested in every sub-programme. As par. 5 of Section III states, the priority agreements are to be elaborated by so-called coordinative head organizations *(golovnaya organizatsiya)* or general contractors. They were to be responsible for the whole complex of implementation, including the harmonizing of interests. Each of the 93 sub-programmes have a Soviet head organization (Antonov 1986a) whose competence and integration into the existing multilateral institutional and legal system was then not yet determined. The proposals that they, for instance, instruct the subcontractors of other countries, or that they have the right to re-channel funds, were clearly incompatible with the major features of the CMEA arrangements. Subcontracting can by no means mean subordination. The issue of equivalent exchange cannot be circumvented at the micro-level either. Certainly, these issues lead to the well-known problem of finances and thus to those of the CMEA mechanism as such. The Programme refers to this in paragraphs 1 and 3 of Section III, calling for the "further improvement" of cooperation in planning as well as for establishing the financial and legal conditions necessary for direct interfirm contacts. Moreover, to make this point stronger, in par. 8 of Section I it reiterates the 1971 Comprehensive Programme, whose economic goals—in the wording of the 1984 Summit Document—are just as urgent today as they were in 1971, i.e. they are unfulfilled. No wonder that even some of those Soviet observers who used to be quite opposed to the Hungarian proposals of the late 1960s later emphatically noted that cooperation in the manufacturing sector requires management methods quite different from the traditional—i.e. present—ones, which are based on the peculiarities of the exchanges in primary products.[1] This conceptual change has evolved from the new real economic problems within the CMEA region and from the new Soviet trade priorities *vis-à-vis* Eastern Europe. Without going into details on this subject already covered in a separate chapter of this book, it may suffice to note that with the exhaustion of the reserves of the traditional integration in the energy and raw materials sphere, it seemed only cooperation in manufacturing that could have given new impetus to CMEA trade. Moreover, due to the constraints on Soviet-Western trade, the East European import of manufactured products is inevitably becoming more important for the USSR. Thus, the propensity to recognize the systemic factors necessary for this type of trade has understandably grown.

The Programme was a project not only for the European CMEA. The role of the developing nations of the CMEA is also dealt with in par. 4, Section I, stating that the Programme should contribute to their speedier growth. The wording underlines the need for improving the efficiency in use of the existing foreign aid and implies that there is a need for a more equitable distribution in the recipient countries. This point was reiterated also by the January 1986 Hanoi meeting of the Committee for Cooperation in Planning.

A further remarkable aspect of the Programme was its repeated call for global cooperation in the high-technology areas, in contrast to the earlier line, although the detailed analysis of the sub-programmes in Section II given at the press conference which followed the extraordinary Council Session of December 1985[2] pointed out that the Programme incorporated several of the import-substituting joint programmes previously approved at the 1982–83 CMEA Sessions as well as the 1974 nuclear engineering programme. Several of the new sub-programmes are open to the West, primarily in the areas of biotechnology and energy-saving technologies, but also in electronics. Since the aim of the Programme is one of catching up, cooperation with Western firms would have been positively required.

It does not seem appropriate here to go into the technicalities involved in the selection of the priority areas. Some aspects immediately related to the topical issues of integration, specifically trade, however, have to be dealt with. As a follow-up to the Economic Summit which adopted the first joint CMEA document put savings ahead of supply increments as the principal avenue to overcoming the energy and raw material shortage in the region, the Programme extends the savings programmes which the June 1985

Council Session approved for 1986–90 to the year 2000. These were supplemented by sub-programmes aiming at improving the quality and the reliability of finished products and semi-products. Nuclear energy was to replace oil in the energy balances, since the latter will be in ever shorter supply. Since brown coal is extremely inefficient and polluting, and the possibility of larger-scale imports from outside the region is usually excluded because of a shortage of hard currency, there seems to be no alternative to nuclear energy even after the Chernobyl catastrophe.[3] Accordingly, a decrease of investment in the energy sector was envisaged, and instead of further investment contributions to this area, regional coordination of national development investment in nuclear engineering was planned.

It is undoubtedly a favourable sign that agriculture and the health sector are not treated separately, but as integral parts of the overall technological development strategy. Improving agricultural technology is one condition for changing the region's present quantity-oriented national development patterns, whose efficiency is ever more questionable. Other systemic and policy considerations have been left to the competence of the national rather than the regional decision-makers.

Section III deals with the implementation of the Programme, though clearly not exhaustively. Par. 2 specifies that the bilateral agreements detailing the precise modes of implementation must be concluded "without delay". As was reflected in the various commentaries made at the time, there was a tendency to see the Programme as having primarily a political function, and the speed of elaborating decisions and agreements was thought by some to have precedence over the issues of substance. On the other hand, their earlier experience with the joint projects prompted GDR decision-makers to call attention to the fact that its realization would have presumed the preliminary fixing of all the practical conditions of joint action, i.e.: a) the clear setting of targets at enterprise level, involving output of the highest world standard; b) laying down exact obligations as to quality, delivery dates, supply conditions, and so on; c) sanctions to be taken against those not living up to their commitments, and incentives for those overfulfilling them; d) resolving the issues of financing, the transmission and use of the jointly achieved technological results on the basis of mutual advantage (Weiz 1986, p. 404).

Small wonder that such a complicated task could not be resolved in the space of a few weeks, especially since the actual harmonization of interests required the elaboration of issues in detail. As the 119th Session of the Executive Committee noted, "Important work needs yet to be done in order to realize the Programme in time and in its full scope" (Communiqué 1986).

Delay seems to be a favourable sign that substantial issues are being resolved, without the pressure of some arbitrarily set timing.

Paragraph 3 of Section III unambiguously specifies that delivery obligations stemming from the Programme were to form part of the national plans, but the way this was to be done was not fixed. This was certainly a positive feature, since various ways had to be found for the diverse national economic mechanisms. Specifying a general norm of behaviour would only be dysfunctional, for the division of competences between the national management organs and the economic units certainly cannot be determined jointly at the integrational level. The same point is reiterated in para. 6 of Section I concerning the need for the continuous review of the Programme's aims. This is to be done with reference to the inevitable technological changes, and the idea corresponds to the concept of revolving plans used by the large Western companies.

The new approach was not aimed at supplementing the existing mechanism of CMEA cooperation with yet another long-term programme, but at revitalizing the endeavours to restructure the CMEA. Since it was adopted after the conclusion of coordination of the plans, it would have been necessary to introduce some corrections (Marcsuk 1986), since the Programme was meant to be not just a mere reiteration of the earlier-concluded bilateral and multilateral cooperation agreements. Wha twas involved was, in fact, the creation of conditions favourable for direct interfirm contacts in the member states. Thus, as a first step to the implementation of the Programme, the Committee for Cooperation in Planning adopted a proposal for developing cooperation and direct enterprise relations.[4] According to this, it was the task of the "head organization" to work out the world market prices of the products to be exchanged, the prices for spare parts as well as the technological documentation of the products based on comparisons with international standards. It was to elaborate an agreement proposition to be submitted for approval to the national decision-making bodies of the participants. It is at this stage that the matters of technological parameters and financing must take their definitive form. Determining assortment, technological development and ways of launching experimental production, as well as exchanging related documentation and information were left to direct inter-firm contacts. Detailed pricing should have been a matter for enterprises, which could rely on the global value quotas set by the respective national control organs. On this proposal, the coordinative head organization was to bear responsibility for the innovation-production-sale cycle as a whole, but has not been empowered with the right to issue instructions, only to make proposals.

Two points have caused practical difficulties: a) the balance of rights and responsibilities of the head organizations were in disequilibrium, given the plurality of competences and management methods in the individual member states; b) as prices do not reflect scarcities, enterprises were not in a position to make economically sound decisions on their own. It is not at all clear how equivalence of exchange and the balanced state of bilateral trade could be determined, though this is, after all, a national interest of each member state. It must also be noted that in practice, price setting by the enterprises as distinct from the Bucharest price principle was tantamount to an endeavour to revitalize the so-called "cooperation price principle". This means either an attempt to set prices for spare parts as a percentage of the value of the end-product,[5] which is in conflict with supply-demand relations, or to apply Soviet wholesale prices, or both. Since the latter proposal's absurdity has been established several times at a number of political fora and in the economic literature, it now appears not in theoretical writings, but in the practical proposals of business executives, who wish to overcome the accounting difficulties of the former system. But however understandable this motive is, the smaller countries can never subscribe to it. One of the reasons is that until the Soviet State Bank applies an exchange rate of 1 : 1 between the Soviet ruble and the much inflated TR, applying Soviet wholesale prices would drastically depress the nominal price level of East European manufacturing exports. Given that foreign trade accounts for only 3–4 percent of the output of most Soviet enterprises, it would be unrealistic to expect them to behave differently. Thus, I do not see much possibility for eschewing the Bucharest price principle and central bargains until the whole mechanism of cooperation is thoroughly reformed. Until that date, partial improvements and measures must willy-nilly be in keeping with the logic of the CMEA system as a whole.

The implementation of the Programme followed a different logic in each of the domestic economic systems. In the GDR, for example, the role of the central organs was underlined, and the tasks deriving from the Programme were broken down to 700 compulsory tasks

(Weiz 1986). In the Soviet Union, it is the State Committee for Science and Technology that organized the work: 30 sectoral ministries and 11 of the 16 newly-formed interbranch scientific-production associations also play this role, with direct foreign trade rights (Antonov 1986a). In Hungary, there was a certain misunderstanding among enterprises after the adoption of the Programme. It was widely assumed that cooperation agreements similar to the practice of the 1950s and 1960s—when efficiency and gains were not even calculated (Szelecki 1986, pp. 15, 40)—would be revived, or at least that participation in a politically supported CMEA programme would provide them with substantial tax returns and/or additional invest-ments that did not need to bring the international rate of return. The inclination to evade the efficiency requirements set by the plan and the system of regulators was so widespread, that the Secretary of State for Industry had to denounce it publicly, and had to re-state the well-known principle that by joining the Programme no one could expect an exemption from the generally valid financial regulators, nor lay claim to some preferential treatment (Szabó I. 1986). In other words, the traditional way of dovetailing the Hungarian and the CMEA mechanism prevailed, namely, that the enterprises take part in elaborating the material substance of the state obligation. State organs can conclude only framework agreements, whose financing is a function of enterprise liquidity and—exceptionally—of occa-sional state decisions, taken jointly by the functional organs. Tak-ing on the concrete delivery obligation contracted by the state organs is a function of the respective enterprises' decisions, i.e. of their interest in, and their ability to finance the projects in keeping with the generally valid regulations. Thus for the Hungarian economic system, it is very important that relevant progress be made in the area of direct interfirm contacts.

DIRECT INTERFIRM CONTACTS

The idea of establishing direct contacts among the enterprises and firms of the CMEA countries dates back to the discussions of the late 1960s. It was an organic part of the original Hungarian concept of transforming the CMEA into a sort of East-European common market. The jointly adopted Comprehensive Programme of 1971 speaks of something else: relations among management organs and also among enterprises within the framework of planning. In practice, this was more likely to mean contacts at the state administrative level, and company-level contacts were restricted to a search for better ways of plan-fulfilment.

At the discussions preceding the Economic Summit of 1984, the issue was raised again, mostly in the context of the medium-level control organs, or as a form supplement to the planned ways of cooperation. Following the Summit Decisions in 1984, some new decrees promoting this form were passed in the Soviet Union. The regulations stressed the strict subordination of these forms to planning, although the sectoral ministries were empowered to sign zero-sum cooperation agreements (i.e. ones for which they did not require extra inputs), and a group of enterprises received exemptions and incentives to enter into such contacts. All in all, these forms were restricted to the exchange of information or documentation among producers engaged in the same activity: they could form joint techno-logical centres or councils, etc. (Grinev 1984). A major feature of these regulations was that these contacts were resolutely divorced from foreign-trade flows, and were extraneous—sometimes formal—in nature. This is understandable enough, since a system based on mandatory planning and balancing is inherently unable to absorb any degree of spontaneity that would affect the macro-proportions of the planned processes. This certainly holds for an international system comprised predominantly of economies of this type.

With the emergence of the concept of "restructuring" in the Soviet Union, and with the adoption of the Programme, the issue of direct interfirm contacts had to be reconsidered as well. It was generally accepted that the system of interstate agreements was unable to sub-stitute for direct interfirm contacts as far as interestedness and flexi-bility were concerned. Furthermore, few authorities doubted that in the absence of market controls, no efficient cooperation was feasible, especially in the high-technology areas (Stoilov 1985, pp. 62–63). Soviet authors pointed out that the Programme would have required not only a different approach, but also a different quality of direct interfirm contacts than had previously existed. It would have been thus necessary to guarantee firms the freedom to establish and main-tain production and scientific contacts, and to recognize that the legal side of the issue had to be subordinate to enhancing the real economic autonomy of the enterprises within the domestic economic systems (Abolikhina and Bakovetzki 1986). Other economists have gone as far as to propose a complete overhaul of the former intra-CMEA cooperation system, so as to enable the primary units of production (the companies) to sign delivery and specialization contracts on their own initiative without the intermediation of the central management organs (Gavrilov 1986). Thus, it seems, there was every reason to be enthusiastic from a Hungarian point of view, since these proposals are in accordance with our own proposals of the 1960s.

In theory, it is very easy to define the Hungarian concept of direct interfirm contacts. The point is the initiative of the independent enterprise, which establishes the contact of its own will, judging its results on the basis of profitability calculated in forints, given the general rules of regulation. Theoretically, it presumes a series of preconditions. No matter how obvious or rational they might seem, they are known to be missing under the CMEA arrangements. The above-quoted new Soviet deliberations certainly point in the direction of bringing about the full set of preconditions, and in Soviet economic literature, positions clearly favouring market integration and attention to the necessary systemic conditions have reemerged (Grinberg and Lyubskii 1985). However, these still represent the minority view.

More important is the fact that not even the most liberal interpretation of the above summarized Programme could see it as a herald of market integration. As documented above, it calls for the "perfecting" of planning, and refers to the Comprehensive Programme of 1971, which, as is known, was hardly a platform of market integration. The hopes that the national economic mechanisms of the CMEA member states would come to converge through a regulated market have been proved to have been vain. During the 80s the divergent economic systems, with mandatory indicators predominating in the majority of the member states, were as given. From the practical point of view, this was the environment determining the logic of the mechanism of CMEA cooperation. This is the context that the new initiatives must be interpreted in and fitted into, despite the fact that they also play a role in the Soviet debates on restructuring the domestic economic system.

What room did the domestic economic management systems leave for enterprises to enter into full-fledged direct contacts (in the Hungarian sense) with the firms of the other CMEA countries? Discussions of this problem will be somewhat constrained by the fact that the state of the relevant legislation as well as its availability varies from country to country.

In the Soviet Union, besides the inevitable self-justifications, some very critical evaluations have been given of the earlier regulations, which relegated enterprise initiative to a minor role. An article in the daily of the Soviet trade unions went as far as to point out that all the talk of change remained on paper, since the 1984 decree did not extend conditions necessary for interfirm contacts, and enterprise autonomy was lacking.[6]

The legislation that has been passed has the following main features (Nikonov and Stromov 1986): 1. Intrasectoral and intersectoral direct contacts were clearly separated. While international relations between companies of the same sector may be established with the permission of the sectoral ministry, contacts to be established with foreign companies of another branch must go through the respective foreign trade organizations. Within the given limits, Soviet producer firms may decide on assortment, technological development and quality issues.

As far as intersectoral contracts were concerned, there were four major forms:

a) Soviet producers sign a global contract in value terms through their foreign trade enterprises with partner foreign trade companies or producers with foreign trade rights. This extends to spare parts, components or technical services. The agreements are made for a one year term, and the prices are set in accordance with the Bucharest pricing principles, prior to signing the contract.

b) Sectoral ministries agree on deliveries within a given limit, without prior fixing of the commercial conditions, which are elaborated ex post facto by the foreign trade companies. This form has been applied mainly in Soviet—GDR relations.

c) A joint scientific-technological association is set up, like Interrobot.

d) Bilateral or multilateral interstate agreements are made, with the concrete material content and the commercial conditions being elaborated by the firms. The Programme is an example of this type.

Forms *b* and *c* were to gain in weight with the September 1986 Government Decrees on the reorganization of Soviet foreign trade. The quoted analysts as well as experienced managers have emphasized that direct interfirm contacts could evolve only under strict central control, which ensures that they are concentrated on the priority areas. Though this was not quite in keeping with the earlier outlined theoretical approach, it does determine practical regulation. The enhanced pricing, balancing and supervisory role of the sectoral ministries fits well into the picture, and constitutes a continuation of the old ways rather than a break with them.

In Czechoslovakia, the federal government has been very supportive of the idea of direct interfirm relations, and has been most critical of the developments of the preceding 15 years for neglecting this form of cooperation (Štrougal 1984b). The professional economists have been equally critical. To quote some major points made in one authoritative analysis: "A campaign for establishing direct contacts is no substitute for its missing systemic preconditions." "The agent of interfirm relations is the basic economic unit, making decisions on considerations of profitabilty, and giving no preferential treatment." Finally, "the material coverage for such an independent decision must be provided by appropriate measures being taken in the material-technical supply system" (Válek 1985). In the wake of these criticisms, there was a fair degree of interest in seeing how the "framework-rules" that were in force since July 1986 regulate these problems. Explicating the rules that were promulgated some weeks earlier, an editorial of the party daily noted emphatically that direct interfirm relations were not to be established without prior consultations with higher-standing organs; on the contrary, it was the sectoral ministry that was to organize and coordinate these activities.[7] Commenting on the new rules in detail, the Deputy Premier in charge of the area published a lengthy study in an economic weekly (Rohliček 1986). From this, we find the Czechoslovak approach to bear an extraordinary similarity to both the theory and practice of former Soviet regulation. Though the new rules significantly simplified the procedure of acquiring the right to enter into direct contacts, such contacts must be intrasectoral. Their object may be spare parts or components. Their aim is to promote the fulfilment of the foreign-trade plans. As Rohliček notes, direct contracts had to be prepared in a planned way even if their financial burden falls exclusively on the economic unit. Even in this case, the project had to be harmonized with the state plan. For production units, the first step was to establish such contacts through foreign trade firms. Certain delivery and cooperation deals stemming from the Programme could be signed by the general directors without the prior permission of the sectoral minister. They could set prices higher than specified in the plan indicators, and must bear the financial consequences. As far as the pricing and financing of the planned flows are concerned, the rules are yet to be elaborated.

The GDR continued to be supportive of the idea of direct contact in the same spirit as was the case in the 1970s. A new aspect was the emphasis on direct relations between the various countries' Academies of Sciences and universities, and the element of concrete use as a decision criterion has also been mentioned. As it was reflected in the materials of the Eleventh Party Congress of the SUPG, the GDR never contemplated a restructuring of its "tried and tested" mechanism, but aims at its continuous "perfecting". Thus, the GDR's standpoint on direct contacts makes perfect sense, given the inner logic of the economic mechanism.

As far as Hungary is concerned, the issue of direct relations was regulated by the law-decree of 1972 and the 1974 law on foreign trade, which were elaborated with hopes of progress and with the Comprehensive Programme of 1971 in mind. It is not necessary to obtain the sectoral ministry's permission before establishing direct contacts. Moreover, given the uniform state management of industry under a single ministry, the sectoral aspect of decision-making does not play a role. Since the system of material-technical supply was abolished and substituted by a system of wholesale trade, the input requirements of direct interfirm contacts may be assured by the company itself at will. It is possible for all Hungarian firms to establish such contacts, without any spatial or sectoral restrictions. The freedom of maintaining contacts with foreign companies is remarkable. In other words, most of the alleviations that have recently come to the fore in CMEA partner countries have already been in force in Hungary for some time.

In Hungarian regulation, a major dividing line is drawn between direct contacts and foreign-trade activity, something which is inevitable given the economic substance of the present mechanism of intra-CMEA cooperation. Accordingly, companies are empowered to exchange information and documentation about their technological, trade, marketing and tourist activities, and matters of plant-organization. They may also elaborate proposals for cooperation, or concrete measures to implement the obligations resulting from the coordination of plans, as well as participate in the preparatory phase of elaborating long-term trade agreements, cooperate in standardization, in buying and using licences and know-how, and in organizing "exchange of assortments". Only holders of a general preliminary permit—i.e. of foreign trade rights with the ability to use foreign currency—are able to sign contracts to meet obligations deriving from direct contacts. Thus a foreign trade deal means a contract between domestic and foreign partners in order to sell or buy commodities, services or rights involving material values, cooperation in production, ventures abroad or trading by foreigners in Hungary. Thus, direct contacts may embrace a large variety of activities leading to a foreign trade deal in a later period. In the case of a foreign trade deal, two possibilities are open to a Hungarian firm: a) it can obtain foreign trade rights for the given occasion; b) under Decree No. 7 of 1985 of the Ministry of Foreign Trade,[8] it can initiate the significantly simplified procedure of obtaining permanent foreign trade rights. The substance of the latter is as follows. If an applicant posesses all the professional, material and personnel conditions qualifying it for this activity, the Ministry has no right to reject the application. Thus it seems justified to assume that Hungary would be able to accommodate far more direct interfirm contacts and foreign trade deals initiated at the firm level than is actually possible under the present state of multilateral arrangements within the CMEA.[2]

Having surveyed the legal aspects it might also be interesting to describe the economic substance of direct interfirm contacts under the conditions of the CMEA. For the 80s, this could be formulated as follows. It is a relation between producers, traders or research institutes that emanates from other sources and motives than the coordination of plans or other forms of centrally planned cooperation. The essential difference was precisely its being other than the planned forms in respect of location, timing, commodity coverage, and occasionally also in respect of its subjects. Thus, direct contacts aimed at finding possibilities for exchange additional to the centrally determined flows that must be distinguished from them. The objective of direct contacts was to explore possibilities that are centrally unavailable, or unforeseeable for reasons of time, scope or knowledge of detail. It goes without saying that their financing had to proceed in conformity with the rules generally in force both within the respective countries and in the CMEA, and companies had to decide for themselves whether or not they find such a relationship profitable or lucrative from some other point of view (e.g. information, choice, etc.).

These considerations are of immediate practical significance. In the available literature—including some of the above-quoted sources—it is quite often that direct contacts are treated in the same breath as other micro-integrational forms such as joint ventures or cooperation agreements. Most frequently, the relations between the coordinative "head organizations" of the Programme and their subcontractors are described in terms of direct contacts. However, it must be noted that the interstate agreements deriving from the Programme were to be incorporated in the coordination of plans and in the five-year protocols on foreign trade (par. 2 of Section III); thus, "direct contacts" in these cases play mostly a plan preparatory and plan implematary role along the lines of the 1970s. Joint enterprises, too, are prospective forms of micro-integration for the time when the conditions of their independent and profit-oriented functioning come into being. Cooperation in production, specialization and joint firms are all important and independent forms of cooperation that should not be confused with direct contacts.

What would the failure to distinguish the various institutions of integration imply in practice? First, a redistribution of the competences in the matter of foreign trade rights within the nation states. Second, if it became pervasive, it would induce changes in the bilateral trade positions and proportions established through the coordination of plans. This would not be a problem if all the systemic conditions of a market-type reform of the CMEA were present, but this is not the case. According to the joint position taken by the member states at the Economic Summit of 1984, it was the task of the coordination of plans and not of other forms of cooperation to determine the major proportions of exchange. This position was fully in keeping with the qualitative characteristics of the national economic mechanisms of most of the CMEA countries during the 80s. Moreover, given that the Hungarian regulations described above were the exception rather than the rule, a great many reserves exist at the CMEA level for developing the possibilities of direct interfirm contacts in the Hungarian sense. These advanced form of integration, however, could not be regulated in a way qualitatively different from the whole environment of which they constitute an organic part.

CHANGES IN THE INTEGRATION'S INSTITUTIONS

The institutional arrangements bear the imprint of the earlier phase of development in a number of ways. For one, the idea that "The more joint organizations, the stronger the integration" is a typical reflection of the "extensive" period, has been with us for a long time. Second, for the same reason, the issue of dissolving certain organs has not even theoretically been raised. Third, the setup of the Standing Committees reflect to a great extent the sectoral division of the Soviet industrial administration, whose extensiveness was a target of criticism at the Twenty-Seventh Party Congress. Fourth, a number of "conferences" are regularly organized, and function more or less as *de facto* standing committees. Fifth, at a lower level, working sessions and specialists' meetings take place, frequently without much practical use. Several formal activities flourish, especially in the areas of standardization, technological and scientific cooperation; certain subjects are studied for years without any practical result. Sixth, the staff of the Secretariat has grown at a pace far outstripping the actual intensity of regional trade flows, its internal setup based on the principle of sectoral division. Seventh, given the demonetization of the mechanism of cooperation, the ability of the lower levels to reach a compromise has lessened. Accordingly, a very large number of issues are submitted to the high political fora for decision. The latter process certainly tends to decrease the efficiency of these high-level organs. The Sessions of the Executive Committee and the Committee for Cooperation in Planning take place only at discrete intervals, and frequently, neither the time available nor the level of representation (Deputy Premiers) is adequate for solving such a quantity of detailed problems.

The Soviet statements made at the 1985 WTO PCB meeting, at the Forty-First Council Session, at the Twenty-Seventh Party Congress of the CPSU and at the Eleventh Party Congress of the SUPG all called for a change in the working style and methods of the multilateral organizations of the CMEA. "Less armchair-administration, less pseudo-activity, a more businesslike approach and more practical results"—this might well sum up the call for change. Since, characteristically, the changes in the Soviet economic mechanism involved the formation of intersectoral top organs with a small personnel but with significant powers to coordinate and instruct—see *Gosagroprom* and the Bureau for Machine Building—it was not without justification to expect similar types of changes in the CMEA, too. One obvious way of doing this would be to merge several of the sectoral standing committees and working groups into one, and to reorganize the Secretariat to perform coordinative functions only (Antonov 1986b). This could be achieved by its internal reorganization along functional, rather than sectoral lines. Better coordination could be attained by giving more competence to the Deputy Standing Representatives[9] meeting in Moscow, as this forum could decide many of the issues that are passed on to the political level, and thus improve the quality of the decisions made by the Executive Committee. All coordinative centres that have a standing apparatus should be dissolved, and the activities of the participants be coordinated in the course of regular working contacts. All activities that yield no results should cease. The Committee for Scientific and Technological Cooperation should make a detailed review of all ongoing projects from this point of view. It should be accepted as a general rule that each standing organ that has members of government or other persons with nation-wide responsibility on its board is compelled to decide in the matters on its agenda.

Some changes of an organizational nature could, in my judgement, have improved the efficiency of joint decision-making even under the present systemic conditions. First, a common analysis of the state of affairs might be approved at the political level prior to elaborating joint measures. Second, it would be worthwhile to study the implementability of any proposed measure, with due attention paid to the usually neglected sociological factors. In this way, the conditions of realization could be set *ex ante*, or alternately, the decision could be appropriately modified in due time. Ways could be found to ensure the responsibility of those submitting proposals at the political level, so that proposals lacking a sound technological and economic basis and/or the support of each interested member state should not get to the political level at all. To this end, it would make sense for the Secretariat always to coordinate its proposals with the Deputy Standing Representatives, and submit its ideas to the Executive Committee or to the Committee for Cooperation in Planning only on condition of the Deputy Representatives' agreement. This way, a fair amount of *ex post* interest harmonization could be seen to *ex ante*.

Following this normative digression, it might be instructive to survey the actual developments. The Fortieth (Warsaw) Session of June 1985 decided to set up the Committee for Cooperation in Engineering. The Committee is comprised of national delegates headed by Deputy Premiers. The aim was—in compliance with the theoretical statements above—to create a top organ with sufficient powers both nationally and at the CMEA level to coordinate the activities of the sectors. The Committee consists of 16 sectoral bureaus (Kirpichnikov 1985), a number identical with that of the former sectoral standing organs. The very level of representation makes it clear that an organ on the level of the Committee for Cooperation in Planning and the Executive Committee has come into being.

Following the adoption of the Programme, in January 1986 the 118th meeting of the Executive Committee decided to set up further two new standing committees for coordinating two new priority areas: one for biotechnology, and one for new materials and material-saving technologies. It seems to me that if Antonov's above-quoted proposal for a smaller number of committees would have materialized, cooperation in these two areas could have developed also as part of the Standing Committee for Health Care and the Committee for Cooperation in

Engineering and/or Committee for Cooperation in Science and Technology. Such and other reorganizations would have assured the present level of cooperation with a smaller staff and more efficiency.

Although much has been said about the need to streamline the Secretariat, not too much has been achieved yet. Moreover, the Director of the CMEA International Research Institute has even proposed that the Secretariat be developed into a sort of general staff of integration, with an independent role (Shiryaev 1986b). These and other of his proposals aiming at transforming the Secretariat into what Brussels is for the EC do not, in my judgement, follow the above-described line of rationalization, and it is not very difficult to see the selfish motives behind statements of this sort.

All in all, the 119th session of the Executive Committee was quite right in deciding that "Further and novel measures are needed to achieve a thoroughgoing improvement of the functioning of the Council". It is difficult to foretell at the time of writing what practical results the reorganization measures have yielded. It seems legitimate to assume that streamlining and improving the Soviet mechanism, for instance, the detailed, practical regulation restructuring Soviet foreign trade management in keeping with the Politbureau decisions of 19 August 1986 was bound to take precedence over the realignment of the joint organs, since the outcome of the former will have a decisive impact on the latter. It is clear that a new Soviet concept of the CMEA was in the making.

Important though changes in the institutional system of multilateral integration may be, further decisions were needed in other areas of the international integration mechanism, including finances. And if we add the economic truism that changing the integration mechanism is not just a matte rof political decision since the mechanism reflects the state of development in the domestic economic systems, and recalls that the common institutions also necessarily reflected the entire range of conflicting national interests and priorities, it was clear that restructuring the CMEA was bound to be a process of more than one year's effort. These are summarized in the following chapter.

NOTES

1 Shiryaev, Yu., Strany SEC: Kurs na dinamichnoe razvitie ekonomiki. *Mezhdunarodnaya Zhizn*, 1985/11, p. 25. For the Hungarian proposal see: Csikós-Nagy, B.: The realization of mutual advantages in the economic cooperation among CMEA countries. In Kiss, T., Földi, T., and Schweitzer,

2 As reported in: *Ekonomicheskoye sotrudnichestvo stran-chlenov SEV*, 1986/3.
3 This is a descriptive statement, and does not imply my agreement with this point. Going into the details of an alternative strategy—as I did in several earlier writings—would go beyond the scope of this discussion.
4 Sovershenstvovanie mekhanizma sotrudnichestva. Editorial in *Ekonomicheskoe sotrudnichestvo stran-chlenov SEV*, 1986/5, pp. 21–24.
5 Klyuchevoy oblast sotrudnichestva. Editorial in *Ekonomicheskoye sotrudnichestvo stran-chlenov SEV*, 1985/8. Quote is from p. 5 of the Hungarian edition.
6 *Trud*, 19 August 1986.
7 Rozvijet primé vztáhy (Developing direct relations) Editorial in *Rudé Právo*, 9 June 1986.
8 A 7/1985. sz. KKM rendelet a külkereskedelmi jog megadásának és gyakorlásának rendjéről (Decree No. 7/1985 of the Ministry of Foreign Trade on the granting of foreign trade rights and their practice). *Magyar Közlöny*, 1985/56 — the official gazette of the People's Republic of Hungary.
9 The standing representative of each member country at the CMEA is a Deputy Premier. Since they have major functions within the national governments, the acting standing representatives residing in Moscow and dealing with current issues are their deputies, the *de facto* ambassadors to the CMEA. They are part of the national governments, while the officials of the Secretariat are formally not national "representatives".

CHAPTER ELEVEN

Hungary in the COMECON

The dynamism of *perestroika* is sweeping away structures and attitudes that not so long ago were considered to be immutable. Thus, international relations are no longer conceived of as essentially bipolar, and the "necessary antagonism" of the differing social systems beginning to disappear from among the axioms of Soviet ideology. Another dogma that has undergone reevaluation is the Suslovian theory of advanced socialism, according to which mandatory planning constitutes the specifica of all the East European economies. Little wonder, then, that the ongoing changes in the Soviet Union have been called truly revolutionary by some competent outside observers (Kaser 1987; and Meissner 1987), and have been likened to turning points in Soviet history as significant as the introduction of NEP in the early 1920s; or the switch to collectivization and heavy industrialization under Stalin in the late 20s and early 30s.

This being so, it is hardly surprising that even the Comecon, that self-confessed bastion of immobility, is undergoing a process of restructuring. The longstanding dissatisfaction of several member states with the arrangements and efficacy of the integration has intensified, fanned as it is by the refreshing Moscow winds. To put it in a nutshell, the new Soviet leadership has reevaluated the role of the CMEA and its member states within the overall Soviet strategy. The generally poor performance of the region in the 1980s, especially as far as technological progress and other qualitative indicators are concerned, has increased Soviet awareness of the costs of immobility. This performance is seen as clearly inadequate for supporting the Soviet aspiration to keep pace with global technological progress, a necessary precondition of maintaining the country's place in the international power-contest. The new East-West *détente* also necessitates the USSR's possessing a stable "backyard", rather than a region rent by the strains and unrest of protracted economic hardship.

The rather harsh Soviet criticism of the functioning of the CMEA
—first expressed at the October 1985 meeting of the Political Consultative Board of the Warsaw Treaty Organization in Sofia—is,
thus, not to be taken for a sheer change in rhetoric, a verbal adjustment to the domestic vocabulary of the *perestroika*. It is a reflection
of the Soviet Union's vital political, strategic and economic interest
in improving the East European region's actual performance. As such,
it is a sincere attempt to do away with the ossified, out-of-date
practices of regional cooperation.

The new initiatives and the policy shifts came in an environment
which was anything but a *tabula rasa*. As I have tried to elaborate
in detail in an earlier chapter, by the mid-eighties the differences
among national approaches and the conflicts of commercial interest
had come to the fore. Any feasible integrational solution thus presumes
a new synthesis, and a willingness to come to a compromise from
widely diverging national standpoints. It also requires that immediate
commercial policy interests be given their due. Even optimally, and
independently of the subjective intentions of the parties involved,
what is feasible will fall far short of what is theoretically desirable
(i.e. of what would lead to qualitative improvements).

The work of restructuring the CMEA was started at Soviet initiative
at the extraordinary Council session of December 1985, with the
first palpable results becoming evident at the extraordinary session
that convened in October of 1987 in Moscow. The official Hungarian
position has been clearly presented both from a political standpoint
(Marjai 1987) and from the standpoint of economists (Osváth, Patai
and Szegvári 1987), and stands in no need of reiteration. Instead,
I should like to expound on my personal understanding of the ongoing changes, aware that this will not necessarily coincide with the
official Hungarian view.

The communiqué published after the October 1987 Council Session
(Communiqué 1987), is only half as long as what is considered normal
for CMEA communiqués. Of the six newspaper columns, two contain
the list of participants, and two discuss issues of foreign policy;
only two are left for intra-Comecon affairs in the strict sense of the
term. Quite meagre results for two years of intensive effort both at
the expert and the political levels. The brevity of the account indicates how few were the areas in which the ten member states could
come to an understanding within this particular period of time.
With so many issues of substance left for later discussion we may
well regard it as an interim account. In fact, all substantial and orga-

nizational aspects of the new integrational platform, the Joint Concept for Socialist International Division of Labour for the Years 1991–2005, were left to be determined later. In October 1987, only the proposal for its elaboration has been endorsed at the political level (Marjai 1987). In other words, the efforts at restructuring will continue, and the principle of gradual change emphasized by the communiqué was a reflection of the understanding that the enduring pluralism of the various national ways will not permit a sudden breakthrough to some new integrational mechanism, despite the political dynamism of the Soviet side. In practical terms, this means that the Joint Concept was meant to be a programmatic document similar to the Comprehensive Programme of 1971, one that would also have served as a basis for harmonizing economic policies and for dovetailing five-year plans (Antonov 1987). This point certainly needs clarification. In the following, I shall therefore discuss both more general issues, and short-term commercial policy problems. The two are intertwined, as they were in 1969–71, when elaborating the longer-term integrational strategies also bore the imprint of immediate commercial policy considerations.

THE CONTROVERSY ABOUT THE PROSPECTIVE MODEL OF INTEGRATION

It is not all obvious what the radically new parlance implies for regional cooperation within the CMEA.

Following the January and June 1987 sessions of the Central Committee of the CPSU, an analytical model of indirect planning emerged in the Soviet Union. We can take this as indicative of the objectives and methods of Soviet management practice in the course of the changeover from the present arrangements to the target model. By virtue of the above decision, the Soviet target model and Hungarian practice have come significantly closer to each other (although the Hungarian target model implies a critical reevaluation, rather than the apologia of the existing practice). In the case of the CMEA, the analytical framework has not yet reached this degree of concreteness.

First and foremost among the reasons is that in the CMEA, too, as in any regional grouping, the national commercial interests and official governmental philosophies of the member states vary considerably. The same empirical experience will lead to quite dissimilar diagnoses, let alone therapies.

In the compromise formulation of the communiqué of October 1987, the coordination of medium-term plans was to remain a major of cooperation, although it is to be improved to leave room for the growing role of decentralized decisions. Harmonization was to proceed on three levels: among governments, among sectoral organs and among enterprises. Not very much more was said in the joint position about this, but the interpretations that have been given by individual countries varied quite a bit.

In the original Soviet version (Konstantinov 1987, pp. 24–25), the three levels of coordination would not, in fact, have changed the hierarchical subordination of the various decision-making levels. What they did imply was an increase in the number of the participating organs, with primacy for the sectoral ministries, and a wider scope for coordination. This idea had met with Bulgarian and Czechoslovak support. The Bulgarian advocates of this line of thought have proposed forming a uniform economic complex of the national economies of CMEA member states, through the coordination of structural, investment, foreign trade and even of foreign debt policies (Alev 1986). Czechoslovak close-to-official analysts contemplating the variants of long-term integration strategies have also described the basic variant as one in which the CMEA region would evolve according to its internal logic: the core of the integration would be a joint structural policy, as contrasted to the present practice of a sectorally segmented partial harmonization of certain of its elements (Chalupsky 1987). Although on this latter view the predominance of physical planning would gradually give way to the parallel development of planning and monetary instruments, it reflects the foreign trade concerns of the more outward-looking Comecon partners that the communiqué of 1987 restated the need to develop external ties, in particular to the EC. Allusions to earlier top-level agreements, such as the Documents of the 1984 CMEA Summit, also served as counterweights to the above extreme proposals.

Countires with very centralized decision-making systems, such as the GDR or Romania, could hardly have an interest in giving up the prerogatives the national planning centres have to determine the international flow of commodities to practically the last detail. To do so would be to lay themselves open to those elements of unpredictability in international trade which take no account of national priorities. These two countries have also pronounced foreign policy profiles to maintain for obvious reasons. As far as Hungary is concerned, from the systemic point of view quite the opposite was the problem. Namely, that the major intra-CMEA proportions tend to be fixed in physical terms, whereas in the Hungarian economy, fiscal policy and monetary categories are coming to play a determinant role, despite the many controversial solutions tried in preceding years (Csaba 1986a), which go a long way towards explaining why the performance of the Hungarian economy has fallen so far short of the expectations generated by reform theories. The two logics—the one of physical, the other of fiscal planning—have been mutually exclusive. Thus, from the Hungarian point of view, the monetization of cooperation as well as the decentralization of decision-making as steps to autonomous direct interfirm relations remain the crux of any CMEA reform. As a matter of fact, far from being a purely Hungarian problem, it is a paradox of the present Comecon arrangements in general that the principal integrating method of coordinating plans is based on fictitious five-year plan documents, while the actual economic processes in each and every Eastern European country are directed by short-term economic policies and regulatory instruments (Szegvári 1987, p. 92.).

In this context, the idea of predetermining economic flows according to sectors and countries in a matrix-like way from a single economic centre of integration seemed to be a bit utopian. From the Hungarian point of view, it is rather reassuring that even formerly not very reform-minded Soviet authors are nowadays questioning the very validity of the entire model of intra-CMEA integration (Nekipelov 1987 p. 78, p. 82); others of the same breed go as far as to expressly state that it is the whole idea of an inward-looking strategy and the system of shortage economy that are to blame for the current problems of integration (Shiryaev 1987, p. 785). This was a favourable sign, a step in the right direction, even if short-term Soviet practice is far from acting on such conceptual insights.

Another fundamental question was what degree of convergence of the national economic systems is at all desirable. In other words, are certain changes within the domestic economic mechanisms the *conditio sine qua non* of any meaningful change in the integration arrangements? Those answering in the affirmative are, as usual, divided into two groups. Those favouring convergence along traditional lines are exemplified by the earlier-cited Bulgarian and Czech authors (Alev 1986; and Chalupsky 1987), the other traditionalist approach is that of a Polish expert who is usually close to the official position (Bożyk 1986): the idea of creating a uniform integration market by opening up the national markets, a proposal taken up by reform-minded Soviet officials as well.

From the Hungarian point of view, the latter proposal is appealing, but its feasibility is more than questionable. In the late sixties, when Hungarian economists had made similar proposals, the idea was based on the presumption that market reforms were the inevitable concomitant of a higher level of development, i.e. were necessitated by the growing complexity of economic structures. This assumption proved to be wrong. Today, the plurality of national ways among the CMEA member states appears to be here to stay; an "all or nothing" stand, thus, is hardly a very constructive or helpful position to maintain. From the practical point of view the Soviet official stand, which lays emphasis on the exchange of experiences and on various common projects while definitely steering clear of some artificial unification (Bogomolov 1987), is more to the point. This idea is reflected in the earlier-cited position of gradualism in the communiqué of 1987, which is far from appealing on the theoretical level, but in practice was the most feasible at that time.

What, then, is meant by the proposal accepted by the Council session for the coordination of plans at other than the central levels? The growing role of the sectoral ministries is a typical feature of the new Soviet foreign trade legislation. Understandably, the Soviet position is that issues of investment policy and of technological progress were to be determined at this level (Antonov 1987).

From the Hungarian point of view, the growing role of the sectoral ministries is not a very promising proposition for two reasons. First, in Hungary sectoral ministries were instrumental in perverting the first phase of the reform in the mid-seventies. It is, therefore, difficult for Hungarian economists to see the regulations of the Soviet law on the state owned enterprise (Zakon 1987)—which also stipulates the increased foreign trade involvement of this particular management level by granting the sectoral ministries foreign currency funds and the right to initiate joint ventures with foreign partners—as the strongest element of a promising reform legislation. Second, in a more decentralized economic mechanism, sectoral ministries have an inherent propensity to disequilibrate planned bilateral trade flows, thereby eroding the bargains struck by the central planning organs in coordinating plans (see Chapter 4). Since the drop in oil prices has already spilled over to contractual prices in the CEMA leaving the small East European states with unintended surpluses in their transferable ruble accounts, such an institutional arrangement is hardly in the commercial policy interest of any of them. The point of the communiqué that calls for a growing role for sectoral ministries is a compromise based on the understanding that branches were to play a relevant role in important member states for quite some time to come (Marjai 1987). Since the January 1988 government reorganization further cut back the number of ministries in Hungary, practically no agents have remained that can engage in intermediate level co-ordinative activities in CMEA fora.

As far as interfirm relations are concerned, this has already been the subject of separate analysis in earlier chapters. In the present context, two points should be made. For one thing, as Soviet officials have justly noted (Kamentsev 1987) this form of cooperation continues to be restricted to exchange of experiences rather than the firms' organizing cooperation, which is due primarily to unresolved issues of pricing and material-technical supply and/or company rights. For another, several member states have not provided the firms with rights that would permit them to function more organically and independently on external (Comecon) markets. This has to do with the management concepts of the given countries. Leaving apart the quasi war economies of Cuba and Vietnam, we shall find a recent article of the state secretary of the State Planning Commission of the GDR to illustrate the point. On this analysis (Hrablei 1987), East German combines have had direct relations with socialist partners since the mid-sixties; direct relations have developed successfully, and extend to 35 per cent of all industrial employees and 50 per cent of all industrial fixed assets. Joint analyses, the exchange of information and of experiences, as well as joint technological research are all part of direct interfirm contacts. The GDR did not intend to go beyond that range of these contacts which, however, the Soviets tend to find too narrow. As far as Romania is concerned, the major features of the regulation of interfirm contacts have been made public in a speech by Nicolae Ceausescu, delivered at his meeting with the Premiers heading the delegations to the 1986 Council Session (Ceauşescu 1986). Accordingly, Romanian firms and *centrale* may enter into foreign contact following the detailed priorities of the national programmes and research projects, and through the foreign trade organizations. The priority of the national plans was to be guaranteed, and in intra-CMEA deals, compulsory interstate agreements had to pave the way for company action aimed at implementing central tasks in a creative manner. To put the gist of all this another way, a country that does not even contemplate economic decentralization can't be forced into it by a regional cooperation organ.

The Hungarian regulation of direct interfirm relations is based on the Foreign Trade Act of 1974. It is in line with the above-described realities, since no national legislation can be more "progressive" than the environment in which it functions. In the same way, the call for free pricing by companies so often voiced in the economic literature can only be perverted if other conditions remain unchanged. For instance, if control organs set the exchange-rate substituting coefficients at the product level, then "free" pricing can only lead to unilateral advantage for the stronger (more centralistic) partner at the macroeconomic level (Szelecki 1987, p. 43).

Cost-insensitive large enterprise with a one-sided vested interest in exporting for transferable rubles (without caring about counter deliveries) may actually disequilibrate trade balances as much as sectoral organs. Thus here, too, the official Hungarian restraint was justified. We cannot endorse the accusation that the Hungarian position was not sufficiently radical (Levcik 1987), since the conceptual issues under actual discussion did not call for more "reformism" than was feasible under the circumstances, and given the extent to which the idea of restructuring has found acceptance.

The reform of the CMEA's currency system was one of the conceptual issues under discussion. The October 1987 Council Session did achieve some consensus, although not one that met Polish and Hungarian expectations. It has been agreed that national currencies may, in fact, be used for accounting in direct interfirm relations. This is a very small step forward, since the major element of the Hungarian proposal (Osváth, Patai and Szegvári 1987), that year-end accounts be settled at least in part (25 percent) in convertible currency from 1988 on, has not been supported by most countries.

There is a chance that in the medium run, the Soviet and the transferable ruble will be more realistically evaluated both *vis-à-vis* each other and the convertible currencies. The Bucharest pricing principle also remained in effect—but this is already a subject for short-term considerations.

As far as institutional streamlining goes, a very moderate progress took place. It was expected that the Council Session of 1988 would decide on these issues. The number of Standing Committees were expected to be cut by a third (Maróthy 1987). Discussion of staff reductions and of the working procedures that might make for the better *ex ante* harmonization of national views was also on the agenda. However, judging by the tone of self-confidence and self-satisfaction that again characterized the writings of the re-elected Secretary of the CMEA (Sychov 1987), the present author must concede that in his earlier analyses (Csaba 1986b), he had overestimated both the speed and the extent of the possible organizational changes. The vested interest of the sectoral ministries in maintaining their international representation will not make it easy to cut back personnel and to merge committees, although functional and operational rationalization would call for wider integration-level support for this Hungarian proposal.

SHORT-TERM POLICY DISPUTES OF THE LATE 80S

"The devil's in petty detail", says the German proverb, and it quite sums up why multilateral integrational practice was so slow to show the changes one might expect in view of the CMEA's novel policy objectives. The policy differences of the CMEA countries were not confined to commercial issues, but also relate to the ways restructuring should be organized. One of the problems, of course, is deciding who should head and manage the streamlining activities. According to the October 1987 decisions, coordination of plans is to be reorganized by the Committee for Cooperation in Planning, while the reorganization of the standing organs is to fall to the Secretariat and its leadership (Marjai 1987). No matter how reasonable this solution may sound—after all, who knows planning better than planners themselves—this option was dangerous.

There is hardly any organization that would readily cut itself back by half. It is a well-known empirical fact also in market economies that no company management, let alone the executive of state organs, tends to see itself critically, and even if it does a plethora of sociological factors militates against a cutback. External expertise, reorganization and/or new management are needed if a serious overhaul is intended or is deemed necessary. In the CMEA, however, no independent expert/political body has been called into life, not even one of an *ad hoc* nature, for the purpose of coordinating such an overhaul. And although nobody with a background in sociology will be really surprised by the fact that CMEA organs tend to survive and expand irrespective of external circumstances, the above-described small organizational shortcoming of the newly-approved "cutback" was decisive for its outcome. The Secretariat of the CMEA has never been very famous for its anti-bureaucratic and businesslike stands. It seems to be a warning sign that the Secretary and the various

official publications of the Secretariat repeatedly call for the reinforcement of the joint organs, playing up their role in the task of
mastering the difficulties of cooperation without ever mentioning
that the greater their putative importance the fewer the measures
they pass, without detailing what activities they themselves find
bureaucratic, and without even hinting that any existing joint organs
might possibly be superfluous.

Other areas where the future is predetermined by past decisions
are those dealt with in the CMEA's comprehensive programme for
scientific and technological progress, to the year 2000 (see: Long-
term Programme), which reflects the Soviet concern with the technological gap between East and West. The programme envisaged overhauling the existing integrational arrangements, and named the
expansion of direct interfirm relations as the major way to do so.
However, there has been little change in the actual methods of cooperation. At the political level, it is the sluggishness with which interstate
and interfirm contracts are signed that has come in for most criticism.
In business practice, however, other problems have proved to be
of greater significance. As it is detailed by a recent analysis of the
Secretariat, in most cases the coordinatory "head organization"
(golovnaya organizatsiya) could not even produce an acceptable
technical and economic feasibility study of the cooperation projects;
thus, neither costs, nor benefits, nor by implication, their distribution
among the participants could be exactly quantified. Neither the
commissioning, nor the executing parties could be identified, since
the determination of actual solvent demand was far too uncertain.[1]
This is partly due to the fact that "effective demand" is determined,
in the final analysis, when the national plans are dovetailed together.
Thus—as other analysts have noted—the coordinative head organizations along with their putative activities have remained bodies
alien to the intra-CMEA mechanism, since they have no way of
securing either the financial, or the physical coverage of their contract
(Il'in 1987, p. 17).

The Long-term Programme has given rise to some special problems
from Hungary's point of view. The idea of accelerating technological
progress is, of course, dear to our hearts, and the promised radical
overhaul of the integration mechanism was expected to remedy
the longstanding problem of the incongruence of the Hungarian and
the CMEA methods of management.

However, the Programme was promulgated at a time when the
Seventh Five-Year Plan containing ambitious growth targets had

already beeen approved, though the restrictive financial arrangements that were necessary to maintain the equilibrium of the current
account were still in force. Thus, many enterprises joined the Programme in the hope of thereby being able to circumvent stringent
financial discipline. For them, the traditional features of the CMEA
mechanism, i.e. relying on long-term interstate agreements based on
the predetermination of supplies in physical terms, has been rather
an advantage. The pressure for financial efficiency is done away
with, as it is the control organs that have made the decisions involved
in such companies producing what they produce and it is they that
bear both the responsibility and the risks involved. Initially, thus,
many companies saw participating in the Long-term Programme as
a new opportunity to claim additional subsidies. When it turned out
that no additional financing was to be had over and above the funds
already available within the framework of various medium-term
national priority research projects, they changed tactics. They tried
to use the Programme to justify those exports to other Comecon
countries which were not paid for in actual counterdeliveries, but
only in nominal transferable rubles. As Head of the National Committee for Technological Development has noted with some em-
barrassment, although it is common knowledge that the Soviet
Union has the greatest R + D potential among all the CMEA states,
of all the cooperation projects proposed by Hungarian firms 90
percent is related to the export of Hungarian R + D, and only 10
percent to importing from CMEA partners (Müller 1987). This is
a clear-cut example of the conventional attitude of large-scale state-
owned companies, which try to boost their activities by unilateral
exports for TR without any regard for the bilateral equilibrium of
sales (an understandable attitude, but one completely unacceptable
from the macroeconomic point of view). Owing to the changed
bargaining positions of the various CMEA partners due to the spillover effects of the collapse of oil prices, the above proposals were
bound to fail. But when non-conventional, innovative, behaviour
was needed, when true technological cooperation (rather than the
traditional exports renamed) was at issue, the loss of interest was
quite conspicuous. The failure of the cooperation mechanism to
change has thwarted the achievement of the CMEA's novel aims—
something the chief Soviet negotiator has also noted (Antonov 1987a).

The above also implies that until the problem of currency convertibility is solved—something that seems to be a long way off—Hungary
cannot serve as a bridge for Western technology transfers to the Soviet

Union, because it is not in her interest to spend dollars for rubles if conversion in the opposite direction cannot take place. It is worth mentioning that the Soviet regulations of October 1987, also preclude such one-sided possibilities; (Clement, 1988–89, Csaba, 1988)[2] this frequently-made suggestion is, thus, simply out of touch with intra-Comecon realities.

In the daily bargains of state trading, some of the more traditional issues took much more time and energy than any analysis aiming at pinpointing (relative or absolute) novelties can and/or should survey. Discussing the evergreen subject of agricultural prices, the way the admittedly absurd pricing principles can be applied in practice to new technology or to spare parts, and the problems of energy supplies unfortunately sometimes continued to take more time and effort than is devoted to the creative search for new ideas. This was all the more unfortunate in that within the given model of co-operation, every way leads to a dead end. For an economist it must be surprising that, for example, the issue of the function of prices is not even raised, while various obviously tactically motivated pro-positions about price relatives proliferate. It is a reflection of the real state of things that the traditional mandatory planning model is still intact in the majority of the member states, despite a great deal of verbal criticism all throughout the 80s.

PROSPECTS

From the Hungarian point of view, it is promising that the policy of doing nothing has become the least acceptable option for the Gorbachevian Soviet Union. Considering its dynamism, in the longer run the evolving Soviet reform process is bound to exert its impact on the Comecon's mechanism as well. However, when it comes to defining Hungary's policy objectives *vis-à-vis* both East and West, one must take as one's point of departure the fact that the process of renewal within the CMEA will take much more time than world economic pressures will allow a small country for working out her adjustment policies. Thus, the consolidation and stabilization pro-gramme of the Hungarian government had to take on a different pace already between 1988–90 (Csaba, 1989b, Köves, 1988).

Within the CMEA, the lack of sufficient technological progress, the disregard for quality and the failure to reward performance is likely to lead to ever greater pressure for change. Thus what seems only theoretically possible today will be inevitable practice tomorrow. A more circumspect strategic orientation would involve the reinterpretation and thorough rethinking of just what is in the national interest. A non-trivial answer presumes that it is the structural changes in the world economy and the imperative of adjustment to them that serve as the compass, rather than the desire for stability, security and other old-fashioned values. In reality, the future is much less predetermined by present considerations than bargaining positions at international fora tend to be—and this in itself is encouraging. To adopt market principles including trade in convertible currency or to perish as a relict of the *ancien regime*: this is the real alternative for the East European regional cooperation system in the 1990s.

NOTES

1 Prioritetnye napravleniya mezhdunarodnoi kooperatsii i mekhanism upravleniya (editorial), *Ekonomicheskoe sotrudnichestvo stran-chlenov SEV* 1987/9, p. 5.
2 Cf. Csaba 1988b for the details.

Appendix

Table 1. Share of CMEA in world exports, 1950–1985 (in percent)

	1950	1960	1965	1970	1975	1981	1983	1985
Total CMEA	6.8	10.1	10.5	9.8	8.9	8.1	9.6	8.8
of which								
Soviet Union	3.0	4.3	4.4	4.1	3.8	4.0	5.05	4.5
Eastern Europe	3.8	5.8	6.1	5.7	5.1	4.1	4.65	4.3

Source: own calculations based on: *UN Monthly Bulletin of Statistics*, June 1978, May 1983, July 1984, July 1986.

Table 2. Share of CMEA in world imports (1950–1985) (in percent)

	1950	1960	1965	1970	1975	1981	1983	1985
Total CMEA	6.3	10.3	10.5	9.6	10.1	8.0	8.7	8.1
of which								
Soviet Union	2.3	4.2	4.1	3.6	4.1	3.6	4.2	4.0
Eastern Europe	4.0	6.1	6.4	6.0	6.0	4.4	4.5	4.1

Source: own calculations based on: *UN Monthly Bulletin of Statistics*, June 1978, May 1983, July 1984, July 1986.

Table 3. Value of Soviet exports by country groups, 1970–1985 (in billion US dollars)

	Total exports	Developed market economies	Developing countries*	Eastern Europe	Asian CPE's
1970	12,8	2,716	2,688	6,759	0,638
1975	33,318	9,582	6,188	16,449	1,100
1979	64,762	21,362	12,871	28,314	2,215
1981	79,003	26,938	15,856	33,613	2,592
1983	91,330	29,996	11,790	39,219	3,251
1985	87,201	22,357	19,559	38,872	6,413

Source: own calculation based on: *UN Monthly Bulletin of Statistics*, June 1978, May 1983, July 1984, July 1986.

* Yugoslavia is calculated as part of developing countries, for 1985 as part of market economies

Table 4. Geographical distribution of Soviet exports 1970–1985
(based on dollar values, in percent)

	Developed market economies	Developing countries	Eastern Europe	Asian CPE's
1970	21.2	21.0	52.8	5.0
1975	28.8	18.5	49.4	3.3
1979	33.0	19.9	43.7	3.4
1980	35.3	18.5	42.1	4.1
1981	34.1	20.0	42.6	3.3
1983	32.8	21.7	42.9	3.6
1985	25.6	22.4	44.6	7.4

Source: own calculations based on: *UN Monthly Bulletin of Statistics,* June 1978,
May 1983, July 1984 and July 1986.

Table 5. Value of Soviet imports by country groups, 1970–1985
(in billion dollars)

	Total exports	Developed market economies	Developing countries*	Eastern Europe	Asian CPE's
1970	11.732	3.073	1.789	6.635	0.235
1975	36.971	14.514	6.177	15.680	0.599
1978	57.744	21.849	8.121	26.647	1.126
1981	72.960	18.957	13.629	29.320	1.054
1983	80.267	28.335	13.010	37.085	1.541
1985	82.578	23.021	18.056	39.235	2.266

Source: own calculations based on: *UN Monthly Bulletin of Statistics,* June 1978,
May 1983, July 1984 and July 1986.

* Yugoslavia is calculated as part of developing countries, from 1985 as
part of market economies.

Table 6. Geographical distribution of Soviet imports by country groups, 1970–1985 (in percent)

	Developed market economies	Developing countries	Eastern Europe	Asian CPE's
1970	26.2	15.2	56.6	2.0
1975	39.3	16.7	42.4	1.7
1979	37.8	14.1	46.1	2.0
1981	39.7	18.7	40.2	1.6
1983	35.3	16.2	46.2	1.9
1985	27.9	21.9	47.5	2.7

Source: own calculations based on: *UN Monthly Bulletin of Statistics*, June 1978, May 1983, July 1984 and July 1986

Table 7. Value of East European exports by country groups, 1970–1985 (in billion US dollars)

	Total	Developed market economies	Developing countries	Soviet Union	Eastern Europe	Asian CPE's
1970	18,168	4,762	1,397	6,655	5,000	0,374
1975	45,029	11,945	4,282	15,680	12,306	0,816
1979	71,391	20,017	7,468	26,647	15,663	1,596
1981	80,382	21,596	11,821	29,320	16,247	1,398
1983	83,852	19,467	8,728	37,083	17,078	1,496
1985	82,672	18,930	11,585	33,616	16,893	1,653

Source: as at Table 1.

Table 8. Geographical distribution of East European exports by country groups (based on dollar figures, in percent)

	Total	Developed market economies	Developing countries	Soviet Union	Eastern Europe	Asian CPE's
1970	100	26.2	7.7	36.5	27.5	2.1
1975	100	26.5	9.5	34.8	27.3	1.8
1979	100	28.0	10.5	37.3	21.9	2.2
1981	100	26.9	14.7	36.5	20.2	1.7
1983	100	23.2	10.4	44.2	20.5	1.8
1985	100	22.9	14.0	40.7	20.4	2.0

Source: as at Table 1.

Table 9. Value of East European imports by country groups, 1970–1985 (in billions of US dollars)

	Total	Developed market economies	Developing countries	Eastern Europe	Soviet Union	Asian CPE's
1970	17,186	4,066	1,158	4,981	6,662	0,319
1975	47,259	14,378	3,39	12,403	16,375	0,718
1979	73,125	20,589	6,67	17,638	26,864	1,364
1980	82,014	22,347	10,708	18,379	29,070	1,510
1981	76,314	18,999	8,568	17,584	29,836	1,327
1983	78,304	19,664	8,028	18,130	31,628	0,854
1985	83,321	19,767	9,073	18,925	34,058	1.498

Source: as at Table 1.

Table 10. Geographical distribution of East European imports by country of origin, 1970–1985 (in percent)

	Total	Developed market economies	Developing countries	Eastern Europe	Soviet Union	Asian CPE's
1970	100	23.7	6.7	29.0	38.8	1.9
1975	100	30.4	7.2	26.2	34.6	1.5
1979	100	28.2	9.1	24.1	36.8	1.9
1980	100	27.2	13.1	22.4	35.4	1.8
1981	100	24.9	11.2	23.0	39.1	1.7
1983	100	25.1	10.2	10.2	40.4	1.1
1985	100	23.7	10.9	22.7	40.8	1.8

Source: as at Table 1.

Table 11. Tendencies in exports of machinery and transport equipment (SITC-7) by CMEA and developing countries to the world, 1970–1984 (in billion dollars)

| | Developing countries | | | CMEA countries of which | | | | | |
| | | | | Eastern Europe | | | Soviet Union | | |
	1	2	3	1	2	3	1	2	3
1970	54,944	1,431	2.6	17,725	6,872	38,7	12,80	2,775	21.7
1975	210,477	7,131	3.4	44,048	18,152	41,2	33,310	6,378	19.1
1978	301,649	15,776	5,2	60,218	26,640	44.2	52,216	10,410	19.9
1981	544,357	31,628	5.6	77,660	33,630	43.2	79,003	10,912	13.8
1982	486,483	32,136	6.6	78,152	34,038	43.6	86,949	11,368	13.1
1984	486,956	49,451	10.5	83,361	36,995	44,3	91,649	11,563	12.6

Source: *UN Monthly Bulletin of Statistics*, June 1979, May 1983 and May 1984, May 1986.

1 = value of total exports
2 = value of SITC 7 exports
3 = 2 : 1 (in percent)

Table 12. Trends in exports of machinery and transport equipment (SITC-7) by CMEA and developing countries to developed market economies (1970–84)

| | Developing countries | | | CMEA countries of which | | | | | |
| | | | | Eastern Europe | | | Soviet Union | | |
	1	2	3	1	2	3	1	2	3
1970	39,758	0,757	1.9	4,316	0,486	11.3	2,716	0,13	5.3
1975	147,710	3,654	2.5	10,617	1,644	15.5	9,582	0,547	5.7
1978	214,563	8,747	4.1	14,944	2,379	15.9	14.356	0,752	5.2
1981	367,400	16,052	4.4	19,300	2,941	15.2	26,936	0,740	2.7
1982	312,152	17,442	5.6	19,383	2,688	13.9	29,365	0,777	2.6
1984	305,683	31,358	10.3	20,634	2,332	11.3	30,078	0,701	2.3

Source: UN *Monthly Bulletin of Statistics*, June 1978, May 1983, May 1984 and May 1986.

1 = value of total exports
2 = value of SITC 7 exports
3 = 2 : 1 (in percent)

Table 13. Comparison of machinery (SITC-7) exports of CMEA and developing economies to competitive markets (1970–84)

Year	Developing countries				
	1	2	3	4	5
1980	27,547	14,097	51.1	7,669	27.8
1984	49,451	31,358	63.4	20,629	41.7
dynamics $\frac{1984}{1980}$	179.5%	222.4%		269%	
$\frac{1984}{1970}$	34.6 times	41.4 times			
CMEA countries, Eastern Europe					
1980	33,894	3,007	8.9	0,251	0.7
1984	36,995	2,332	6.3	0,144	0.4
dynamics $\frac{1984}{1980}$	109.1%	77.6%		57.3%	
$\frac{1984}{1970}$	5.4 times	4.8 times			
Soviet Union					
1980	12,227	0,781	6.4	0,007	0,06
1984	11,563	0,701	6.0	0,007	0.06
dynamics $\frac{1984}{1980}$	94.6%	89.8%			
$\frac{1984}{1970}$	4.2 times	4.9 times			

Source: *UN Monthly Bulletin of Statistics*, May 1986.

1 = value of total machinery exports to the world, in bn $
2 = value of total machinery exports to developed market economies, in bn $
3 = 2 : 1 (in percent)
4 = value of machinery exports to the USA, in bn US $
5 = 4 : (share of US among all export markets, in percent)

Table 14. World trade: annual rates of change in volume and prices, 1976–1986[c]
(Percentage)

	1976—1980	1981—1984	1985[b]	1986[c]
Volume of exports				
World	5.1	2.0	2.6	3.5
Developed market economies	6.6	3.0	4.2	4.0
Developing countries	1.9	—1.6	—0.9	4.0
Capital-surplus countries	—1.7	—16.1	—6.0	3.0
Other net energy exporters	2.1	0.4	—2.0	4.0
Net energy importers	7.4	9.6	2.0	4.5
Centrally planned economies[d]	5.7	4.4	—0.8	0.0
Volume of imports				
World	5.5	2.8	3.4	4.0
Developed market economies	5.6	3.0	5.5	6.0
Developing countries	5.5	2.9	—3.8	—1.9
Capital-surplus countries	11.5	4.9	—13.5	—12.0
Other net energy exporters	5.9	1.6	—1.0	—10.0
Net energy importers	3.8	2.8	—1.7	4.5
Centrally planned economies[d]	4.8	2.5	4.8	3.0
Unit value of exports				
World	12.2	—3.3	—1.6	7.0
Developed market economies	9.8	—3.5	—1.1	14.0
Developing countries	19.1	—3.2	—2.7	—11.0
Capital-surplus countries	23.5	—1.9	—1.8	—33.0
Other net energy exporters	21.0	—1.4	—3.1	—23.5
Net energy importers	11.2	—4.9	—2.5	6.0
Centrally planned economies[d]	8.7	—1.1	—1.3	—2.0
Unit value of imports				
World	11.7	—3.7	—2.4	7.0
Developed market economies	12.1	—4.0	—2.6	7.0
Developing countries	12.5	—3.4	—1.8	8.0
Capital surplus countries	10.8	—3.7	—1.7	13.0
Other net energy exporters	11.1	—3.7	—1.9	11.5
Net energy importers	13.4	—3.3	—1.8	5.5
Centrally planned economies[d]	6.8	—1.7	—1.5	3.0
Terms of trade				
Developed market economies	—2.1	0.5	1.5	6.5
Developing countries	5.9	0.2	—0.9	—-18.0
Capital surplus countries	11.5	1.9	0.0	—40.5
Other net energy exporters	8.9	2.4	—1.2	—31.0
Net energy importers	—1.9	—1.7	—0.7	0.5
Centrally planned economies[d]	1.7	0.6	0.2	—5.0

Source: *UN World Economic Survey*, New York, 1986, p. 45.

[a] Rates of change in unit values on indices expressed in dollars.
[b] Preliminary estimates.
[c] Forecasts, rounded to the nearest half percentage point.
[d] Eastern Europe and the Soviet Union only.

Table 15. Indebtedness of CMEA states (in billion US $)

	1981	1983	1985	1987ᵖ
Bulgaria	3.1	2.4	3.6	6.0
GDR	15.4	12.1	13.5	18.5
Poland	25.4	26.4	29.7	37.6
Romania	10.1	8.8	6.6	5.7
Soviet Union	26.5	23.5	28.4	128.6
Czechoslovakia	4.5	3.6	3.5	5.3
Hungary	8.6	8.2	11.7	17.5
	93.6	85.0	97.0	219.2

Source: OECD Financial Market Trends, February 1988
  ᵖ = forecast

Bibliography

Abolikhina, G. and Bakovetzki, O. 1986. Kursom integratzii. *Ekonomicheskaya Gazeta* 25.

Abonyi, Á. and Sylvain, I. 1977. CMEA integration and policy options for Eastern Europe: a development strategy for dependent states. *The Journal of Common Market Studies*, No. 4.

Abonyi, Á. and Sylvain, I. 1980. Political economy perspectives on integration. In Marer, P. and Montias, J. M. eds.

Alev, F. 1986. Uglublenie soglasovaniya ekonomicheskoi politiki stran-chlenov SEV. *Ekonomicheskie Nauki* 12.

Allakhverdyan, D. A. 1976. *Finansovo-kreditnii mekhanizm razvitogo sotsializma.* Moscow: Finansy.

Allen, M. 1980. Discussion of Brainard 1980. In Marer, P. and Montias, J. M. eds.

Angelov, T. 1982. Rol' koordinatsii kapitalnykh vlozhenii v formirovanii osnovnykh napravlenii i printsipov soglasovannoi strukturnoi politiki stran-chlenov SEV. In Belovič, A. 1982, pp. 32–37.

Antal, L. 1983. Conflicts of financial planning and regulation. The "nature" of restrictions. *Acta Oeconomica* Vol. 30, No. 3–4.

Antonov, A. 1986a. Increase of intensification. *CMEA — Economic Cooperation 1.*

Antonov, A. 1986b. Sodruzhestvo umnozhaet sily. *Sotsialisticheskaya Industriya*, February 13.

Antonov, A. 1986c. S'ezd strategicheskikh reshenii. *Ekonomicheskoe sotrudnichestvo stran chlenov SEV* 5, p. 15.

Antonov, A. K. 1987. The new mechanism of cooperation (interview). *New Times* 42.

Asztalos, L. 1981. Néhány gondolat a szocialista viszonylatú nem kereskedelmi elszámolások továbbfejlesztéséről (Some thoughts on developing non-commercial accounts with socialist countries). *Egyetemi Szemle* 3.

Ausch, S. 1971. Problems of bilateralism and multilateralism in the external trade and payments system of the CMEA countries. In Vajda, I. and Simai, M. eds. 1971, pp. 61–100.

Ausch, S. 1972. *Theory and practice of CMEA co-operation.* Budapest: Akadémiai Kiadó.

Badrus, G. 1983. Viabilitatea deplina a principiilor fundamentale ale collaborarii si cooperarii in cadrul C.A.E.R. (The complete viability of the fundamental principles of cooperation within the CMEA). *Era Socialista* 4, pp. 21—25.

Bagudin, P. 1982. The CMEA member-countries' co-operation in the sphere of capital investments and foreign trade. *Foreign Trade of the USSR 8.*

Bagudin, P. 1983. The CMEA countries' coordinated plan for multilateral integration measures for 1981–85. *Foreign Trade of the USSR 1.*

Baibakov, N. 1978. Dolgosrochnye tseleviye programmy sotrudnichestva: novyi etap v razvitii sotsialisticheskoy ekonomicheskoy integratsii stranchlenov SEV. *Planovoe Khozyaistvo 9.*

Bakhtov, K. and Zoloev, V. 1977. The fuel exports of the USSR in the contemporary stage. *Foreign Trade of the USSR 2.*

Bakovetzkii, O. 1985. Pryamye svyazi: opyt i perspektivy. *Ekonomicheskaya Gazeta 50.*

Bakovetzkii, O. and Gavrilov, V. 1983. Rasshirenie pryamykh svyazei mezhdu khozyaistvennymi zvenyami SSSR i stran SEV. *Planovoe Khozayistvo 10.*

Bakovetzkii, O. and Grinev, V. 1982. O pryamykh proizvodstvennykh svyazakh. *Voprosy Ekonomiki 4.*

Balassa, Á. 1979. *A magyar népgazdaság tervezésének alapjai* (Basic features of macroeconomic planning in Hungary). Budapest: Közgazdasági és Jogi Könyvkiadó.

Balassa, B. 1977. *Policy Reform in Developing Countries.* Oxford: Pergamon Press.

Balásházy, M. 1984. A szerződéses kapcsolatok néhány problémája a KGST-ben (Some problems of contractual relations in the CMEA). Priority Research Project on Public Economic Law of the Hungarian Academy of Sciences, concluding studies, series No. 1. Budapest, Sept.

Bálek, J. 1976. Vládni úvěr jako dulezity nástroj socialistické ekonomické integráce (State credit as an important tool of socialist economic integration). *Finance a Úvěr 3.*

Bánfi, T. 1981. *Valutaárfolyam-elmélet és -politika* (Exchange-rate theory and policy). Budapest: Közgazdasági és Jogi Könyvkiadó.

Bautina, N. and Samovol, V. 1986. Povyshenie deistvennosti planovovo mekhanizma sotrudnichestva stran SEV. *Mirovaya Ekonomika Mezhdunarodnye Otnosheniva 6.* p. 93.

Bársony, J. 1980. A transzferábilis rubel (The transferable ruble). Institute for Economic and Market Research publications, May.

Bartha, F. 1975. A KGST-országok közötti sokoldalú elszámolások megvalósításának egy lehetséges útja (A possible way of implementing multilateral payments among CMEA countries). *Külgazdaság 1.*

Bartha, F. 1984. A KGST továbbfejlesztésének távlatai (Prospects for improving the CMEA). *Külpolitika 3.*

Bauer, T. 1981. *Tervgazdaság, beruházás, ciklusok* (Planned economy, investments, cycles). Budapest: Közgazdasági és Jogi Könyvkiadó.

Bauer, T., Patkós, A., Soós, K. A., Tárnok, É. and Vince, P. 1980. Jármű-program és gazdaságirányítás. Megfigyelések a gazdaságirányítási rendszer, a vállalatközi kapcsolatok és a műszaki fejlesztés összefüggéseiről (The central development programme for vehicles and economic control. Observations on the interrelationships between the economic mechanism, interfirm relations and technological progress). Publication series of the Institute of Economics of the Hungarian Academy of Sciences, Budapest, new volume, No. 19.

Bauer, T. and Soós, K. A. 1981. The current debate among Soviet economists over the transformation of the system of economic control. *Eastern European Economics*, 1.

Bauer, T. and Szamuely, L. 1978. The structure of industrial administration in European CMEA countries: change and continuity. *Acta Oeconomica*, Vol. 20. No. 4.

Bautina, N. et al. 1983. Obobshchenie opyta sovershenstvovaniya natsional-nykh khozyaistvennykh mekhanizmov stran-chlenov SEV, i vyyavlenie vozmozhnykh napravlenii ikh sblizheniya. Research report at the CMEA International Economic Research Institute, Moscow.

Bautina, N. and Shiryaev, Yu. 1982. Deepening CMEA economic cooperation. *International Affairs* (Moscow) 11.

Bautina, N. and Shiryaev, Yu. 1984. Voprosy ispol'zovaniya tovarno-denezh-nykh rychagov v realizatsii integratsionnykh meropriyatii. *Planovoe Khozyaistvo* 3.

Becsky, Gy. 1982. Az Európai Pénzügyi Rendszer a 80-as évek elején: műkö-dése, tapasztalatai és perspektívái (The EMS in the early 80s: its function-ing, experiences, and prospects). *Közgazdasági Szemle*, 10.

Belovič, A. ed. 1982. Aktual'nye voprosy sovershenstvovaniya koordinatsii kapital'nykh vlozhenii stran-chlenov SEV. CMEA International Economic Research Institute, Moscow.

Belovič, A. 1983. Koordinatsiya kapitalnykh vloznenii stran-chlenov SEV. *Voprosy Ekonomiki*, 3.

Belovič, A., Voropaev, V. and Zvorigin, Yu. eds. 1984. Sovershenstvovanie ekonomicheskikh uslovii investitsionnovo sotrudnichestva stran-chlenov SEV i planirovaniya meropriyatii v etoi oblasti. CMEA International Economic Research Institute, Moscow.

Berend, I. T. 1971. Contribution to the history of East-Central European integration. In: Vajda, I. and Simai, M. eds.

Bergson, A. 1980. The geometry of Comecon trade. *European Economic Review*, No. 14.

Betkenhagen, J. 1984. Oil and gas in CMEA intra-block trade. *DIW Economic Bulletin*, February.

Betkenhagen, J. 1985. The impacts of energy on East-West trade: retrospect and prospects. In Saunders, Ch. ed.

Bialer, S. 1984. Die osteuropäische Krise: ein sowjetisches Dilemma. In Höh-mann, H. H. and Vogel, H. eds.

Biró, A. 1976. Megjegyzések a magyar—szovjet külkereskedelmi árszínvonal problematikájához (Comments on price level in Hungarian—Soviet trade). Institute for World Economy of the Hungarian Academy of Sciences, Budapest, July (manuscript).

Bochkov, V. F. 1982. Finansovyi mekhanizm sotrudnichestva. *Ekonomiches-kaya Gazeta*, 28.

Bogdanowicz-Bindert, Ch. 1985/86. Rethinking the world debt. *Foreign Af-fairs*, Fall/Winter.

Bognár, J. 1979. Relations of the CMEA to the world economy at the begin-ning of a new era. *Acta Oeconomica*, Vol. 23. No. 1–2.

Bogomolov, O. 1964. A KGST-országok gazdasági együttmflködési tapasz-talatairól (On the experiences of economic cooperation among CMEA countries). *Közgazdasági Szemle*, 5.

Bogomolov, O. 1967. *Teoriya i metodologiya mezhdunarodnogo sotsialisticheskogo razdeleniya truda.* Moscow: Ekonomika.

Bogomolov, O. 1983a. Közös stratégiával (By means of a joint strategy). An interview by Matkó, I. and Szalay, H. *Magyar Hírlap,* 11 March.

Bogomolov, O. 1983b. Ob ekonomicheskom razvitii i sotrudnichestve stran—chlenov SEV. *Kommunist,* 7.

Bogomolov, O. 1983c. The coordination of economic policies. *New Times,* 5.

Bogomolov, O. 1985a. Soglasovanie ekonomicheskikh interesov i politiki pri sotsialisme. *Kommunist,* 10.

Bogomolov, O. 1985b. Nauchno-tekhnicheskiy progress v khozyaistvennom razvitii i ekonomicheskom sotrudnichestve stran-chlenov SEV. *Ekonomicheskoe sotrudnichestvo stran-chlenov SEV,* 9.

Bogomolov, O. 1986a. Rol' SSSR v sotsialisticheskoi ekonomicheskoi integratsii. *Ekonomicheskoe sotrudnichestvo stran-chlenov SEV,* 2.

Bogomolov, O. 1986b. A szovjet gazdaság reformjáról és a KGST-együttműködésről (On the Soviet economic reform and on CMEA cooperation). An interview by Zalai, I. and Miklós, G. *Népszabadság,* 13 Sept.

Bogomolov, O. 1987. World Socialism at a Turning Point. *International Affairs,* 12.

Böhm, E. 1981. Die Einnahmeverluste der Sowjetunion bei ihren RGW-Ölexporten. *Osteuropa Wirtschaft,* 2.

Borisov, O. 1984. Soyuz novogo tipa. *Voprosy Istorii KPSS,* 4.

Bornstein, M. 1984. Restriktion oder Kooperation: Handel. In Höhmann, H. H. and Vogel, H. eds.

Bornstein, M. 1985a. *The Transfer of Western Technology to the USSR.* Paris: OECD.

Bornstein, M. 1985b. Improving the Soviet economic mechanism. *Soviet Studies,* 1.

Böröczffy, F. ed. 1982. *A szocialista integrációról.* "Vélemények és viták" sorozat (On socialist integration. The "Opinions and discussions" series.) Budapest: Kossuth Könyvkiadó.

Borozdin, O. 1986. Planovoe tsenoobrazovanie v novoi sisteme khozyaistvovaniya. *Kommunist,* 16

Botos, K. 1978. *Pénzügyek a KGST-ben* (Finances in the CMEA). Budapest: Közgazdasági és Jogi Könyvkiadó.

Botos, K. 1979. A KGST-tagországok valutáinak egységes árfolyamáról (On the uniform exchange rate of currencies of the CMEA member states). *Pénzügyi Szemle,* 8–9.

Botos, K. 1980. A transzferábilis rubel reális árfolyamáról (On the realistic exchange rate of the TR). *Közgazdasági Szemle* 9.

Botos, K. 1982. On the further development of the currency and financial system of the CMEA. *Soviet Studies* 2.

Botos, K., Patai, M. and Szalkai, I. 1980. *Pénzügyeink és a nemzetközi gazdasági kapcsolatok* (Finances in Hungary and international economic relations). Budapest: Közgazdasági és Jogi Könyvkiadó.

Bożyk, P. 1977. Sovmestnye predpriyatiya i kapitalnye vlozheniya stran SEV: uchastie Pol'shi. *Planovoe Khozyaistvo* 4.

Bożyk, P. 1986. Handel wzajemny krajów RWPG. *Sprawy Międzynarodowe* 11.

Brabant, J. van 1971. Long-term development credits and socialist trade. *Weltwirtschaftliches Archiv*, Band 107, No. 1.

Brabant, J. van 1977. The transferable rouble — the COMECON currency controversy. *International Currency Review* 1.

Brabant, J. van 1981. Target programming — a new instrument of socialist economic integration ? In *Jahrbuch der Wirtschaft Osteuropas*, Band 9, 2 Halbband. München: Olzog Verlag, pp. 141–184.

Brabant, J. van 1984. The USSR and socialist economic integration: a comment. *Soviet Studies* 1.

Brainard, L. 1980. CMEA financial system and integration. In Marer, P. and Montias, J. M. eds.

Brendel, G. 1979. Die planmässige Ausnützung der Ware-Geld-Beziehungen in der Wirtschaftszusammenarbeit der RGW-Länder.*Wirtschaftswissenschaft* 5.

Brown, A. and Kaser, M. eds. 1982. *Soviet policy for the 1980s*. Oxford: St Anthony's Macmillan Series.

Brus, W. 1972. *The market in a socialist economy*. London–Boston: Routledge and Kegan Paul.

Brus, W. 1985. Wirtschaftsreformen in der Sowjetunion. *Europäische Rundschau*, 1.

Bunce, V. 1985. The empire strikes back: the transformation of the Eastern bloc from a Soviet asset to a Soviet liability. *International Organization* (MIT) 1.

Bunich, P. G. 1986. Eskiz mekhanizma upravleniya. *Literaturnaya Gazeta*, Feb. 12.

Butenko, A. 1982. Economic integration and national sovereignity. *New Times* 30.

Ceauşescu, N. 1986. Speech delivered at his meeting the Premiers on the occasion of the 42nd Council Session. *Scînteia*, 5. December.

Chalupsky, Z. 1987. Predpokladany vývoj mezinárodní socialisticke ekonomické integráce. *Politická Ekonomie* 5.

Chukanov, O. 1982. Integratsiya kak faktor intensifikatsii ekonomiki stran SEV. *Kommunist* 17.

Chukanov, O. 1985. A new stage of development of the economic cooperation of CMEA member countries. *CMEA — Economic Cooperation* 1.

Chukanov, O. 1986. Scientific and technical progress in the CMEA countries . *International Affairs* (Moscow) 3.

Chvojka, P. 1980. General problems of interdependence among individual components of the CMEA international monetary system. *Acta Oeconomica*, Vol. 25. No. 3–4.

Chvojka, P. 1982. A KGST-országok nemzetközi piacának tervszerű irányítása (The planned management of the international market of CMEA countries). In Böröczffy, F. ed. pp. 89–115.

Clement, H. 1988–89. Changes in the Soviet Foreign Trade system. *Soviet and East European Foreign Trade*, Vol. XXIV. No, 4.

Communiqué (1978), issued from the 32nd Session of the CMEA. Central Party dailies, 30 June.

Communiqué (1983), issued from the 37th Session of the Council. Central Party dailies, 21 Oct.

Communiqué (1985), issued from the 40th Session of the Council. Central Party dailies, 29 June. In English, in *New Times*, 1985/27.

Communiqué (1985b), from the meeting of the Political Consultative Board of the Warsaw Treaty Organization, held in Sofia. Central Party dailies, 26 Oct.

Communiqué (1986), issued from the 119th Meeting of the Executive Committee of the CMEA. Central Party dailies, 23 May.

Communiqué (1987), issued from the 43rd Session of the Council. Central Party dailies, 15 October.

Csaba, L. 1980. Impacts of world economic changes on CMEA. *Acta Oeconomica*, Vol. 25, No. 3–4.

Csaba, L. 1981. Planning and finances in the decade after the adoption of the Comprehensive Programme in the CMEA. *Acta Oeconomica*, Vol. 27, No. 3–4.

Csaba, L. 1983. Adjustment to the world economy in Eastern Europe. *Acta Oeconomica*, Vol. 30, No. 1.

Csaba, L. 1984. The role of the CMEA in the world economy in the 1980s. *The ACES Bulletin* 2–3. Summer/Fall.

Csaba, L. 1985. Three studies on the CMEA. *Trends in World Economy*, No. 52. Budapest: Hungarian Scientific Council for the World Economy.

Csaba, L. 1986a. Le processus de la réforme hongroise et son évolution prévisible en 1985–87. *Revue d'Études Comparatives Est-Ouest* 2.

Csaba, L. 1986b. CMEA and East-West Trade. *Comparative Economic Studies*, No. 3.

Csaba, L. 1987. Die dritte Phase der ungarischen Wirtschaftsreform, *Südost-Europa* 7–8.

Csaba, L. 1988a. Restructing of the Soviet foreign trade mechanism and possibilities for interfirm relations in the CMEA. *Acta Oeconomica* 39, No. 1–2.

Csaba, L. 1988b. CMEA in the year 2000. *The Nordic Journal of Soviet and East European Studies*, Vol. 5, No. 1.

Csaba, L. 1989a. Die Entstehung der sowjetischen Wirtschaftsreform. *Österreiche Osthefte*, Vol. 31, No. 1.

Csaba, L. 1989b. Quo vadis, Comecon? *Le Courier des Pays de l'Est*, No. 343.

Csikós-Nagy, B. 1973a. *Socialist economic policy*. Budapest–London: Akadémiai Kiadó — Longman Group.

Csikós-Nagy, B. 1973b. The realization of mutual advantages in the economic cooperation among CMEA countries. In Kiss, T., Földi, T. and Schweitzer I. eds.

Csikós-Nagy, B. 1975. *Socialist price theory and price policy*. Budapest: Ak-a démiai Kiadó.

Csikós-Nagy, B. 1983. Hungary's adjustment to new world market relations. *Acta Oeconomica*, Vol. 30, No. 1.

Csikós-Nagy, B. 1968. *Általános és szocialista árelmélet* (General and socialist theory of prices). Budapest: Kossuth Könyvkiadó.

Daianu, D. 1984. External equilibrium and control of domestic absorption. *Revue Roumaine des Sciences Sociales, Serie des Sciences Économiques 2.*

Dăscălescu, C. 1982. Statement made at the 36th, Budapest Session of the CMEA. *Scînteia*, 13 June.

Dascălescu, C. 1984. Statement made at the 39th, Havana Session of the CMEA. *Scînteia*, 30 Oct.

Davidov, D. 1978. Contribution to the national conference on national economic planning, as reviewed in: Usavershenstvuvane planiranego na narodnoto stopanstvo (Improving the planning of the national economy). *Ikonomicheska Misal* 9.

Dementsev, V. V. 1986a. Vremya obyazyvaet rabotat' po novomu. *Den'gi i Kredit*, 10.

Dementsev, V. V. 1986b. Usilit' bankovskoe vozdeistvie na ekonomiku. *Ekonomicheskaya Gazeta*, 39.

Diebold, W. 1980. *Industrial policy as an international issue*. New York–St. Louis, etc.: McGraw-Hill Book Company for the Council on Foreign Relations.

Dietz, R. 1979. Price changes in Soviet trade with the CMEA and the rest of the world since 1975. In Hardt, J. P. ed.

Dietz, R. 1984. Advantages/disadvantages in USSR trade with Eastern Europe: the aspect of prices. *WIIW Forschungsberichte*, No. 97, Aug.

Dimov, I. 1983. Problemy na koordinatziyata na kapitalnite vlozheniya v stranite-chlenki na SIV (Problems of coordination of investments among CMEA countries). *Planovo Stopanstvo* 7.

Dobozi, I. 1973. Az energiahordozók a KGST gazdaságában (Fuels in the economy of the CMEA). *Valóság* 1.

Dobozi, I. 1978. Problems of raw material supply in Eastern Europe. *The World Economy* 1.

Dobozi, I. 1983. World raw material markets until the year 2000 — implications for Eastern Europe. *Raw Materials Report* (Stockholm), Vol. 2, No. 2.

Dobozi, I. 1984. A KGST-n belüli nyersanyag- és energiaegyüttműködés idő-szerű kérdései (Topical issues of intra-CMEA energy and raw material cooperation). *Külgazdaság* 1.

Documents of the Economic Summit meeting of the CMEA countries. *International Affairs* (Moscow), 1984/7, and *Czechoslovak Economic Digest*. (Prague), 1984/6.

Doichev, M. 1984. Koordinatsiyata na narodnostopanskite planove — glaven metod za upravleniya integratsionnite protsessi v ramkite na SIV (The coordination of national economic plans as the basic method of management of integrational processes within the CMEA). *Vneshna Trgoviya* 1.

Dolgosrochnaya tselevaya programma sotrudnichestva stran-chlenov SEV v oblasti sel'skogo khozyaistva i pishchevoi promyshlennosti. *BIKI*, 30 Oct., 1982.

Drábek, Z. 1983. External disturbances and balance of payments adjustment in the Soviet Union. *Aussenwirtschaft* 2.

Drechsler, L. et al. 1983. Production cooperations among CMEA countries: aims and realities. *Acta Oeconomica*, Vol. 30, No. 2.

Drechsler, L. and Szatmári, T. 1982. Iparpolitika és nemzetközi gazdasági együttmflködés (Industrial policy and international economic cooperation). Part II. *Iparpolitikai Tájékoztató* No. 5.

Dubrowsky, H.-J. and Zschockelt, W. 1980. Tezisy o nekotorykh problemakh valyutno-finansovykh otnoshenii mezhdu stranami-chlenami SEV. Paper presented at the international conference in Sopron.

Dudinskii, I. 1983. Uchastie SSSR v sotsialisticheskoi integratsii. (Review article on the book by Zubkov, A. and Shastitko, V., published under the same title by Nauka Publishing House, Moscow in 1981.) *EKO* 5.

Dyakin, B. and Medvedev, B. 1986. Deepening economic integration as the material basis for the CMEA countries' further cohesion. *International Affairs* (Moscow).

Ehlert, W. 1978. A KGST-országok hitelkapcsolatai és a KGST-bankok szerepe (Credit relations among CMEA countries and the role of CMEA banks). In *A szocialista integráció fejlesztésének elméleti és gyakorlati kérdései* (Theoretical and practical problems of developing the socialist integration). Budapest: Közgazdasági és Jogi Könyvkiadó.

Ekonomicheskii eksperiment (Economic experiment). *Ekonomicheskaya Gazeta,* 1984/47. Supplement.

Ekonomicheskii eksperiment: itogi pervogo goda i perspektivy dal'neishego razvitiya (Economic experiment: the results of the first year and prospects for further development). Round table discussion in the editorial office. *Voprosy Ekonomiki* and *Planovoe Khozyaistvo,* both 1985/4.

Enev, S. 1980a. Nekotorye aktual'nye voprosy dal'neishego sovershenstvovaniya valyutno-finansovoi sistemy stran-chlenov SEV. Paper presented at the international conference in Sopron.

Enev, S. 1980b. Po vprosa za stabil'nosta na kollektivnata valyuta na stranitechlenki ot SIV (On the issue of the stability of the purchasing power of the common currency of the CMEA member-countries). *Ikonomicheska Misal* 1.

Enyedi, A. 1979. Helyettesíthető-e a dollár és az arany? (Is it possible to find a substitute for the dollar and gold?) *Pénzügyi Szemle* 6.

Erdős, P. 1982. *Wage, profit, taxation,* Budapest: Akadémiai Kiadó.

Fallenbuchl, Z. 1977. L'intégration économique en Europe de l'Est, *Revue d'Études Comparatives Est-Ouest* 2.

Faluvégi, L. 1977. *Állami pénzügyek és gazdaságirányítás* (State finances and economic management). Budapest: Közgazdasági és Jogi Könyvkiadó.

Faluvégi, L. 1980. *Pénzügyeink a 70-es években* (Finances in Hungary in the 1970s). Budapest: Kossuth Könyvkiadó.

Faluvégi, L. 1984. A KGST-országok együttműködéséről (Cooperation among CMEA countries). *Pártélet,* 8–9.

Farkas, Gy. 1978. A transzferábilis rubel fejlődési lehetőségei (Development possibilities of the transferable ruble). *Külgazdaság,* No 12.

Fekete, J. 1980. Crisis of the international monetary system — impact of world economic changes on Hungarian economic policy. *Acta Oeconomica,* Vol. 24, No. 3–4.

Fiedler, Ch. 1982. Labilität der kapitalistischen Währungs- und Finanzsystemen und Ost-West-Beziehungen. *IPW Berichte* 6.

Fingerland, J. 1984. CMEA looks ahead realistically and with optimism. *Czechoslovak Economic Digest* 3.

Fock, J. 1973. Statement on return from the CMEA Session. *Népszabadság* 9 June.

Földi, T. and Kiss, T. eds. 1969. *Socialist world market prices.* Budapest: Akadémiai Kiadó.

Friss, I. 1974. Sotsialisticheskaya ekonomicheskaya integratsiya i postroenie sotsializma v Vengrii. *Acta Oeconomica,* Vol. 12. No. 1.

Friss, I. 1976. Bevezető (Introduction). In Friss, I. ed. *Gazdaságpolitikánk tapasztalatai és tanulságai, 1957–60* (Experiences and lessons of the Hungarian economic policy of the years 1957 to 60). Budapest: Közgazdasági és Jogi Könyvkiadó.

Furmanová, J. 1981. Funkce mezinárodniho palivove-surovinového komplexu v rozvoje socialistické ekonomické integrace (The role of the fuel and energy complex in the development of socialist economic integration). *Zahraniční Obchod* 3.

Garbuzov, V. 1983. Valyutno-finansovaya sistema stran SEV. *Ekonomicheskaya Gazeta* 5.

Gavrilov, E. and Motorin, I. 1979. Vzaimosvyaz' dolgosrochnykh tselevykh program sotrudnichestva stran SEV s natsionalnym planirovaniem. *Izvestiya AN SSSR, Seriya Ekonomicheskaya 3.*

Gavrilov, V. 1986. Prjamym svyazyam-khozyaistvennii dogovor. *Ekonomicheskaya Gazeta* 29.

Gavrilov, V. and Leznik, A. 1982. Planovye osnovy neposredstvennykh proizvodstvennykh svyazei SSSR i drugikh stran SEV. *Planovoe Khozyaistvo* 9.

Geidarov, M. 1981. Vazhnyi instrument tovarno-denezhnogo mekhanizma. *Den'gi i Kredit* 6.

Georgiev, G. 1978. Dolgosrochnye tzelevye programmy sotrudnichestva — vazhnye osnovy dal'neyshego razshireniya sotrudnichestva BNR s bratskimi sotsialisticheskimi stranami. *Planovoe Khozyaistvo* 9.

Glushkov, N. 1982. Planovoe tsenoobrazovanie i upravlenie ekonomikoi. *Voprosy Ekonomiki* 8.

Goldmann, J. and Kouba, K. 1969. *Economic growth in Czechoslovakia.* Prague: Academia.

Goldmann, J. 1975. The Czechoslovak economy in the 1970s. *Czechoslovak Economic Digest* 1.

Gorbachev, M. S. 1986. Speech to the Krasnodar Party cell. *Pravda*, 19 September.

Gorbachev, M. 1988. Address to the 19th All-Union Party Conference. *Pravda*, 29 June.

Goryunov, F. 1984. The reserves of integration. *New Times* 44.

Götz, H.-H. 1983. Der RGW plant eine neue Etappe der multilateralen Zusammenarbeit. *Frankfurter Allgemeine Zeitung*, 10. May.

Graziani, G. 1982. *COMECON: domination et dépendences.* Paris: Maspero.

Grinberg, R. and Lyubskii, M. 1985. Tseny i valyutnye otnosheniya v sotrudnichestve stran SEV. *Voprosy Ekonomiki* 6.

Grinev, V. 1984. Vygoda vzaimnaya. *Ekonomicheskaya Gazeta* 52.

Hágelmayer, I. 1974. A pénz értékmérő funkciója a szocialista világpiacon (The function of money as a measure of value on the socialist world market). *Pénzügyi Szemle* 5.

Hágelmayer, I. 1976. Gazdasági növekedésünk és a nemzetközi pénzügyek néhány összefüggése (Economic growth in Hungary and some interrelationships in international finances). *Gazdaság* 3.

Hágelmayer, I. 1976–77. Internal effects of external inflation and of deterioration in the terms of trade. *Soviet and East European Foreign Trade* Vol. XII, No. 4. Winter.

Hannigan, J. and McMillan, C. 1981. Joint investments in resource development: sectoral approaches to socialist integration. In Hardt, J. P. ed.

Hanson, P. 1982. Foreign economic relations. In Brown, A. and Kaser, M. eds.

Hanson, P. 1984. Restriktion der Kooperation: Technologietransfer. In Höhmann, H.-H. and Vogel, H. eds.

Hanson, P. 1985. *On the limitations of the Soviet economic debate.* University of Birmingham, Centre for Russian and East European Studies Discussion Papers, General Series No. 2. July.

Hanson, P. 1986. Economic relations between communist and capitalist nations in Europe. *Bericht des Bundesinstituts für ostwissenschaftliche und internationale Studien* (Köln) 44.

Hardt, J. P. ed. 1979. *Soviet economy in a time of change.* Washington, D. C.: Government Printing Office for the Joint Economic Committee of the US Congress.

Hardt, J. P. ed. 1981. *East European economic assessment — Part II. Regional assessment.* Washington, D. C.: Government Printing Office for the Joint Economic Committee of the Congress of the US.

Hardt, J. P. 1984. Alternativen für die westliche Allianz: Erfahrungen der Vergangenheit — Szenarien für die Zukunft. In Höhmann, H.-H. and Vogel, H. eds.

Hardt, J. P. and Gold, D. 1986. East-West trade policy and implications for the CMEA region. Washington, D. C.: JEC Congressional Research Service. March.

Henyš, O. 1983. More intensive coordination of economic development of the CMEA member-countries. *Czechoslovak Economic Digest* 4.

Hewett, E. 1984. *Energy economics and foreign policy in the Soviet Union.* Washington, D. C.: The Brookings Institution.

Hewett, E. 1986. Reform or rhetoric: Gorbachev and the Soviet economy. *The Brookings Review,* Fall.

Höhmann, H.-H. and Vogel, H. 1984. *Osteuropas Wirtschaftsprobleme und die Ost-West-Beziehungen.* Baden-Baden: Nomos Verlagsgesellschaft. Schriftenreihe des Bundesinstituts für ostwissenschaftliche und internationale Studien, No. 14.

Höhmann, H.-H. 1985. *Ein Exponent der Umgestaltung. Aktuelle Analysen des Bundesinstituts für ostwissenschaftliche und internationale Studien.* Köln, 25.

Holeček, J. 1982. Coordination of plans for 1986–90. *Czechoslovak Economic Digest,* 8.

Holzman F. 1978. CMEA's hard currency deficits and rouble convertibility. In Watts, N. (ed.).

Holzman, F. 1962. Soviet foreign trade pricing and the question of discrimination. *Review of Economics and Statistics.* May.

Hosková, A. 1986. Ekonomické predpoklady rozvijanija priamich hospodárskych vztahov v ramci krajín RVHP (The economic preconditions of developing direct economic relations among the CMEA countries). *Ekonomicky Časopis* 4.

Hrablei, A. 1987. XI. s"ezd SEPG: realizatsiya reshenii v oblasti integratsii. *Planovoe Khozyistvo* 11.

Il'in, M. 1987. The head organizations and their role in realizing the tasks of the comprehensive programme for scientific and technological progress of the CMEA countries. *Foreign Trade of the USSR* 8.

Inotai, A. 1978. The EEC in the 1970s. *Trends in World Economy,* No. 20.

Inotai, A. 1983. Nem OECD-országok késztermékexportja az OECD országokba (Exports of manufactures by non-OECD members to OECD countries) Parts I–II–III. *Iparpolitikai Tájékoztató* 10–11–12.

Inotai, A. 1986a. *Regional integrations in the new world economic environment.* Budapest: Akadémiai Kiadó.

Inotai, A. 1986b. Die RGW-Länder im internationalen Handel mit Maschinenbauprodukten. *Osteuropa Wirtschaft* 4.

Inozemtsev, N. 1981. Kursom ekonimicheskoi integratsii. *Planovoe Khozyaistvo* 8.

Inozemtsev, N. 1984. Koordinatsiya narodnokhozyaistvennykh planov stranchlenov SEV: novye problemy i zadachi. *Planovoe Khozyaistvo* 10.

Ionescu, N. 1983. Coordinarea planul di dezvoltarea economice dintre traile membre ale CAER (The coordination of plans for economic development among CMEA member-states). *Revista Economica* 32.

Iskra, W. 1985. Contribution to the round table discussion organized by World Marxist Review. In: Scientific . . .

Ivanchenko, V. M. 1986. Razvivat' funkcii osnovnogo zvena. *Ekonomicheskaya Gazeta*, 32.

Jánossy, F. 1970. Widersprüche in der ungarischen Wirtschaftsstruktur: wie sie entstanden und wie könnten sie überwunden werden ? *Acta Oeconomica*. Vol. 4. No. 4.

Jecminek, V., Petráš, M. and Takács, G. 1982. Kollektivnimi usiliyami. (O M.S.P.I.M. na 1981–85 gg.) *Ekonomicheskoe sotrudnichestvo stran-chlenov SEV* 1.

Kádár, B. 1984. *Structural changes in the world economy*. Budapest: Akadémiai Kiadó—St. Martin's Press, New York.

Kádár, B. 1986. East-West economic relations in the second half of the 1980s. Paper presented at the Franco-Hungarian colloquium held in Budapest, 29 April.

Kal'chev, V. 1977. Tselevite kreditirane mezhdu stranite-chlenki ot SIV i uchastieto nashata strana v nego (Extension of target credits among the CMEA member countries and the participation of Bulgaria in it). *Ikonomicheska Misal* 2.

Kamentsev, V. M. 1987. Problemy vneshneekonomicheskoi deyatel'nosti. *Kommunist* 15.

Kapitanov, V. 1985. Strany SEV-kurs na uskorenie nauchno-technicheskogo progressa. *Mezhdunarodnaya Zhizn'* 3.

Karagedov, R. 1985. Pervye itogi, problemy, perspektivy. *EKO* 5.

Karavaev, V. 1978. O formakh i mekhanizme investitsionnovo sotrudnichestva stran SEV. *Izvestiya AN SSSR, Seriya Ekonomicheskaya* 5.

Karavaev, V. 1979. *Integratsiya i investitsii: problemy sotrudnichestva stran SEV*. Moscow: Nauka.

Kaser, M. 1987. "One economy, two systems": parallels between Soviet and Chinese reform, *International Affairs*. London No. 3.

Kazandzhieva, K. 1980. Valyutno-kreditnye otnosheniya Vostok-Zapad i valyutno-finansovye otnosheniya stran-chlenov SEV. Paper presented at the international conference in Sopron.

Kevevári, B. 1977. A beruházási hozzájárulások aktuális kérdései (Topical issues of investment contributions). Manuscript. Research Institute for Finances, Budapest, July.

Key field of cooperation. Editorial. *CMEA-Economic Cooperation* 1986/1.

Keynes, J. M. 1973. *Collected Writings*. Vol. 7. *The General Theory*. London: Macmillan, for the Royal Economic Society.

Kheifetz, B. 1983. Tendentsii strukturnoi politiki stran SEV v oblasti promyshlennosti v 80-e gody. *Izvestiya AN SSSR, Seriya Ekonomicheskaya* 3.

Khbanov, J. 1986. Delo o hlopke I–II. *Izvestiya*, Sept. 5–6.

Khlistov, A. P. 1986. Starie voprosy v novykh usloviyakh khozyaistrovaniya. EKO, 8.

Kiss-Pavelcsák, Á. 1981. *Nemzetközi ipari együttműködési politika a KGST-ben* (International policy for industrial cooperation in the CMEA). Budapest: Kossuth Könyvkiadó.

Kiss, T. 1971a. *International division of labour in open economies with special regard to the CMEA*. Budapest: Akadémiai Kiadó.

Kiss, T. 1971b. A termelési viszonyok szerepe a KGST-integráció fejlődésében (The role of relations of production in the development of CMEA integration). *Gazdaság* 1.

Kiss, I. 1972. *Hol tart a KGST-integráció?* (What is the present state of CMEA integration?) Budapest: Kossuth Könyvkiadó.

Kiss, T. 1973. The development of the forms of economic relations in the CMEA integration. In Kiss, T., Földi, T. and Schweitzer, I. eds.

Kiss, T. 1974. A KGST nemzetközi szervezetei továbbfejlesztésének néhány kérdése (Some problems of improving the international organizations of the CMEA). *Gazdaság- és Jogtudomány* 3–4.

Kiss, T. 1976. International cooperation in planning in the CMEA. *Eastern European Economics* 1.

Kiss, T., Földi, T., Schweitzer, I. eds. 1973. *The market of socialist economic integration*. Budapest: Akadémiai Kiadó.

Knyżiak, Z. 1975. Elementy mezhdunarodnogo planirovaniya v natsionalnykh planakh razvitiya. *Planovoe Khozyaistvo* 9.

Knyazev, Yu. and Bakovetskii, O. 1982. Sblizhenie struktur khozyaistvennykh mekhanizmov stran SEV. *Planovoe Khozyaistvo* 6.

Kogan, J. 1983. Sblizhenie struktur khozyaistvennykh mekhanizmov stran SEV (Conference review). *Voprosy Ekonomiki* 6.

Kolesnikov, V. I. and Lapidis, M. H. 1986. Finansovyi aspekt sozdaniya tselostnoi sistemy upravleniya narodnym khozyaistvom. *Finansy SSSR*. No. 10, p. 12.

Konstantinov, Yu. 1980. DTzPS i ikh valyutno-finansovoe obespechenie, *Den' gi i Kredit* 2.

Konstantinov, Yu. 1981a. Valyutnii kurs v ekonomicheskikh otnosheniyakh stran SEV. *Den'gi i Kredit* 2.

Konstantinov, Yu. 1981b. The transferable rouble in the system of international economic relations. *Foreign Trade of the USSR* 7.

Konstantinov, Yu. 1981c. Perevodnyi rubl' v khozyaistvennom mekhanizme sotsialisticheskoi ekonomicheskoi integratsii. *Planovoe Khozyaistvo* 4.

Konstantinov, Yu. 1981d. O funktsii perevodnogo rublya kak mery stoimosti. *Finansy SSSR* 6.

Konstantinov, Yu. 1982a. Valyutnaya sistema sotsializma. *Den'gi i Kredit* 1.

Konstantinov, Yu. 1982b. Perevodnyi rubl' — valyuta sotsialisticheskogo sodruzhestva. *Voprosy Ekonomiki* 11.

Konstantinov, Yu. 1984. Novye rubezhi ekonomicheskoi integratsii stranchlenov SEV. *Den' gi i Kredit* 11.

Konstantinov, Yu. 1986. XXVII s"ezd KPSS ob ekonomicheskoi integratsii stran SEV. *Den'gi i Kredit* 9.

Konstantinov, Yu. 1987. Vneshneekonomicheskii kompleks SSSR v novykh usloviyakh. *Den' gi i Kredit* 1.

Kormnov, Yu. 1985. Sotrudnichestvo stran SEV i struktura proizvodstva. *Voprosy Ekonomiki* 10.

Kornai, J. 1972. *Rush versus harmonic growth.* Budapest: Akadémiai Kiadó.

Kornai, J. 1980. *Economics of shortage.* Amsterdam: North Holland Publishing House.

Kovács, Gy. 1984. Koordinatsiya planov — glavnyi metod garmonizatsii ekonomicheskikh politik. *Ekonomicheskoe sotrudnichestvo stran-chlenov SEV* 12.

Kovács, Gy. 1985. Fejlődő szocialista integráció (Socialist economic integration on the path of development). *Népszabadság,* 22 June.

Kővári, L. 1976. A KGST-országokkal folytatott tervegyeztetés és az V. ötéves terv (Coordination of plans with CMEA countries and the Fifth Five Year Plan). *Külgazdaság* 1.

Kővári, L. 1982. KGST-helyzetkép (A situation report on the CMEA). *Magyar Hírlap,* 22 October.

Kővári, L. 1985. A tervegyeztetés súlypontjai (Priority areas in dovetailing plans). *Figyelő,* 27 June.

Kővári, L. and Mosóczy, R. 1976. Az 1975–80. évi magyar–szovjet tervkoordináció jelentősége gazdasági együttmflködésünk fejlesztésében (The significance of coordination of plans for 1975–80 between Hungary and the Soviet Union in the development of our economic cooperation). *Külgazdaság* 2.

Köves, A. 1978. Integration into the world economy and the direction of economic development in Hungary. *Acta Oeconomica,* Vol. 20, No. 1–2.

Köves, A. 1979. Hungarian and Soviet foreign trade with developed capitalist countries: common and different problems. *Acta Oeconomica,* Vol. 23, No. 3–4.

Köves, A. 1980. *A világgazdasági nyitás: kihívás és kényszer* (Opening up to the world economy: challenge and necessity). Budapest: Közgazdasági és Jogi Könyvkiadó.

Köves, A. 1981. Turning inward or turning outward ? Reflections on the foreign economic strategy of CMEA countries. *Acta Oeconomica,* Vol. 26, No. 1–2.

Köves, A. 1982. Alternative foreign economic strategies for CMEA countries. *Konjunkturpolitik* 5.

Köves, A. 1983a. "Implicit subsidies" and some issues of economic relations within the CMEA. *Acta Oeconomica,* Vol. 31, No. 1–2.

Köves, A. 1983b. Az Egyesült Államok és a kelet-nyugati kereskedelem (The United States and East-West trade). Budapest: Institute for Economic and Market Research Publications.

Köves, A. 1985a. The import restriction squeeze and import maximizing ambitions. *Acta Oeconomica,* Vol. 34, No. 1.

Köves, A. 1985b. *The CMEA countries in the world economy: turning inwards or turning outwards.* Budapest: Akadémiai Kiadó.

Köves, A. 1988: Eine neue Situation im Handel Ungarns mit den RGW-Länder: Was ist zu tun ? *Europäische Rundschau,* No 3.

Kozma, F. 1971. A komplex programról és a közgazdasági kutatás feladatairól (On the Comprehensive Programme and on the task of economic research). *Közgazdasági Szemle* 12.

Kozma, F. 1974. Új vonások születése a szocialista integrációban (Incipient new features of socialist integration). *Gazdaság- és Jogtudomány* 3–4.

Kozma, G. 1976. *Bilaterális mérlegegyensúly és külkereskedelmi hatékonyság* (Bilateral equilibrium of the balance of payments and the efficiency of foreign trade). Budapest: Közgazdasági és Jogi Könyvkiadó.

Kozma, F. 1978a. A magyar népgazdaság szelektív fejlesztése a szocialista gazdasági integrációban (Selective development of the Hungarian economy in the socialist economic integration). *Társadalmi Szemle* 10.

Kozma, F. 1978b. *Mire képes a magyar népgazdaság* (What is the Hungarian economy capable of ?) Budapest: Kossuth Könyvkiadó.

Kresák, J. 1978. Stoime na začátku dlouhé a složité česty (We stand at the beginning of a long and difficult road). *Hospodárské noviny* 25.

Kulka-Fiedler, Ch. 1985. Zur Entwicklung der Ost-West Kreditbeziehungen. *IPW Berichte* 10.

Kunz, W. 1985. Contribution to the round-table discussion organized by *World Marxist Review*. In *Scientific*. 1985.

Kuznetsov, N. and Nartsissov, L. 1983. Sovmestnoe planirovanie otdel'nykh otraslei i podotraslei. *Ekonomicheskoe sotrudnichestvo stran-chlenov SEV*, 2.

Kuznetsov, V. 1984. International plan coordination. *International Affairs* (Moscow) 6.

Ladygin, B. 1981. Planomernost' sotsialisticheskoi ekonomicheskoi integratsii. *Obshchestvenye Nauki* 1.

Lakos, I. 1975. Út a konvertibilitáshoz (The road to convertibility). Institute for Economic and Market Research Publications, November.

Lantos, I. and Pörzse, O. 1975. *A szocializmus valutáris kérdései* (The issue of currencies under socialism). Budapest: Tankönyvkiadó.

Lányi, K. 1976. Az agráripari komplexumok és a KGST (Agro-industrial complexes and the CMEA). Institute for Economic and Market Research Publications, January.

Lányi, K. 1984. Hungarian agriculture: superfluous growth or export surplus ? *Acta Oeconomica*, 34, No. 3–4.

Latsis, O. 1986. Po novomu vzglyanut' ... *Kommunist*, 13.

Latsis, O. 1987. Kak shagaet perestroika ? *Kommunist*, 4.

Lavigne, M. 1983. The Soviet Union inside Comecon. *Soviet Studies*, No. 2.

Levcik, F. 1986. Neue Impulse für eine Wirtschaftsreform in der Sowjetunion. *Wirtschaft und Gesellschaft* 3.

Levcik, F. 1987. Neue Akzente bei der 42. Ratstagung des RGW in Bukarest ? *Osteuropa Wirtschaft* 1.

Litviakov, P. et al. 1977. Rol' i mesto DTsPS v sotrudnichestve stran-chlenov SEV v oblasti planovoi deyatel'nosti. Research Report CMEA International Economic Research Institute, Moscow.

Long-term Programme 1985. — The Comprehensive Programme for Scientific and Technological Progress in the CMEA Member Countries until the Year 2000. Central Party dailies of the respective countries, 19. Dec.

Lozanov, K. 1982. Osnovnye voprosy sovershenstvovaniya koordinatsii kapital'nykh vlozhenii stran-chlenov SEV. In Belovič, A. ed.

Lozanov, K. 1984. Problemy investitsionnovo storudnichestva stran-chlenov SEV. In Belovič, A., Voropaev, V. and Zvorigin, Yu. eds.

Luft, Ch. 1982. Zum Verhältnis und zur organischen Verbindung von zwei- und mehrseitigen Formen wirtschaftlicher Zusammenarbeit der Mitgliedsländer des RGW. *Wirtschaftswissenschaft* 5.

Luft, Ch. 1983. Contribution to the discussion in the international conference on converging economic mechanisms, held in Moscow, in Dec., 1982. In Kogan, J.

Lyubskii, M. Sulyaeva, M. and Shastitko, V. 1978. *Valyutnye i kreditnye otnosheniya stran SEV.* Moscow: Nauka.

Machlup, F. ed. 1976. *International Economic Integration: Worldwide, Regional, Sectoral.* London: Macmillan.

Machová, D. 1976. Plánovitost, vyrobni vztahy, sémantika a integráce (Planned development, relations of production, vocabulary and integration). *Politická Ekonomie* 9.

Mangushev, K. 1983. The oil market: the business cycle and long-term factors. *World Marxist Review* 4.

Manipulation (the) of the world's oil supplies. *International Currency Review,* June, 1979.

Marcsuk, G. 1986. A KGST-országok tudományos-műszaki haladási komplex programja (The Comprehensive Programme of scientific and technological progress of CMEA countries). An interview in APN-MTI *KGST-Együttműködés* 5.

Marer, P. 1974. The political economy of Soviet relations with Eastern Europe. In: *Testing theories of imperialism.* Lexington: D. C. Heath.

Marer, P. and Montias, J. M. 1980a. Theory and measurement of East European integration. In: Marer, P. and Montias, J. M. eds.

Marer, P. and Montias, J. M. eds. 1980b. *East European integration and East-West trade.* Bloomington: Indiana University Press.

Marjai, J. 1984a. Hungary and the CMEA. *New Times* 40.

Marjai, J. 1984b. Nem meditálni, cselekedni kell! (Let us act, not theorize!) *Figyelő* 34.

Marjai, J. 1987. A KGST munkájának továbbfejlesztéséről (On improving the functioning of CMEA), an interview by Földes, I., *Népszabadság,* 17 October.

Marrese, M. and Vanous, J. 1983. *Soviet subsidization of trade with Eastern Europe: a Soviet perspective.* Institute of International Studies, University of California, Berkeley.

Mateev, E. 1975. An interview with the Soviet news agency. *MTI-APN KGST-Együttműködés* 6.

Material 27-ogo sj'ezda KPSS. Moscow: Politizdat, 1986.

Meisel, S. 1979. *A KGST 30 éve* (Thirty years of the CMEA). Budapest: Kossuth Könyvkiadó.

Meissner, B. 1987. Gorbatschows "Perestrojka": Reform oder Revolution? *Aussenpolitik,* 3.

Mendershausen, H. 1959. Terms of trade between the Soviet Union and smaller communist countries: 1955–57. *Review of Economics and Statistics,* May.

MIEP MSS: Voprosy kompleksnovo razvitiya valyutno-finansovykh otnosheniy stran-chlenov SEV na sovremennom etape. (Conference paper prepared by a research team of the CMEA International Economic Research Institute for the international conference on CMEA finances, held in Oct. 1981 in Sopron.)

Milyukov, A. 1986. Problemy radikalnoi reformy. *Ekonomicheskaya Gazeta* 20.

Moguchaya sila sodruzhestva. *Izvestiya,* 1 March, 1983.

Moldovan, R. 1970. Economic cooperation between the socialist countries. *Revue Roumaine des Sciences Sociales, Série des Sciences Economiques* 2.

Mosóczy, R. 1975. Gazdasági együttmflködésünk fejlesztése a KGST-országokkal (Developing Hungary's economic cooperation with CMEA countries). *Közgazdasági Szemle* 7–8.

Mosóczy, R. 1976. A KGST-országok tervezési együttműködésének jelentősége gazdasági kapcsolataink fejlesztésében (The significance of cooperation in planning among CMEA countries in expanding our economic relations). *Külgazdaság* 3.

Mosóczy, R. 1983. Possibilities of and trends in the development of international economic cooperation in the 1980s. *Acta Oeconomica*, Vol. 30, No. 3–4.

Motorin, I. 1980. Metodologiya planirovaniya protsessov integratsii. *Obshchestvennye Nauki* 1.

Müller, Fr. 1988. Änderungen in dem Weltenergiemarkt und ihre Auswirkungen auf die Ost-West-Wirtschaftsbeziehungen in den 80-er Jahren in Inotai, A., Nötzold, J. and Schröder, K. eds.

Müller, H. 1984. Vazhnyi metod sovershenstvovaniya sotrudnichestva. *Ekonomicheskoe sotrudnichestvo stran-chlenov SEV* 12.

Müller, L. 1987. Első tapasztalatok a komplex programról (The first lessons of the Comprehensive Programme). *Figyelő*, 31.

Nagy, F. 1978. A szocialista gazdasági integráció fejlesztésének fontos állomása (An important stage in the development of socialist economic integration). *Társadalmi Szemle* 8–9.

Náray, P. 1987, Organizational and institutional reform of the Hungarian trade regime. *The Journal of World Trade Law*, No. 3.

Nekipelov, A. 1987. Perestroika mekhanizma integratsii. *Ekonomicheskoe sotrudnichestvo stran-chlenov SEV* 5.

Niederhauser, E. 1977. Kelet-Európa fogalma a magyar történetírásban (The concept of Eastern Europe in Hungarian historiography). *Magyar Tudomány* 1.

Nikolova, N. 1982. Problemi na kollektivnata parichna edinitsa na SIV — perevodnata rubla (The problems of the common accounting unit of the CMEA — the TR). *Finansy i Kredit* 8.

Nikonov, A. and Stromov, A. 1986. Prjamye svyazi-perspektivnoe napravlenie sotrudnichestva. *Vneshnyaya Torgovlya* 6.

Nötzold, G. 1983. Perspektiven der sozialistischen ökonomischen Integration und die intersystemaren Wirtschaftsbeziehungen. *Wissenschaftliche Zeitschrift der Karl Marx Universität Leipzig, Gesellschaft- und Sprachwissenschaftliche Reihe*, Vol. 32, No. 4.

Nötzold, J. 1988. Auswirkungen technologischer Entwicklungen auf die Ost-West-Beziehungen. In Inotai, A., Nötzold, J. and Schröder, K. eds.

Nove, A. 1964. Principal problems of Soviet planning. In Nove, A. *Was Stalin really necessary.* London: Allen and Unwin.

Nove, A. 1977. *The Soviet economic system.* London: Allen and Unwin.

Nyers, R. 1970. *Twenty questions and answers* (A series of interviews, conducted by Bagota, B. and Garam, J.). Budapest: Pannonia Editions.

Nyers, R. 1975. The CMEA countries on the road to economic integration. *Trends in World Economy*, No. 16.

Nyers, R. 1977. Vliyanie mnogostoronnykh integratsionnykh meropriyatii SEV na vengerskoe narodnoe khozyaistvo v 1976–80 godakh. *Acta Oeconomica*, Vol. 18, No. 1.

Nyers, R. 1983a. Tendencies of tradition and reform in CMEA cooperation. *Acta Oeconomica*, Vol. 30, No. 1.

Nyers, R. 1983b. The past, present and future of the East European economies: the Hungarian case. (Interview) *Acta Oeconomica*, Vol. 31, No. 3–4.

Nyilas, A. 1979. A közös beruházások hatékonysága (Efficiency of joint investments). *Figyelő* 44.

Nyilas, J. 1978. Az 1974–75. évi tőkés világgazdasági válság hatása a tőkés országok közötti erőviszonyokra (The impact of the 1974–75 crisis of the world capitalist economy on the balance of forces among capitalist countries). *Közgazdasági Szemle* 2.

Nyilas, J. 1982. *World economy and its main development tendencies.* Budapest: Akadémiai Kiadó.

Obodowski, J. 1985. Press-conference of the then-Chairman of the Executive Committee following the meeting of this body in Moscow. *Népszabadság*, 17 January.

Obzina, J. 1985. The main line of economic cooperation. *World Marxist Review* 3.

O dal'neishem 1986a. sovershenstvovanii ekonomicheskogo mekhanizma v agropromyshlennom komplekse strany. *Ekonomicheskaya Gazeta*, No. 15.

OECD: East-West Technology Transfer (Draft Synthesis Report). Paris, Sept., 1984, p. 270.

Oleynik, I. 1982. Obmen opytom stran sotsializma. *Voprosy Ekonomiki* 3.

O merakh 1986b. po korennomu sovershenstvovaniyu vneshneekonomicheskoy deyatel'nosti. *Ekonomicheskaya Gazeta*, 40.

Osnovnye plozheniya korennoi perestroiki upravleniya ekonomikoi (postanovlenie TsK KPSS). *Pravda*, 27 June, 1987.

Osváth, L.—Patai, M., Szegvári, I. 1987. A KGST reformja — magyar nézőpontból, I–IV (The reform of the CMEA — from a Hungarian point of view, parts I–IV), *Figyelő*, 49–52.

Pachta, P. 1980. Rozvoj spolupráce členských státu RVHP v oblastí neobchodních plátu (The development of cooperation among CMEA countries in non-commercial payments). *Zahraniční Obchod* 7–8.

Páfai, I. 1974. *A szocialista gazdasági integráció* (Socialist economic integration). Budapest: Kossuth Könyvkiadó.

Palócz-Németh, É. 1981. Exports of manufactures of CMEA and developing countries to developed industrial countries. *Acta Oeconomica*, Vol. 26, No. 1–2.

Părăluta, M. 1975. The main method of organizing cooperation among CMEA countries is the coordination of development plans. Part I–II. *Scînteia*, 1 and 3, June, 1975. As translated into Hungarian in: *MTI Cikkek a Szocialista Sajtóból* 26.

Pasieczny, L. 1985. Contribution to the round-table discussion, organized by *World Marxist Review*. In Scientific . . . 1985.

Pavelcsák, Á. and Kiss, T. 1977. *Nemzetközi gazdaságpolitika és tervezési együttműködés* (International economic policy and cooperation in planning). Budapest: Kossuth Könyvkiadó.

Pécsi, K. 1964. A beruházási együttműködés néhány nemzetközi pénzügyi vonatkozása (International financial aspects of cooperation in investments). *Közgazdasági Szemle* 4.

Pécsi, K. 1979a. *A magyar–szovjet gazdasági kapcsolatok 30 éve* (Thirty years of Hungarian–Soviet economic cooperation). Budapest: Közgazdasági és Jogi Könyvkiadó.

Pécsi, K. 1979b. A valutáris és pénzügyi viszonyok időszerű kérdései a KGST-ben (Topical issues of currency and financial relations in the CMEA). *Külgazdaság* 9.

Pécsi, K. 1979c. Nekotorye aspekty ustanovleniya tsen vo vzaimnoi torgovle stran-chlenov SEV. *Mirovaya Ekonomika i Mezhdunarodnye Otnosheniya* 9.

Pécsi, K. 1980–81. The future of socialist integration. *Eastern European Economics*, Vol. 19, No, 2–3. Winter-Spring.

Pécsi, K. 1983. Ekonomicheskie aspekti razvitiya pryamykh i neprosredstvennykh svyazei mezhdu predpriyatiyami stran-chlenov SEV. *Trends in World Economy*, No. 45.

Penchev, V. 1984. Koordinatsiya narodnokhozyaistvennykh planov. *Ekonomicheskoe sotrudnichestvo stran-chlenov SEV* 12.

Petrakov, N. 1966. *Nekotorye aspekty diskussii ob ekonomicheskikh metodakh khozyaistvovaniya*. Moscow: Ekonomika.

Poteryam — nadezhnyi zaslon. *Sotsialisticheskaya Industriya*, 1 March, 1983.

Pörzse, O. 1979. A KGST-országok valutáris-pénzügyi együttműködése (Monetary and financial cooperation among CMEA countries). Unpublished M.A. thesis at the Karl Marx University of Economics, Budapest.

Progress plus invulnerability. *New Times*, 40.

Ptaszek, J. 1981. Doswiadzenia i kierunki zmian systemu walutno-finansowego (The lessons and the main lines of change in the financial and currency system). *Rynki Zagraniczne*, 3 November.

Rácz, M. 1982. *A KGST gazdasági szervezetei és a vállalatközi együttműködés* (Economic organizations of the CMEA and interfirm cooperation) Budapest: Közgazdasági és Jogi Könyvkiadó. For a condensed version see: Inter-country relations at the microeconomic level: the intra-CMEA and the Hungarian experience. *Trends in World Economy*, No. 51, 1985, containing only 1 of the 3 quotations from the Hungarian edition.

Rácz, M. 1985. A vállalatok részvétele a KGST-n belüli együttmflködésben (Company participation in intra-CMEA cooperation). *Medvetánc* 4.

Radev, S. 1980. Problemi na uchastieto na NRB v savmestnoto stroitelstvo na stranite-chlenki ot SIV (Problems of PR of Bulgaria's participation in the joint investments of the CMEA member countries). *Vnshna Targoviya* 4.

Rédei, J. 1972. A konvertibilitás megteremtésének lehetőségei a KGST-ben (Possibilities for introducing convertibility in the CMEA). *Közgazdasági Szemle* 5.

Rédei, J. 1973. The system of foreign trade agreements. In Kiss, T., Földi, T. and Schweitzer, I. eds. 1973, pp. 167–175.

Rekunkov, A. 1986. Na strazhe pravoporyadka i sotsial'noi spravedlivosti. *Kommunist*, 1.

Richter, S. 1980. Hungary's trade with CMEA partners in convertible currencies. *Acta Oeconomica*, Vol. 25, No. 3–4.

Richter, S. 1984. Jugoszlávia gazdasága: kísérletek a válság leküzdésére (The Yugoslav economy: attempts at overcoming the crisis). *Gazdaság 2.*

Rohliček, R. 1986. Ku slovu prizhádzaju priame vztáhy (On the notion of direct contacts). *Hospodářské Noviny*, 6 June.

Rosefielde, S. 1973. *Soviet foreign trade in a Heckscher-Ohlin perspective.* Lexington Books, Lexington (Mass.): D. C. Heath and Co.

Rusakov, K. 1984. New cornerstones of cooperation and development. *World Marxist Review* 10.

Rusmich, L. 1983. Value aspects of the development of socialist integration. *Acta Oeconomica*, Vol. 31, No. 3–4.

Rybakov, O. 1982. Problemy koordinatsii narodnokhozyaistvennykh planov stran-chlenov SEV. *Planovoe Khozyaistvo* 11.

Rybakov, O. 1984. Dolgovremennaya strategiya uglubleniya sotsialisticheskoi ekonomicheskoi integratsii stran-chlenov SEV. *Planovoe Khozyaistvo* 8.

Rybakov, O. and Shiryaev, Yu. 1984. New frontiers of socialist economic integration. *International Affairs* (Moscow) 9.

Ryzhkov, N. 1985. Statement at the 41st (extraordinary) Session of the CMEA. *Pravda*, 16 December.

Ryzhkov, N. 1986. Speech at the 27th Congress of the CPSU. *in Materiali* ... 1986.

Salgó, I. 1982. A kelet-európai tervgazdaságok kiépítésének külgazdasági vonatkozásai és a regionális gazdasági együttműködés (Foreign trade aspects of introducing planned economy in Eastern Europe and regional economic cooperation). *Közgazdasági Szemle* 6.

Salgó, I. 1989. *Külkereskedelmi vállalat, külkereskedelmi szervezet.* (Foreign trade enterprise, foreign trade organization). Budapest: Közgazdasági és Jogi Könyvkiadó.

Saunders, Ch. ed. 1983. *Regional integration in East and West.* London–Basingstoke: Macmillan. WIIW Workshop Series. No. 6.

Saunders, Ch. ed. 1985. *East-West trade and finance in the world economy. A new look for the 1980's.* London–Basingstoke: Macmillan. WIIW Workshop Series, No. 8.

Savitskii, V. 1976. Ekonomicheskie problemy razvitiya zapadnosibirskogo nefteprovoda. *Ekonomika neftyanoi promyshlennosti* 9.

Savov, M. 1975. A szocialista internacionalizmus gyakorlata (Socialist internationalism in practice). *MTI-APN KGST-Együttműködés* 7.

Schönfeld, R. 1984. Gemeinsame Investitionen im RGW und die Beteiligung südosteuropäischer Mitgliedsländer. In Schönfeld, R. ed. *RGW-Integration und Südosteuropa.* München: R. Oldenbourg Verlag.

Schröder, K. 1983. Die Umschuldungen mit den Ländern des RGW — Ursachen, Ziele, Modalitäten. *Aussenpolitik*, 2.

Schröder, K. 1984. Restriktion oder Kooperation: Kredit- und Finanzbeziehungen. In Höhmann, H.-H. and Vogel, H. eds.

Schweitzer, I. and Róth, A. 1979. Miért nincs elég pótalkatrész ? (Why is there a shortage of spare parts?) *Figyelő* 29.

Schiavone, G. 1985. COCOM and its future. Strategic controls or economic warfare ? In *Annali* of the Institute of European Studies, A. de Gasperc Roma, Vol. 7.

Scientific 1985. and technical cooperation is the key task in the development of socialist integration. (Round-table discussion in the editorial office). *World Marxist Review*, 12.

Šedivy, Z. 1978. Sotrudnichestvo ChSSR so stranami SEV v razrabotke planov na period za 1980. *Planovoe Khozyaistvo* 9.

Šedivy, Z. 1984. On the socialist economy: the processes of a new era. *World Marxist Review* 11.

Shatalin, S. and Gaidar, E. 1986. Uzlovye problemy reformy. *Ekonomicheskaya Gazeta* 29.

Shein, N. 1980. *Nekotorye problemy razvitiya i sovershenstvovaniya vzaimnykh valyutno-finansovykh otnoshenii stran-chlenov SEV na sovremennom etape razvitiya sotsialisticheskoi integratsii.* Paper presented at the international conference in Sopron, 1980.

Sheinin, E. 1982. Strany SEV v mirokhozyaistvennykh svyazakh. *Obshchestvennye Nauki 4.*

Shelkov, O. 1980. O sokhranenii real'noi stoimosti perevodnogo rublya. Paper presented at the international conference in Sopron, 1980.

Shilov, V. 1986. Ministerstvo i perestroika. *Sovetskaya Rossiya*, Aug. 5.

Shiryaev, Yu. 1973. *Ekonomicheskii mekhanizm sotsialisticheskoi integratsii.* Moscow: Ekonomika.

Shiryaev, Yu. 1977. *Mezhdunarodnoe sotsialisticheskoe razdelenie truda.* Moscow, Nauka.

Shiryaev, Yu. 1979. Strany SEV v sisteme mirovikh uhozyaistvennikh sviazai. *Mirovaia Ekonomika i Mezhdunarodnie Otnoshenia, 4.*

Shiryaev, Yu. 1981. *Szocialista integráció és nemzetközi munkamegosztás* (Socialist integration and international division of labour). Budapest: Kossuth Könyvkiadó.

Shiryaev, Yu. 1983. In the stage of intensification. *World Marxist Review* 4.

Shiryaev, Yu. 1984. Ekonomicheskaya integratsiya stran SEV i intensifikatsiya sotsialisticheskogo proizvodstva. *Voprosy Ekonomiki* 9.

Shiryaev, Yu. 1986a. Nauchno-technicheskii progress i sotsialisticheskaya integratsiya. *Voprosy Ekonomiki* 5.

Shiryaev, Yu. 1986b. Mekhanizm integratsii: novye kriterii. *Ekonomicheskaya Gazeta* 30.

Shiryaev, Yu. 1987. Problemy razrabotki i realizatsii novoi strategii sotrudnichestva i razvitiya stran-chlenov SEV. *Ekonomika i Matematicheskie Metody* 5.

Shiryaev, Yu. and Bautina, N. 1982. Deepening CMEA economic cooperation. *International Affairs* (Moscow) 11.

Shmelyov, N. 1979a. New tendencies in the world economy and their impact on the economic interests of CMEA countries. *Acta Oeconomica*, Vol. 23, No. 3–4.

Shmelyov, N. 1979b. *Sotsializm i mezhdunarodnye ekonomicheskie otnosheniya.* Moscow. Mezhdunarodnye Otnosheniya.

Shmelyov, N. 1984. Credits and politics. *International Affairs* (Moscow) 4.

Shmelyov, N. 1987. Avansy i dolgi. (Credits and debts). *Novyi Mir* 6.

Shmelyov, N. 1988a. Novye trevogi. *Novyi Mir* 4.

Shmelyov, N. 1988b. The Other Danger. *Moscow News* 1.

Shokhin, A. 1986. Dogovor postavki v usloviyakh ekonomicheskogo eksperimenta v promishlennosti. *Sovetskoe Gosudarstvo i Pravo*, 7.

Silyaev, I. 1986. Zadachi byuro po mashinostroeniyu (Interview). *Izvestiya* 11 March.

Silvestrov, S. 1982. Mezhdunarodnaya kooperatsiya proizvodstva stranchlenov SEV. *Ekonomicheskie Nauki 3.*

Sitnin, V. 1984. Novyi rubezh sotsialisticheskoi ekonomicheskoi integratsii. *Izvestiya AN SSSR, Seriya Ekonomicheskaya* 6.

Slyunkov, N. 1988a. Perestroika i partiinoe rukovodstvo ekonomikoi. *Kommunist*, No. 1.

Smiganovskii, V. 1986. Na tamozhne. *Izvestiya*, Aug. 22.

Smirnov, B. and Nesterovich, N. 1988. V interesakh potrebitelya. *Ekonomicheskaya Gazeta*, No. 5.

Soós, K. A. 1986. *Terv, kampányok, pénz* (Plan, campaigns, finances). Budapest: Közgazdasági és Jogi Könyvkiadó.

Soós, K. A. 1987. The "policy of grievances". Contribution to the first halt of the Hungarian reform in 1969. *Soviet Studies* 3.

Sorokin, G. 1969. Leninskie printsipy sotrudnichestva sotsialisticheskikh stran. *Planovoe Khozyaistvo* 3.

Soviet foreign trade performance in 1987: non-socialist trade surplus soars to a record $ 8.5 billion as dollar export earnings increase 17% while import outlays remain unchanged. *Plan Econ Report* 1988/14.

Sovmestnyi opyt sodruzhestva. 1983. *Izvestiya*, 17 September.

Špaček, P. 1979. Neobchodni pláti a kursi Rady (The non-commercial payments and exchange rates of the Council). *Socialistická Ekonomická Integráce* 1.

Špaček, P. 1982. Problemy a perspektivy měnového sistemů RVHP (Problems and prospects of the CMEA monetary system): *Hospodářské noviny* 22.

Špaček, P. 1984. MBHS — základni článek platebniho a úvěrového mechanismu členskych států RVHP (The International Bank for Economic Cooperation as a fundamental link in the payments and credit system of the CMEA member states). *Finance a Úvěr* 7.

Stancu, S. 1978. Un eveniment remarcabil in dezvoltarea collaborarii si cooperarii economice dintre traile membre ale C.A.E.R. (A remarkable event in the development of the cooperation among the CMEA member countries). *Revista Economica* 28.

Starżyk, K. 1977. Wieloletnie kierunkowe programy wspólpracy krajów RWPG (Long-term target programmes of cooperation among the CMEA countries). *Gospodarka Planowa* 10.

Stoilov, S. 1985. Sotsialisticheskaya integratsiya i eyo vliyanie na rost i effektivnost'. In Grozdanov, K. ed. *Ekonomicheskaya Misl'*, No. 2. Sofia: Izd. Bolgarskoi Akademii Nauk.

Stoilov, S. et al. 1984. Problema vneshneekonomicheskoi sbalansirovannosti v stranakh SEV. *Izvestiya AN SSSR, Seriya Ekonomicheskaya* 6.

Stoph, W. 1982. Statement at the 36th Session of the CMEA. *Neues Deutschland*, 9 June.

Stoph, W. 1984. Statement at the 39th Session of the CMEA. *Neues Deutschland*, 30 October.

Stoyanov, G. 1983. Zadacha, koyato savremieto postavit na dneven red (A task set by the times). *Rabotnichesko Delo*, 7 February.

Stračar, J. 1980. Long-term special purpose programmes of cooperation promote expansion of trade among CMEA countries. *Foreign Trade of the USSR* 6.

Ströhm, C.-G. 1987. Dritter Weg in die Sackgasse. *Die Welt*, Aug. 18.

Štrougal, L. 1984a. A gazdaságpolitika koordinálása az együttmüködés minőségileg fij formája (Coordination of economic policies is a qualitatively new form of cooperation). *Új Szó*, 5 July.

Štrougal, L. 1984b. Statement delivered at the 39th Session of the CMEA in Havana. *Ekonomicheskoe sotrudnichestvo stran-chlenov SEV*, 1985/1.

Štrougal, L. 1985. Statement at the 40th (Warsaw) Session of the Council. *Ekonomicheskoe sotrudnichestvo stran-chlenov SEV* 11.

Sukhotin, Yu. and Dementev, V. 1988. Ekonomicheskaya reforma i sily tormozheniya. *Ekonomicheskaya Gazeta* 7.

Sychov, V. 1986. Novye rubezhi nauchno-tekhnicheskogo sotrudnichestva. *Ekonomicheskoe sotrudnichestvo stran-chlenov SEV* 1.

Sychov, V. 1987. KP NTP stran-chlenov SEV do 2000 goda. *Voprosy Ekonomiki* 7.

Szabó, I. 1986. A mi húzóágazataink (The dynamic sectors in Hungary). An interview by K. G. Kocsis. *Magyar Hírlap*, 20 August.

Szalajda, Z. 1986. Priorities in development. *CMEA-Economic Cooperation* 1.

Szamuely, L. 1974. *First models of the socialist economic systems*. Budapest: Akadémiai Kiadó.

Szamuely, L. 1983. The situation of the Eastern European economies and the prospects of foreign trade. *The New Hungarian Quarterly*, No. 92. Winter.

Szegvári, I. 1972. A komparatív előnyök problematikája (The issue of comparative advantages). Unpublished doctoral thesis at the Karl Marx University of Economics, Budapest.

Szegvári, I. 1981. A komparatív előnyökről — vitáink kapcsán (On the theory of comparative advantages — à propos discussions in Hungarian economic literature). *Külgazdaság* 12.

Szegvári, I. 1987. *A tervkoordináció és fejlesztésének lehetősége* (Coordination of plans and its possibilities for development). *Tervgazdasági Fórum* 3.

Szekér, Gy. 1976. A KGST komplex program öt éve (Five years of the Comprehensive Programme of the CMEA). *Társadalmi Szemle* 7–8.

Szekér, Gy. 1982. *Iparfejlesztés — műszaki fejlesztés* (Industrial development and technological progress). Budapest: Kossuth Könyvkiadó.

Szelecki, Gy. 1986. *Mit kell tudni a KGST-ről* (What has to be known of the CMEA?) Budapest: Kossuth Könyvkiadó.

Szelecki, Gy. 1987. A KGST-együttműködés megifjulásának főbb tényezői (Major factors of renewal in CMEA cooperation). *The Political Academy of the Hungarian Socialist Workers' Party*, February.

Szikszay, B. 1982. Aspects of the international coordination of national economic plans. *Acta Oeconomica*, Vol. 28, No. 1–2.

Szita, J. 1971. A szocialista gazdasági integráció közgazdaságtudományi kérdéseihez (On the economics of socialist economic integration). *Társadalmi Szemle* 11.

Szita, J. 1975. A KGST XXIX., budapesti ülésszakáról (On the Twenty-Ninth, Budapest, Session of the CMEA). *Gazdaság* 3.

Szita, J. 1976. A gazdasági integráció útján (On the road of economic integration). *Közgazdasági Szemle* 9.

Szücs, J. 1983. The three historical regions of Europe. *Acta Historica* 3–4.

Tardos, M. 1969. A model of intra-regional foreign trade. In Földi, T. and Kiss, T. eds.

Tardos, M. 1972. A gazdasági verseny problémái hazánkban (Problems of competition in the Hungarian economy). *Közgazdasági Szemle* 7–8.

Tardos, M. and Nagy, Á. 1976. *A magyar–szovjet külkereskedelem árszínvonalá-*

ról (On the price level in Hungarian–Soviet trade). Budapest: Institute for Economic and Market Research Publications.

Tauchmann, J. 1983a. Ke společné strukturální strategii zemí RVHP (Contribution to the common structural strategy of the CMEA countries). *Nová Mysl* 6.

Tauchmann, J. 1983b. Teorie komparativních nákladu a mezinárodní socialistická delba práce (The theory of comparative costs and international socialist division of labour). *Politická Ekonomie* 8.

Tesner, I. 1982. A beruházási együttmflködés néhány jellemző vonása a szocialista gazdasági integrációban (Some characteristic features of cooperation in investments in socialist economic integration). In Böröczffy, F. ed.

Thede. S. 1982. Comments on the paper of Belovič, A. In: Belovič, A. ed., pp. 67–69.

Thürmer, Gy. 1985. Három évtized a béke és a biztonság védelmében (Three decades in the defence of peace and security). *Külpolitika* 3.

Tikhonov, N. 1982. Statement delivered at the Budapest Session of the CMEA. *Népszabadság*, 19 October.

Tikhonov, N. 1984. Statement at the Havana Session of the CMEA. *Pravda*, 30 October.

Tikhonov, N. 1985. Statement at the ordinary Warsaw Session of the CMEA. *Pravda*, 26 June.

Tömpe, I. 1979. On the economic nature of investment contributions. *Acta Oeconomica*, Vol. 23, No. 3–4.

Totu, I. 1984. Dezvolatarea si perfectionarea colaborarii dintre traile socialiste membre ale C.A.E.R. (Development and improving of cooperation among socialist countries in the CMEA). *Revista Economica* 4.

Ultanbaev, R. 1984. Sozidatel'noe vzaimodeistvie. *Ekonomicheskaya Gazeta* 6.

Vajda, I. and Simai, M. eds. 1971. *Foreign trade under central planning.* Cambridge University Press.

Válek, V. 1982. Platebne-úvěrovy mechanismus RVHP (The payments and credit system of the CMEA). *Finance a Úvěr* 6.

Válek, V. 1985. Primé vztáhy chozrasčotnich organizáci mezi zainteresovánimi členskymi státú RVHP (Direct relations among the cost-accounting organizations of the interested CMEA member states). *Politická Ekonomie* 2.

Valki, L. 1974. A szuverenitásról (On sovereignty). *Külpolitika* 3.

Valki, L. 1982. The problem of treaty-making between the CMEA and the Common Market. *Acta Iuridica*, Vol. XXIV, Fasc. 1–2.

Valouch, J. 1979. Spolupráce členskych státú RVHP v oblasti plánovaci cinnosti (Cooperation of CMEA member states in planning). *Politická Ekonomie* 9.

Vályi, P. 1971. A szocialista gazdasági integráció kérdéseiről (On problems of socialist economic integration). Interview. *Társadalmi Szemle* 8–9.

Vazin, N. and Bibik, L. 1984. Dal'neishee razvitie vneshneekonomicheskikh svyazei stran sotsialisticheskogo sodruzhestva v svete Ekonomicheskogo soveshchaniya na vysshem urovne. *Ekonomicheskie Nauki* 10.

Vincze, I. 1977. A közös valuta — a transzferábilis rubel — jelenlegi közgazdasági jellemzői (The present economic characteristics of the common currency — the TR). *Pénzügyi Szemle* 11.

Vincze, I. 1978. Multilaterality, transferability and exchangeability in the CMEA. *Acta Oeconomica*, Vol. 20, No. 1–2.

Vincze, I. 1983. A KGST-országok gazdaságirányítási rendszereiről (On the economic management systems of CMEA countries). *Figyelő* 11 August.

Vincze, I. 1984. *The international payments and the monetary system in the integration of socialist countries.* Budapest—The Hague: Akadémiai Kiadó—Martinus Nijhoff Publishers.

Vladimirov, O. 1985. Vedushchii faktor mirovogo revolutsionnogo dvizheniya. *Pravda,* 21 June.

Vladimirov, V. 1987. Cooperation in the whole innovation cycle. *CMEA Economic Cooperation,* 3.

Vogel, H. 1984. Alternative westliche Strategien in the Wirtschaftsbeziehungen zu Osteuropa: Die europäische Perspektive. In Höhmann, H.-H. and Vogel, H. eds.

Vörös, I. 1981. *A szocialista piaci magatartás joga* (The law of socialist market behaviour). Budapest: Közgazdasági és Jogi Könyvkiadó.

Voskresenskii, L. 1988. The Constitution of the Cooperative. *New Times,* 8.

Vozniak, V. 1984. Neftegazovoe stroitel'stvo v Zapadnoi Sibiri. *Voprosy Eko nomiki* 12.

Wallace, W. V. and Clarke, R. 1986. *Comecon, trade and the West.* London: Frances Pinter Publishers Ltd.

Watts, N. ed. 1978. *Economic relations between East and West.* London—Basingstoke: Macmillan.

Weiz, H. 1986. Neue Dimensionen der sozialistischen ökonomischen Integration. *Einheit* 4–5,

Wettig, G. 1986. Die kleineren Warschau-Pakt-Staaten in den Ost-West-Beziehungen. *Aussenpolitik* 1.

Wiesel, I. and Wilcsek, J. 1978. *A monetáris rendszer fejlődése és a konvertibilitás* (The development of the monetary system and convertibility). Budapest: Kossuth Könyvkiadó.

Wiles, P. 1973. On purely financial convertibility. In Laulan, Y. ed. *Banking, money and credit in Eastern Europe.* Brussels: NATO Directorate of Economic Affairs.

Winiecki, J. 1983. Central planning and export orientation. *Oeconomica Polona* 2.

Yakovets, Yu. 1974. Tseny v planovom khozyaistve. Moscow: Ekononika.

Yakushin, A. 1978. Toplivo-energeticheskaya problema i mezhdunarodnoe sótrudnichestvo. *Izvestiya AN SSSR, Seriya Ekonomicheskaya* 4.

Zakon 1987. SSSR 'O gosudarstvennom predpriyatii' (ob"edinenii). *Izvestiya,* 1 July

Zhivkova, S. and Kazandzhieva, K. 1980. Nyakoi aspekti na edinnaya valuten kurs pri sotsializma (Some aspects of the uniform exchange rate under socialism). *Finansy i Kredit* 1.

Zhuravlyov, J. and Kalashnikov, A. 1986. Pryamye svyazi — pryamaya vygoda. *Trud,* 19 August.

Zsoldos, L. 1962. *The economic integration of Hungary into the Soviet block.* Ohio University Press.

Żurawicki, L. 1983. Multinationals in the European integration areas. In Saunders, Ch. ed.

Zverev, A. 1981. Comprehensive programme and the CMEA countries monetary-financial cooperation. *Foreign Trade of the USSR* 6.

Zwass, A. 1978–79. Money, banking and credit in the Soviet Union and Eastern Europe. *Eastern European Economics,* Vol. 17, No. 1–2, Fall/Winter.

Index

SOVIET AND EAST EUROPEAN STUDIES

THE FOLLOWING SERIES TITLES ARE NOW OUT OF PRINT: